Single Page Web Applications

Single Page Web Applications

JAVASCRIPT END-TO-END

MICHAEL S. MIKOWSKI
JOSH C. POWELL

MANNING
Shelter Island

For online information and ordering of this and other Manning books, please visit www.manning.com. The publisher offers discounts on this book when ordered in quantity. For more information, please contact

Special Sales Department
Manning Publications Co.
20 Baldwin Road
PO Box 261
Shelter Island, NY 11964
Email: orders@manning.com

∞ Recognizing the importance of preserving what has been written, it is Manning's policy to have the books we publish printed on acid-free paper, and we exert our best efforts to that end. Recognizing also our responsibility to conserve the resources of our planet, Manning books are printed on paper that is at least 15 percent recycled and processed without the use of elemental chlorine.

Manning Publications Co.
20 Baldwin Road
Shelter Island, NY 11964

Development editor: Karen Miller
Technical proofreader: John J. Ryan III
Production editor: Janet Vail
Copyeditor: Benjamin Berg
Proofreader: Toma Mulligan
Typesetter: Gordan Salinovic
Cover designer: Marija Tudor

ISBN 9781617290756
Printed in the United States of America
1 2 3 4 5 6 7 8 9 10 – MAL – 18 17 16 15 14 13

To my parents, wife, and children.
You have taught me so much, and I love you all.

—M.S.M.

To my wife, Marianne. Thank you for your extraordinary patience with all the time I took writing the book. I love you.

—J.C.P.

brief contents

contents

foreword

I wrote my first JavaScript single page web application (SPA) in 2006, although we didn't call it that at the time. This was quite a change for me. Earlier in my career I had focused on low-level Linux kernel hacking and parallel and distributed computing, and the user interface was always a simple command line. After receiving tenure at the University of San Francisco in 2006, I started an ambitious distributed computing project called River (http://river.cs.usfca.edu) that required an interactive graphical interface to facilitate distributed machine management and debugging.

Alex Russell had just coined the term "comet" and we were inspired and determined to use this technology and the web browser for the interface. We had quite a challenge trying to wrangle JavaScript to enable real-time interaction. Though we were able to get something working, it wasn't as effective as we had hoped. The challenge was that we had to develop just about everything ourselves, as the libraries and techniques available today simply didn't exist. The first version of jQuery, for example, wasn't released until later that year.

In July 2011, I was Director of Research at SnapLogic, Inc. (http://snaplogic.com) when Mike Mikowski joined the company as UI Architect. We worked together on the team that designed the next generation data integration product. Mike and I spent countless hours discussing core issues in software engineering and language design. We learned a lot from each other. Mike also shared drafts of the book you're now reading and that is when I learned about his and Josh's method of building SPAs. It was clear that they had developed several generations of commercial SPAs and had used this experience to refine techniques and architectures that are comprehensive, clear, and comparatively simple.

Since my time with Project River in 2006, the ingredients to develop browser-native SPAs have matured to the point where they are generally superior to third-party plug-ins like Java or Flash. There are many fine books that focus on these ingredients, like HTML, CSS, JavaScript, jQuery, NodeJS, and HTTP. Unfortunately, few books do a good job of showing how to bring these ingredients together.

This book is the exception. It shows in detail the well-tested recipes needed to build compelling SPAs using JavaScript end-to-end. It shares insights gained over many generations of SPA refinement. One could say Mike and Josh have made many mistakes so that you don't have to. With this book, you can focus on the purpose of the application instead of its implementation.

The solutions in this book use modern web standards, and should be long-lived and work across many browsers and devices. I really wish today's technologies and this book existed when we worked on Project River in 2006. We would have certainly used them both!

GREGORY D. BENSON
PROFESSOR, DEPARTMENT OF COMPUTER SCIENCE
UNIVERSITY OF SAN FRANCISCO

preface

Josh and I met when I was job hunting and he offered me a web architect position in the summer of 2011. Though I ultimately decided to take another offer, we got along really well and had some interesting discussions about single page web applications (SPAs) and the future of the internet. One day, Josh naively suggested we write a book together. I foolishly agreed, and we sealed our collective fates for hundreds of weekends to come. We expected this would be a rather slim book, under 300 pages. The idea was to provide an over-the-shoulder view of an experienced developer creating a production-ready SPA using JavaScript end-to-end. We would use only best-in-class tools and techniques to provide a world-class user experience. The concepts would apply to anyone developing a JavaScript SPA, whether they developed it as we do in the book, or decided to use one of the framework libraries that are available.

When first published in the Manning Early Access Program, nearly a thousand people purchased the book in the first month. We listenened to their feedback and also spoke to thousands of developers and influencers at meetups, universities, and industry conferences to learn why SPAs fascinate people. What we heard was a thirst for knowledge about this topic. We found that developers are yearning to learn a better way to build their web applications. So we added coverage of more topics. For example, the chapter-length appendix B was added to show in detail how to set up headless SPA testing because many felt the coverage of testing in the manuscript wasn't enough.

We still have an over-the-shoulder view of development of a production-ready SPA, and we also cover quite a few additional topics that our readers really wanted. And our "little" book grew to around double our original estimate. We hope you enjoy it.

MICHAEL S. MIKOWSKI

acknowledgments

The authors would like to thank

- Joey Brooks, the recruiter responsible for introducing the two of us. It's all your fault, Joey.
- John Resig and all the jQuery developers, for creating a fantastically focused, extensible, and capable library. jQuery makes SPA development faster, more reliable, and a lot more fun.
- Ian Smith, for writing and maintaining TaffyDB, a powerful tool for in-browser data manipulation.
- Niels Johnson (a.k.a "Spikels"), who offered to proofread our material in exchange for early access. I think we got the better part of the deal, as his reviews were amazingly detailed and very useful for final editing.
- Michael Stephens at Manning, who helped us get our first outline together and set up the structure of the book.
- Bert Bates, who knows how to write technical books better than most people on the planet. He really helped us consider our audience as we wrote.
- Karen Miller, our development editor, who worked with us the majority of the time on this book, pushing us and others involved in the process and keeping things moving along.
- Benjamin Berg, our copyeditor; Janet Vail, our production editor, who was fantastically communicative and effective in getting the book to press; and everyone else at Manning who helped out with the book.

- Ernest Friedman-Hill, our technical illustration advisor, who provided the ideas behind some of the most compelling illustrations in the book.
- John J. Ryan, for his careful technical proofread of the final manuscript shortly before it went into production.
- All the reviewers, who provided detailed analysis of our writing and our code so we could simplify and enhance it as needed: Anne Epstein, Charles Engelke, Curtis Miller, Daniel Bretoi, James Hatheway, Jason Kaczor, Ken Moore, Ken Rimple, Kevin Martin, Leo Polovets, Mark Ryall, Mark Torrance, Mike Greenhalgh, Stan Bice, and Wyatt Barnett.
- The thousands of MEAP purchasers, conference attendees, and colleagues, who challenged us to optimize the solutions presented in the book.

Mike would also like to thank

- Josh Powell, for asking me to write this book. What a great idea and a wonderful learning experience. Now can I have my life back, please?
- Greg Benson, for writing the foreword, and reminding me that it isn't spelled "forward."
- Gaurav Dhillon, John Schuster, Steve Goodwin, Joyce Lam, Tim Likarish, and others at the SnapLogic team, who understood the value of economy and elegance of design.
- Anees Iqbal, Michael Lorton, David Good, and others from the GameCrush team. Product development at GameCrush wasn't perfect, but it is the closest I have ever seen.
- My parents, for buying a computer and refusing to buy any software for it. This was great motivation to learn how to code.
- Everyone I forgot. Murphy's Law, subsection 8, clearly indicates I have forgotten someone very important but will remember them only after publication. For this, I am truly sorry and hope you will forgive me.

Josh would like to thank

- Mike Mikowski, for agreeing to write this book with me. I am so glad I did not have to undertake writing an entire book on my own. Sucker! I mean...thank you.
- Luca Powell, my brother, for having the courage to follow his dreams and build a business and to be himself. He is an inspiration.
- The rest of my family and friends, without whom I wouldn't be the person I am today.
- John Kelly, for giving me the freedom to finish up the book and understanding that these things take time. Wow, do they take time!
- Mark Torrance, for mentoring me as I grew an experienced engineering team and for giving me the freedom to begin writing this book.
- Wilson Yeung and Dave Keefer, for pushing me to learn deeper in the web stack. You've had a major impact on my career and software engineering knowledge and experience.

about this book

When we considered writing this book we intended to focus about two-thirds on the development of the SPA client. The other third was to focus on the web server and the services needed to provide an SPA. But we couldn't decide what to use for our web server. We had written scores of web servers for traditional and SPA sites using Ruby/Rails, Java/Tomcat, mod_perl, and other platforms, but they all had shortcomings, especially when supporting an SPA, that left us wanting more.

We had recently switched to a "pure" JavaScript stack using Node.js as the web server and MongoDB as the database. Though there were challenges, we found the experience liberating and compelling. The benefits of the common language and data format were usually so profound that they significantly outweighed any language-specific features we lost from the polyglot-stack.

We felt that presenting the "pure" JavaScript stack provided by far the most value to our readers, because we know of no other book that shows how to put all the pieces together. And we expect this stack will continue to gain popularity and become one of the most commonly used stacks for single page applications.

Roadmap

Chapter 1 is an introduction to Single Page Applications. JavaScript SPAs are defined and compared to other kinds of SPAs. Traditional web sites and SPAs are compared, and the opportunities, benefits, and challenges of using an SPA are discussed. The reader is guided through the development of an SPA that is usable by the end of the chapter.

Chapter 2 covers the capabilities and features of JavaScript essential to building an SPA. Since nearly all of the code in an SPA is written in JavaScript, and not just an afterthought added on to provide some user interaction, it's extremely important to understand how the language works. Variables, format, and functions are discussed, as well as more advanced topics such as execution context, closures, and object prototypes.

Chapter 3 introduces the SPA architecture used throughout the book. It also introduces the Shell as the primary user interface module. The Shell coordinates feature modules and browser-wide events and data such as the URL and cookies. An event handler is implemented and the anchor interface pattern is used to manage page state.

Chapter 4 details feature modules which provide well-defined and scoped capabilities to the SPA. Well-written feature modules are compared to third-party JavaScript. Isolation is advocated to help ensure quality and modularity.

Chapter 5 illustrates how to build the Model module that consolidates all business logic into a single namespace. The Model isolates its clients from data management and interaction with the server. The People API is designed and developed here. The Model is tested using the Fake data module and the JavaScript console.

Chapter 6 completes the work on the Model. The Chat API is designed and developed here and again tested using the Fake Data modules and the JavaScript console. The Data module is introduced, and the application is adjusted to use "live" data from the web server.

Chapter 7 introduces Node.js as the web server. Since most of the code in an SPA is in the client side, the backend can be written in any language that performs well enough to keep up with the demands of the application. Writing the backend in JavaScript keeps our programming environments consistent and simplifies full-stack development. If you've never used Node.js before, this is an excellent introduction, and even if you're an experienced Node.js developer, this chapter provides insight into the server's role in an SPA.

Chapter 8 pushes further down the stack into the database. We use MongoDB because it's a production proven database that stores data in JSON documents, the same format in which the data will be consumed by the client. We provide a basic introduction for people who haven't used MongoDB, before delving into the role of the database in an SPA.

Chapter 9 covers some conceptual details of an SPA that are different than a traditional MVC web application: optimizing SPAs for search engines, collecting analytics on SPAs, and error logging in SPAs. We also cover some areas of interest to traditional web applications that are especially important in SPA development: quickly serving static content through CDNs, and caching at every level of the stack.

Appendix A goes into our JavaScript coding standards in great detail; they may or may not work for you but we've found them to be an invaluable guide to structuring the JavaScript in an SPA in a way that's testable, maintainable, and very readable. We cover why a coding standard is important, organizing and documenting code, naming variables and methods, protecting namespaces, organizing files, and using JSLint to validate JavaScript. We also include a two-page reference to keep on hand as you code.

Appendix B covers testing in an SPA. Testing an SPA could be a book on its own, but it's such an important and critical topic that we couldn't ignore it. We cover setting up test modes, selecting a testing framework, creating a test suite, and adjusting SPA modules for test settings.

Audience

This book is intended for web developers, architects, and product managers with at least a smattering of JavaScript, HTML, and CSS experience. If you've never even dabbled in web development, this book is not for you, although you're welcome to buy it anyway (go ahead, daddy needs a new car). Many books are available that do a great job teaching beginner website development and design, but this isn't one of them.

This book does aspire to be a great guide to designing and building large-scale Single Page Web Applications (SPAs) using JavaScript end-to-end. We use JavaScript as the language of the database, the web server, and the browser application. About two-thirds of the book is devoted to client development. The last third shows how to build a server using JavaScript tools such as Node.js and MongoDB. If you're locked in to another server platform, most of the logic should be easy to translate, although the messaging service almost requires an event-driven web server.

Code conventions and downloads

Source code in listings or in text appears in a `fixed-width font like this` to separate it from ordinary text. Code annotations accompany the listings, highlighting important concepts.

Source code for the examples in this book can be downloaded from the publisher's website at www.manning.com/SinglePageWebApplications.

Software and hardware requirements

If you're using a recent Mac OSX or Linux computer, you should have little or no trouble with any of the exercises in the book, assuming you install the specified software as we go along.

If you're using Windows, you should have little or no trouble with any exercises in parts 1 and 2 of the book. Part 3 requires some tools that are not available or limited on Windows. We recommend using a freely available virtual machine (see http://www.oracle.com/technetwork/server-storage/virtualbox/downloads/index.html) and Linux distribution (we recommend Ubuntu Server 13.04, see http://www.ubuntu.com/download/server).

Author Online

Purchase of *Single Page Web Applications* includes free access to a private web forum run by Manning Publications where you can make comments about the book, ask technical questions, and receive help from the authors and from other users. To access the forum and subscribe to it, point your web browser to www.manning.com/SinglePageWebApplications. This page provides information on how to get on the forum once you're registered, what kind of help is available, and the rules of conduct on the forum.

Manning's commitment to our readers is to provide a venue where a meaningful dialog between individual readers and between readers and the author can take place. It's not a commitment to any specific amount of participation on the part of the authors whose contribution to the Author Online forum remains voluntary (and unpaid). We suggest you try asking the authors some challenging questions lest their interest stray!

The Author Online forum and the archives of previous discussions will be accessible from the publisher's website as long as the book is in print.

About the authors

MICHAEL S. MIKOWSKI is an award-winning industrial designer and SPA architect with 13 years' experience as a full-stack web developer and architect. He spent nearly four years as development manager for an HP/HA platform that served hundreds of millions of requests per day using mod_perl application servers in large clusters.

He began working on commercial single page web applications (SPAs) in 2007 when he developed the AMD "Where to Buy" site when hosting constraints prevented most other solutions. After that, he was enamoured with the possibilities of SPAs and proceeded to design and develop many similar solutions. He firmly believes that design for quality, creative destruction, minimalism, and targeted testing techniques can remove complexity and confusion from SPA development.

Mike is a contributor to a number of open source projects, and has published a number of jQuery plugins. He has presented at HTML5 developer conferences in 2012 and 2013, Developer Week 2013, University of San Francisco, and various companies. Recently he has worked as a UI architect, consultant, and Director of UX engineering.

JOSH C. POWELL has worked with the web since IE 6 was the good browser. A software engineer and web architect with over 13 years of experience, he loves the craft of developing web applications and building teams to do the same. He's currently immersed in playing with different single page web application technologies and loving every minute of it.

By some quirk of nature, he's energized by public speaking and has presented on single page applications and JavaScript at conferences such as the HTML 5 Developers Conference and NoSQL Now!, to universities and to Silicon Valley companies like Engine Yard, RocketFuel, and many others. He's also written articles for www.learningjquery.com and various online magazines.

about the cover illlustration

The figure on the cover of *Single Page Web Applications* is captioned "Gobenador de la Abisinia," or the governor of Abyssinia, today called Ethiopia. The illustration is taken from a Spanish compendium of regional dress customs first published in Madrid in 1799. The book's title page states:

> *Coleccion general de los Trages que usan actualmente todas las Nacionas del Mundo desubierto, dibujados y grabados con la mayor exactitud por R.M.V.A.R. Obra muy util y en special para los que tienen la del viajero universal.*

Which we translate, as literally as possible, thus:

> *General collection of costumes currently used in the nations of the known world, designed and printed with great exactitude by R.M.V.A.R. This work is very useful especially for those who hold themselves to be universal travelers.*

Although nothing is known of the designers, engravers, and workers who colored this illustration by hand, the "exactitude" of their execution is evident in this drawing. The "Gobenador de la Abisinia" is just one of many figures in this colorful collection. Their diversity speaks vividly of the uniqueness and individuality of costumes from different countries around the world just 200 years ago.

We at Manning celebrate the inventiveness, the initiative, and the fun of the computer business with book covers based on the rich diversity of life of two centuries ago brought back to life by the pictures from this collection.

Part 1

Introducing SPAs

In the time it takes to read this page, 35 million person minutes will be spent waiting for traditional website pages to load. That's enough spinning icon time for the Curiosity Lander to fly to Mars and back 96 times. The productivity cost of traditional websites is astonishing, and the cost to a business can be devastating. A slow website can drive users away from your site—and into the welcoming wallets of smiling competitors.

One reason traditional websites are slow is because popular MVC server frameworks are focused on serving page after page of static content to an essentially dumb client. When we click a link in a traditional website slideshow, for example, the screen flashes white and everything reloads over several seconds: the navigation, ads, headlines, text, and footer are all rendered again. Yet the only thing that changes is the slideshow image and perhaps the description text. Worse, there's no indicator when some element of the page becomes functional. For example, sometimes a link can be clicked as soon as it appears on a web page; other times we have to wait until the redrawing is 100% complete plus five seconds. This slow, inconsistent, and clunky experience is becoming unacceptable for an increasingly sophisticated web consumer.

Prepare to learn about another—and dare we say better—approach to developing web applications, the single page web application (SPA). An SPA delivers a desktop application in the browser. The result is a highly responsive experience that surprises and delights users instead of confusing and annoying them. In part 1 we learn:

- What an SPA is and the advantages it provides over traditional websites
- How an SPA approach can make our web application a great deal more responsive and compelling

- How to improve our JavaScript skills for SPA development
- How to build an example SPA

Product design is increasingly seen as the decisive factor in the success of commercial and enterprise web applications. SPAs are often the best choice to provide the optimal user experience. As a result, we expect the demand for user-focused design to drive SPA adoption and sophistication.

1 Our first single page application

This chapter covers

- Defining single page web applications
- Comparing the most popular single page application platforms—Java, Flash, and Javascript
- Writing our first JavaScript single page application
- Inspecting the application using Chrome Developer Tools
- Exploring the user benefits of single page applications

This book is intended for web developers, architects, and product managers with at least a smattering of JavaScript, HTML, and CSS experience. If you've never even dabbled in web development, this book is *not* for you, although you're welcome to buy it anyway (go ahead, daddy needs a new car). Many books are available that do a great job teaching beginner website development and design, but this isn't one of them.

This book *does* aspire to be a great guide to designing and building large-scale single page web applications [SPAs] using JavaScript end to end. In fact, as figure 1.1

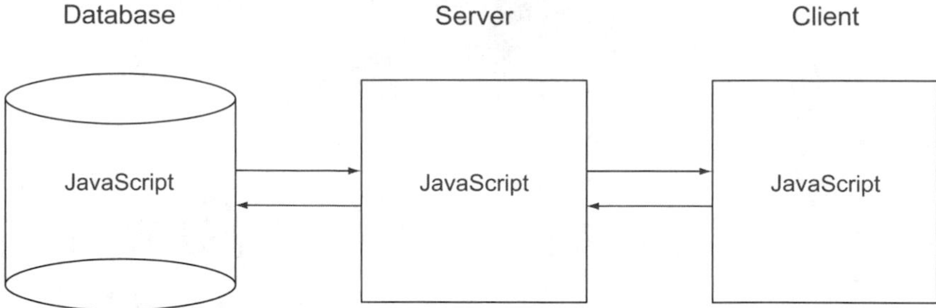

Figure 1.1 JavaScript end-to-end

depicts, we use JavaScript as the language of the database, the web server, *and* the browser application.

We've spent the last six years leading the development of numerous large-scale commercial and enterprise SPAs. During that time we've constantly updated our practices to meet the challenges we've found. We share these practices in this book as they have helped us develop faster, provide a better user experience, ensure quality, and improve team communication.

1.1 Definition, a little history, and some focus

An SPA is an application delivered to the browser that doesn't reload the page during use. Like all applications, it's intended to help the user complete a task, such as "write a document" or "administer a web server." We can think of an SPA as a fat client that's loaded from a web server.

1.1.1 A little history

SPAs have been around for a long time. Let's look at some early examples:

- *Tic-Tac-Toe*—http://rintintin.colorado.edu/~epperson/Java/TicTacToe.html. Hey, we didn't say this would be pretty. This application challenges us to beat a formidable and ruthless computer nemesis in a game of Tic-Tac-Toe. The Java plugin is required—see http://www.java.com/en/download/index.jsp. You may have to grant permission for your browser to run this applet.
- *Flash Spacelander*—http://games.whomwah.com/spacelander.html. This is one of the earlier Flash games, written by Duncan Robertson circa 2001. The Flash plugin is required—see http://get.adobe.com/flashplayer/.
- *JavaScript mortgage calculator*—http://www.mcfedries.com/creatingawebpage/mortgage.htm. This calculator seems almost as old as JavaScript itself, but it works nicely. *No plugin is required.*

The astute reader—and even a few slovenly ones[1]—will notice that we've provided examples of three of the most popular SPA platforms: Java applets, Flash/Flex, and

[1] If you're reading this chapter as you eat potato chips off your chest, you're slovenly.

JavaScript. And those same readers may have noticed that *only the JavaScript SPA works without the overhead or security concerns of a third-party plugin.*

Today, JavaScript SPAs are often the best choice of the three. But JavaScript took a while to become competitive, or even possible, for most SPA uses. Let's take a look at why.

1.1.2 What took JavaScript SPAs so long?

Flash and Java applets had evolved nicely by the year 2000. Java was being used to deliver complex applications and even a complete office suite via the browser.[2] Flash had become the platform of choice for delivering rich browser games and, later, video. On the other hand, JavaScript was still mostly relegated to little more than mortgage calculators, form validation, roll-over effects, and pop-up windows. The problem was that we couldn't rely on JavaScript (or the rendering methods it used) to provide critical capabilities consistently on popular browsers. Even so, JavaScript SPAs promised a number of enticing advantages over Flash and Java:

- *No plugin required*—Users access the application without concern for plugin installation, maintenance, and OS compatibility. Developers also don't need to worry about a separate security model, which reduces development and maintenance headaches.[3]
- *Less bloat*—An SPA using JavaScript and HTML should use significantly fewer resources than a plugin that requires an additional run-time environment.
- *One client language*—Web architects and most developers have to know many languages and data formats—HTML, CSS, JSON, XML, JavaScript, SQL, PHP/Java/Ruby/Perl, and so on. Why write applets in Java, or Flash applications in ActionScript, when we're already using JavaScript elsewhere on our pages? Using a single programming language for everything on the client is a great way to reduce complexity.
- *A more fluid and interactive page*—We've all seen a Flash or Java application on a web page. Often the application is displayed in a box somewhere and many details are different than the HTML elements that surround it: the graphical widgets are different, the right-click is different, the sounds are different, and interaction with the rest of the page is limited. With a JavaScript SPA, the entire browser window is the application interface.

As JavaScript has matured, most of its weaknesses have been either fixed or mitigated and its advantages have increased in value:

- *The web browser is the world's most widely used application*—Many people have a browser window always open and use it throughout the day. Access to a JavaScript application is one more bookmark click away.

---

[2] Applix (VistaSource) Anywhere Office

[3] Can you say "same origin policy"? If you've ever developed in Flash or Java, you almost certainly are familiar with this challenge.

- *JavaScript in the browser is one of the world's most widely distributed execution environments*—By December 2011, nearly one million Android and iOS mobile devices were being activated every day. Each of these devices has a robust JavaScript execution environment built into the OS. More than one billion robust JavaScript implementations have shipped in the last three years on phone, tablet, laptop, and desktop computers around the world.
- *Deployment of JavaScript is trivial*—A JavaScript application can be made available to more than a billion web users by hosting it on an HTTP server.
- *JavaScript is useful for cross-platform development*—Now we can create SPAs using Windows, Mac OS X, or Linux, and we can deploy a single application not only to all desktop machines but also to tablets and smart phones. We can thank converging implementations of standards across browsers, and mature libraries such as jQuery and PhoneGap that smooth over inconsistencies.
- *JavaScript has become surprisingly fast and can, at times, rival compiled languages*—Its speedup is thanks to ongoing and heated competition between Mozilla Firefox, Google Chrome, Opera, and Microsoft. Modern JavaScript implementations enjoy advanced optimizations such as JIT compilation to native machine code, branch prediction, type-inference, and multi-threading.[4]
- *JavaScript has evolved to include advanced features*—These features include the JSON native object, native jQuery-style selectors, and more consistent AJAX capabilities. Push messaging has become far easier with mature libraries like Strophie and Socket.IO.
- *HTML5, SVG, and CSS3 standards and support have advanced*—These advancements allow for the rendering of pixel-perfect graphics that can rival the speed and quality produced by Java or Flash.
- *JavaScript can be used throughout a web project*—Now we can use the excellent Node.js web server and data stores such as CouchDB or MongoDB, both of which communicate in JSON, a JavaScript data format. We can even share libraries between the server and the browser.
- *Desktop, laptop, and even mobile devices have become more powerful*—The ubiquity of multi-core processors and gigabytes of RAM means processing that used to be accomplished on the server can now be distributed to the client browsers.

JavaScript SPAs are becoming increasingly popular due to these advantages, and the demand for experienced JavaScript developers and architects has blossomed. Applications that were once developed for many operating systems (or for Java or Flash) are now delivered as a single JavaScript SPA. Startups have embraced Node.js as the web server of choice, and mobile application developers are using JavaScript and PhoneGap to create "native" applications for multiple mobile platforms using a single code base.

---

[4] See http://iq12.com/blog/as3-benchmark/ and http://jacksondunstan.com/articles/1636 for some comparisons to Flash ActionScript 3.

JavaScript isn't perfect, and we don't have to look far to find omissions, inconsistencies, and other aspects to dislike. But this is true of all languages. Once you become comfortable with its core concepts, employ best practices, and learn what parts to avoid, JavaScript development can be pleasant and productive.

Generated JavaScript: One destination, two paths

We've found it easier to develop SPAs using JavaScript directly. We call these *native* JavaScript SPAs. Another surprisingly popular approach is to use *generated* JavaScript, where developers write code in another language which is then converted to JavaScript. This conversion occurs either at runtime or during a separate generation stage. Notable JavaScript generators include:

- *Google Web Toolkit (GWT)*—See http://code.google.com/webtoolkit/. GWT generates JavaScript from Java.
- *Cappuccino*—See http://cappuccino.org/. Cappuccino uses Objective-J, a clone of the Objective-C language from Mac OS X. Cappuccino itself is a port of the Cocoa application framework, again from OS X.
- *CoffeeScript*—See http://coffeescript.org/. CoffeeScript turns a custom language that provides some syntactic sugar into JavaScript.

Given that Google uses GWT for Blogger, Google Groups, and many other sites, we can safely say that generated JavaScript SPAs are widely used. This raises the question: *why bother writing in one high-level language and then converting it to another*? Here are a number of reasons generated JavaScript remains popular, and why these reasons aren't as compelling as they once were:

- *Familiarity*—The developers can use a more familiar or simpler language. The generator and framework allows them to develop without having to learn the vagaries of JavaScript. The problem is that something eventually gets lost in translation. When this happens, the developers have to inspect the generated JavaScript and understand it to get things to work right. We feel we're more effective when we work directly in JavaScript instead of working through a language abstraction layer.
- *Framework*—The developers appreciate that GWT provides the cohesive system of matching libraries built for server and client. This is a persuasive argument, particularly if the team already has a lot of expertise and products that are in production.
- *Multiple targets*—The developers can have the generator write for multiple targets, such as one file for Internet Explorer and one for the rest of the world's browsers. Although generating code for different targets sounds nice, we think it's even more effective to deploy a single JavaScript source for all browsers. Thanks to converging browser implementations and mature cross-browser libraries like jQuery, it's now much easier to write a sophisticated SPA that runs across all major browsers without modification.

(continued)

- *Maturity*—The developers consider JavaScript insufficiently structured for large-scale application development. Yet JavaScript has evolved to become a much better language, with impressive strengths and manageable weaknesses. Developers from strongly typed languages like Java sometimes feel the lack of type safety is unforgivable. And some developers from inclusive frameworks like Ruby on Rails bemoan the apparent lack of structure. Thankfully, we can mitigate these issues through a combination of code validation tools, code standards, and the use of mature libraries.

We believe native JavaScript SPAs are usually the better choice today. And that's what we design and build in this book.

1.1.3 Our focus

This book shows how to develop engaging, robust, scalable, and maintainable SPAs using JavaScript end to end.[5] Unless otherwise noted, when we refer to an SPA from this point forward, we mean a *native* JavaScript SPA, where the business and presentation logic is written directly in JavaScript and executed by the browser. This JavaScript renders the interface using browser technologies such as HTML5, CSS3, Canvas, or SVG.

SPAs can use any number of server technologies. Because so much of the web application moves to the browser, the server requirements are often significantly reduced. Figure 1.2 illustrates how the business logic and generation of HTML migrates from the server to the client.

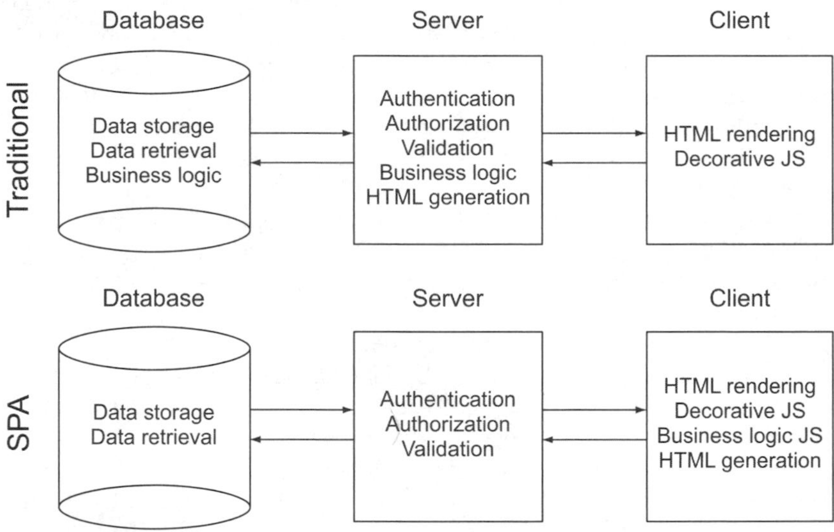

Figure 1.2 Responsibilities of the database, server, and client

[5] Another title for this book might have been *Building Single Page Web Applications Using Best Practices.* But that seemed too wordy.

We focus on the backend in chapters 7 and 8, where we use a web server and database with JavaScript as their control languages. You may not have this choice or may prefer a different backend. That's okay—most of the SPA concepts and techniques we use in this book work well regardless of what backend technologies you use. But if you want to use JavaScript end-to-end, we've got you covered.

Our client libraries include jQuery for DOM manipulation with plugins for history management and event handling. We use TaffyDB2 to provide high-performance, data-centric models. Socket.IO provides seamless near-real-time messaging between the web server and the client. On the server, we use Node.js for our event-based web server. Node.js uses the Google V8 JavaScript engine and excels at handling tens of thousands of concurrent connections. We also use Socket.IO on the web server. Our database is MongoDB, a noSQL database that uses the JavaScript native data format, JSON, to store data and also has a JavaScript API and command-line interface. All of these are proven and popular solutions.

SPA development requires JavaScript coding at a scale at least an order of magnitude greater than a traditional website, as much of the application logic moves from the server to the browser. The development of a single SPA may require many developers to code concurrently and may result in well over 100,000 lines of code. Conventions and discipline previously reserved for server-side development become a must for working at this scale. On the other hand, the server software is simplified and relegated to authentication, validation, and data services. Keep this in mind as we proceed through our examples.

1.2 Build our first SPA

It's now time to develop an SPA. We'll use best practices and explain them as we go.

1.2.1 Define the goal

Our first SPA will have the modest goal of providing a chat slider at the bottom right of the browser window, similar to one you might see on Gmail or Facebook. When we load the application, the slider will be retracted; when we click on the slider, it'll extend, as shown in figure 1.3. Clicking again will retract it.

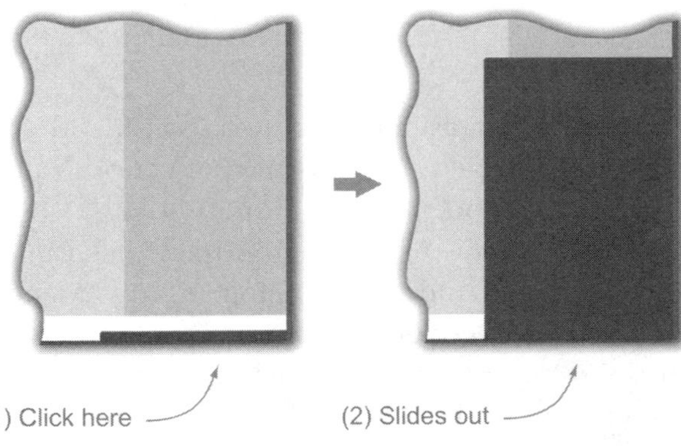

Figure 1.3 The chat slider retracted and extended

SPAs usually do many other things besides opening and closing a chat slider—like sending and receiving chat messages. We'll omit such pesky details to keep this introduction relatively simple and brief. To pervert a famous saying, one can't conquer SPAs in a day. Fear not, we'll return to sending and retrieving messages in chapters 6 and 8.

In the next few sections, we'll set up a file for SPA development, introduce some of our favorite tools, develop the code for the chat slider, and highlight some best practices. We've given you a lot to absorb here, and you're not expected to understand everything right now—particularly some of the JavaScript tricks we're using. We'll have a lot more to say about each of these topics in the next few chapters, but for now, relax, don't sweat the small stuff, and take in the lay of the land.

1.2.2 Start the file structure

We'll create our application in a single file, spa.html, using only jQuery as our one external library. Usually, it's better to have separate files for CSS and JavaScript, but starting with a single file is handy for development and examples. We start by defining where we'll place our styles and our JavaScript. We'll also add a `<div>` container where our application will write HTML entities, as shown in listing 1.1:

Listing 1.1 A toe in the pool—spa.html

```
<!doctype html>
<html>
<head>
  <title>SPA Chapter 1 section 1.2.2</title>
  <style type="text/css"></style>
  <script type="text/javascript"></script>
</head>
<body>
  <div id="spa"></div>
</body>
</html>
```

Add a `script` tag to contain our JavaScript.

Add a `style` tag to contain our CSS selectors. Loading CSS before JavaScript generally results in faster page rendering, and is best practice.

Create a div with an ID of `spa`. The JavaScript will control the contents of this container.

Now that we have the file ready, let's set up Chrome Developer Tools to inspect the application in its current state.

1.2.3 Set up Chrome Developer Tools

Let's use Google Chrome to open our listing—spa.html. We should see a blank browser window, because we haven't added any content. But activities *are* going on under the hood. Let's use Chrome Developer Tools to inspect them.

We can open Chrome Developer Tools by clicking on the wrench in the upper-right corner of Chrome, selecting Tools, and then Developer Tools (Menu > Tools > Developer Tools). This will display the Developer Tools, as shown in figure 1.4. If we don't see the JavaScript console, we can display it by clicking on the Activate console button at the bottom left. The console should be blank, which means we have no

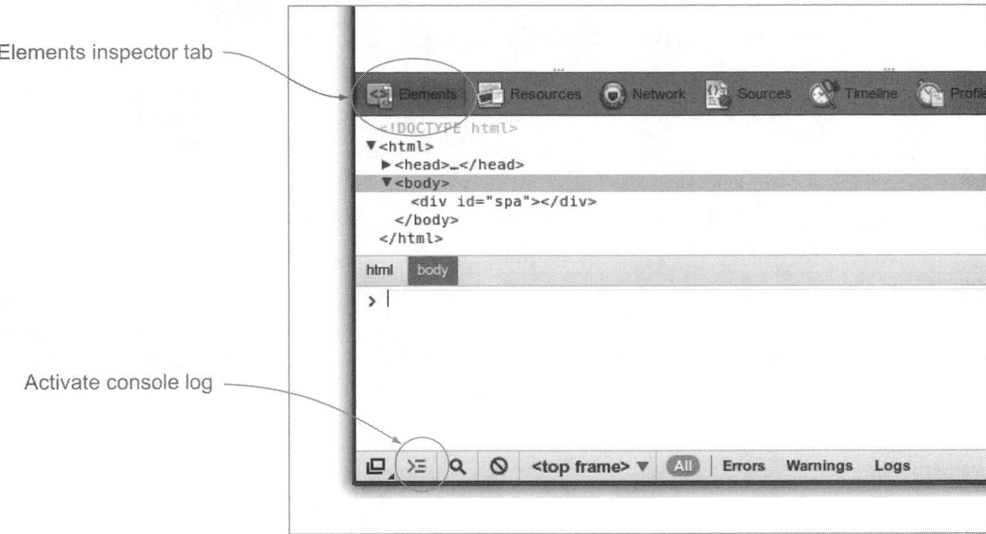

Figure 1.4 Google Chrome Developer Tools

JavaScript warnings or errors. This is good, because currently we have no JavaScript. The Elements section above the console shows the HTML and structure of our page.

Although we use Chrome Developer Tools here and throughout the book, other browsers have similar capabilities. Firefox, for example, has Firebug, and both IE and Safari provide their own version of Developer Tools.

When we present listings in this book, we'll often use the Chrome Developer Tools to ensure our HTML, CSS, and JavaScript all play nicely together. Now let's create our HTML and CSS.

1.2.4 Develop the HTML and CSS

We'll need to add a single chat slider container to our HTML. Let's begin by styling the containers in the `<style>` section in the spa.html file. The adjustments to the `<style>` section are shown in the following listing:

Listing 1.2 HTML and CSS—spa.html

```
<!doctype html>
<html>
<head>
  <title>SPA Chapter 1 section 1.2.4</title>
  <style type="text/css">
    body {
      width    : 100%;
      height   : 100%;
      overflow : hidden;
      background-color : #777;
    }
```

Define the <body> tag to fill the entire browser window and hide any overflow. Set the background color to mid-gray.

```
    #spa {
      position : absolute;
      top      : 8px;
      left     : 8px;
      bottom   : 8px;
      right    : 8px;
      border-radius : 8px 8px 0 8px;
      background-color : #fff;
    }
    .spa-slider {
      position : absolute;
      bottom   : 0;
      right    : 2px;
      width    : 300px;
      height   : 16px;
      cursor   : pointer;
      border-radius : 8px 0 0 0;
      background-color : #f00;
    }
  </style>
  <script type="text/javascript"></script>
</head>
<body>
  <div id="spa">
    <div class="spa-slider"></div>
  </div>
</body>
</html>
```

Define a container to hold all the content of our SPA.

Define the `spa-slider` class so the chat slider container is anchored to the bottom-right corner of its container. Set the background color to red, and round the top-left corner.

When we open spa.html in our browser, we should see the slider retracted, as shown in figure 1.5. We're using a liquid layout where the interface adapts to the display size and the slider always stays anchored at the bottom-right corner. We didn't add any borders to our containers because they add to container width and can impede development, as we have to resize containers to accommodate those borders. It's handy to add borders after the basic layout is created and verified, as we do in later chapters.

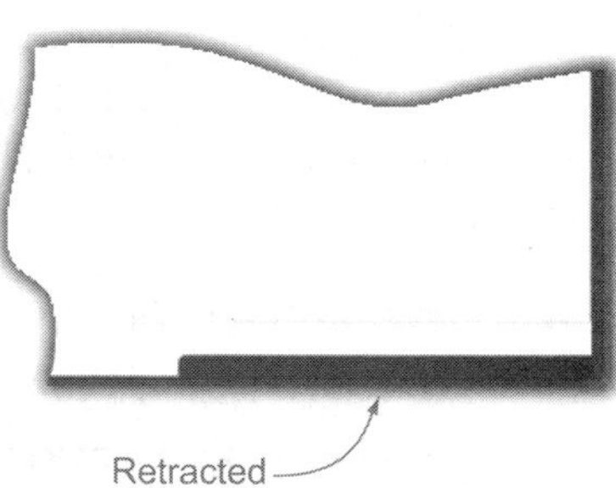

Figure 1.5 Chat slider retracted—spa.html

Now that we have the visual elements in place, it's time to use JavaScript to make the page interactive.

1.2.5 Add the JavaScript

We want to employ best practices with our JavaScript. One tool that will help is *JSLint*, written by Douglas Crockford. JSLint is a JavaScript validator that ensures that our code doesn't break many sensible JavaScript best practices. And we also want to use *jQuery*, a Document Object Model (DOM) toolkit written by John Resig. jQuery provides simple cross-browser tools to easily implement the slider animation.

Before we get into writing the JavaScript, let's outline what we want to do. Our first script tag will load the jQuery library. Our second script tag will contain *our* JavaScript which we'll break into three parts:

1. A header that declares our JSLint settings.
2. A function called spa that creates and manages the chat slider.
3. A line to start the spa function once the browser's Document Object Model (DOM) is ready.

Let's take a closer look at what we need the spa function to do. We know from experience that we'll want a section where we declare our module variables and include configuration constants. We'll need a function that toggles the chat slider. And we'll need a function that receives the user click event and calls the toggle function. Finally, we'll need a function that initializes the application state. Let's sketch an outline in more detail:

Listing 1.3 JavaScript development, first pass—spa.html

```
/* jslint settings */

// Module /spa/
// Provides chat slider capability
  // Module scope variables
    // Set constants
    // Declare all other module scope variables

  // DOM method /toggleSlider/
  // alternates slider height

  // Event handler /onClickSlider/
  // receives click event and calls toggleSlider

  // Public method /initModule/
  // sets initial state and provides feature
    // render HTML
    // initialize slider height and title
    // bind the user click event to the event handler

// Start spa once DOM is ready
```

This is a good start! Let's keep the comments just as they are and add our code. We have kept the comments in bold for clarity.

Listing 1.4 Javascript development, second pass— spa.html

```
/* jslint settings */

// Module /spa/
// Provides chat slider capability
//
var spa = (function ( $ ) {
  // Module scope variables
  var
    // Set constants
    configMap = { },
    // Declare all other module scope variables
```

```
      $chatSlider,
      toggleSlider, onClickSlider, initModule;

    // DOM method /toggleSlider/
    // alternates slider height
    //
    toggleSlider = function () {};

    // Event handler /onClickSlider/
    // receives click event and calls toggleSlider
    //
    onClickSlider = function ( event ) {};

    // Public method /initModule/
    // sets initial state and provides feature
    //
    initModule = function ( $container ) {
      // render HTML
      // initialize slider height and title
      // bind the user click event to the event handler
    };
  }());

  // Start spa once DOM is ready
```

Now let's make a final pass at spa.html as shown in listing 1.5. We load the jQuery library and then we include our own JavaScript, which has our JSLint settings, our spa module, and a line to start the module once the DOM is ready. The spa module is now fully functional. Don't worry if you don't "get" everything right away—there's lots to take in here, and we'll be covering everything in more detail in upcoming chapters. This is just an example to show you what can be done:

Listing 1.5 JavaScript development, third pass—spa.html

```
<!doctype html>
<html>
<head>
  <title>SPA Chapter 1 section 1.2.5</title>
  <style type="text/css">
...
  </style>

  <script type="text/javascript" src=
    "http://ajax.googleapis.com/ajax/libs/jquery/1.9.1/jquery.min.js">
  </script>

  <script type="text/javascript">
  /*jslint         browser : true, continue : true,
    devel  : true, indent  : 2,    maxerr   : 50,
    newcap : true, nomen   : true, plusplus : true,
    regexp : true, sloppy  : true, vars : true,
    white  : true
  */
  /*global jQuery */

// Module /spa/
```

Include the jQuery library from the Google Content Delivery Network (CDN), which lightens the load on our servers and is often faster. Because many other websites use jQuery from the Google CDN, chances are high that the user's browser has already cached this library and will use it without having to make an HTTP request.

Include JSLint settings. We use JSLint to ensure our code is free of common JavaScript mistakes. Don't worry about what the settings mean right now. Appendix A covers JSLint in more detail.

```
// Provides chat slider capability
//
var spa = (function ( $ ) {
  // Module scope variables
  var
    // Set constants
    configMap = {
      extended_height : 434,
      extended_title : 'Click to retract',
      retracted_height : 16,
      retracted_title : 'Click to extend',
      template_html : '<div class="spa-slider"><\/div>'
    },

    // Declare all other module scope variables
    $chatSlider,
    toggleSlider, onClickSlider, initModule;

  // DOM method /toggleSlider/
  // alternates slider height
  //
  toggleSlider = function () {
    var
      slider_height = $chatSlider.height();

    // extend slider if fully retracted
    if ( slider_height === configMap.retracted_height ) {
      $chatSlider
        .animate({ height : configMap.extended_height })
        .attr( 'title', configMap.extended_title );
      return true;
    }

    // retract slider if fully extended
    else if ( slider_height === configMap.extended_height ) {
      $chatSlider
        .animate({ height : configMap.retracted_height })
        .attr( 'title', configMap.retracted_title );
      return true;
    }

    // do not take action if slider is in transition
    return false;
  }

  // Event handler /onClickSlider/
  // receives click event and calls toggleSlider
  //
  onClickSlider = function ( event ) {
    toggleSlider();
    return false;
  };
  // Public method /initModule/
  // sets initial state and provides feature
  //
  initModule = function ( $container ) {

    // render HTML
```

Package our code into the `spa` namespace. More details on this practice are provided in chapter 2.

Declare all variables before they are used. Store module configuration values in `configMap` and state values in `stateMap`.

Group all Document Object Model [DOM] manipulation methods in a section.

Add the code to extend the chat slider. It inspects the slider height to determine if it's fully retracted. If so, it uses a jQuery animation to extend it.

Add the code to retract the chat slider. It inspects the slider height to determine if it's fully extended. If so, it uses a jQuery animation to retract it.

Group all event handler methods in a section. It is good practice to keep the handlers small and focused. They should call other methods to update the display or adjust business logic.

Group all public methods in a section.

```
      $container.html( configMap.template_html );

      $chatSlider = $container.find( '.spa-slider' );
      // initialize slider height and title
      // bind the user click event to the event handler
      $chatSlider
        .attr( 'title', configMap.retracted_title )
        .click( onClickSlider );

      return true;
    };

    return { initModule : initModule };
  }( jQuery ));

  // Start SPA once DOM is ready
  //
  jQuery(document).ready(
    function () { spa.initModule( jQuery('#spa') ); }
  );
  </script>
</head>

<body>
  <div id="spa"></div>
</body>
</html>
```

Add code to fill the `$container` with the slider template HTML.

Find the chat slider div and store it in a module-scope variable, `$chatSlider`. A module-scope variable is available to all functions in the `spa` namespace.

Set the title of the slider, and bind the `onClickSlider` handler to a click event on the chat slider.

Export public methods by returning an object from our spa namespace. We export only one method—initModule.

Start the SPA only after the DOM is ready using the jQuery ready method.

Clean up the HTML. Our JavaScript now renders the chat slider, so it has been removed from the static HTML.

Don't worry too much about JSLint validation, as we'll detail its use in coming chapters. But we'll cover a few noteworthy concepts now. First, the comments at the top of the script set our preferences for validation. Second, this script and settings pass validation without any errors or warning. Finally, JSLint requires that functions be declared before they're used, and therefore the script reads "bottom up" with the highest level functions at the end.

We use jQuery because it provides optimized, cross-browser utilities for fundamental JavaScript features: DOM selection, traversal, and manipulation; AJAX methods; and events. The jQuery `$(selector).animate(...)` method, for example, provides a simple way to do something that's otherwise quite complex: animate the height of the chat slider from retracted to extended (and vice versa) within a specified time period. The motion starts slowly, accelerates, and then slows to a stop. This type of motion—called *easing*—requires knowledge of frame-rate calculations, trigonometric functions, and the vagaries of implementation across popular browsers. If we wrote it ourselves, it would require dozens of additional lines.

The `$jQuery(document).ready(function)` also saves us a lot of work. It runs the function only after the DOM is ready for manipulation. The traditional way to do this was to use the `window.onload` event. For a variety of reasons, `window.onload` isn't an efficient solution for more demanding SPAs—although it makes little

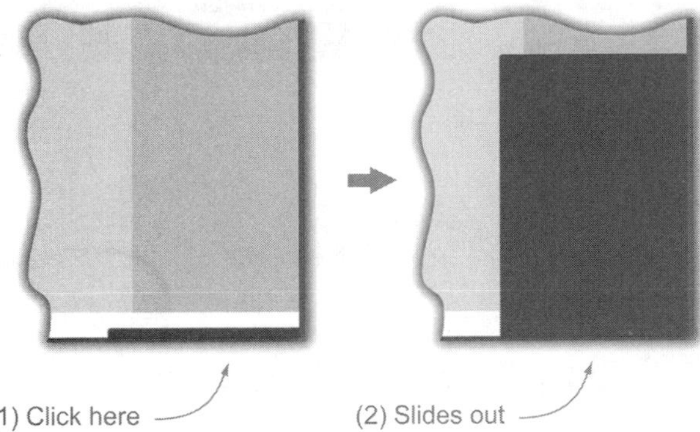

Figure 1.6 The completed chat slider in action—spa.html

difference here. But writing the correct code to use across all browsers is painfully tedious and verbose.[6]

jQuery's benefits, as the previous example shows, usually significantly outweigh its costs. In this case, it shortened our development time, reduced the length of our script, and provided robust cross-browser compatibility. The cost of using it is somewhere between low and negligible, as its library is small when minimized and users likely have it already cached on their devices anyway. Figure 1.6 shows the completed chat slider.

Now that we've completed the first implementation of our chat slider, let's look at how the application actually works using the Chrome Developer Tools.

1.2.6 *Inspect our application using Chrome Developer Tools*

If you're comfortable using Chrome Developer Tools, you may skip this section. If not, we *highly* encourage you to play along at home.

Let's open our file, spa.html, in Chrome. After it loads, let's immediately open up the Developer Tools (Menu > Tools > Developer Tools).

The first thing you may notice is how the DOM has been changed by our module to include the `<div class="spa-slider" ... >` element, as shown in figure 1.7. As we continue, our application will be adding a *lot* more dynamic elements like this one.

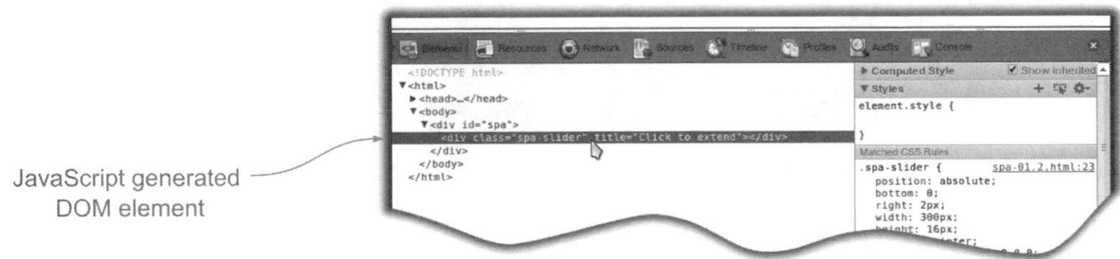

Figure 1.7 Inspecting the elements—spa.html

---

[6] See www.javascriptkit.com/dhtmltutors/domready.shtml to get a taste of the pain.

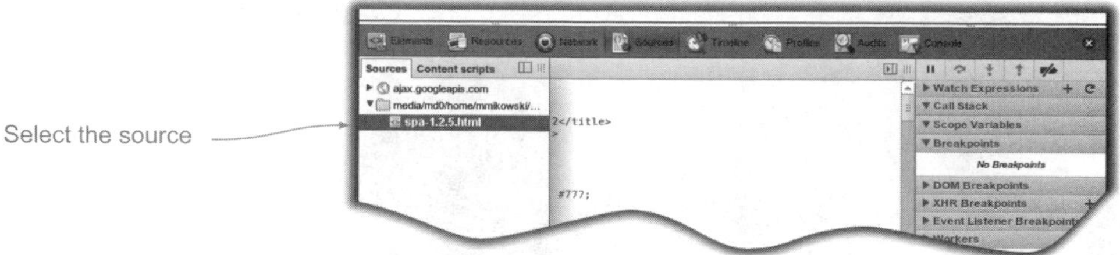

Figure 1.8 Selecting a source file—spa.html

We can explore the JavaScript execution by clicking on the Sources button in the top menu of the Developer Tools. Then select the file that contains the JavaScript, as shown in figure 1.8.

In later chapters we'll be placing our JavaScript into separate files. But for this example it's in our HTML file as shown in figure 1.9. We'll need to scroll down to find the JavaScript we want to inspect.

Figure 1.9 Viewing the source file—spa.html

When we navigate to line 76, we should see an `if` statement, as shown in figure 1.10. We should like to inspect the code *before* this statement is executed, so we click on the left margin to add a breakpoint. Whenever the JavaScript interpreter reaches this line in the script, it'll pause so we can inspect elements and variables to better understand what's happening.

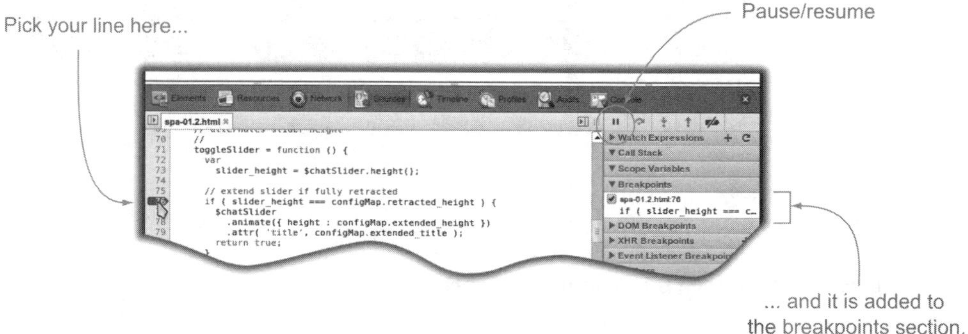

Figure 1.10 Setting a breakpoint—spa.html

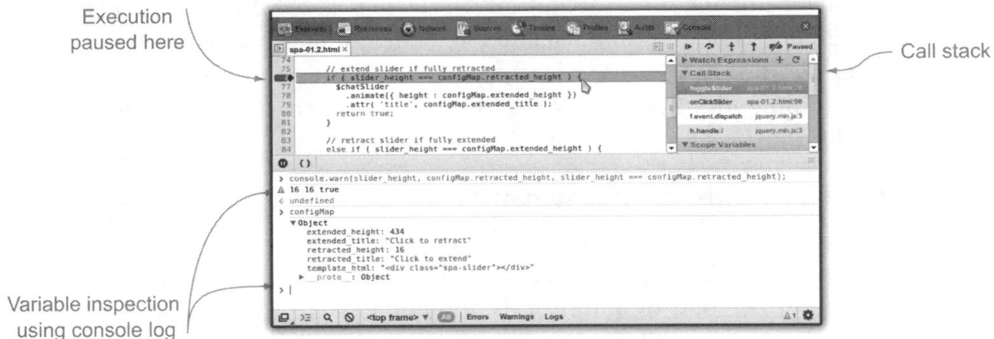

Figure 1.11 Inspecting values on break—spa.html

Now let's go back to the browser and click on the slider. We'll see that the JavaScript has paused at the red arrow at line 76, as in figure 1.11. While the application is paused, we can inspect variables and elements. We can open the console section and type in various variables and press Return to see their values in this paused state. We see that the `if` statement condition is true (`slider_height` is 16, and `configMap.retracted_height` is 16), and we can even inspect complex variables like the `configMap` object, as shown at the bottom of the console. When we're done inspecting, we can remove the breakpoint by clicking on the left margin of line 76, and then clicking the Resume button at the top right (above Watch Expressions).

Once we click Resume, the script will continue from line 76 and finish toggling the slider. Let's return to the Elements tab and look at how the DOM has changed, as shown in figure 1.12. In this figure we can see that the CSS `height` property, which was provided by the `spa-slider` class (see Matched CSS Rules on the lower right), has been overridden by an element style (element styles have higher priority over styles that come from classes or IDs). If we click on the slider again, we can watch the height change in real-time as the slider retracts.

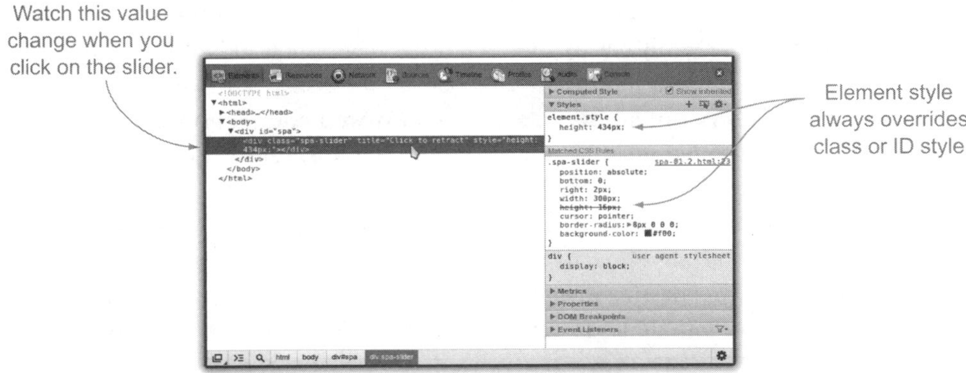

Figure 1.12 Viewing DOM changes—spa.html

Our short introduction to Chrome Developer Tools shows only a small portion of their ability to help us understand and change what's occurring "under the hood" of our application. We'll continue to use these tools as we develop this application, and we recommend you spend some quality time with the online manual at http://mng.bz/PzIJ. It's time well spent.

1.3 The user benefits of a well-written SPA

Now that we've built our first SPA, let's consider the primary benefit of an SPA over a traditional website: it provides a substantially more engaging user experience. An SPA can deliver the best of both worlds: the immediacy of a desktop application *and* the portability and accessibility of a website.

- *An SPA can render like a desktop application*—The SPA redraws the parts of the interface that need to change only as needed. A traditional website, in comparison, redraws the entire page on many user actions, resulting in a pause and a "flash" while the browser retrieves from the server and then redraws everything on the page. If the page is large, the server is busy, or the internet connection is slow, this flash can take several seconds or more, and the user has to guess when the page is ready to use again. This is a horrible experience when compared to the rapid rendering and immediate feedback of an SPA.
- *An SPA can respond like a desktop application*—The SPA minimizes response time by moving working (transient) data and processing from the server to the browser as much as possible. The SPA has the data and business logic needed to make most decisions locally and therefore quickly. Only data validation, authentication, and permanent storage must remain on the server, for reasons we discuss in chapters 6-8. A traditional website has most of the application logic on the server and the user must wait for a request/response/redraw cycle in response to much of their input. This can take several seconds, compared to the near immediate response of the SPA.
- *An SPA can notify users of its state like a desktop application*—When an SPA *does* have to wait on a server, it can dynamically render a progress bar or busy indicator so the user isn't befuddled by a delay. Compare this to a traditional website, where the user actually has to *guess* when the page is loaded and usable.
- *An SPA is nearly universally accessible like a website*—Unlike most desktop applications, users can access an SPA from any web connection and a decent browser. Today, the list includes smart phones, tablets, televisions, laptops, and desktop computers.
- *An SPA can be instantly updated and distributed like a website*—The user doesn't have to do anything to realize the benefits—when they reload the browser it works. The hassle of maintaining multiple concurrent versions of software is largely eliminated.[7] The authors have worked on SPAs that have been built and

[7] But not completely: what happens if the server-client data exchange format changes, yet many users have the prior version of software loaded in their browser? This can be accommodated with some forethought.

updated multiple times in a single day. Desktop applications often require a download and administrative access to install a new version, and the interval between versions can be many months or years.

- *An SPA is cross-platform like a website*—Unlike most desktop applications, a well-written SPA can work on any operating system that provides a modern HTML5 browser. Though usually this is considered a developer benefit, it's extremely useful for many users who have a combination of devices—say Windows at work, a Mac at home, a Linux server, an Android phone, and an Amazon tablet.

All of these benefits mean that you may want to make your next application an SPA. Clunky websites that re-render an entire page after each click tend to alienate increasingly sophisticated users. The communicative and responsive interface of a well-written SPA, along with the accessibility of the internet, helps keep our customers where they belong—using our product.

1.4 Summary

The single page application has been around for some time. Flash and Java have, until recently, been the most widely used SPA client platforms because their capability, speed, and consistency exceeded those of JavaScript and browser rendering. But recently, JavaScript and browser rendering have reached a tipping point where they've overcome their most troublesome deficiencies while providing significant advantages over other client platforms.

We focus on creating SPAs using native JavaScript and browser rendering, and when we refer to an *SPA* we mean a native JavaScript SPA unless otherwise noted. Our SPA tool chain includes jQuery, TaffyDB2, Node.js, Socket.IO, and MongoDB. All of these are proven, popular solutions. You may choose to employ alternatives to these technologies, but the fundamental structure of an SPA would remain regardless of specific technology decisions.

The simple chat slider application we developed demonstrates many features of a JavaScript SPA. It responds immediately to user input, and it uses data stored in the client instead of the server to make decisions. We used JSLint to ensure that our application didn't contain common JavaScript mistakes. And we used jQuery to select and animate the DOM and to handle the event when a user clicks on the slider. We explored using the Chrome Developer Tools to help us understand how our application was working.

An SPA can provide the best of both worlds—the immediacy of a desktop application *and* the portability and accessibility of a website. The JavaScript SPA is available on over a billion devices that support a modern web browser and that don't require any proprietary plugins. With a little effort, it can support desktops, tablets, and smart phones running many different operating systems. SPAs are easily updated and distributed, usually without requiring any action from the user. All of these benefits explain why you may want to make your next application an SPA.

In the next chapter, we'll explore some key JavaScript concepts that are needed for SPA development, but are frequently ignored or misunderstood. We'll then build on this foundation to improve and extend the example SPA we developed in this chapter.

2 Reintroducing JavaScript

This chapter covers

- Variable scoping, function hoisting, and the execution context object
- Explaining variable scope chains and why we use them
- Creating JavaScript objects using prototypes
- Writing self-executing anonymous functions
- Using the module pattern and private variables
- Exploiting closures for fun and profit

This chapter reviews unique JavaScript concepts that we need to know if we're to build a native JavaScript single page application of significant scale. The snippet of code in listing 2.1 from chapter 1 shows the concepts we'll be covering. If you understand all of these *how* and *why* concepts then you might skim or skip this chapter and get straight to work on an SPA in chapter 3.

To follow along at home you can cut and paste all of the listings in this chapter into the console log of Chrome Development Tools and press Return to see them execute. We highly encourage you to join in the fun.

Listing 2.1 Application JavaScript

```
...
  var spa = (function ( $ ) {                         <-- Self-executing anonymous functions, module pattern
    // Module scope variables
    var
      configMap = {                                   <-- Prototype-based inheritance, variable hoisting, variable scope
        extended_height  : 434,
        extended_title   : 'Click to retract',
        retracted_height : 16,
        retracted_title  : 'Click to extend',
        template_html    : '<div class="spa-slider"></div>'
      },
      $chatSlider,
      toggleSlider, onClickSlider, initModule;
 ...

    // Public method
    initModule = function ( $container ) {            <-- Anonymous functions, module pattern, closures

      $container.html( configMap.template_html );
      $chatSlider = $container.find( '.spa-slider' );

      $chatSlider
        .attr( 'title', configMap.retracted_title )
        .click( onClickSlider );

      return true;
    };

    return { initModule : initModule };               <-- Module pattern, scope chain

  }( jQuery ));                                       <-- Self-executing anonymous functions
...
```

Coding standards and JavaScript syntax

JavaScript syntax can be confusing to the uninitiated. It's important to understand variable declaration blocks and object literals before moving on. Feel free to skip this sidebar if you're already familiar with them. For a complete rundown on what we consider to be important JavaScript syntax and good coding standards, see appendix A.

VARIABLE DECLARATION BLOCKS

```
var spa = "Hello world!";
```

JavaScript variables are declared following the `var` keyword. A variable can contain any type of data: arrays, integers, floats, strings, and so on. The variable type isn't specified, so JavaScript is considered a *loosely typed* language. Even after a value is assigned to a variable, the type of value can be changed by assigning a value with a different type, so it's also considered a *dynamic* language.

JavaScript variable declarations and assignments can be chained together following the `var` keyword by separating them with commas:

(continued)

```
var book, shopping_cart,
    spa = "Hello world!",
    purchase_book = true,
    tell_friends = true,
    give_5_star_rating_on_amazon = true,
    leave_mean_comment = false;
```

There are many viewpoints on the best format for a variable declaration block. We prefer variables that are declared but not defined to be at the top, followed by variable declarations with definitions. We also prefer having commas at the end of the line, as shown here, but we aren't religious about it and the JavaScript engine doesn't care.

OBJECT LITERALS

An *object literal* is an object defined by a comma separated list of attributes contained in curly braces. Attributes are set with a colon instead of an equals sign. Object literals can also contains arrays, which are a comma-separated list of members surrounded by square brackets. Methods can be defined by setting a function as the value of one of the attributes:

```
var spa = {
    title: "Single Page Web Applications",        //attribute
    authors: [ "Mike Mikowski", "Josh Powell" ],  //array
    buy_now: function () {                        //function
      console.log( "Book is purchased" );
    }
}
```

Object literals and variable declaration blocks are used extensively throughout the book.

2.1 Variable scope

A good place to start our discussion is with the behavior of variables and when variables are in or out of scope.

Variables are scoped by functions in JavaScript and they're either global or local. *Global* variables are accessible everywhere, and *local* variables are only accessible where they are declared. The only block that defines scope for a variable in JavaScript is a function. That's it. Global variables are defined outside of a function, whereas local variables are defined inside of a function. Simple, right?

Another way to look at it is that functions are like a prison, and the variables defined inside of the function are like prisoners. Just like a prison contains the prisoners and doesn't let them escape outside of the prison walls, a function contains the local variables and doesn't let them escape outside the function, as the following code shows:

```
var regular_joe = 'I am global!';

function prison() {
  var prisoner = 'I am local!';
}

prison();
console.log( regular_joe );     <-- Outputs "I am global!"
console.log( prisoner );        <-- Outputs "Error: prisoner is not defined"
```

JavaScript 1.7, 1.8, 1.9+, and block scope

JavaScript 1.7 introduces a new block-scope constructor, the `let` statement. Unfortunately, even though standards exist for JavaScript 1.7, 1.8, and 1.9, not even 1.7 is consistently deployed across all browsers. Until browsers are compatible with these JavaScript updates, we'll pretend that JavaScript 1.7+ doesn't exist. Still, let's take a look at how it works.

```
let (prisoner = 'I am in prison!') {
  console.log( prisoner );      <-- Outputs "I am in prison!"

}
console.log( prisoner );        <-- Outputs "Error: prisoner isn't defined"
```

To use JavaScript 1.7, put the version in the `type` attribute of the script tag:

```
<script type="application/javascript;version=1.7">
```

This is only a brief taste of JavaScript 1.7+; there are many additional changes and new features.

If only it were that simple. The first gotcha you'll likely encounter with JavaScript scoping is that it's possible to declare a global variable while inside of a function simply by omitting the var declaration, as figure 2.1 shows. And as with all programming languages, global variables are almost always a Bad Idea.

```
Global scope
  Function scope
    function leaky() {
        var local=1;
        global=2;
    }
  global=2;
```

Figure 2.1 If you forget the `var` keyword when you declare a local variable in a function, you create a global variable instead.

```
function prison () {
  prisoner_1 = 'I have escaped!';
  var prisoner_2 = 'I am locked in!';
}

prison();
console.log( prisoner_1 );      <-- Outputs: "I have escaped!"

console.log( prisoner_2 );      <-- Outputs an error: prisoner_2 is not defined
```

This isn't good—don't let your prisoners escape. Another place this gotcha shows up often is when we forget the `var` when declaring the counter in `for` loops. Try the following definitions for the `prison` function one at a time:

```
// wrong
function prison () {
  for( i = 0; i < 10; i++ ) {
    //...
  }
}
prison();
console.log( i );  // i is 10
delete window.i;

// permissible
function prison () {
  for( var i = 0; i < 10; i++ ) {
    //...
  }
}
prison();
console.log( i );  // i is not defined

// best
function prison () {
  var i;
  for ( i = 0; i < 10; i++ ) {
    // ...
  }
}
prison();
console.log( i );  // i is not defined
```

We like this version better because declaring the variable at the top of the function makes its scope perfectly clear. Declaring a variable inside the `for` loop initializer might fool some people into thinking the variable's scope is limited to the `for` loop, as it would be in some other languages.

We extend this logic to solve and combine all of the JavaScript declarations and most assignments at the top of the function they're declared in, so that the scope of the variable is clear:

```
function prison() {
  var prisoner = 'I am local!',
      warden   = 'I am local too!',
      guards   = 'I am local three!'
  ;
}
```

By consolidating the local variable definitions using commas, we make them easy to see and, perhaps more importantly, make it less likely that a typo could inadvertently sneak in and create a global variable instead of a local one. Also, did you notice how nicely lined up they were? See how the semicolon at the end acts to the eye like a closing tag for the variable declaration block? We talk about this and other methods of

```
function hoisted() {                function hoisted() {
        console.log(v);                     var v;
        var v=1;                            console.log(v);
}                                           v=1;
                                    }
```

Figure 2.2 JavaScript variable declarations are "hoisted" to the beginning of the function they appear in, but initializations stay where they are. The JavaScript engine doesn't actually rewrite the code: the declaration is rehoisted every time the function is invoked.

formatting JavaScript for readability and understandability in the JavaScript Coding Standards in appendix A. Another interesting feature of JavaScript, variable hoisting, is related to this method of declaring local variables. Let's look at that next.

2.2 Variable hoisting

When a variable is declared in JavaScript, its declaration is said to be *hoisted* to the top of its functional scope and the variable is assigned the value of `undefined`. This has the effect of making it so that a variable declared anywhere in a function exists throughout the entire function, though its value is undefined until it's assigned a value, as illustrated in figure 2.2.

```
function prison () {
  console.log(prisoner);          // Outputs "prisoner is undefined"
    var prisoner = 'Now I am defined!';

  console.log(prisoner);          // Outputs "Now I am defined!"
}
prison();
```

Contrast the code in the figure with an attempt to access a variable not declared locally or globally, which results in a runtime JavaScript error that will stop JavaScript from executing at that statement:

```
function prison () {

  console.log(prisoner);          // Outputs "error: prisoner is not defined" and the JavaScript engine stops executing code.

}
prison();
```

Because variable declarations are always hoisted to the top of your functional scope, the best practice is to always declare your variables at the top of your functions, preferably with a single `var` statement. This matches what JavaScript does and avoids the type of confusion we illustrated in the previous figure.

```
function prison () {
  console.log(prisoner);          // Outputs "undefined"
  var prisoner, warden, guards;

  console.log(prisoner);          // Outputs "undefined"
  prisoner = 'prisoner assigned';
```

```
  console.log(prisoner);      <-- Outputs "prisoner assigned"
}
prison();
```

This scope and hoisting behavior can sometimes combine to cause some surprising behavior. Take the following code:

```
var regular_joe = 'Regular Joe';        <-- regular_joe is defined in the global scope
function prison () {
   console.log(regular_joe);           <-- 'Regular Joe' global variable regular_joe is logged inside of the prison function
}
prison();
```

When prison is executed and `regular_joe` is requested by `console.log()`, the JavaScript engine first checks whether `regular_joe` has been declared in the local scope. Because `regular_joe` isn't declared in the local scope, the JavaScript engine then checks the global scope and finds that it's defined there and returns that value. This is called *walking up the scope chain*. But what if the variable is also declared in the local scope?

```
var regular_joe = 'regular_joe is assigned';
function prison () {
   console.log(regular_joe);          <-- Outputs "undefined". The declaration of regular_joe is hoisted to the top of the function and that hoisted declaration is checked before looking for regular_joe in the global scope.
   var regular_joe;
}
prison();
```

Does this seem counterintuitive or confusing? Let's walk through the way JavaScript handles hoisting under the covers.

2.3 Advanced variable hoisting and the execution context object

All the concepts we've covered so far are generally regarded as necessary to know in order to be successful as a JavaScript developer. Let's take it a step beyond that and see what happens under the hood: you'll be one of the few who understands how JavaScript really works. We'll start with one of JavaScript's more "magical" features: variable and function hoisting.

2.3.1 Hoisting

Like all forms of magic, the trick becomes almost disappointing when the secret is revealed. The secret is that the JavaScript engine makes two passes over code when it comes into scope. On the first pass it initializes variables and on the second pass it executes code. I know, simple; I have no idea why it's not usually described in these terms. Let's go into more detail on what the JavaScript engine does during the first pass because it has some interesting repercussions.

On the first pass, the JavaScript engine walks through the code and does three things:

1. Declares and initializes the function arguments.
2. Declares the local variables, including anonymous functions assigned to a local variable, but doesn't initialize them.
3. Declares and initializes functions.

Listing 2.2 The first pass

```
function myFunction( arg1, arg2 ) {
  var local_var = 'foo',
      a_function = function () {
        console.log( 'a function' );
      };

  function inner () {
    console.log('inner');
  }

}
myFunction( 1,2 );
```

① **Declares and initializes the function arguments**

② **Declares the local variables, including anonymous functions assigned to a local variable, but doesn't initialize them.**

③ **Declares and initializes functions**

Values are *not* assigned to local variables during the first pass because code may have to be executed to determine the value and the first pass doesn't execute code. Values are assigned to the arguments, because any code needed to determine an argument's value was run before the argument was passed into the function.

We can demonstrate that the values of the arguments are set in the first pass by comparing them to the code demonstrating function hoisting from the end of the last section.

Listing 2.3 Variables are undefined before they are declared

```
var regular_joe = 'regular_joe is assigned';
function prison () {
   console.log(regular_joe);
   var regular_joe;
}
prison();
```

Outputs "undefined". The declaration of `regular_joe` is hoisted to the top of the function and that hoisted declaration is checked before looking for `regular_joe` in the global scope.

`regular_joe` is undefined before it's declared in the prison function, but if `regular_joe` is also passed in as an argument, it has a value before it's declared.

Listing 2.4 Variables have a value before they're declared

```
var regular_joe = 'regular_joe is assigned';
function prison ( regular_joe ) {
  console.log(regular_joe);
  var regular_joe;

  console.log(regular_joe);
}

prison( 'the regular_joe argument' );
```

Outputs "the regular_joe argument". Arguments are assigned a value during the first pass. Without understanding the two passes the JavaScript engine makes, it looks like the regular_joe argument would be overwritten by the `regular_joe` local variable declaration being hoisted.

Outputs "the regular_joe argument". Surprise! Since `regular_joe` was assigned a value from the argument, it's not overwritten with undefined when it's declared. This declaration is redundant.

If your head is spinning from this, that's okay. Though we've explained that the JavaScript engine makes two passes over a function when it executes, and that on the first pass it stores the variables, we haven't seen *how* it stores the variables. Seeing how the JavaScript engine stores variables will hopefully clear up any remaining confusion. The JavaScript engine stores variables as attributes on an object referred to as the *execution context object*.

2.3.2 Execution context and the execution context object

Every time a function is invoked, there's a new execution context. The execution context is a concept, the concept of a running function—it's not an object. It's like thinking of an athlete in a running context or a jumping context. We could say a running athlete instead of an athlete in a running context, just like we could say a running function, but that's not how the jargon works. We say the *execution context*.

The execution context is made up of everything that happens while that function is executing. This is separate from a function declaration, because the function declaration describes what *will* happen when the function is executed. The execution context *is* the execution of the function.

All of the variables and functions defined in a function are considered part of the execution context. The execution context is a part of what developers are referring to when they talk about a function's *scope*. A variable is considered "in scope" if it's accessible in the current execution context, which is another way of saying the variable is in scope if it's accessible while the function is running.

The variables and functions that are part of the execution context are stored on the *execution context object*, an implementation of the ECMA standard for the execution context. The execution context object is an object in the JavaScript engine, and not a variable directly accessible in JavaScript. It's easy enough to access indirectly, as every time you use a variable you're accessing an attribute of an execution context object.

Earlier, we discussed how the JavaScript engine makes two passes over an execution context, declaring and initializing the variables, but where does it store these variables? The JavaScript engine declares and initializes the variables as attributes on the execution context object. For an example of how the variables are stored, take a look at table 2.1.

Table 2.1 Execution context object

<table>
<tr><th>Code</th><th>Execution context object</th></tr>
<tr><td><pre>var example_variable = "example",
    another_example = "another";</pre></td><td><pre>{
  example_variable: "example",
  another_example: "another"
};</pre></td></tr>
</table>

It's possible that you've never heard of the execution context object. It's not something commonly discussed in the web developer community, probably because the execution context object is buried in the implementation of JavaScript and not directly accessible during development.

Understanding the execution context object will be key to understanding the rest of the chapter, so let's walk through the lifecycle of an execution context object and the JavaScript code that creates it.

Listing 2.5 Execution context object—first pass

```
outer(1);

function outer( arg ) {

  var local_var = 'foo';

  function inner () {
    console.log('inner');
  }

  inner();

}
```

```
{
}
```

An empty execution context object is created when `outer` is invoked.

```
{
  arg : 1
}
```

Arguments are declared and assigned

```
{
  arg : 1,
  local_var: undefined
}
```

Local variables are declared but not assigned

```
{
  arg : 1,
  local_var : undefined,
  inner : function () {
    console.log('inner');
  }
}
```

Functions are declared and assigned, but not executed.

Nothing happens; code isn't executed on the first pass

Now that the arguments and functions have been declared and assigned, and the local variables have been declared, a second pass is made, executing the JavaScript and assigning the definitions of the local variables.

Listing 2.6 Execution context object—second pass

```
{
  arg: 1,
  local_var: undefined,
  inner: function () {
    console.log('inner');
  }
}
```

```
outer(1);

function outer( arg ) {

  var local_var = 'foo';

  function inner () {
    console.log('inner');
  }

  inner();

}
```

```
{
  arg: 1,
  local_var: 'foo',
  inner: function () {
    console.log('inner');
  }
};
```

Local variables are assigned as code is executed.

```
{
  arg: 1,
  local_var: 'foo',
  inner: function () {
    console.log('inner');
  }
}
```

The attributes representing variables on this execution context object remain the same, but when function inner is invoked, a new execution context object is created inside of this one.

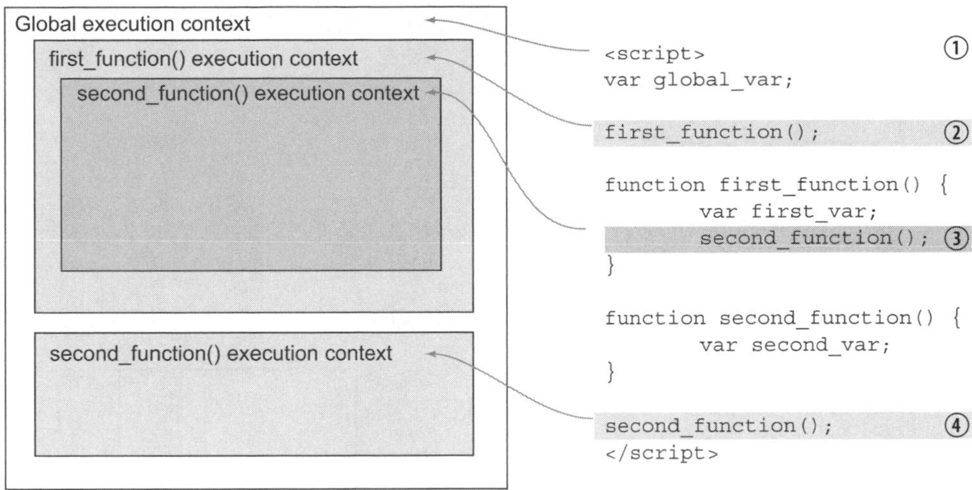

Figure 2.3 Calling a function creates an execution context.

This can go many layers deep, as functions can be invoked inside of an execution context. Invoking a function inside of an execution context creates a new execution context nested inside the existing execution context. Okay, head spinning again; it's picture time. See figure 2.3.

1. Everything inside of the `<script>` tag is in the global execution context.
2. Invoking `first_function` creates a new execution context inside the global execution context. When `first_function` runs, it has access to the variables of the execution context in which it was invoked. In this case, `first_function` has access to the variables defined in the global execution context and the local variables defined in `first_function`. These variables are said to be *in scope*.
3. Invoking `second_function` creates a new execution context inside of the `first_function` execution context. `second_function` has access to the variables from the `first_function` execution context because it was invoked inside of it. `second_function` also has access to variables in the global execution context and the local variables defined in `second_function`. These variables are said to be *in scope*.
4. `second_function` is invoked again, this time in the global execution context. This `second_function` doesn't have access to the variables in the `first_function` execution context because this time `second_function` wasn't invoked in the `first_function` execution context. Said another way, this time when `second_function` is called, it doesn't have access to the variables defined in `first_function` because it wasn't called inside of `first_function`.

   This `second_function` execution context doesn't have access to the variables from the previous time `second_function` was invoked either, because they occur in different execution contexts. Said another way, when you call a function, you

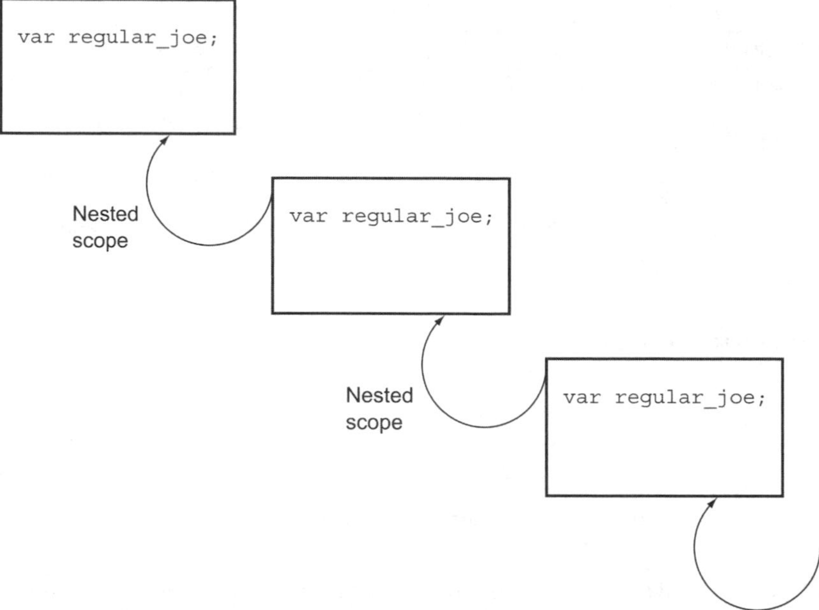

Figure 2.4 During runtime JavaScript searches the scope hierarchy to resolve variable names.

don't have access to local variables created the last time the function was called, and the next time you call this function you won't have access to the local variables from this function call. These inaccessible variables are said to be *out of scope*.

The order in which the JavaScript engine looks in the execution context objects to access variables that are "in scope" is referred to as the *scope chain*, which, together with the *prototype chain*, describes the order in which JavaScript accesses variables and their attributes. We'll discuss these concepts in the next few sections.

2.4 The scope chain

Up until now we've mostly limited our discussion of variable scope to *global* and *local*. This is a good starting point, but scoping is more nuanced, as implied in the discussion of nested execution contexts in the last section. Variable scope is more accurately thought of as a chain, as seen in figure 2.4. When looking for the definition of a variable, the JavaScript engine first looks at the local execution context object. If the definition isn't there, it jumps up the scope chain to the execution context it was created in and looks for the variable definition in that execution context object, and so on until it finds the definition or reaches the global scope.

Let's modify an earlier example to illustrate the scope chain. The code in listing 2.7 will print the following:

```
I am here to save the day!
regular_joe is assigned
undefined
```

Listing 2.7 Scope chain example—regular_joe defined at each calling scope

```
var regular_joe = 'I am here to save the day!';

// logs 'I am here to save the day!'
console.log(regular_joe);
function supermax(){
  var regular_joe = 'regular_joe is assigned';

  // logs 'regular_joe is assigned'
  console.log(regular_joe);

  function prison () {
    var regular_joe;
    console.log(regular_joe);
  }

  // logs 'undefined'
  prison();
}
supermax();
```

`regular_joe` is set in the global scope.

Calling scope: global. Closest match in scope chain: the global `regular_joe`.

Calling scope: global -> `supermax()`. Closest match in scope chain: the `regular_joe` defined in `supermax()`.

Calling scope: global -> `supermax()` -> `prison()`. Closest match in scope chain: the `regular_joe` defined in `prison()`.

During runtime, JavaScript searches the scope hierarchy to resolve variable names. It starts with the current scope, and then works its way back to the top-level scope, the `window` (browsers) or `global` (node.js) object. It uses the first match it finds and the search stops. Note that this implies that variables in more deeply nested scopes can hide variables in more global scopes by replacing them for their current scope. This can be either good or bad, depending on whether you're expecting it to happen. In real code you should strive to make variable names unique to the extent possible: the code we just looked at, in which the same name is introduced into three different nested scopes, is hardly an example of best practice and is used only to illustrate the point.

In the listing, the value of a variable called `regular_joe` is requested from three scopes:

1 The last line of the listing, `console.log(regular_joe)`, is in the global scope. JavaScript starts searching for a `regular_joe` property of the global execution context object. It finds one with the value `I am here to save the day` and uses it.
2 At the last line of the `supermax` function, we see `console.log(regular_joe)`. This call is within the `supermax` execution context. JavaScript starts searching for a `regular_joe` property of the `supermax` execution context object. It finds one with the value of `regular_joe is assigned` and uses that.
3 At the last line of the `prison` function, we see `console.log(regular_joe)`. This call is within the `prison` execution context within the `supermax` execution context. JavaScript starts searching for a `regular_joe` property of the `prison` execution context object. It finds one with a value of `undefined` and uses that.

In this example, the value of `regular_joe` is defined for all three scopes. In the next version of the code, in listing 2.8, we define it only in the global scope. Now the program prints "I am here to save the day!" three times:

Listing 2.8 Scope chain example—regular_joe defined only in one scope

```
var regular_joe = 'I am here to save the day!';
// logs 'I am here to save the day!'
console.log(regular_joe);
function supermax(){

  // logs 'I am here to save the day!'
  console.log(regular_joe);

  function prison () {
    console.log(regular_joe);
  }

  // logs 'I am here to save the day!'
  prison();
}
// logs 'I am here to save the day'. Twice.
supermax();
```

regular_joe is set in the global scope.

Calling scope: global, which is found.

Calling scope: global -> supermax(). Closest match in scope chain: the global regular_joe.

Calling scope: global -> supermax() -> prison(). Closest match in scope chain: the global regular_joe.

It's important to remember that when we request a variable value, the result may come from anywhere in the scope chain. It's up to us to control and understand where in the chain our values are derived from, lest we shall fall into tortured coding chaos. The JavaScript coding standards in appendix A outline a number of techniques to help us in this effort, and we'll use them as we go along.

Global variables and the window object

What we typically call *global* variables are properties of the top-level object of the execution environment. The top-level object of the browser is the `window` object; in node.js, the top-level object is called `global`, and variable scope works differently.

The `window` object contains many properties which themselves contain objects, methods (`onload`, `onresize`, `alert`, `close`...), DOM elements (`document`, `frames`...) and other variables. All these properties are accessed by using the syntax `window.`*property*.

```
window.onload = function(){
  window.alert('window loaded');
}
```

The top-level object for node.js is called `global`. Because node.js is a network server and not a browser, the functions and properties which are available are significantly different.

When JavaScript in a browser checks for the existence of a *global* variable, it looks at the `window` object.

```
var regular_joe = 'Global variable';
console.log( regular_joe );          // 'Global variable'
console.log( window.regular_joe ); // 'Global variable'
console.log( regular_joe === window.regular_joe ); // true
```

JavaScript has a parallel concept to the scope chain, known as the *prototype chain*, that defines where an object looks for the definitions of its attributes. Let's take a look at prototypes and the prototype chain.

2.5 JavaScript objects and the prototype chain

JavaScript objects are prototype-based, whereas the other most widely used languages today all use class-based objects. In a class-based system, an object is defined by describing what it'll look like with a class. In prototype-based systems, we create an object that looks like what we want all objects of that type to look like, and then tell the JavaScript engine that we want more objects that look like that.

Not to stretch a metaphor too far, but if architecture were a class-based system, an architect would draw up the blueprints of a house and then have houses built based on that blueprint. If architecture were prototype-based, the architect would build a house and then have houses built to look like that one.

Let's build on our earlier prisoner example and compare what it takes in each system to create a single prisoner with properties for the name, prisoner ID, length of prison sentence in years, and number of years probation.

Table 2.2 Simple object creation: class versus prototype

<table>
<tr><th>Class-based</th><th>Prototype-based</th></tr>
<tr><td><pre>public class Prisoner {
  public int sentence = 4;
  public int probation = 2;
  public string name   = "Joe";
  public int id   = 1234;
}

Prisoner prisoner = new Prisoner();</pre></td><td><pre>var prisoner = {
  sentence : 4,
  probation : 2,
  name   : 'Joe',
  id   : 1234
};</pre></td></tr>
</table>

The prototype-based object is simpler and quicker to write when there's only one instance of an object. In class-based systems you have to define a class, define a constructor, and then instantiate an object that is a member of that class. A prototype-based object is simply defined in place.

The prototype-based system shines for the simple one object use case, but it can also support the more complex use case of having multiple objects that share similar characteristics. Let's take the previous example of prisoners and let the code change the `name` and `id` of the prisoners, but keep the same preset years in sentence and years until probation.

As you can see in table 2.3, the two kinds of programming follow a similar sequence, and if you're used to classes, adjusting to prototypes shouldn't be much of a stretch. But the devil is in the details, and if you're coming from a class-based system and jump into JavaScript without learning the prototype-based approach, it's easy to

Table 2.3 Multiple objects: class versus prototype

<table>
<tr><th>Class-based</th><th>Prototype-based</th></tr>
<tr><td><pre>/* step 1 */
public class Prisoner {
  public int sentence = 4;
  public int probation = 2;
  public string name;
  public string id;

  /* step 2 */
  public Prisoner(string name,
    string id) {

    this.name = name;
    this.id   = id;
  }
}</pre></td><td><pre>// * step 1 *
var proto = {
  sentence : 4,
  probation : 2
};

//* step 2 *
var Prisoner =
    function(name, id){
  this.name = name;
  this.id   = id;
};

//* step 3 *
Prisoner.prototype = proto;</pre></td></tr>
<tr><td><pre>/* step 3 */
Prisoner firstPrisoner
 = new Prisoner("Joe","12A");

Prisoner secondPrisoner
 = new Prisoner("Sam","2BC");</pre></td><td><pre>// * step 4 *
var firstPrisoner =
  new Prisoner('Joe','12A');

var secondPrisoner =
  new Prisoner('Sam','2BC');</pre></td></tr>
<tr><td>1 Define the class
2 Define the class constructor
3 Instantiate the objects</td><td>1 Define prototype object
2 Define the object constructor
3 Link constructor to prototype
4 Instantiate the objects</td></tr>
</table>

get tripped up on something that seems like it should be simple. Let's step through the sequence and see what we can learn.

In each method, we first create the template for our objects. The template is called the *class* in class-based programming and the *prototype object* in prototype-based programming, but they serve the same purpose: acting as a framework from which objects will be created.

Second, we create a constructor. In class-based languages, the constructor is defined inside of the class so it's clear when instantiating the object which constructor goes with which class. In JavaScript, the object constructor is set outside of the prototype, so an additional step is needed to link them together.

Finally, the objects are instantiated.

JavaScript's use of the `new` operator is a departure from its prototype-based roots, perhaps as an attempt to make it more comprehensible to developers familiar with class-based inheritance. Unfortunately, we think it clouds the issue and makes something that should be unfamiliar (and therefore studied) appear to be familiar, causing developers to jump in until they run into issues and spend hours trying to figure out a bug caused by mistaking JavaScript for a class-based system.

As an alternative to using the `new` operator, the method `Object.create` has been developed and is used to add a more prototype-based feel to JavaScript object creation. We use the `Object.create` method exclusively throughout the book. Creating prisoners from the prototype-based example from table 2.3 using `Object.create` would look like this:

Listing 2.9 Using `Object.create` to create objects

```
var proto = {
  sentence  : 4,
  probation : 2
};

var firstPrisoner = Object.create( proto );
firstPrisoner.name = 'Joe';
firstPrisoner.id = '12A';

var secondPrisoner = Object.create( proto );
secondPrisoner.name = 'Sam;
secondPrisoner.id = '2BC';
```

`Object.create` takes the prototype as an argument and returns an object; in this way you can define the common attributes and methods on a prototype object and use it to create many objects sharing the same properties. Having to set the `name` and `id` on each of them manually is a pain because having to repeat code isn't very clean. As an alternative, a common pattern for using `Object.create` is to use a factory function that creates and returns the final object. We name all our factory functions `make<object_name>`.

Listing 2.10 Use of `Object.create` with a factory function

```
var proto = {
  sentence  : 4,
  probation : 2
};

var makePrisoner = function( name, id ) {

  var prisoner = Object.create( proto );
  prisoner.name = name;
  prisoner.id = id;

  return prisoner;
};

var firstPrisoner = makePrisoner( 'Joe', '12A' );

var secondPrisoner = makePrisoner( 'Sam', '2BC' );
```

makePrisoner is the factory function; it creates prisoner objects.

The object creation is identical to the previous listing, just wrapped inside of the factory function.

Now we can create new prisoners by calling the makePrisoner function and passing in their name and `id`.

Though there are a number of alternative methods to create objects in JavaScript (it's another oft-debated developer topic), it's generally considered a best practice to use `Object.create`. We prefer this method as it clearly illustrates how the prototype is set. The `new` operator is, unfortunately, perhaps the most commonly used method to create objects. We say unfortunate because it misleads developers into thinking the language is class-based and obscures the nuances of the prototype-based system.

Object.create for older browsers

`Object.create` works in IE 9+, Firefox 4+, Safari 5+, and Chrome 5+. In order to be compatible across older browsers (we're looking at you IE 6, 7, and 8!), we need to define `Object.create` when it doesn't exist and leave it unchanged for browsers that have already implemented it.

```
// Cross-browser method to support Object.create()

var objectCreate = function ( arg ){
  if ( ! arg ) { return {}; }
  function obj() {};
  obj.prototype = arg;
  return new obj;
};

Object.create = Object.create || objectCreate;
```

Now that we've seen how JavaScript uses prototypes to create objects sharing the same properties, let's dig into the prototype chain and talk about how the JavaScript engine implements finding the value of attributes on an object.

2.5.1 *The prototype chain*

Attributes on an object are implemented and function differently in prototype-based JavaScript than in a class-based system. There are enough similarities that most of the time we can get along without a clear understanding, but when the differences rear their ugly heads, we pay the price in frustration and lost productivity. Just like learning the basic differences between prototypes and classes is worth it up front, so is learning about the prototype chain.

JavaScript uses the *prototype chain* to resolve property values. The prototype chain describes how the JavaScript engine looks from object to the object's prototype to the prototype's prototype in order to locate the value of a property of the object. When we request an object's property, the JavaScript engine first looks for the property directly on the object. If it can't find the property there, it looks at the prototype (stored in the `__proto__` property of objects) and sees if the prototype contains the requested property.

If the JavaScript engine can't find the property in the objects prototype, it checks the prototype's prototype (the prototype is just an object, so it has a prototype as well). And so on. This prototype chain ends when JavaScript reaches the generic `Object` prototype. If JavaScript can't find the requested property anywhere in the chain, it returns `undefined`. The details can get intricate as the JavaScript engine checks up the prototype chain, but for the purposes of this book we just need to remember that if a property isn't found on the object, the prototype is checked.

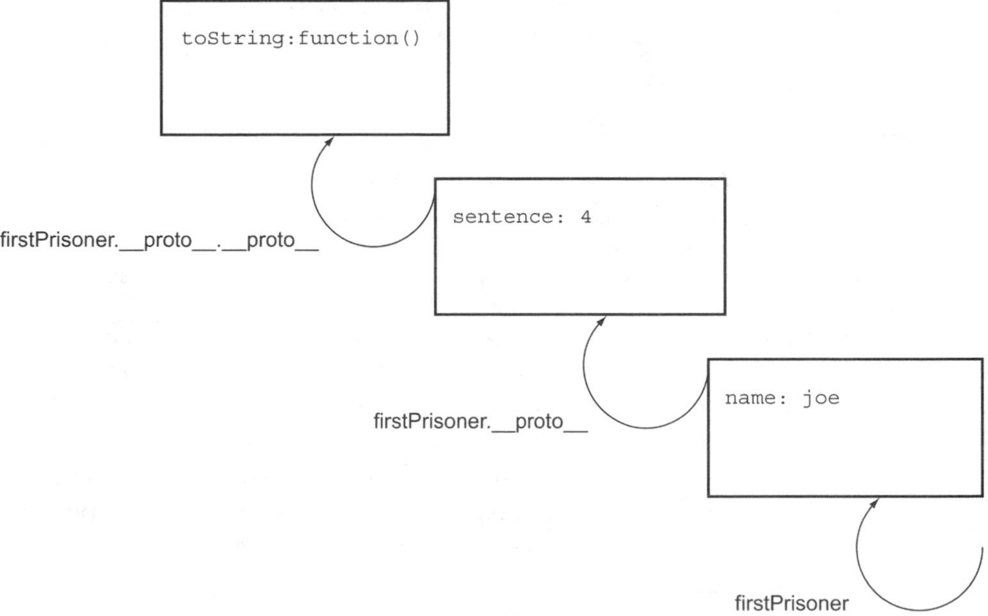

Figure 2.5 During runtime JavaScript searches the prototype chain to resolve property values.

This climb up the prototype chain is similar to the JavaScript engine's climb up the scope chain to find a variable's definition. As you can see in figure 2.5, the concept is nearly identical to the scope chain from figure 2.4.

You can climb the prototype chain manually with the `__proto__` property.

```
var proto = {
  sentence  : 4,
  probation : 2
};

var makePrisoner = function( name, id ) {

  var prisoner = Object.create( proto );
  prisoner.name = name;
  prisoner.id = id;

  return prisoner;
};

var firstPrisoner = makePrisoner( 'Joe', '12A' );

// The entire object, including properties of the prototype
// {"id": "12A", "name": "Joe", "probation": 2, "sentence": 4}
console.log( firstPrisoner );

// Just the prototype properties
// {"probation": 2, "sentence": 4}
console.log( firstPrisoner.__proto__ );

// The prototype is an object with a prototype.  Since one
```

```
// wasn't set, the prototype is the generic object prototype,
// represented as empty curly braces.
// {}
console.log( firstPrisoner.__proto__.__proto__ );

// But the generic object prototype has no prototype
// null
console.log( firstPrisoner.__proto__.__proto__.__proto__ );

// and trying to get the prototype of null is an error
// "firstPrisoner.__proto__.__proto__.__proto__ is null"
console.log( firstPrisoner.__proto__.__proto__.__proto__.__proto__ );
```

If we request `firstPrisoner.name`, JavaScript will find the name of the prisoner directly on the object and return `Joe`. If we request `firstPrisoner.sentence`, JavaScript won't find the property on the object, but would find it in the prototype and return the value of `4`. And if we request `firstPrisoner.toString()`, we'll get the string `[object Object]` because the base Object prototype has that method. Finally, if we request `firstPrisoner.hopeless`, we'll get `undefined`, as that property is nowhere to be found in the prototype chain. These results are summarized in table 2.4.

Table 2.4 Prototype chain

Requested property	Prototype chain
`firstPrisoner`	`{ id: '12A', name: 'Joe', __proto__: { probation: 2, sentence: 4, __proto__: { toString : function () {} } } }` — **`firstPrisoner` object created above, its prototype, and the prototype's prototype, the JavaScript base object.**
`firstPrisoner.name`	`{ id: '12A', name: 'Joe', __proto__: { probation: 2, sentence: 4, __proto__: { toString : function () {} } } }` — **name is accessed directly on the `firstPrisoner` object.**

Table 2.4 Prototype chain *(continued)*

Requested property	Prototype chain

`firstPrisoner.sentence`	`{`
	`  id: '12A',`
	`  name: 'Joe',`
	
	`  __proto__: {`
	`    probation: 2,`
	`    sentence: 4,`
	
	`    __proto__: {`
	`      toString : function () {}`
	`    }`
	`  }`
	`}`
	`sentence` attribute isn't accessible on the `firstPrisoner` object, so it looks to the prototype, where it finds it.

`firstPrisoner.toString`	`{`
	`  id: '12A',`
	`  name: 'Joe',`
	
	`  __proto__: {`
	`    probation: 2,`
	`    sentence: 4,`
	
	`    __proto __ :`
	`      toString : function () {`
	`        [ native code ]`
	`      }`
	`    }`
	`  }`
	`}`
	`toString()` isn't available on the object or its prototype, so it looks at the prototype's prototype, which happens to be the base JavaScript object.

`firstPrisoner.hopeless`	`{`
	`  id: '12A',`
	`  name: 'Joe',`
	
	`  __proto__: {`
	`    probation: 2,`
	`    sentence: 4,`
	
	`    __proto __ :`
	`      toString : function () {`
	`        [ native code ]`
	`      }`
	`    }`
	`  }`
	`}`
	`hopeless` isn't defined on the object . . .
	. . . or the prototype . . .
	. . . or the prototype's prototype, so its value is undefined.

Another way to demonstrate the prototype chain is to see what happens when we change a value on an object set by the prototype.

Listing 2.11 Overwriting the prototype

```
var proto = {
  sentence  : 4,
  probation : 2
};

var makePrisoner = function( name, id ) {

  var prisoner = Object.create( proto );
  prisoner.name = name;
  prisoner.id = id;

  return prisoner;
};

var firstPrisoner = makePrisoner( 'Joe', '12A' );

// Both of these output 4
console.log( firstPrisoner.sentence );
console.log( firstPrisoner.__proto__.sentence );
firstPrisoner.sentence = 10;

// Outputs 10
console.log( firstPrisoner.sentence );

// Outputs 4
console.log( firstPrisoner.__proto__.sentence );
delete firstPrisoner.sentence;

// Both of these output 4
console.log( firstPrisoner.sentence );
console.log( firstPrisoner.__proto__.sentence );
```

`firstPrisoner.sentence` doesn't find a sentence attribute on the `firstPrisoner` object, so it looks at the object's prototype and finds it.

Set the object's `sentence` property to 10.

Confirm that the value was set to 10 on the object...

...but the prototype of that object remains untouched and is still 4

To get the attribute back to the value of the prototype, we delete the attribute from the object.

The next time, the JavaScript engine can no longer find the attribute on the object and must look back up the prototype chain to find the attribute on the prototype object.

So what happens, I can hear you thinking, if we change the value of the attribute on the prototype object?

PROTOTYPE MUTATIONS

One powerful—and potentially dangerous—behavior that prototype inheritance provides is the ability to mutate *all* objects based on a prototype at once. For those familiar with static variables, attributes on the prototype act like static variables for objects created from the prototype. Let's check out our code one more time.

```
var proto = {
  sentence  : 4,
  probation : 2
};

var makePrisoner = function( name, id ) {
```

```
  var prisoner = Object.create( proto );
  prisoner.name = name;
  prisoner.id = id;

  return prisoner;
};

var firstPrisoner = makePrisoner( 'Joe', '12A' );

var secondPrisoner = makePrisoner( 'Sam', '2BC' );
```

If, after the preceding example, we inspect `firstPrisoner` or `secondPrisoner`, we'll find that the inherited property `sentence` is set to 4.

```
...
// Both of these output '4'
console.log( firstPrisoner.sentence );
console.log( secondPrisoner.sentence );
```

If we change the prototype object, for example by setting `proto.sentence = 5`, then all objects created after *and before* will reflect this value. Thus `firstPrisoner.sentence` and `secondPrisoner.sentence` are set to 5.

```
...
proto.sentence = 5;

// Both of these output '5'
console.log( firstPrisoner.sentence );
console.log( secondPrisoner.sentence );
```

This behavior has good and bad points. The important thing is that it's consistent across JavaScript environments and that we know about it so we can code accordingly.

Now that we know how objects inherit properties from other objects using prototypes, let's look at how functions work, because they may also behave differently than you'd expect. We'll also investigate how these differences can provide some useful capabilities that we take advantage of throughout the book.

2.6 Functions—a deeper look

Functions are first-class objects in JavaScript. They can be stored in variables, given attributes, and even be passed as arguments into function calls. They're used to control variable scope and provide private variables and methods. Understanding functions is one of the keys to understanding JavaScript and an important foundation for building professional single page applications.

2.6.1 Functions and anonymous functions

An important feature of a function in JavaScript is that it's an object, just like any other object. We all have probably seen a JavaScript function declared like this:

```
function prison () {}
```

But we can also store functions in variables:

```
var prison = function prison () {};
```

We can decrease the redundancy (and the chance we'll mismatch the names) by making it an *anonymous function*, which is just the label given to a function declaration without a name. Here's an anonymous function being saved to a local variable:

```
var prison = function () {};
```

Functions saved to a local variable are called the same way we would expect a function to be called:

```
var prison = function () {
  console.log('prison called');
};
prison();                          <-- Outputs "prison called"
```

2.6.2 Self-executing anonymous functions

One problem we constantly face in JavaScript is that everything defined in the global scope is available everywhere. Sometimes you don't want to share with everyone and you don't want third-party libraries to share their internal variables with you because it's easy to step over each other's libraries and cause difficult-to-diagnose problems. Using what we know about functions, we could wrap the entire program in a function, call that function, and then our variables wouldn't be accessible to any external code.

```
var myApplication = function () {
  var private_variable = "private";
};

myApplication();

//outputs an error saying the variable in undefined.
console.log( private_variable );
```

But that's a wordy and awkward way to have to do it. It'd be nice if we didn't have to define a function, save it to a variable, and then execute that function. It sure would be nice to have a shorthand approach. Guess what... we do!

```
(function () {
  var private_variable = "private";
})();

//outputs an error saying the variable in undefined.
console.log( private_variable );
```

This is referred to as a *self-executing anonymous function* because it's defined without being given a name or saved to a variable, and is executed immediately. All we do is surround the function with parentheses, followed by a pair of parentheses to execute the function as shown in table 2.5. The syntax isn't that surprising when seen next to an explicitly called function.

Self-executing anonymous functions are used to contain variable scope and prevent variables from leaking out into other places in the code. This can be used to create JavaScript plugins that won't conflict with application code because they don't add any variables to the global namespace. In the next section we'll demonstrate an even

Table 2.5 Explicit invocation versus self-executing functions. These have the same effect: creating a function and then calling it immediately

Explicit invocation	Self-executing function

`var foo = function () {`
`  // do something`
`};`
`foo();`
	`(function () {`
	`  // do something`
	`})();`

more advanced use case that we use throughout the book. It's called the *module pattern* and it gives us access to define private variables and methods. First, let's see how variable scope works in a self-executing anonymous function. If this looks familiar it's because it's exactly the same as before, just using the new syntax:

```
// error message "local_var is not defined"
console.log(local_var);

(function () {

  // local_var is undefined
  console.log(local_var);

  var local_var = 'Local Variable!';

  // local_var is 'Local Variable!'
  console.log(local_var);
}());

// error message "local_var is not defined"
console.log(local_var);
```

When the local variable is declared inside of the function, it is not accessible outside of that function.

Inside of the self-executing anonymous function and before the declaration, the variable is undefined because the variable is declared during the JavaScript engine's first pass over the function and not initialized until it hits the declaration during the second pass.

After the variable is declared and assigned a value inside the function, the value of that variable is available.

Outside of the self-executing anonymous function, the variable is not defined.

Compare that with:

```
console.log(global_var);
var global_var = 'Global Variable!';

console.log(global_var);
```

`global_var` is undefined, but is still declared.

`global_var` is "Global Variable!"

Here the global namespace is polluted with the `global_var` variable and runs the risk of conflicting with other variables of the same name used in our code or in external JavaScript libraries used in our projects. *Pollution of the global namespace* is a term you might hear often in JavaScript circles—this is what it refers to.

One problem that can be solved with a self-executing anonymous functions is that global variables can be overwritten by a third-party library, or even unintentionally by your own code. By passing a value into a self-executing anonymous function as a parameter, you're guaranteeing that the value of that parameter will be what you expect it to be for that execution context because outside code can't affect it.

First, let's see how to pass a parameter into a self-executing anonymous function.

```
(function (what_to_eat) {

  var sentence = 'I am going to eat a ' + what_to_eat;
  console.log(sentence);
})('sandwich');
```

The value sandwich is passed into the anonymous function as the first parameter, `what_to_eat`.

Outputs "I'm going to eat a sandwich".

If that syntax throws you for a loop, it's just passing the value `sandwich` into the anonymous function as the first parameter. Let's compare that syntax against a normal function:

```
var eatFunction = function (what_to_eat) {
  var sentence='I am going to eat a ' + what_to_eat;
  console.log( sentence );
};
eatFunction( 'sandwich' );

// is the same as

(function (what_to_eat) {
  var sentence = 'I am going to eat a ' + what_to_eat;
  console.log(sentence);
})('sandwich');
```

The only difference is that the variable `eatFunction` has been removed and the function definition is surrounded by parentheses.

One famous example of preventing a variable from being overwritten uses the jQuery and Prototype JavaScript libraries. They both make extensive use of the one character variable `$`. If you include both of them in your application, then the library that was added last gets control over the `$`. The technique of passing in a variable to the self-executing anonymous function can be used to ensure that jQuery can use the `$` variable for a block of code.

For this example, you should know that the jQuery and `$` variables are aliases of each other. By passing the jQuery variable into the self-executing anonymous function that uses it as the `$` parameter, you prevent the `$` from being taken over by the Prototype library:

```
( function ( $ ) {

  console.log( $ );
})( jQuery );
```

`$` is the prototype function up until this point.

`$` is the jQuery object within the function scope. This is a simple example: even functions defined inside of the self-executing anonymous function will reference the jQuery object through the `$`.

2.6.3 The module pattern—bringing private variables to JavaScript

It's great that we can wrap our application in a self-executing anonymous function to protect our application from third-party libraries (and protect them from us), but a single page application is huge and can't be defined in one file. It sure would be nice if there were a way to break up that file into modules, each with their own private variables. Okay, you can see where I'm going with this... we can!

Let's see how to break our code up into multiple files, but still take advantage of the self-executing anonymous function to control the scope of our variables.

> **Still not used to that self-executing anonymous function syntax?**
>
> Let's take another look at it. This funny looking syntax:
>
> ```
> var prison = (function() {
>   return 'Mike is in prison';
> })();
> ```
>
> Is practically the same as this syntax:
>
> ```
> function makePrison() {
>   return 'Mike is in prison';
> }
> var prison = makePrison();
> ```
>
> In both cases that value of prison is "Mike is in prison". The only practical difference is that instead of saving the `makePrison` function when it only needs to be used one time, the function is created and invoked without saving it anywhere.

```
var prison = (function () {
  var prisoner_name = 'Mike Mikowski',
      jail_term = '20 year term';

  return {
    prisoner: prisoner_name + ' - ' + jail_term,
    sentence: jail_term
  };
})();

// this is undefined, no prisoner_name for you.
console.log( prison.prisoner_name );

// this outputs 'Mike Mikowski - 20 year term'
console.log( prison.prisoner );

// this outputs '20 year term'
console.log( prison.sentence );
```

The return value of the self-executing anonymous function is stored in the prison variable.

The self-executing anonymous function is returning an object with just the attributes we want on the prison variable.

`prison.prisoner_name` is undefined because it is not an attribute on the object returned by the self-executing anonymous function.

Our self-executing anonymous function is immediately executed and returns an object with the properties `prisoner` and `sentence`. The anonymous function isn't stored in the prison variable because the anonymous function was executed—*the return value of the anonymous function* is stored in the `prison` variable.

Instead of adding the variables `prisoner_name` and `jail_term` to the global scope, only the variable `prison` is added. In bigger modules, the reduction in global variables can be even more significant.

One problem with our object is that the variables defined in the self-executing anonymous function are gone once the function stops executing, so they can't be changed. `prisoner_name` and `jail_term` aren't properties of the object saved to the variable `prison`, so they can't be accessed this way. They *are* variables used to define the attributes `prisoner` and `sentence` on the object returned from the anonymous function, and those attributes can be accessed on the `prison` variable.

```
...

// outputs undefined
console.log( prison.jail_term );
prison.jail_term = 'Sentence commuted';

// this now outputs 'Sentence commuted', but...
console.log( prison.jail_term );

// this outputs 'Mike Mikowski - 20 year term'... sorry Mike
console.log( prison.prisoner );
```

`prison` is an object, so you can still define a `jail_term` attribute on it...

`prison.jail_term` is undefined because it's not an attribute on the object returned by the self-executing anonymous function.

...but `prison.prisoner` still won't be updated.

`prison.prisoner` doesn't get updated for a few reasons. First, `jail_term` isn't an attribute on the `prison` object or prototype; it was a variable in the execution context that created the object and saved to the prison variable, and that execution context no longer exists because the function finished executing already. Second, these attributes are set one time when the anonymous function is executed and are never updated. To make them update, we have to turn the attributes into methods that access the variables every time they're invoked.

```
var prison = (function () {
  var prisoner_name = 'Mike Mikowski',
      jail_term = '20 year term';

  return {
     prisoner: function () {
       return prisoner_name + ' - ' + jail_term;
    },
    setJailTerm: function ( term ) {
       jail_term = term;
    }
  };
})();

// this outputs 'Mike Mikowski - 20 year term'
console.log( prison.prisoner() );

prison.setJailTerm( 'Sentence commuted' );

// this now outputs 'Mike Mikowski - Sentence commuted'
console.log( prison.prisoner() );
```

Returning an object with two methods.

Every time `prisoner()` is invoked, it looks up the `prisoner_name` and `jail_term` again.

Every time `setJailTerm()` is invoked, it looks up the jail_term and sets it.

Even though the self-executing anonymous function is done executing, the variables `prisoner_name` and `jail_term` remain accessible to the `prisoner` and `setJailTerm` methods. `prisoner_name` and `jail_term` now act like private attributes for the prison object. They can only be accessed by methods on the object returned from the anonymous function and aren't directly accessible on the object or the object's prototype. And you'd heard closures were hard. Wait, I'm sorry... I haven't explained how that's a closure yet, have I? Okay, let's take a few steps back and walk up to it.

WHAT IS A CLOSURE?

As an abstract concept, closures can be difficult to wrap your head around, so before answering the question "What is a closure?" we'll need to set some background. Please bear with us, as you'll get the answer to this question by the end of this section.

As programs run, they take up and use the computer's memory for all sorts of things, such as storing the values of variables. If programs ran and never freed up memory that was no longer needed, the computer would eventually crash. In some languages, like C, memory management has to be handled by the programmer and a lot of time is spent by programmers writing code to make sure that memory is freed up when it can.

Other languages, like Java and JavaScript, implement a system for automatically freeing up memory by removing code from the computer's memory when it's no longer needed. These automated systems are called *garbage collectors*, presumably because unneeded variables taking up space stink. There are opinions as to which system is better, automated or manual, but that's beyond the scope of this book. It's enough to know that JavaScript has a garbage collector.

When a function is finished executing, a naive approach to memory management would be to remove everything that was created inside of that function from memory. After all, the function is finished executing, so it would seem that we don't need access to anything inside of that execution context anymore.

```
var prison = function () {
  var prisoner = 'Josh Powell';
};

prison();
```

Once `prison` is done executing, we no longer need access to the `prisoner` variable, so Josh is free to go. This pattern is verbose, so let's turn it back into that self-executing anonymous function pattern.

```
(function () {
  var prisoner = 'Josh Powell';
})();
```

Same thing here: the function is executed and when it's done the prisoner variable doesn't need to be kept in memory any longer. Bye bye, Josh!

Let's stick this in our module pattern.

```
var prison = (function () {
  var prisoner = 'Josh Powell';

  return { prisoner: prisoner };
})();

// outputs 'Josh Powell'
console.log( prison.prisoner );
```

We're going to become very familiar with saving a variable or function to a property of the same name on the object returned from the module pattern: we use it throughout the book.

We still don't need access to the `prisoner` variable after the anonymous function has executed. Because the string `Josh Powell` is now stored in `prison.prisoner`, there's no reason to keep the `prisoner` variable in the module in memory because it's no longer accessible. Though it may seem otherwise, the value of `prison.prisoner` is the string `Josh Powell`; it doesn't point to the `prisoner` variable.

```
var prison = (function () {
  var prisoner = 'Josh Powell';

  return {
    prisoner: function () {
      return prisoner;
    }
  }
})();

// outputs 'Josh Powell'
console.log( prison.prisoner() );
```

Now, the `prisoner` variable is accessed every time `prison.prisoner` is executed. `prison.prisoner()` returns the current value of the `prisoner` variable. If the garbage collector came and removed it from memory, invoking `prison.prisoner` would return `undefined` instead of `Josh Powell`.

Now, finally, we can answer the question "What is a closure?" A closure is the process of preventing the garbage collector from removing a variable from memory by keeping access to the variable outside the execution context in which it was created. A closure is created when the `prisoner` function is saved on the `prison` object. The closure is created by saving a function, with dynamic access to the `prisoner` variable, outside of the current execution context, which prevents the garbage collector from removing the `prisoner` variable from memory.

Let's look at a few more examples of closures.

```
var makePrison = function ( prisoner ) {
  return function () {
    return prisoner;
  }
};

var joshPrison = makePrison( 'Josh Powell' );
var mikePrison = makePrison( 'Mike Mikowski' );

// outputs 'Josh Powell', prisoner variable is saved in a closure.
// The closure is created because of the anonymous function returned
// from the makePrison call that accesses the prisoner variable.
console.log( joshPrison() );
```

```
// outputs 'Mike Mikowski',the prisoner variable is saved in a closure.
// The closure is created because of the anonymous function returned
// from the makePrison call that accesses the prisoner variable.
console.log( mikePrison() );
```

Another common use of closures is to save variables for use when an Ajax call returns. When using methods in a JavaScript object, `this` refers to the object:

```
var prison = {
  names: 'Mike Mikowski and Josh Powell',
  who: function () {
    return this.names;
  }
};

// returns 'Mike Mikowski and Josh Powell'
prison.who();
```

If your method makes an Ajax call using jQuery, then `this` no longer refers to your object; it refers to the Ajax call:

```
var prison = {
  names: 'Josh Powell and Mike Mikowski',
  who: function () {
    $.ajax({
      success: function () {
        console.log( this.names );
      }
    });
  }
};

// outputs undefined, 'this' is the ajax object
prison.who();
```

So how do you refer to the object? Closures to the rescue! Remember, a closure is created by taking a function that has access to a variable in the current execution context and saving it to a variable outside of the current execution context. In the following example, it's created by saving `this` to `that`, and accessing `that` in the function that executes when the Ajax call is returned. The Ajax call is asynchronous, so the response comes outside of the execution context where the Ajax call is made.

```
var prison = {
  names: 'Mike Mikowski and Josh Powell',
  who: function () {
    var that = this;
    $.ajax({
        success: function () {
         console.log( that.names );
      }
    });
  }
};

// outputs 'Mike Mikowski and Josh Powell'
prison.who();
```

The Ajax call is asynchronous, so the call to `who()` is finished executing by the time the response comes back.

Even though `who()` has finished executing by the time the Ajax call has returned, the `that` variable wasn't garbage collected and is available for use by the `success` method.

Hopefully, we've presented closures in a way that makes it easy to grasp what they are and how they work. Now that we have a grasp of what a closure is, let's dig into the mechanics of closures and see how they're implemented.

2.6.4 Closures

How do closures work? Now we understand *what* a closure, but not *how* it is implemented. The answer lies with execution context objects. Let's take a look at an example from the last section:

```
var makePrison = function (prisoner) {
  return function () {
    return prisoner;
  }
};

var joshPrison = makePrison( 'Josh Powell' );
var mikePrison = makePrison( 'Mike Mikowski' );

// outputs 'Josh Powell'
console.log( joshPrison() );

// outputs 'Mike Mikowski'
console.log( mikePrison() );
```

When `makePrison` is invoked, an execution context object for that *specific* invocation is created and `prisoner` is assigned the value passed in. Remember that an execution context object is part of the JavaScript engine and isn't directly accessible in JavaScript.

In the preceding example, we make two calls to `makePrison`, saving the results to `joshPrison` and `mikePrison`. Because the return value of `makePrison` is a function, when we assign it to the `joshPrison` variable, the reference count to that *specific* execution context object is one, and because the count remains greater than zero, that *specific* execution context object is retained by the JavaScript engine. If that count were to drop to zero, then the JavaScript engine would know that object could be garbage collected.

When `makePrison` is called again and assigned to `mikePrison`, a new execution context object is created and the reference count to that execution context object is also set to one. At that point, we have two pointers to two execution context objects, both with a reference count of one, even though both were created by executing the same function.

If we were to invoke `joshPrison` again, it would use the value set on the execution context object created when `makePrison` was invoked and saved to `joshPrison`. The only way to purge the retained execution context object (besides closing the web page, smarty pants) is to delete the `joshPrison` variable. When we do, the reference count to that execution context object drops to 0, and it may be removed at JavaScript's leisure.

Let's get a few execution context objects going at once and see what happens:

Listing 2.12 Execution context objects

```
var curryLog, logHello, logStayinAlive, logGoodbye;

curryLog = function ( arg_text ){
  var log_it = function (){ console.log( arg_text ); };
  return log_it;
};

logHello       = curryLog('hello');
logStayinAlive = curryLog('stayin alive!');
logGoodbye     = curryLog('goodbye');

// This creates no reference to the execution context,
// and therefore the execution context object can be
// immediately purged by the JavaScript garbage collector
curryLog('fred');

logHello();      // logs 'hello'
logStayinAlive(); // logs 'stayin alive!'
logGoodbye();    // logs 'goodbye'
logHello();      // logs 'hello' again

// destroy reference to 'hello' execution context
delete window.logHello;

// destroy reference to 'stayin alive!' execution context
delete window.logStayinAlive;

logGoodbye();    // logs 'goodbye'
logStayinAlive(); // undefined - execution context destroyed
```

We must remember that a unique execution context object is created every time a function is called. After the function completes, the execution object is immediately discarded *unless the caller retains a reference to it.* If a function returns a number, you can't typically retain a reference to a function's execution context object. On the other hand, if a function returns a more complex structure like a function, an object, or an array, creating a reference to the execution context is often accomplished—sometimes mistakenly—by storing the return value to a variable.

It's possible to create chains of execution context references many layers deep. And this is a good thing when we want it (think *object inheritance*). But there are times when we don't want closures like this, as they could create runaway memory usage (think *memory leak*). Rules and tools are presented in appendix A that can help you avoid unintended closures.

Closures—one more time!

Before moving on, because closures are such an important and confusing part of JavaScript, let's take one more stab at an explanation. If you've got closures down cold, feel free to move on.

(continued)

```
var   menu, outer_function,
      food = 'cake';

outer_function = function () {
  var fruit, inner_function;

  fruit = 'apple';

  inner_function = function () {
    return { food: food, fruit: fruit };
  }

  return inner_function;
};

menu = outer_function();

// returns { food:  'cake', fruit: 'apple' }
menu();
```

When `outer_function` is executed, it creates an execution context. `inner_function` is defined inside of that execution context

Because `inner_function` is defined inside the `outer_function` execution context, it has access to all of the variables in scope in `outer_function`—in this case `food`, `fruit`, `outer_function`, `inner_function`, and `menu`.

When `outer_function` is finished executing, you might expect everything inside of that execution context to be destroyed by the garbage collector. You'd be wrong.

It's not destroyed because a reference to the `inner_function` has been saved in the global scope in the variable `menu`. Because the `inner_function` needs to retain access to all of the variables that were in scope where it was declared, it "closes over" the `outer_function` execution context to prevent the garbage collector from removing it. This is a closure.

That brings us back to our first example, so let's examine why `scoped_var` is accessible after the Ajax call returns.

```
function sendAjaxRequest() {
  var scoped_var = 'yay';
  $.ajax({
    success: function () {
      console.log(scoped_var);
    }
  });
}
sendAjaxRequest();
```

Logs "yay" when the Ajax call successfully completes

It's accessible because the success method is defined in the execution context created when `sendAjaxRequest` was called, and `scoped_var` was in scope at the time. If closures are still unclear to you, don't be dismayed. Closures are one of the more difficult

JavaScript concepts, and if after reading this section a few times you still don't get it, just move on; it could be a concept that you need some more practical experience with in order to understand. Hopefully, by the end of this book you'll have enough practical experience that it'll become second nature to you.

And this concludes our head-long and sometimes deep dive into the particulars of JavaScript. The review wasn't comprehensive, but instead focused on the concepts we've found necessary to develop large-scale SPAs. We hope you enjoyed the ride.

2.7 Summary

In this chapter we've covered some concepts that, though not unique to JavaScript, are sometimes not found in other widely used programming languages. Knowledge of these topics will be important to writing a single page application—without this knowledge you could end up feeling lost as we build out the application.

Understanding variable scoping, and variable and function hoisting, is fundamental to demystifying variables in JavaScript. Understanding the execution context object is important for understanding how scoping and hoisting work.

Knowing how to create objects in JavaScript using prototypes makes it possible to write reusable code in native JavaScript. Without an understanding of prototype-based objects, engineers often revert to using a library to write reusable code, depending on a class-based model provided by a library that's actually a wrapper on top of the prototype-based model. If, after learning the prototype-based method, you still prefer to use a class-based system, you'll still be able to take advantage of the prototype-based model for the simple use cases. For building our single page application, we'll be using the prototype-based model for two reasons: we believe it's simpler to use for our use cases, and it's the JavaScript way and we're coding in JavaScript.

Writing self-executing anonymous functions will contain your variable scope, help prevent you from inadvertently polluting the global namespace, and help you write libraries and a codebase that don't conflict with other libraries.

Understanding the module pattern and how to use private variables allows you to cultivate a thoughtful public API for your objects and to hide all of the messy internal methods and variables that other objects don't need access to. This keeps your API nice and clean and makes it obvious which methods you should be consuming and which are meant to be private helper methods for the API.

Finally, we spent a good deal of time diving into one of the most difficult JavaScript concepts: closures. If you don't fully understand closures just yet, hopefully there will be enough practical experience throughout the book to cement your understanding.

With these concepts in mind, let's move on to the next chapter and start building a production-quality SPA.

Part 2

The SPA client

An SPA client provides much more than a traditional website user interface (UI). Though some say that SPA clients can be as responsive as desktop applications, it's more accurate to say that well-written SPA clients are desktop applications.

Like desktop applications, SPA clients differ substantially from traditional web pages. When we replace a traditional website with an SPA, the entire software stack changes—from the database server through the HTML templating. Companies that have had the vision to successfully transition from traditional websites to SPAs have understood that the old practices and structures must change. They've refocused engineering talent, discipline, and testing on the client. The server remains important, but it's focused on providing JSON data services.

So let's forget everything we know about traditional website client development. All right, not *everything*—it's still good to know JavaScript, HTML5, CSS3, SVG, CORS, and a bunch of other acronyms. But we need to remember as we proceed through these chapters that *we'll be building a desktop application*, not a traditional website. In part 2 we learn how to:

- Build and test a highly scalable, testable, and capable SPA client
- Make the Back button, bookmarks, and other history controls work as expected
- Design, implement, and test robust feature modules and their APIs
- Make our UI work seamlessly on mobile devices and desktops
- Organize modules and namespaces to greatly improve testing, team development, and design-for-quality.

One thing we don't discuss is how to use a particular SPA framework library. We have many reasons for this (see the sidebar in chapter 6 for an in-depth discussion). We want to explain the inner workings of well-written SPAs instead of the implementation intricacies that apply to only a single framework library. Instead, we use an architecture refined over six years and many commercial products. This architecture encourages testability, readability, and design-for-quality. It also makes dividing work between many client developers simple and enjoyable. With this approach, readers who *want* to use a framework library can make an informed decision and use it with greater success.

3

Develop the Shell

This chapter covers

- Describing the Shell module and its place in our architecture
- Structuring your files and namespaces
- Creating and styling feature containers
- Using an event handler to toggle a feature container
- Using the anchor interface pattern to manage application state

In this chapter, we describe the *Shell*, a required component of our architecture. We develop a page layout that contains our feature containers, and then adjust the Shell to render them. Next we show how the Shell manages feature containers by having it extend and retract the chat slider. We then have it capture the user click event to open and close the slider. Finally, we use the URI anchor as our state API using the *anchor interface pattern*. This provides users the browser controls they expect—controls like Forward and Back buttons, browser history, and bookmarks.

By the end of this chapter we'll have built the foundation for a scalable and manageable SPA. But let's not get too far ahead of ourselves. First we must understand the Shell.

3.1 Grok the Shell

The *Shell* is the master controller for our SPA and is required in our architecture. We can compare the role of the Shell module to the shell of an airplane:

An airplane's shell (also called the monocoque or airframe) provides shape and structure to the vehicle. Assemblies like the seats, tray tables, and the engines are attached to it using various fasteners. All assemblies are built to work as independently as possible because nobody likes it when Aunt Milly opens her tray table and it causes the jet to promptly bank hard to the right.

The Shell module provides shape and structure to our application. Feature modules like chat, sign-in, and navigation are "attached" to the Shell with APIs. All feature modules are built to work as independently as possible because nobody likes it when Aunt Milly types "`ROTFLMAO!!! UR totally pwned!`" into her chat slider and the application promptly closes her browser window.

The Shell is just one piece of an architecture which we refined over many commercial projects. This architecture—and where the Shell fits in—is shown in figure 3.1. We like to write the Shell first because it's central to our architecture. It coordinates the *feature modules* with the business logic and universal browser interfaces like the URI or cookies. When the user clicks the Back button, signs in, or does anything else that changes the bookmark-able state of the application, the Shell coordinates the change.

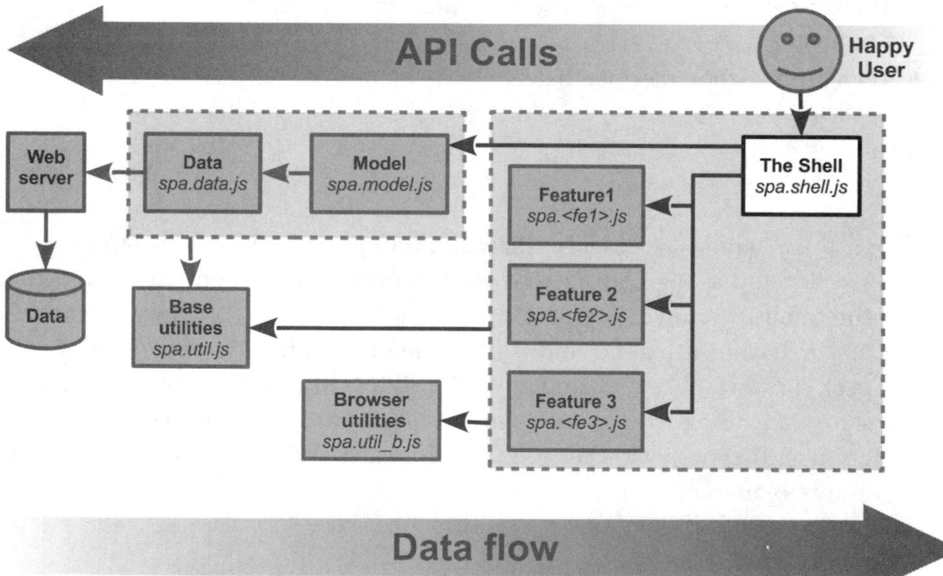

Figure 3.1 The Shell in our SPA architecture

Those of you comfortable with the Model-View-Controller (MVC) architecture may consider the Shell the master controller, as it coordinates the controllers of all the subordinate feature modules.

The Shell is responsible for the following:

- Rendering and managing the feature containers
- Managing the application state
- Coordinating feature modules

The next chapter will detail the coordination of feature modules. This chapter covers rendering the feature containers and managing the application state. First let's prepare our files and namespaces.

3.2 Set up the files and namespaces

We'll set up our files and namespaces according to the code standards found in appendix A. In particular, we'll have one JavaScript file per JavaScript namespace, and use self-executing anonymous functions to prevent pollution of the global namespace. We'll also set up CSS files in a parallel structure. This convention speeds development, improves quality, and eases maintenance. Its value increases as we add more modules and developers to the project.

3.2.1 Create the file structure

We've selected spa for the root namespace of our application. We synchronize the JavaScript and CSS file names, the JavaScript namespace, and the CSS selector names. This makes it much easier to track which JavaScript goes with which CSS.

PLAN THE DIRECTORIES AND FILES

Web developers often place their HTML file in a directory and then place their CSS and JavaScript in subdirectories. We see no reason to break convention. Let's create the directories and files as shown in listing 3.1:

Listing 3.1 Files and directories, first pass

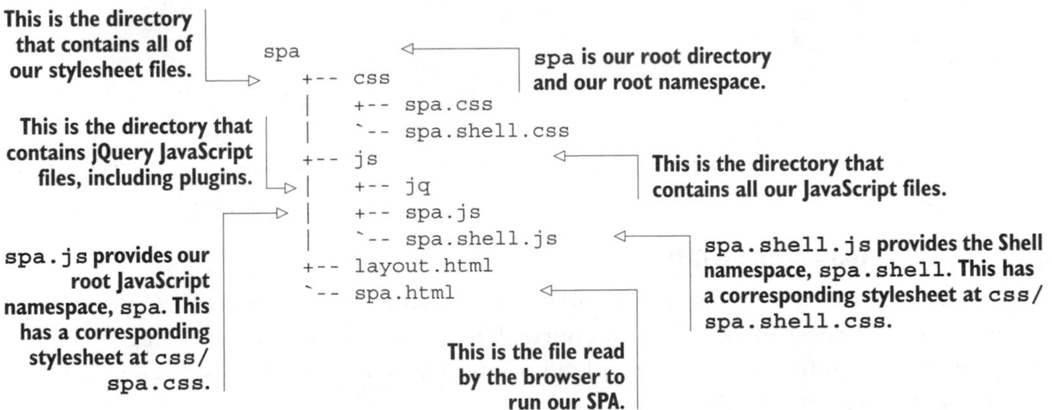

Now that we have the basics in place, let's get jQuery installed.

INSTALL JQUERY AND A PLUGIN

jQuery and its plugins are often offered as either minified or regular files. We almost always install the regular files because this helps in debugging, and we minimize as part of our build system anyway. Don't worry about what they do yet—we'll get to that later in the chapter.

The jQuery library provides useful cross-platform DOM manipulation and other utilities. We're using version 1.9.1, which is available from http://docs.jquery.com/Downloading_jQuery. Let's place it in our jQuery directory:

```
...
  +-- js
  |    +-- jq
  |    |    +-- jquery-1.9.1.js
  ...
```

The jQuery `uriAnchor` plugin provides utilities to manage the anchor component of the URI. It's available from github at https://github.com/mmikowski/urianchor. Let's place it in the same jQuery directory:

```
...
  +-- js
  |    +-- jq
  |    |    +-- jquery.uriAnchor-1.1.3.js
  ...
```

Our files and directories should now look like listing 3.2:

Listing 3.2 Files and directories after adding jQuery and plugin

```
spa
  +-- css
  |    +-- spa.css
  |    `-- spa.shell.css
  +-- js
  |    +-- jq
  |    |    +-- jquery-1.9.1.js
  |    |    `-- jquery.uriAnchor-1.1.3.js
  |    +-- spa.js
  |    `-- spa.shell.js
  +-- layout.html
  `-- spa.html
```

Now that we have all of our files in place, it's time to start writing some HTML, CSS, and JavaScript.

3.2.2 *Write the application HTML*

When we open our browser document (spa/spa.html) we can bask in all the SPA goodness we've wrought so far. Of course, because this is an empty file, the goodness provided is limited to a bug-free, highly secure blank page that does absolutely nothing. Let's change the "blank page" part.

The browser document (spa/spa.html) will always remain small. Its only role is to load libraries and stylesheets, and then start our application. Let's fire up our favorite text editor and add all the code we'll need to get through this chapter, as shown in listing 3.3:

Listing 3.3 Application HTML—spa/spa.html

```
<!doctype html>
<html>
<head>
  <title>SPA Starter</title>

  <!-- stylesheets -->
  <link rel="stylesheet" href="css/spa.css" type="text/css"/>
  <link rel="stylesheet" href="css/spa.shell.css" type="text/css"/>

  <!-- third-party javascript -->
  <script src="js/jq/jquery-1.9.1.js"          ></script>
  <script src="js/jq/jquery.uriAnchor-1.1.3.js"></script>

  <!-- our javascript -->
  <script src="js/spa.js"       ></script>
  <script src="js/spa.shell.js"></script>
  <script>
    $(function () { spa.initModule( $('#spa') ); });
  </script>

</head>
<body>
  <div id="spa"></div>
</body>
</html>
```

Load stylesheets first. This optimizes performance. If we add third-party stylesheets, we should load them first.

Load third-party JavaScript next. At present, the only third-party scripts we're loading are jQuery and the plugin for anchor manipulation.

Load our JavaScript libraries next. They should be ordered by depth of namespace. This is important because our namespace object, `spa`, must be declared before we can declare its children, for example, `spa.shell`.

Initialize the application once the DOM is ready. Those familiar with jQuery will notice our code uses shorthand, as `$(function (...` could've been written as `$(document).ready(function (...`

The performance conscious developers in the audience might ask "Why don't we put scripts at the end of the body container like traditional web pages?" That is a fair question, because this usually allows the page to render faster, as static HTML and CSS can be displayed before the JavaScript finishes loading. SPAs don't work like that, though. They generate the HTML with JavaScript, and therefore placing the scripts outside the header doesn't result in faster rendering. Instead, we keep all of the external scripts in the head section to improve organization and legibility.

3.2.3 *Create the root CSS namespace*

Our root namespace is spa, and per our convention from appendix A our root stylesheet should be called spa/css/spa.css. We previously created this file, but now it's time to populate it. Because this is our root stylesheet, it'll have a few more sections than our other CSS files. Let's again use our favorite text editor to add the rules we need, as shown in listing 3.4:

Listing 3.4 The root CSS namespace—spa/css/spa.css

```
/*
 * spa.css
 * Root namespace styles
```

```
*/

/** Begin reset */
  * {
    margin  : 0;
    padding : 0;
    -webkit-box-sizing : border-box;
    -moz-box-sizing    : border-box;
    box-sizing         : border-box;
  }
  h1,h2,h3,h4,h5,h6,p { margin-bottom : 10px; }
  ol,ul,dl { list-style-position : inside;}
/** End reset */

/** Begin standard selectors */
  body {
    font : 13px 'Trebuchet MS', Verdana, Helvetica, Arial, sans-serif;
    color            : #444;
    background-color : #888;
  }
  a { text-decoration : none; }
    a:link, a:visited { color : inherit; }
    a:hover { text-decoration: underline; }

  strong {
    font-weight : 800;
    color       : #000;
  }
/** End standard selectors */

/** Begin spa namespace selectors */
  #spa {
    position : absolute;
    top      : 8px;
    left     : 8px;
    bottom   : 8px;
    right    : 8px;

    min-height : 500px;
    min-width  : 500px;
    overflow   : hidden;

    background-color : #fff;
    border-radius    : 0 8px 0 8px;
  }
/** End spa namespace selectors */

/** Begin utility selectors */
  .spa-x-select {}
  .spa-x-clearfloat {
    height     : 0      !important;
    float      : none   !important;
    visibility : hidden !important;
    clear      : both   !important;
  }
/** End utility selectors */
```

Reset most selectors. We don't trust browser defaults. CSS authors will recognize this as a common practice, though not without controversy.

Adjust standard selectors. We again don't trust browser defaults, and we also want to ensure a common look across the application for certain types of elements. These can—and will—be adjusted by more specific selectors in other files.

Define namespace selectors. Generally, this is the selector for an element using the root name, for example, `#spa`.

Provide utility selectors for use across all other modules. These are prefixed with `spa-x-`.

Per our code standards, all CSS IDs and class names in this file are preceded by the spa- prefix. Now that we've created the root application CSS, we'll create the corresponding JavaScript namespace.

3.2.4 Create the root JavaScript namespace

Our root namespace is spa, and per our convention from appendix A, our root JavaScript should be called spa/js/spa.js. The minimal JavaScript required is `var spa = {};`. But, we want to add a method to initialize the application, and we want to ensure that the code will pass JSLint. We can use the template from appendix A and pare it down because we don't need all the sections. Let's open the file with our second-most-favorite text editor and populate it as shown in listing 3.5:

Listing 3.5 The root JavaScript namespace—spa/js/spa.js

```
/*
 * spa.js
 * Root namespace module
*/

/*jslint           browser : true,   continue : true,
  devel  : true,    indent : 2,       maxerr  : 50,
  newcap : true,     nomen : true,   plusplus : true,
  regexp : true,    sloppy : true,       vars : false,
  white  : true
*/
/*global $, spa */

var spa = (function () {
  var initModule = function ( $container ) {
    $container.html(
      '<h1 style="display:inline-block; margin:25px;">'
        + 'hello world!'
      + '</h1>'
    );
  };

  return { initModule: initModule };
}());
```

Set JSLint switches per the module template in appendix A.

Tell JSLint to expect the spa and $ global variables. If we find ourselves adding our own variables to this list after spa, we're probably doing something wrong.

Use the module pattern from chapter 2 to create our "spa" namespace. This module exports one method, initModule, which, as the name suggests, is a function that initializes the application.

We want to ensure our code doesn't have any common errors or bad practices. Appendix A shows how to install and run the valuable JSLint utility, which does just that. It describes what all the `/*jslint ... */` switches at the top of our files mean. Besides the appendix, we also discuss JSLint further in chapter 5.

Let's check our code by typing `jslint spa/js/spa.js` at the command line—we shouldn't see any warnings or errors. We can now open our browser document (spa/spa.html) and see the contract-mandated "hello world" demonstration as shown in figure 3.2.

Now that we've greeted the world and are emboldened by the savory flavor of success, let's embark on a more ambitious quest. In the next section, we start building our first "real-world" SPA.

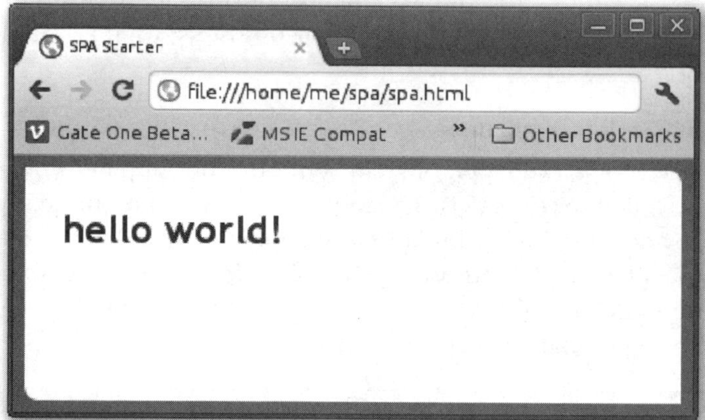

Figure 3.2 Obligatory "hello world" screenshot

3.3 Create the feature containers

The Shell creates and manages the containers our feature modules will use. Our chat slider container, for example, will follow popular convention and be anchored on the bottom right of the browser window. The Shell is responsible for the slider container, but won't manage the behavior inside of the container—that's reserved for the chat feature module, which we'll discuss in chapter 6.

Let's place our chat slider in a layout that's relatively complete. Figure 3.3 shows a wireframe of the containers we'd like to see.

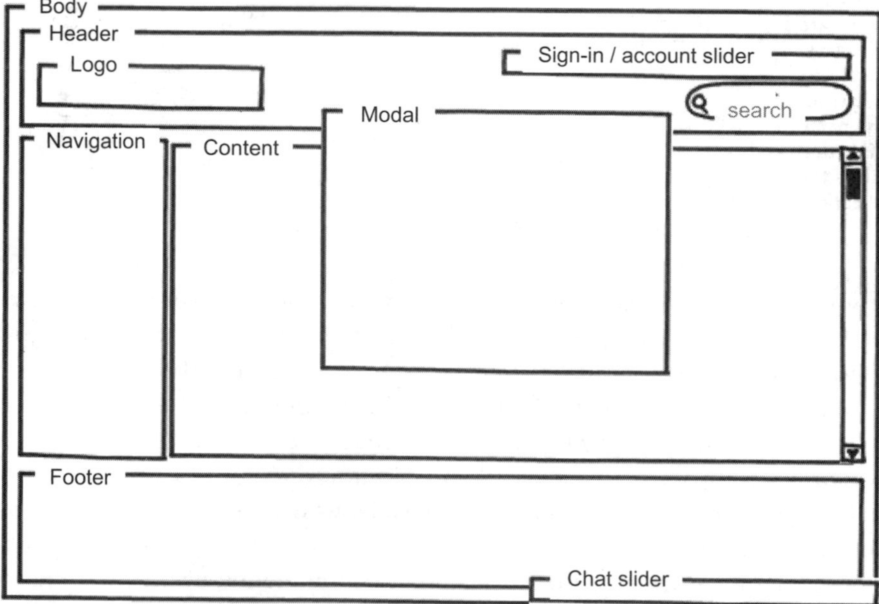

Figure 3.3 Application containers wireframe

Of course, this is only a wireframe. We need to convert this into HTML and CSS. Let's discuss how we might do that.

3.3.1 Pick a strategy

We'll develop the HTML and CSS for our feature containers in a single-layout document file at spa/layout.html. Only after we've tweaked our containers to our liking will we move the code to the Shell's CSS and JavaScript files. This approach is usually the fastest and most efficient means to develop the initial layout because we can proceed without worrying about interactions with most other code.

First we'll write the HTML, and then later we'll add the styles.

3.3.2 Write the Shell HTML

One great feature of HTML5 and CSS3 is that we really *can* separate styling from the content. The wireframe shows the containers we want and how they'll be nested. This is all we need to write the HTML for our containers with confidence. Let's open our layout document (spa/layout.html) and enter the HTML shown in listing 3.6:

Listing 3.6 Create HTML for the containers—spa/layout.html

```
<!doctype html>
  <html>
  <head>
    <title>HTML Layout</title>
    <link rel="stylesheet" href="css/spa.css" type="text/css"/>
  </head>
  <body>
    <div id="spa">
      <div class="spa-shell-head">
        <div class="spa-shell-head-logo"></div>
        <div class="spa-shell-head-acct"></div>
        <div class="spa-shell-head-search"></div>
      </div>
      <div class="spa-shell-main">
        <div class="spa-shell-main-nav"></div>
        <div class="spa-shell-main-content"></div>
      </div>
      <div class="spa-shell-foot"></div>
      <div class="spa-shell-chat"></div>
      <div class="spa-shell-modal"></div>
    </div>
  </body>
  </html>
```

Nest the `logo`, the account settings (`acct`), and the `search` box inside of the head container.

Place the navigation (`nav`) and `content` containers inside the main container.

Create a `footer` container.

Anchor the `chat` container to the bottom right of the outer container.

Create a `modal` container that floats above other content.

Now we should validate the HTML to ensure it's without error. We like to use the venerable Tidy tool, which can find missing tags and other common HTML errors. You can find Tidy online at http://infohound.net/tidy/, or download the source at http://tidy.sourceforge.net/. If you're using a Linux distribution like Ubuntu or Fedora, Tidy is probably readily available in the standard software repositories. Now let's give these containers some style.

3.3.3 *Write the Shell CSS*

We'll write our CSS to provide a *liquid layout* where the width and height of our content will adjust to fill the browser window at all but the most extreme sizes. We'll give our feature containers background colors so we can easily see them. We'll also avoid any borders, because they can change the size of the CSS boxes. This introduces unwanted tedium into our rapid prototype process. Once we're happy with the presentation of our containers, we can return to add borders as necessary.

> **Liquid layouts**
>
> As our layout grows more complex, we may need to use JavaScript to provide its *liquidity*. Often a window resize event handler is used to determine the browser window size and then recalculate and apply new CSS dimensions. We illustrate this technique in chapter 4.

Let's add the CSS to the <head> section of our layout document (spa/layout.html). We can place it right after the `spa.css` stylesheet link as shown in listing 3.7. All changes are shown in **bold**:

Listing 3.7 Create CSS for the containers—spa/layout.html

```
...
  <head>
    <title>HTML Layout</title>
    <link rel="stylesheet" href="css/spa.css" type="text/css"/>
    <style>
      .spa-shell-head, .spa-shell-head-logo, .spa-shell-head-acct,
      .spa-shell-head-search, .spa-shell-main, .spa-shell-main-nav,
      .spa-shell-main-content, .spa-shell-foot, .spa-shell-chat,
      .spa-shell-modal {
        position : absolute;
      }
      .spa-shell-head {
        top    : 0;
        left   : 0;
        right  : 0;
        height : 40px;
      }
      .spa-shell-head-logo {
        top        : 4px;
        left       : 4px;
        height     : 32px;
        width      : 128px;
        background : orange;
      }
      .spa-shell-head-acct {
        top    : 4px;
        right  : 0;
        width  : 64px;
        height : 32px;
```

```
  background : green;
}
.spa-shell-head-search {
  top        : 4px;
  right      : 64px;
  width      : 248px;
  height     : 32px;
  background : blue;
}

.spa-shell-main {
  top    : 40px;
  left   : 0;
  bottom : 40px;
  right  : 0;
}
.spa-shell-main-content,
.spa-shell-main-nav {
  top    : 0;
  bottom : 0;
}
.spa-shell-main-nav {
  width      : 250px;
  background : #eee;
}
.spa-x-closed .spa-shell-main-nav {
  width : 0;
}

.spa-shell-main-content {
  left       : 250px;
  right      : 0;
  background : #ddd;
}
.spa-x-closed .spa-shell-main-content {
  left : 0;
}

.spa-shell-foot {
  bottom : 0;
  left   : 0;
  right  : 0;
  height : 40px;
}
.spa-shell-chat {
  bottom     : 0;
  right      : 0;
  width      : 300px;
  height     : 15px;
  background : red;
  z-index    : 1;
}
.spa-shell-modal {
  margin-top    : -200px;
  margin-left   : -200px;
  top           : 50%;
```

```
        left          : 50%;
        width         : 400px;
        height        : 400px;
        background    : #fff;
        border-radius : 3px;
        z-index       : 2;
      }
    </style>
  </head>
...
```

When we open our browser document (spa/layout.html), we should see a page that looks amazingly similar to our wireframe, as shown in figure 3.4. When we resize the browser window, we can see the feature containers also resize as needed. Our liquid layout does have a limitation—if we make the width or height less than 500 pixels, scrollbars are shown. We do this because we can't squeeze our content below this size.

Figure 3.4 HTML and CSS for containers—spa/layout.html

We can use Chrome Developer Tools to try out some of our newly defined styles that aren't used in the initial display. For example, let's add the class `spa-x-closed` to the `spa-shell-main` container. This will close the navigation bar on the left of the page. Removing the class will return the navigation bar, as shown in figure 3.5.

3.4 Render the feature containers

The layout document (spa/layout.html) we created is a nice foundation. Now we're going to use it in our SPA. The first step is to have the Shell render the containers instead of using static HTML and CSS.

3.4.1 Convert the HTML to JavaScript

We'll need our JavaScript to manage all our document changes; therefore, we need to convert the HTML developed earlier into a JavaScript string. We'll keep the HTML indentation to ease legibility and maintainability as shown in listing 3.8:

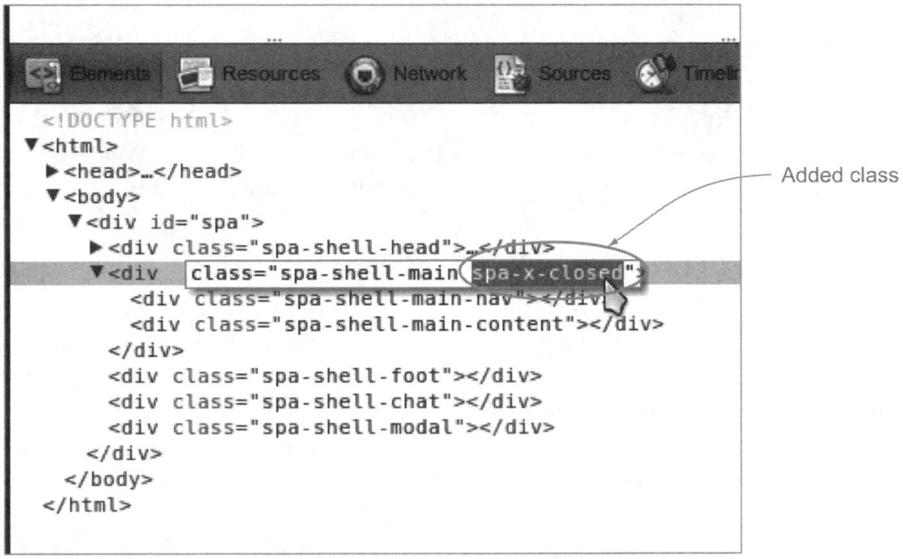

Figure 3.5 Double-click in the HTML to add a class in Chrome Developer Tools

Listing 3.8 Concatenating the HTML template

```
var main_html = String()
  + '<div class="spa-shell-head">'
    + '<div class="spa-shell-head-logo"></div>'
    + '<div class="spa-shell-head-acct"></div>'
    + '<div class="spa-shell-head-search"></div>'
  + '</div>'
  + '<div class="spa-shell-main">'
    + '<div class="spa-shell-main-nav"></div>'
    + '<div class="spa-shell-main-content"></div>'
  + '</div>'
  + '<div class="spa-shell-foot"></div>'
  + '<div class="spa-shell-chat"></div>'
  + '<div class="spa-shell-modal"></div>';
```

We aren't worried about any performance penalty of concatenated strings. Once we get to production, the JavaScript minifier will join the string for us.

Configure your editor!

A professional developer should be using a professional-grade text editor or IDE. Most of these have regular expression and macro support. We should be able to automate converting HTML into a JavaScript string. For example, the venerable `vim` editor can be configured so that two keystrokes will format HTML into a JavaScript concatenated string. We can add the following to our ~/.vimrc file:

(continued)

```
vmap <silent> ;h :s?^\(\s*\)+ '\([^']\+\)',*\s*$?\1\2?g<CR>
vmap <silent> ;q :s?^\(\s*\)\(.*\)\s*$? \1 + '\2'?<CR>
```

Once we restart vim, we can visually select the HTML to change. When we press `;q` the selection will be formatted; when we press `;h` we will undo the format.

3.4.2 Add an HTML template to our JavaScript

It's now time to take a bold step and create our Shell. When we initialize the Shell, we'd like to have it fill the page element of our choice with the feature containers. While we're at it, we'd like to cache the jQuery collection objects. We can use the module template from appendix A along with the JavaScript string we just created to accomplish this. Let's fire up our text editor and create the file shown in listing 3.9. Please pay careful attention to the annotations, as they provide useful details:

Listing 3.9 Starting the Shell—spa/js/spa.shell.js

```
/*
 * spa.shell.js
 * Shell module for SPA
*/

/*jslint         browser : true, continue : true,
  devel  : true, indent  : 2,    maxerr   : 50,
  newcap : true, nomen   : true, plusplus : true,
  regexp : true, sloppy  : true, vars     : false,
  white  : true
*/
/*global $, spa */

spa.shell = (function () {
  //---------------- BEGIN MODULE SCOPE VARIABLES --------------
  var
    configMap = {
      main_html : String()
        + '<div class="spa-shell-head">'
          + '<div class="spa-shell-head-logo"></div>'
          + '<div class="spa-shell-head-acct"></div>'
          + '<div class="spa-shell-head-search"></div>'
        + '</div>'
        + '<div class="spa-shell-main">'
          + '<div class="spa-shell-main-nav"></div>'
          + '<div class="spa-shell-main-content"></div>'
        + '</div>'
        + '<div class="spa-shell-foot"></div>'
        + '<div class="spa-shell-chat"></div>'
        + '<div class="spa-shell-modal"></div>'
    },
    stateMap  = { $container : null },
    jqueryMap = {},

    setJqueryMap, initModule;
```

Declare all variables that are available across the namespace—`spa.shell` in this case—in the "Module Scope" section. See appendix A for a complete discussion of this and other sections in the template.

Place static configuration values in `configMap`.

Indent HTML strings. This aids comprehension and eases maintenance.

Cache jQuery collections in `jqueryMap`.

Place dynamic information shared across the module in `stateMap`.

Declare all module scope variables in this section. Many are assigned later.

```
  //---------------- END MODULE SCOPE VARIABLES --------------

  //------------------- BEGIN UTILITY METHODS ----------------
  //-------------------- END UTILITY METHODS -----------------

  //-------------------- BEGIN DOM METHODS -------------------
  // Begin DOM method /setJqueryMap/
  setJqueryMap = function () {
    var $container = stateMap.$container;
    jqueryMap = { $container : $container };
  };
  // End DOM method /setJqueryMap/
  //-------------------- END DOM METHODS ---------------------

  //------------------- BEGIN EVENT HANDLERS -----------------
  //------------------- END EVENT HANDLERS -------------------

  //------------------- BEGIN PUBLIC METHODS -----------------
  // Begin Public method /initModule/
  initModule = function ( $container ) {
    stateMap.$container = $container;
    $container.html( configMap.main_html );
    setJqueryMap();
  };
  // End PUBLIC method /initModule/

  return { initModule : initModule };
  //------------------- END PUBLIC METHODS -------------------
}());
```

Place functions that create and manipulate page elements in the "DOM Methods" section.

Reserve the "Utility Methods" section for functions that don't interact with page elements.

Use `setJqueryMap` to cache jQuery collections. This function should be in almost every shell and feature module we write. The use of the `jqueryMap` cache can greatly reduce the number of jQuery document transversals and improve performance.

Reserve an "Event Handlers" section for jQuery event handler functions.

Place publicly available methods in the "Public Methods" section.

Create the `initModule` public method, which will be used to initialize the module.

Export public methods explicitly by returning them in a map. At present only `initModule` is available.

Now we have a module that renders the feature containers, but we still have to populate the CSS file and instruct the root namespace module (spa/js/spa.js) to use the Shell module (spa/js/spa.shell.js) instead of presenting the time-honored "hello world" text. Let's get to it.

3.4.3 Write the Shell stylesheet

Using our handy namespacing conventions presented in appendix A, we know we need to put our spa-shell-* selectors into a file named spa/css/spa.shell.css. We can copy the CSS we developed in spa/layout.html directly into that file, as shown in listing 3.10:

Listing 3.10 The Shell CSS, take 1—spa/css/spa.shell.css

```
/*
 * spa.shell.css
 * Shell styles
*/

.spa-shell-head, .spa-shell-head-logo, .spa-shell-head-acct,
.spa-shell-head-search, .spa-shell-main, .spa-shell-main-nav,
.spa-shell-main-content, .spa-shell-foot, .spa-shell-chat,
```

```
.spa-shell-modal {
  position : absolute;
}
.spa-shell-head {
  top    : 0;
  left   : 0;
  right  : 0;
  height : 40px;
}
.spa-shell-head-logo {
  top        : 4px;
  left       : 4px;
  height     : 32px;
  width      : 128px;
  background : orange;
}
.spa-shell-head-acct {
  top        : 4px;
  right      : 0;
  width      : 64px;
  height     : 32px;
  background : green;
}
.spa-shell-head-search {
  top        : 4px;
  right      : 64px;
  width      : 248px;
  height     : 32px;
  background : blue;
}

.spa-shell-main {
  top    : 40px;
  left   : 0;
  bottom : 40px;
  right  : 0;
}
.spa-shell-main-content,
.spa-shell-main-nav {
  top    : 0;
  bottom : 0;
}
.spa-shell-main-nav {
  width  : 250px;
  background : #eee;
}
  .spa-x-closed .spa-shell-main-nav {
     width  : 0;
  }

.spa-shell-main-content {
  left  : 250px;
  right : 0;
  background : #ddd;
}
  .spa-x-closed .spa-shell-main-content {
```

Define shared CSS rules. (annotating `.spa-shell-main-content,`)

Use the parent classes to affect child elements. This is perhaps one of the most powerful capabilities of CSS, and not used nearly often enough. (annotating `.spa-x-closed .spa-shell-main-nav {`)

Indent derived selectors and place immediately below the parent selector. Derived selectors are selectors clearly dependent on a parent for meaning. (annotating `.spa-x-closed .spa-shell-main-content {`)

```
    left : 0;
  }
.spa-shell-foot {
  bottom : 0;
  left   : 0;
  right  : 0;
  height : 40px;
}
.spa-shell-chat {
  bottom     : 0;
  right      : 0;
  width      : 300px;
  height     : 15px;
  background : red;
  z-index    : 1;
}
.spa-shell-modal {
  margin-top    : -200px;
  margin-left   : -200px;
  top           : 50%;
  left          : 50%;
  width         : 400px;
  height        : 400px;
  background    : #fff;
  border-radius : 3px;
  z-index       : 2;
}
```

All Selectors have the `spa-shell-` prefix. This has multiple benefits:

- It shows that these classes are controlled by the Shell module (spa/js/spa.shell.js).
- It prevents namespace collisions with third-party scripts and our other modules.
- When we're debugging and inspecting the document HTML, we can immediately see which elements are generated and controlled by the shell module.

All of these benefits prevent us from descending into the fiery depths of CSS-selector-name-goulash hell. Anyone who's ever managed stylesheets on even a moderate scale should know exactly what we're talking about.

3.4.4 Direct the application to use the Shell

Now let's modify our root namespace module (spa/js/spa.js) to use the Shell instead of slavishly copying "hello world" into the DOM. The following adjustment shown in **bold** should do the trick:

```
/*
 * spa.js
 * Root namespace module
*/
...
/*global $, spa */
```

```
var spa = (function () {
  var initModule = function ( $container ) {
    spa.shell.initModule( $container );
  };

  return { initModule: initModule };
}());
```

We should now be able to open our browser document (spa/spa.html) and see something similar to figure 3.6. We can use Chrome Developer Tools to confirm the document generated by our SPA (spa/spa.html) matches our layout document (spa/layout.html).

Figure 3.6 It's like deja vu all over again—spa/spa.html

With this foundation in place, we'll begin the work to have the Shell manage the feature containers. It might also be a good time to take a break, as the next section is fairly ambitious.

3.5 Manage the feature containers

The Shell renders and controls the *feature containers*. These are "top level" containers—usually DIVs—that hold feature content. The Shell initializes and coordinates all the feature modules in the application. And the Shell directs feature modules to create and manage all content inside feature containers. We'll discuss feature modules further in chapter 4.

In this section, we'll first write a method to extend and retract the chat slider feature container. We'll then build the click event handler so the slider may be opened or closed whenever the user wishes. Then we'll check our work and talk about the next big thing—managing the page state using the URI hash fragment.

3.5.1 Write a method to extend or retract the chat slider

We'll be moderately ambitious with our chat slider function. We need it production-quality, but it doesn't have to be extravagant. Here are the requirements we want to achieve:

1. Enable developers to configure the speed and height of slider motions.
2. Create a single method to extend or retract the chat slider.
3. Avoid a race condition where the slider may be extending and retracting at the same time.
4. Enable developers to pass in an optional callback to be invoked on completion of a slider motion.
5. Create test code to ensure the slider is functioning properly.

Let's adjust the Shell to meet these requirements as shown in listing 3.11.[1] All changes are shown in **bold**. Please review the annotations as they detail how the changes pertain to the requirements:

Listing 3.11 The Shell, revised to extend and retract the chat slider—spa/js/spa.shell.js

```
...
spa.shell = (function () {
  //---------------- BEGIN MODULE SCOPE VARIABLES --------------
  var
    configMap = {
      main_html : String()
      ...
      chat_extend_time     : 1000,
      chat_retract_time    : 300,
      chat_extend_height   : 450,
      chat_retract_height  : 15
    },
    stateMap  = { $container : null },
    jqueryMap = {},

    setJqueryMap, toggleChat, initModule;
  //----------------- END MODULE SCOPE VARIABLES ---------------

  //------------------- BEGIN UTILITY METHODS ------------------
  //-------------------- END UTILITY METHODS -------------------

  //-------------------- BEGIN DOM METHODS --------------------
  // Begin DOM method /setJqueryMap/
  setJqueryMap = function () {
    var $container = stateMap.$container;

    jqueryMap = {
      $container : $container,
      $chat : $container.find( '.spa-shell-chat' )
    };
  };
  // End DOM method /setJqueryMap/

  // Begin DOM method /toggleChat/
  // Purpose   : Extends or retracts chat slider
  // Arguments :
  //   * do_extend - if true, extends slider; if false retracts
```

Store the retract and extend times and heights in the module configuration map per Requirement I: "Enable developers to configure the speed and height of slider motions."

Add the toggleChat method to our list of module-scope variables.

Cache the chat slider jQuery collection in jqueryMap.

Add the toggleChat method per Requirement 2: "Create a single method to extend or retract the chat slider."

[1] Now would be a good time to thank your favorite celestial bodies for jQuery, as this would be a lot harder without it.

```
//   * callback  - optional function to execute at end of animation
// Settings  :
//   * chat_extend_time, chat_retract_time
//   * chat_extend_height, chat_retract_height
// Returns   : boolean
//   * true  - slider animation activated
//   * false - slider animation not activated
//
toggleChat = function ( do_extend, callback ) {
  var
    px_chat_ht = jqueryMap.$chat.height(),
    is_open    = px_chat_ht === configMap.chat_extend_height,
    is_closed  = px_chat_ht === configMap.chat_retract_height,
    is_sliding = ! is_open && ! is_closed;

  // avoid race condition
  if ( is_sliding ){ return false; }

  // Begin extend chat slider
  if ( do_extend ) {
    jqueryMap.$chat.animate(
      { height : configMap.chat_extend_height },
      configMap.chat_extend_time,
      function () {
        if ( callback ){ callback( jqueryMap.$chat ); }
      }
    );
    return true;
  }
  // End extend chat slider

  // Begin retract chat slider
  jqueryMap.$chat.animate(
    { height : configMap.chat_retract_height },
    configMap.chat_retract_time,
    function () {
      if ( callback ){ callback( jqueryMap.$chat ); }
    }
  );
  return true;
  // End retract chat slider
};
// End DOM method /toggleChat/
//-------------------- END DOM METHODS ---------------------

//------------------- BEGIN EVENT HANDLERS -------------------
//------------------- END EVENT HANDLERS --------------------

//------------------- BEGIN PUBLIC METHODS -------------------
// Begin Public method /initModule/
initModule = function ( $container ){
  // load HTML and map jQuery collections
  stateMap.$container = $container;
  $container.html( configMap.main_html );
  setJqueryMap();

  // test toggle
  setTimeout( function () {toggleChat( true ); }, 3000 );
```

Prevent a race condition by declining to take action if the slider is already in motion, per Requirement 3: "Avoid a race condition where the slider may be extending and retracting at the same time."

Invoke a callback after the animation is complete, per Requirement 4: "Enable developers to pass in an optional callback to be invoked on completion of a slider motion."

Extend the slider 3 seconds after page load, and retract it after 8 seconds, per Requirement 5: "Create test code to ensure the slider is functioning properly."

```
    setTimeout( function () {toggleChat( false );}, 8000 );
  };
  // End PUBLIC method /initModule/

  return { initModule : initModule };
  //------------------- END PUBLIC METHODS ---------------------
}());
```

If you *are* playing along at home, let's first check our code with JSLint by typing `jslint spa/js/spa.shell.js` in the command line—we shouldn't see any warnings or errors. Next let's reload the browser document (spa/spa.html) and see the chat slider extend after three seconds and retract after eight seconds. Now that we have the slider moving, we can employ a user's mouse-click to toggle its position.

3.5.2 Add the chat slider click event handler

Most users expect to click on a chat slider and see it extend or retract, as this is the common convention. Here are the requirements we want to achieve:

1. Set tool-tip text to prompt user action, for example "Click to retract."
2. Add a click event handler to call `toggleChat`.
3. Bind the click event handler to the jQuery event.

Let's adjust the Shell to meet these requirements as shown in listing 3.12. All changes are again shown in **bold**, and the annotations detail how the changes pertain to the requirements.

Listing 3.12 The Shell, revised to handle chat slider click events—spa/js/spa.shell.js

```
...
spa.shell = (function () {
  //---------------- BEGIN MODULE SCOPE VARIABLES --------------
  var
    configMap = {
      ...
      chat_retract_height  : 15,
      chat_extended_title  : 'Click to retract',
      chat_retracted_title : 'Click to extend'
    },
    stateMap  = {
      $container        : null,
      is_chat_retracted : true
    },
    jqueryMap = {},
    setJqueryMap, toggleChat, onClickChat, initModule;
  //----------------- END MODULE SCOPE VARIABLES ---------------
  ...
  //--------------------- BEGIN DOM METHODS --------------------
  // Begin DOM method /setJqueryMap/
  ...
  // End DOM method /setJqueryMap/
```

Add retracted and extended title text to the `configMap` per Requirement I: "Set tool-tip text to prompt user action..."

Add `is_chat_retracted` to the `stateMap`. It's good practice to list all keys used in the `stateMap` so they can be easily found and inspected. This is used by our `toggleChat` method.

Add `onClickChat` to our list of module-scope function names.

```
// Begin DOM method /toggleChat/
// Purpose    : Extends or retracts chat slider
...
// State      : sets stateMap.is_chat_retracted
//     * true  - slider is retracted
//     * false - slider is extended
//
toggleChat = function ( do_extend, callback) {
  var
    px_chat_ht = jqueryMap.$chat.height(),
    is_open    = px_chat_ht === configMap.chat_extend_height,
    is_closed  = px_chat_ht === configMap.chat_retract_height,
    is_sliding = ! is_open && ! is_closed;

  // avoid race condition
  if ( is_sliding ) { return false; }

  // Begin extend chat slider
  if ( do_extend ) {
    jqueryMap.$chat.animate(
      { height : configMap.chat_extend_height },
      configMap.chat_extend_time,
      function () {
        jqueryMap.$chat.attr(
          'title', configMap.chat_extended_title
        );
        stateMap.is_chat_retracted = false;
        if ( callback ) { callback( jqueryMap.$chat ); }
      }
    );
    return true;
  }
  // End extend chat slider

  // Begin retract chat slider
  jqueryMap.$chat.animate(
    { height : configMap.chat_retract_height },
    configMap.chat_retract_time,
    function () {
      jqueryMap.$chat.attr(
        'title', configMap.chat_retracted_title
      );
      stateMap.is_chat_retracted = true;
      if ( callback ) { callback( jqueryMap.$chat ); }
    }
  );
  return true;
  // End retract chat slider
};
// End DOM method /toggleChat/
//--------------------- END DOM METHODS ----------------------

//------------------- BEGIN EVENT HANDLERS -------------------
 onClickChat = function ( event ) {
   toggleChat( stateMap.is_chat_retracted );
   return false;
 };
```

Update the `toggleChat` API docs to indicate how `stateMap.is_chat_retracted` is set by this method.

Adjust `toggleChat` to control the hover text as well as the `stateMap.is_chat_retracted` value per Requirement 1: "Set tool-tip text to prompt user action..."

Add the `onClickChat` event handler per Requirement 2: "Add a click event handler to call toggleChat."

```
  //-------------------- END EVENT HANDLERS --------------------

  //------------------- BEGIN PUBLIC METHODS -------------------
  // Begin Public method /initModule/
  initModule = function ( $container ) {
    // load HTML and map jQuery collections
    stateMap.$container = $container;
    $container.html( configMap.main_html );
    setJqueryMap();

    // initialize chat slider and bind click handler
    stateMap.is_chat_retracted = true;
    jqueryMap.$chat
      .attr( 'title', configMap.chat_retracted_title )
      .click( onClickChat );
  };
  // End PUBLIC method /initModule/

  return { initModule : initModule };
  //------------------- END PUBLIC METHODS ---------------------
}());
```

Initialize the event handler by setting `stateMap.is_chat_retracted` and the hover text. Then bind the handler to a click event per Requirement 3: "Bind the click event handler to the jQuery event."

Those playing along at home should again check our code by typing `jslint spa/js/spa.shell.js` at the command line. We again shouldn't see any warnings or errors.

There's an aspect of jQuery event handlers that we think is crucial to remember: the return value is interpreted by jQuery to specify its continued handling of the event. We usually return `false` from our jQuery event handlers. Here's what that does:

- It tells jQuery to prevent the default action—like following a link, or selecting text—from occurring. The same effect can be acquired by invoking `event.preventDefault()` in the event handler.
- It tells jQuery to stop the event from triggering the same event on the parent DOM element (this behavior is often called *bubbling*). The same effect can be acquired by invoking `event.stopPropagation()` in the event handler.
- It concludes the handler execution. If the clicked element has other handlers bound to it after this handler, the next one in line will be executed. (If we don't want subsequent handlers to execute, we can invoke `event.preventImmediatePropagation()`.)

These three actions are usually what we want our event handlers to do. Soon we'll write event handlers where we do not want these actions. These event handlers will return the `true` value.

The Shell doesn't need to necessarily handle the click. It could instead provide the capability to manipulate the slider as a callback to the chat module—and we encourage this. But, because we haven't written that module yet, we have handled the click event in the Shell for now.

Now let's add a little flair to our Shell styles. Listing 3.13 shows the changes:

Listing 3.13 Adding some flair to the Shell—spa/css/spa.shell.css

```
...
.spa-shell-foot {
  ...
}
.spa-shell-chat {
  bottom        : 0;
  right         : 0;
  width         : 300px;
  height        : 15px;
  cursor        : pointer;
  background    : red;
  border-radius : 5px 0 0 0;
  z-index       : 1;
}
  .spa-shell-chat:hover {
    background : #a00;
}
.spa-shell-modal { ... }
...
```

Round a corner to make the slider look nicer.

Change the cursor to a pointer when hovering over the slider. This informs the user that something will happen if they click.

Change the slider color when the cursor hovers over the slider. This reinforces the message to the user that an action is available on click.

When we reload the browser document (spa/spa.html) we can click on the slider and see it extend as shown in figure 3.7:

The slider extends much more slowly than it retracts. We can change the speed of the slider by changing the configuration in the Shell (spa/js/spa.shell.js), for example:

```
...
  configMap = {
    main_html : String()
    ...
    chat_extend_time  : 250,
    chat_retract_time : 300,
    ...
  },
...
```

In the next section, we'll adjust our application to better manage its state. When we're finished, all browser history features like Bookmarks, the Forward button, and the Back button will work for the chat slider as the user expects.

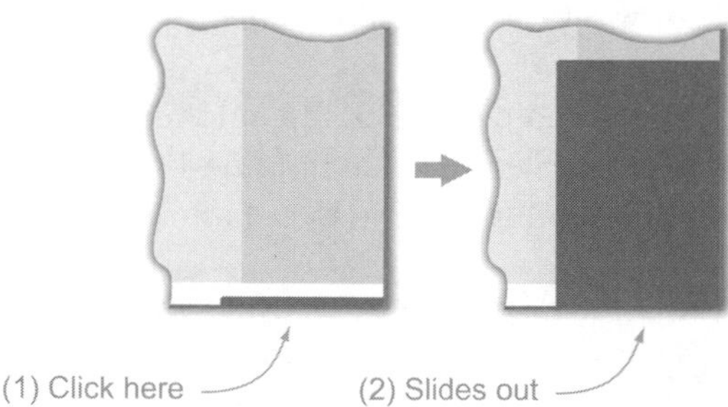

Figure 3.7 Extending the chat slider—spa/spa.html

3.6 Manage application state

In computer science, a *state* is a unique configuration of information in an application. Desktop and web applications generally try to maintain some state between sessions. For example, when we save a word processing document and then open it again at a later date, the document is restored. The application may also restore the window size, our preferences, and the cursor and page location. Our SPA needs to manage state too, because people who use browsers have come to expect certain behaviors.

3.6.1 Understand the behavior browser users expect

Desktop and web applications vary widely in what aspect of state they maintain. A desktop application can omit a Previous button if it doesn't provide a "go back" capability. But in a web application we've got the browser's Back button—one of the most frequently used browser controls—staring our user in the face, begging to be clicked—and we can't remove it.

And the same goes for the Forward button, the Bookmark button, and View history. The users expect these *history* controls to work. If they don't, our users get cranky, and our application will never win a Webby. Table 3.1 illustrates the approximate desktop application counterparts to these history controls.

Table 3.1 Browser versus desktop controls

Browser control	Desktop control	Comments
Back button	Undo	Revert to prior state
Forward button	Redo	Restore state from recent "undo" or "back" motion
Bookmark	Save As	Store application state for future use or reference
View history	Undo History	View steps in undo/redo sequence

Because we do aspire to win a Webby, we have to ensure these history controls work as our users expect. Next we'll discuss strategies to provide the behaviors our users expect.

3.6.2 Pick a strategy to manage history controls

An optimal strategy to provide history controls should meet these requirements:

1. The history controls should work as the user expects, per table 3.1.
2. Development to support history controls should be reasonably inexpensive. It shouldn't require significantly more time or complexity in comparison to development without history controls.
3. The application should perform well. The application shouldn't take longer to respond to user actions, and the user interface shouldn't be more complicated as a result.

Let's consider some strategies using the chat slider and the following user interaction as our example:

1. Susan visits our SPA and clicks on the chat slider to open it.
2. She bookmarks the SPA, and then browses to other sites.
3. Later, she decides to return to our application and clicks on her bookmark.

Let's consider three strategies to make Susan's bookmark work as expected. Please don't worry about memorizing them; we just want to illustrate their relative merits: [2]

Strategy 1—On the click, the event handler directly calls the `toggleChat` routine, and ignores the URI. When Susan returns to her bookmark, the slider will be presented in its default position—closed. Susan isn't pleased because the bookmark didn't work as expected. James the developer isn't pleased either, because his product manager finds the usability of the application unacceptable and is pestering him about it.

Strategy 2—On the click, the event handler directly calls the `toggleChat` routine, and then modifies the URI to record this state. When Susan returns to her bookmark, the application must recognize the parameter in the URI and act on it. Susan is pleased. James the developer is *not* pleased because he must now support two conditions that will open the slider: a run-time click event, and a load-time URI parameter. And James's product manager isn't too happy either because supporting this dual-path approach is slower and prone to bugs and inconsistencies.

Strategy 3—On the click, the event handler changes the URI and then promptly returns. The Shell `hashchange` event handler picks up the change, and dispatches to the `toggleChat` routine. When Susan returns to her bookmark, the URI is parsed by the same routine and the open slider is restored. Susan is pleased because the bookmark works as expected. James the developer is pleased as well, because he can use *one code path to implement all bookmark-able states.* And James's product manager is pleased too, because development is fast and comparatively bug-free.

Our preferred solution is *Strategy 3* as it supports all history controls (requirement A). It addresses and minimizes development concerns (requirement B). And it ensures application performance by adjusting only the parts of the page that need to be changed when a history control is used (requirement C). This solution, where the URI always drives the page state, we call the *anchor interface pattern*, as shown in figure 3.8.

We'll return to this pattern in chapter 4. Now that we have selected our strategy, let's implement it.

3.6.3 Change the anchor when a history event occurs

The anchor component of a URI instructs the browser what part of a page to show. Other common names for the anchor are the *bookmark component* or the *hash fragment.* The anchor always starts with a # symbol, and is shown in **bold** in the following code:

```
http://localhost/spa.html#!chat=open
```

[2] There are other strategies—like the use of a persistent cookie or an iframe—but these are frankly too limited and convoluted to merit consideration.

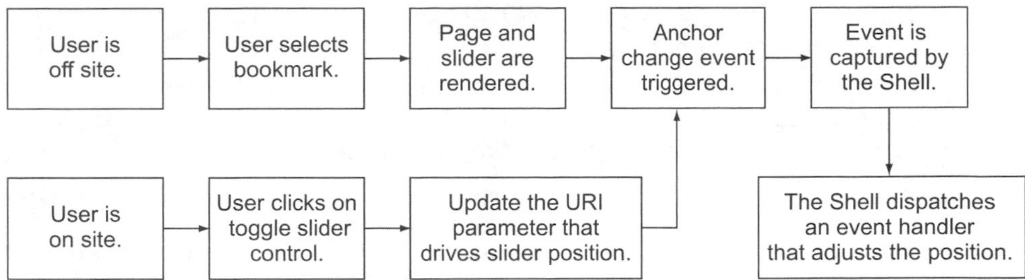

Figure 3.8 The anchor interface pattern

Traditionally, web developers have used the anchor mechanism to enable users to easily "jump" between sections of a long document. For example, a web page that has a table of contents at the top might link all the section titles to their corresponding sections within the document. And each of the sections may have a "back to top" link at the end. Blogs and forums still use this mechanism extensively.

One exceptional feature of the anchor component is that the browser does *not* reload the page when it's changed. The anchor component is a client-side-only control, which makes it an ideal place to store our application state. This technique is used by many SPAs.

We refer to an application state change that we want to keep in the browser history as a *history event*. Because we decided that opening or closing the chat is a history event (you missed the meeting), we can have our click event handler change the anchor to express the chat slider state. We can use the `uriAnchor` jQuery plugin to do the heavy lifting. Let's revise the Shell so a user click changes the URI as shown in listing 3.14. All changes are shown in **bold**.

Listing 3.14 The uriAnchor jQuery plugin at play—spa/js/spa.shell.js

```
...
  //------------------- BEGIN EVENT HANDLERS -------------------
  onClickChat = function ( event ) {
    if ( toggleChat( stateMap.is_chat_retracted ) ) {
      $.uriAnchor.setAnchor({
        chat : ( stateMap.is_chat_retracted ? 'open' : 'closed' )
      });
    }
    return false;
  };
  //-------------------- END EVENT HANDLERS --------------------
  ...
```

Now when we click on the slider, we see the anchor in the URI change—but only if `toggleChat` succeeds and returns true. For example, when we click the chat slider open and then closed, we see the following:

```
http://localhost/spa.html#!chat=closed
```

> **About that exclamation point**
> The exclamation point following the hash symbol (`#!`) in the example URI is used to inform Google and other search engines that this URI may be indexed for search. We'll cover more about search engine optimization in chapter 9.

We need to ensure that when the anchor changes, only the part of the application that needs adjustment is changed. This makes the application much faster and avoids the disturbing "flicker" that happens when parts of the page are unnecessarily cleared and re-rendered. For example, let's say Susan is viewing a list of a thousand user profiles when she opens the chat slider. If she clicks the Back button, the application should simply close the slider—the profiles shouldn't be re-rendered.

We ask ourselves three questions to determine whether the change from an event is worthy of history support:

- How strongly will the user want to bookmark the change that has occurred?
- How strongly will the user want to revert to the page state before the change?
- How expensive will this be?

Although the incremental cost to maintain a state is usually minor using the anchor interface pattern, there are some situations where it can be expensive or impossible. For example, an online purchase would be very difficult to reverse when a user clicks the Back button. In such a situation, we need to avoid a history entry completely. Lucky for us, our `uriAnchor` plugin supports this.

3.6.4 *Use the anchor to drive the application state*

We want the anchor component to always drive the bookmark-able application state. This ensures history functions always work as expected. The following pseudo-code outlines how we like to handle a history event:

- When a history event occurs, change the anchor component of the URI to reflect the changed state:
  - The handler that received the event calls a Shell utility to change the anchor.
  - The event handler then exits.
- A Shell `hashchange` event handler notices the URI change and acts on it:
  - It compares the current state to the state proposed by the new anchor.
  - It tries to change the sections of the application that need adjustment as determined by the comparison.
  - If it can't make the requested changes, it maintains the current state and restores the anchor to match it.

Now that we've sketched out the pseudo-code, let's get to work converting it into the real thing.

CHANGE THE SHELL TO USE THE ANCHOR COMPONENT

Let's revise the Shell to use the anchor component to drive the application state, as shown in listing 3.15. There's a fair bit of new code here, but don't get discouraged—all will be explained in due time:

Listing 3.15 Using the anchor to drive application state—spa/js/spa.shell.js

```
...
spa.shell = (function () {
  //---------------- BEGIN MODULE SCOPE VARIABLES --------------
  var
    configMap = {
      anchor_schema_map : {
        chat : { open : true, closed : true }
      },
      main_html : String()
      ...
    },
    stateMap  = {
      $container         : null,
      anchor_map         : {},
      is_chat_retracted : true
    },
    jqueryMap = {},

    copyAnchorMap, setJqueryMap, toggleChat,
    changeAnchorPart, onHashchange,
    onClickChat,      initModule;
  //----------------- END MODULE SCOPE VARIABLES ---------------

  //------------------- BEGIN UTILITY METHODS ------------------
  // Returns copy of stored anchor map; minimizes overhead
  copyAnchorMap = function () {
    return $.extend( true, {}, stateMap.anchor_map );
  };
  //-------------------- END UTILITY METHODS -------------------

  //--------------------- BEGIN DOM METHODS --------------------
  ...
  // Begin DOM method /changeAnchorPart/
  // Purpose : Changes part of the URI anchor component
  // Arguments:
  //   * arg_map - The map describing what part of the URI anchor
  //     we want changed.
  // Returns : boolean
  //   * true - the Anchor portion of the URI was update
  //   * false - the Anchor portion of the URI could not be updated
  // Action :
  //   The current anchor rep stored in stateMap.anchor_map.
  //   See uriAnchor for a discussion of encoding.
  //   This method
  //     * Creates a copy of this map using copyAnchorMap().
  //     * Modifies the key-values using arg_map.
  //     * Manages the distinction between independent
  //       and dependent values in the encoding.
```

Define the map used by uriAnchor for validation.

Store the current anchor values in a map in the module state, stateMap.anchor_map.

Declare three additional methods: copyAnchorMap, changeAnchorPart, and onHashchange.

Use the jQuery extend() utility to copy an object. This is required because all JavaScript objects are passed by reference, and copying one correctly is non-trivial.

Add the changeAnchorPart utility to atomically update the anchor. It takes a map of what we want to change, for example { chat : 'open' }, and updates only the specified key-value in the anchor component.

```
//     * Attempts to change the URI using uriAnchor.
//     * Returns true on success, and false on failure.
//
changeAnchorPart = function ( arg_map ) {
  var
    anchor_map_revise = copyAnchorMap(),
    bool_return = true,
    key_name, key_name_dep;

  // Begin merge changes into anchor map
  KEYVAL:
  for ( key_name in arg_map ) {
    if ( arg_map.hasOwnProperty( key_name ) ) {

      // skip dependent keys during iteration
      if ( key_name.indexOf( '_' ) === 0 ) { continue KEYVAL; }

      // update independent key value
      anchor_map_revise[key_name] = arg_map[key_name];

      // update matching dependent key
      key_name_dep = '_' + key_name;
      if ( arg_map[key_name_dep] ) {
        anchor_map_revise[key_name_dep] = arg_map[key_name_dep];
      }
      else {
        delete anchor_map_revise[key_name_dep];
        delete anchor_map_revise['_s' + key_name_dep];
      }
    }
  }
  // End merge changes into anchor map

  // Begin attempt to update URI; revert if not successful
  try {
    $.uriAnchor.setAnchor( anchor_map_revise );
  }
  catch ( error ) {
    // replace URI with existing state
    $.uriAnchor.setAnchor( stateMap.anchor_map,null,true );
    bool_return = false;
  }
  // End attempt to update URI...

  return bool_return;
};
// End DOM method /changeAnchorPart/
//-------------------- END DOM METHODS --------------------

//------------------- BEGIN EVENT HANDLERS -------------------
// Begin Event handler /onHashchange/
// Purpose : Handles the hashchange event
// Arguments:
//   * event - jQuery event object.
// Settings : none
// Returns  : false
// Action   :
//   * Parses the URI anchor component
```

Don't set the anchor if it doesn't pass the schema (`uriAnchor` will throw an exception). When this occurs, revert the anchor component to its previous state.

Add the `onHashchange` event handler to handle URI anchor changes. Use the `uriAnchor` plugin to convert the anchor into a map and compare to the previous state to determine action. If the proposed anchor change is invalid, resets the anchor back to its prior value.

```
//    * Compares proposed application state with current
//    * Adjust the application only where proposed state
//      differs from existing
//
onHashchange = function ( event ) {
  var
    anchor_map_previous = copyAnchorMap(),
    anchor_map_proposed,
    _s_chat_previous, _s_chat_proposed,
    s_chat_proposed;

  // attempt to parse anchor
  try { anchor_map_proposed = $.uriAnchor.makeAnchorMap(); }
  catch ( error ) {
    $.uriAnchor.setAnchor( anchor_map_previous, null, true );
    return false;
  }
  stateMap.anchor_map = anchor_map_proposed;

  // convenience vars
  _s_chat_previous = anchor_map_previous._s_chat;
  _s_chat_proposed = anchor_map_proposed._s_chat;

  // Begin adjust chat component if changed
  if ( ! anchor_map_previous
    || _s_chat_previous !== _s_chat_proposed
  ) {
    s_chat_proposed = anchor_map_proposed.chat;
    switch ( s_chat_proposed ) {
      case 'open' :
        toggleChat( true );
      break;
      case 'closed' :
        toggleChat( false );
      break;
      default :
        toggleChat( false );
        delete anchor_map_proposed.chat;
        $.uriAnchor.setAnchor( anchor_map_proposed, null, true );
    }
  }
  // End adjust chat component if changed

  return false;
};
// End Event handler /onHashchange/

// Begin Event handler /onClickChat/
onClickChat = function ( event ) {
  changeAnchorPart({
    chat: ( stateMap.is_chat_retracted ? 'open' : 'closed' )
  });
  return false;
};
// End Event handler /onClickChat/
//-------------------- END EVENT HANDLERS --------------------
```

Revise the `onClickChat` event handler to only modify the `chat` parameter of the anchor.

```
//------------------- BEGIN PUBLIC METHODS -------------------
// Begin Public method /initModule/
initModule = function ( $container ) {
  ... // configure uriAnchor to use our schema
  $.uriAnchor.configModule({
    schema_map : configMap.anchor_schema_map
  });

  // Handle URI anchor change events.
  // This is done /after/ all feature modules are configured
  // and initialized, otherwise they will not be ready to handle
  // the trigger event, which is used to ensure the anchor
  // is considered on-load
  //
  $(window)
    .bind( 'hashchange', onHashchange )
    .trigger( 'hashchange' );

  };
  // End PUBLIC method /initModule/

  return { initModule : initModule };
  //------------------- END PUBLIC METHODS --------------------
}());
```

Configure the `uriAnchor` plugin to test against a schema.

Bind the `hashchange` event handler and immediately trigger it so the module considers the bookmark on initial load.

Now that we've adjusted the code, we should see that all history controls—the Forward button, the Back button, bookmarks, and browser history—all work as expected. And the anchor should "fix itself" if we manually change it to have parameters or values that we don't support—for example, try replacing the anchor in the browser address bar with `#!chat=barney` and press Return.

Now that we have the history controls working, let's discuss how we use the anchor to drive the application state. We'll start by showing how we use the `uriAnchor` to encode and decode the anchor.

UNDERSTAND HOW URIANCHOR ENCODES AND DECODES THE ANCHOR

We use the jQuery `hashchange` event to recognize a change in the anchor component. Application state is encoded using the concept of *independent* and *dependent* key-value pairs. Take for example the following anchor shown in **bold**:

`http://localhost/spa.html`**`#!chat=profile:on:uid,suzie|status,green`**

The *independent* key in this example is `profile`, and it has a value of `on`. Keys that further define the `profile` state are *dependent* keys, and they follow the colon (:) delimiter. This includes the key `uid` with a value of `suzie`, and the key `status` with the value of `green`.

The `uriAnchor` plugin, js/jq/jquery.uriAnchor-1.1.3.js, takes care of encoding and decoding dependent and independent values for us. We can use the `$.uriAnchor.setAnchor()` method to change the browser URI to match the earlier example:

```
var anchorMap = {
  profile  : 'on',
  _profile : {
    uid    : 'suzie',
```

```
    status : 'green'
  }
};
$.uriAnchor.setAnchor( anchorMap );
```

The makeAnchorMap method can be used to read and parse the anchor into a map:

```
var anchorMap = $.uriAnchor.makeAnchorMap();
console.log( anchorMap );

// If the URI anchor component in the browser is
// http://localhost/spa.html#!chat=profile:on:uid,suzie|status,green
//
// Then console.log( anchorMap ) should show the
// following:
//
// { profile  : 'on',
//   _profile : {
//     uid    : 'suzie',
//     status : 'green'
//   }
// };
//
```

Hopefully you now better understand how uriAnchor can be used to encode and decode the application state expressed in the URI anchor component. Now let's take a closer look at how we use the URI anchor component to drive the application state.

UNDERSTAND HOW ANCHOR CHANGES DRIVE APPLICATION STATE

Our history control strategy is that any event that changes a bookmark-able state should do two things:

1. Change the anchor.
2. Promptly return.

We added the changeAnchorPart method to the Shell, which allowed us to update only part of the anchor while ensuring independent and dependent keys and values are properly handled. It unified the logic for anchor management, and *it is the only means by which the anchor is modified by our application.*

When we say "promptly return," we mean that after the anchor has been changed, the event handler's work is done. It doesn't change the page elements. It doesn't update variables or flags. It doesn't pass Go or collect 200 dollars. It simply returns directly back to its calling event. This is illustrated in our onClickChat event handler:

```
onClickChat = function ( event ) {
  changeAnchorPart({
    chat: ( stateMap.is_chat_retracted ? 'open' : 'closed' )
  });
  return false;
};
```

This event handler uses changeAnchorPart to change the chat parameter of the anchor and then promptly returns. Because the anchor component is changed, this initiates a `hashchange` browser event. The Shell listens for `hashchange` events and takes action based on the anchor contents. For example, if the Shell notices the `chat` value has changed from `opened` to `closed` it closes the chat slider.

You might think of the anchor—modified by the `changeAnchorPart` method—as *the* API for bookmark-able states. The beauty of this approach is that it doesn't matter *why* the anchor was changed—it could be that our application modified it, or the user clicked a bookmark, or played with the Forward or Back buttons, or directly typed into the browser address bar. In any case, it always works correctly and uses only a single execution path.

3.7 Summary

We've finished implementing two of the primary responsibilities of the Shell. We created and styled feature containers, and we created a framework to drive application state using the URI anchor. We updated our chat slider to help illustrate these concepts.

Our work with the Shell isn't complete, because we've yet to tackle its third primary responsibility: coordinating feature modules. Our next chapter shows how to build feature modules, how to configure and initialize them from the Shell, and how to call them. Isolating features into their own modules greatly improves reliability, maintainability, scalability, and workflow. It also encourages the use and development of third-party modules. So stick around—this is where the rubber hits the road.

4 Add feature modules

This chapter covers

- Defining feature modules and how they fit into our architecture
- Comparing feature modules and third-party modules
- Explaining the fractal MVC design pattern and its role in our architecture
- Setting up files and directories for feature modules
- Defining and implementing the feature module APIs
- Implementing commonly needed feature module capabilities

Before you begin, you should have completed chapters 1-3 of this book. You should also have the project files from chapter 3 as we'll be building on them. We recommend you copy all the files and the whole directory structure you created in chapter 3 into a new "chapter_4" directory so you may update them there.

A *feature module* provides a well-defined and scoped capability to the SPA. In this chapter we move the chat slider capability introduced in chapter 3 into a feature module and improve its capabilities. Besides the chat slider, examples of other feature modules might include an image viewer, an account management panel, or a workbench where users might assemble graphical objects.

We design our feature modules to interface with our application much like third-party modules do—with well-defined APIs and strong isolation. This allows us to release sooner with higher quality because we can focus on creating our value-add core modules while leaving secondary modules to third parties. This strategy also provides a clear enhancement path, as we can selectively replace third-party modules with better modules as time and resources permit. As an added benefit, our modules are easy to reuse across multiple projects.

4.1 The feature module strategy

The Shell discussed in chapter 3 is responsible for application-wide tasks like management of the URI anchor or cookies, and it dispatches feature-specific tasks to carefully isolated feature modules. These modules have their own View, Controller, and a slice of the Model that the Shell shares with them. An overview of the architecture is shown in figure 4.1:[1]

Sample feature modules might include `spa.wb.js` to handle sketching on a workbench, `spa.acct.js` for account management features like sign-in or sign-out, and `spa.chat.js` for the chat interface. Because we seem to be on a roll with chat, we'll focus on that module in this chapter.

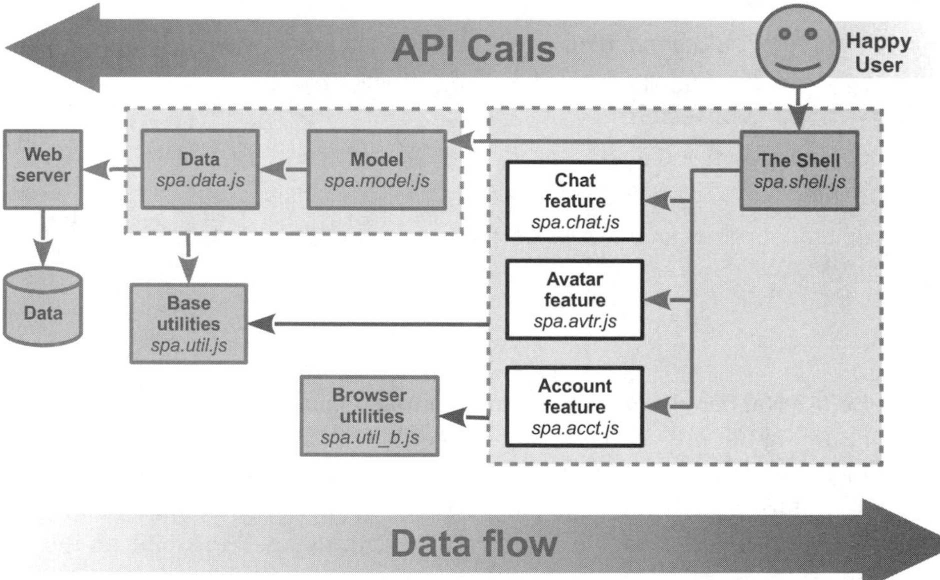

Figure 4.1 Feature modules in SPA architecture (shown in white)

[1] The author has this diagram taped to the wall next to his desk.

4.1.1 A comparison with third-party modules

Feature modules are a lot like third-party modules, which provide all sorts of capabilities to modern websites.[2] Example third-party modules include blog commenting (*DisQus*, or *LiveFyre*), advertising (*DoubleClick* or *ValueClick*), analytics (*Google* or *Overture*), sharing (*AddThis* or *ShareThis*), and social services (*Facebook* "Like" or *Google* "+1" buttons). They're enormously popular because website operators can add high-quality features to their sites at a tiny fraction of the cost, effort, and maintenance than if they were to develop the features themselves.[3] Typically, third-party modules are added to a website by including a script tag in a static web page, or adding a function invocation to an SPA. Many features on many websites wouldn't be possible were it not for third-party modules, as the costs would otherwise be prohibitive.

Well-written third-party modules share these common characteristics:

- *They render in their own container,* which may be provided for them, or they append to the documents themselves.
- *They provide a well-defined API* to control their behaviors.
- *They avoid corrupting the host page* by keeping their JavaScript, data, and CSS carefully isolated.

Third-party modules have some disadvantages. The primary problem is that the "third-party" has its own business goals, which may be at odds with our own. This can manifest itself in many ways:

- *We're dependent on their code and services.* If they fail or go out of business, their service can be lost. If they screw up a release, they can even prevent our site from working. Sadly, this happens a lot more often than it should.
- *They're often slower* than custom modules due to server chatter or feature bloat. If one third-party module is slow, it may slow down our entire application.
- *Privacy is a concern* because each third-party module has its own Terms of Service, in which their lawyers almost always reserve the right to change at a moment's notice.
- *Features often don't integrate seamlessly* due to a mismatch of data, style, or lack of flexibility.
- *Cross-feature communication* may be difficult or impossible if we can't integrate their third-party data to our SPA.
- *Customization* of the module may be difficult or impossible.

Our feature modules keep the positive characteristics of third-party modules, but because there is no third party, we avoid their disadvantages. This means that for a

---

[2] To learn more about third-party modules and how they're created, see *Third-Party JavaScript* by Ben Vinegar and Anton Kovalyov (Manning, 2012).

[3] It's hard to gauge exactly how popular third-party modules are, but it's hard to find a commercial website without at least one. At the time of this writing, for example, we counted at least 16 major third-party modules in use at TechCrunch.com, with at least five analytics services alone—and a whopping 53 script tags.

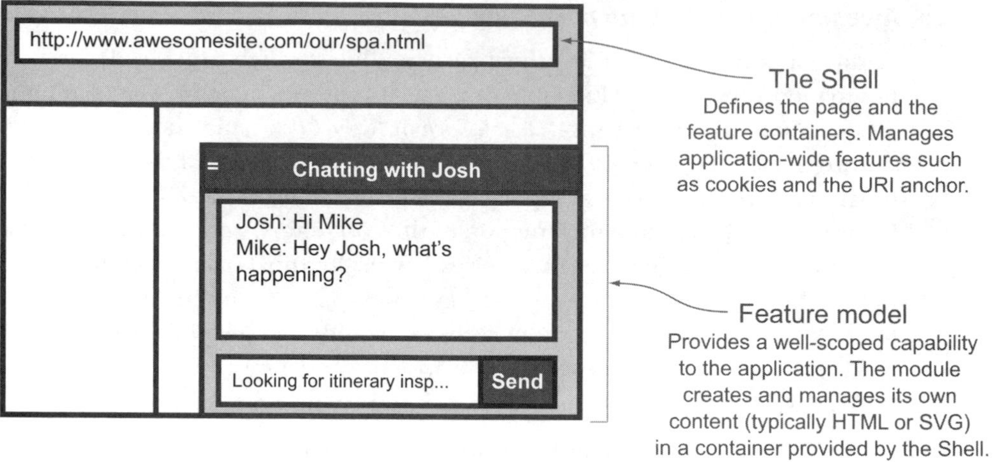

Figure 4.2 Shell and feature module responsibilities

given feature, the Shell provides a container that the feature module populates and controls, as shown in figure 4.2. The feature module provides a consistent API to the Shell for configuration, initialization, and use. The feature is kept isolated from other features by using unique and coordinated JavaScript and CSS namespaces, and by not allowing any external calls except to shared utilities.

Developing feature modules as if they were a third-party module allows us to take advantage of the benefits of third-party-style JavaScript:

- *Teams can be more effective* because developers can distribute responsibility based on the module. Let's face it: if you're working on a team, the only module that isn't third-party to you is the one for which you're responsible. Team members who aren't responsible for a module only need to know its API to use it.
- *The application tends to perform well* as the modules manage only the portion of the application for which they're responsible, and they're optimized for our use without the bloat of unused or unwanted capabilities.
- *Code maintenance and reuse is much easier* because modules are kept neatly isolated. Many of the more sophisticated jQuery plugins, such as a date picker, are effectively third-party applications. Think of how much easier it is to use a date picker plugin than it is to write your own.

And, of course, there's one other, *huge* advantage to developing our feature modules like third-party modules: we're well positioned to use third-party modules for non-core features of our web application, and then selectively replace them—as time and resources allow—with our own feature modules, which can be better integrated, faster, less invasive, or all of the above.

4.1.2 Feature modules and fractal MVC pattern

Many web developers are familiar with the *Model-View-Controller (MVC)* design pattern because it's presented in many frameworks such as Ruby on Rails, Django (Python), Catalyst (Perl), Spring MVC (Java), or MicroMVC (PHP). Because so many readers are familiar with this pattern, we'll explain how our SPA architecture relates to it, particularly to the feature modules.

Let's recall that MVC is a pattern used to develop an application. Its parts include:

- The *Model*, which provides the data and business rules of the application.
- The *View*, which provides the sensory (usually visual, but also often audio) representation of the Model's data.
- The *Controller*, which converts requests from the user into commands that update the Model and/or View of an application.

Developers familiar with a web MVC framework should be comfortable with most of this chapter. The greatest difference between a traditional web developer's view of an MVC framework and our SPA architecture is as follows:

- Our SPA moves as much of the application to the browser as possible.
- We recognize the MVC pattern is repeated as if in a fractal.

A *fractal* is a pattern that displays self-similarity on all levels. A simple example is illustrated in figure 4.3, where from a distance we see a general pattern, and as we look closer we see the pattern repeating at finer levels of detail.

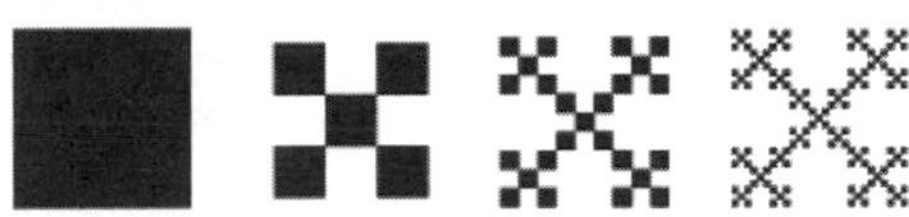

Figure 4.3 Box fractal

Our SPA architecture employs a repeating MVC pattern at multiple levels, so we call it *Fractal Model-View-Controller*, or FMVC. This concept isn't new, and developers have been discussing it with the same name for at least a decade. How much of the fractal we see is a matter of perspective. When we view our web application from a distance, as in figure 4.4, we see a single MVC pattern—the Controller handles the URI and user input, interacts with the Model, and provides us with a View in the browser.

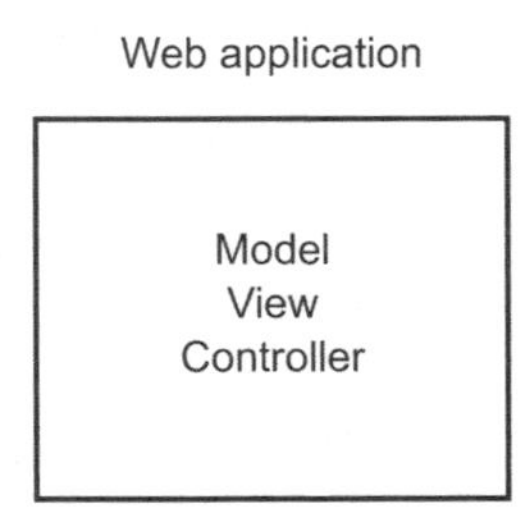

Figure 4.4 Our web application from a distance

When we zoom in a bit, as seen in figure 4.5, we see that the web application is split into two parts: the server side, which employs an MVC pattern to feed data to the client, and an SPA, which employs MVC to allow the user to view and interact with the browser Model. The server's Model includes the data from the database, whereas the View is the presentation of the data that gets sent to the browser, and the Controller is the code that orchestrates data management and communication with the browser. On the client, the Model includes the data that's been received from the server, the View is the user interface, and the Controller is the logic that orchestrates the client data with the interface.

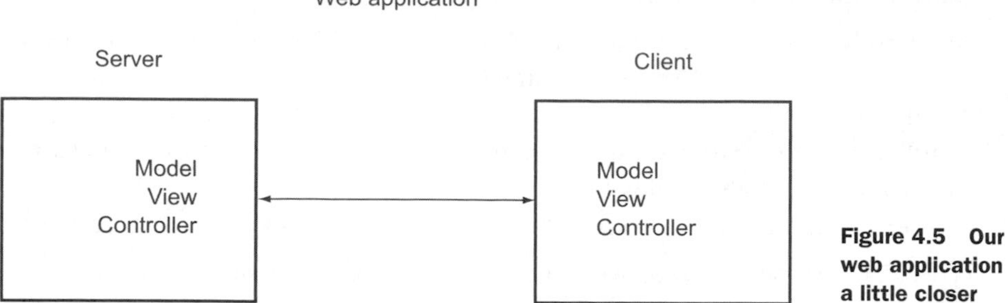

Figure 4.5 Our web application a little closer

When we zoom in closer still, as in figure 4.6, we see yet more MVC patterns. The server application, for example, employs an MVC pattern to provide an HTTP data API. The database that the server application uses employs its own MVC pattern. On the client, the client application uses an MVC pattern, yet the Shell calls subordinate feature modules, which themselves use MVC patterns.

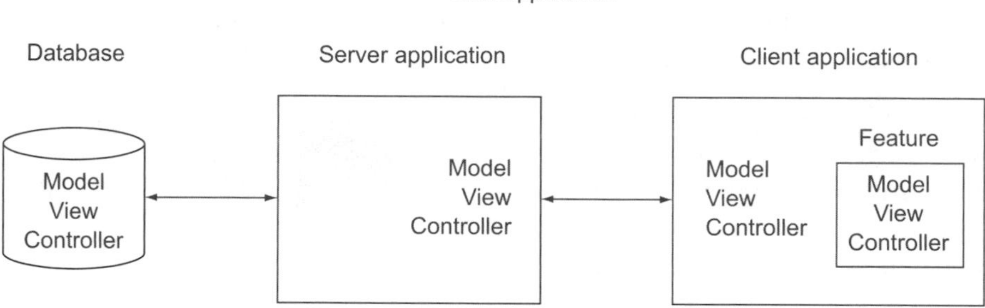

Figure 4.6 Our web application up close and personal

Almost all modern websites fit this pattern, even if the developers don't recognize it. For example, once a developer adds a commenting feature from *DisQus* or *LiveFyre* to their blog—or virtually any other third-party module—they're adding another MVC pattern.

Our SPA architecture embraces this fractal MVC pattern. In other words, our SPA works nearly the same way whether integrating a third-party feature or a feature module we write ourselves. Figure 4.7 shows how our Chat module will employ its own MVC pattern.

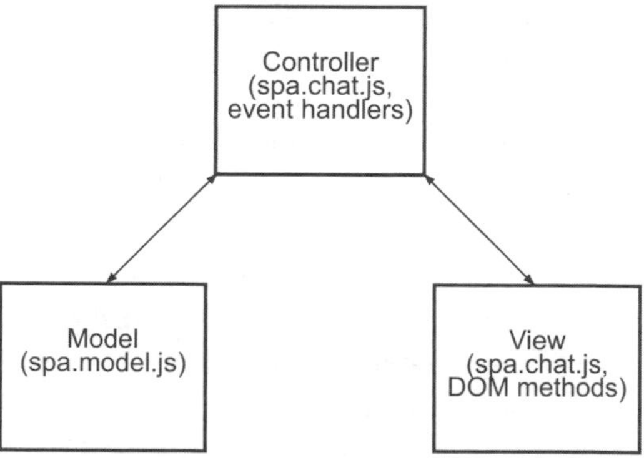

Figure 4.7 The MVC pattern as it appears in our Chat feature module

We've covered where feature modules fit into our architecture, how they're similar to third-party modules, and how they employ fractal MVC. In the next section, we'll put these concepts to use and create our first feature module.

4.2 Set up feature module files

The first SPA feature module we'll create will be the chat feature module, which we'll refer to as *Chat* for the remainder of the chapter. We chose this feature because we already have completed significant work on it in chapter 3, and because the conversion helps highlight the defining characteristics of a feature module.

4.2.1 Plan the file structure

We recommend you copy the whole directory structure you created in chapter 3 into a new "chapter_4" directory so we may update them there. Let's review our file structure as we left it in chapter 3 as shown in listing 4.1:

Listing 4.1 File structure from chapter 3

```
spa
+-- css
|   +-- spa.css
|   `-- spa.shell.css
+-- js
|   +-- jq
|   |   +-- jquery-1.9.1.js
|   |   `-- jquery.uriAnchor-1.1.3.js
|   +-- spa.js
|   `-- spa.shell.js
+-- layout.html
`-- spa.html
```

Here are the changes we wish to make:

- Create a namespaced stylesheet for Chat.
- Create a namespaced JavaScript module for Chat.
- Create a stub for the browser Model.
- Create a utility module that provides common routines for use by all other modules.
- Modify the *browser document* to include the new files.
- Delete the file we used to develop the layout.

When we're finished, our updated files and directories should look like listing 4.2. All the files we'll have to create or modify are shown in **bold**:

Listing 4.2 Revised file structure for Chat

```
spa
+-- css
|   +-- spa.chat.css      <-- Add the stylesheet for Chat.
|   +-- spa.css
|   `-- spa.shell.css
```

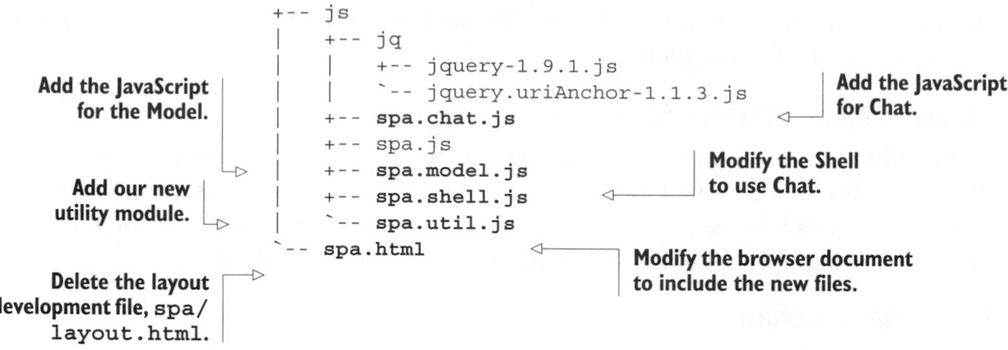

Now that we've identified the files we want to add or modify, let's fire up our trusty text editor and get the job done. We're going to consider each file exactly in the order we've presented it.

4.2.2 Populate the files

Our first file to consider is the Chat stylesheet, spa/css/spa.chat.css. We'll create a file and populate it with the contents shown in listing 4.3. Initially, it will be a *stub*:[4]

Listing 4.3 Our stylesheet (stub)—spa/css/spa.chat.css

```
/*
 * spa.chat.css
 * Chat feature styles
*/
```

Next let's create our Chat feature module, spa/js/spa.chat.js, as shown in listing 4.4, using our module template from appendix A. This is just the first pass, and we'll have it fill the chat slider container with some trivial HTML:

Listing 4.4 Our Chat module, with limited capability—spa/js/spa.chat.js

```
/*
 * spa.chat.js
 * Chat feature module for SPA
*/

/*jslint         browser : true, continue : true,
  devel  : true, indent  : 2,    maxerr   : 50,
  newcap : true, nomen   : true, plusplus : true,
  regexp : true, sloppy  : true, vars     : false,
  white  : true
*/

/*global $, spa */

spa.chat = (function () {
```

Create namespace of this module, `spa.chat`.

[4] A *stub* is purposely incomplete or a placeholder resource. For example, in chapter 5 we create a "stub" data module that fakes communication with the server.

```
//---------------- BEGIN MODULE SCOPE VARIABLES --------------
var
  configMap = {
    main_html : String()
      + '<div style="padding:1em; color:#fff;">'
        + 'Say hello to chat'
      + '</div>',
    settable_map : {}
  },
  stateMap  = { $container : null },
  jqueryMap = {},

  setJqueryMap, configModule, initModule
  ;
//----------------- END MODULE SCOPE VARIABLES ---------------

//------------------- BEGIN UTILITY METHODS ------------------
//-------------------- END UTILITY METHODS -------------------

//--------------------- BEGIN DOM METHODS --------------------
// Begin DOM method /setJqueryMap/
setJqueryMap = function () {
  var $container = stateMap.$container;
  jqueryMap = { $container : $container };
};
// End DOM method /setJqueryMap/
//---------------------- END DOM METHODS ---------------------

//------------------- BEGIN EVENT HANDLERS -------------------
//-------------------- END EVENT HANDLERS --------------------

//------------------- BEGIN PUBLIC METHODS -------------------
// Begin public method /configModule/
// Purpose    : Adjust configuration of allowed keys
// Arguments  : A map of settable keys and values
//   * color_name - color to use
// Settings   :
//   * configMap.settable_map declares allowed keys
// Returns    : true
// Throws     : none
//
configModule = function ( input_map ) {
  spa.util.setConfigMap({
    input_map    : input_map,
    settable_map : configMap.settable_map,
    config_map   : configMap
  });
  return true;
};
// End public method /configModule/

// Begin public method /initModule/
// Purpose    : Initializes module
// Arguments  :
//  * $container the jquery element used by this feature
// Returns    : true
// Throws     : none
```

Store HTML template for chat slider in `configMap`. Feel free to replace our inane stock message with your own.

Create `configModule` method. Whenever a feature module accepts settings, we always use the same method name and the same `spa.util.setConfigMap` utility.

Add `initModule` method. Almost all our modules have this method. It starts the module execution.

```
  //
  initModule = function ( $container ) {
    $container.html( configMap.main_html );
    stateMap.$container = $container;
    setJqueryMap();
    return true;
  };
  // End public method /initModule/

  // return public methods
  return {
    configModule : configModule,
    initModule   : initModule
  };
  //------------------- END PUBLIC METHODS ---------------------
}());
```

Fill chat slider container with our HTML template.

Export module methods, `configModule` and `initModule`. These are standard methods for nearly all feature modules.

Now let's create our Model as shown in listing 4.5. This is also a stub. Like all our modules, the file name (spa.model.js) indicates the namespace it provides (`spa.model`):

Listing 4.5 Our model (stub)—spa/js/spa.model.js

```
/*
 * spa.model.js
 * Model module
*/

/*jslint         browser : true, continue : true,
  devel  : true, indent  : 2,    maxerr   : 50,
  newcap : true, nomen   : true, plusplus : true,
  regexp : true, sloppy  : true, vars     : false,
  white  : true
*/

/*global $, spa */

spa.model = (function (){ return {}; }());
```

Let's create a general utility module so we may share common routines across all modules as shown in listing 4.6. The `makeError` method can be used to easily create error objects. The `setConfigMap` method provides an easy and consistent way to change settings for modules. Because these are public methods, we detail their use for the benefit of other developers:

Listing 4.6 Common utilities—spa/js/spa.util.js

```
/*
 * spa.util.js
 * General JavaScript utilities
 *
 * Michael S. Mikowski - mmikowski at gmail dot com
 * These are routines I have created, compiled, and updated
 * since 1998, with inspiration from around the web.
 *
 * MIT License
```

```
 *
*/

/*jslint          browser : true, continue : true,
  devel  : true,  indent  : 2,    maxerr   : 50,
  newcap : true,  nomen   : true, plusplus : true,
  regexp : true,  sloppy  : true, vars     : false,
  white  : true
 */
/*global $, spa */

spa.util = (function () {
  var makeError, setConfigMap;

  // Begin Public constructor /makeError/
  // Purpose: a convenience wrapper to create an error object
  // Arguments:
  //   * name_text - the error name
  //   * msg_text  - long error message
  //   * data      - optional data attached to error object
  // Returns  : newly constructed error object
  // Throws   : none
  //
  makeError = function ( name_text, msg_text, data ) {
    var error     = new Error();
    error.name    = name_text;
    error.message = msg_text;

    if ( data ){ error.data = data; }

    return error;
  };
  // End Public constructor /makeError/

  // Begin Public method /setConfigMap/
  // Purpose: Common code to set configs in feature modules
  // Arguments:
  //   * input_map    - map of key-values to set in config
  //   * settable_map - map of allowable keys to set
  //   * config_map   - map to apply settings to
  // Returns: true
  // Throws : Exception if input key not allowed
  //
  setConfigMap = function ( arg_map ){
    var
      input_map    = arg_map.input_map,
      settable_map = arg_map.settable_map,
      config_map   = arg_map.config_map,
      key_name, error;

    for ( key_name in input_map ){
      if ( input_map.hasOwnProperty( key_name ) ){
        if ( settable_map.hasOwnProperty( key_name ) ){
          config_map[key_name] = input_map[key_name];
        }
        else {
          error = makeError( 'Bad Input',
            'Setting config key |' + key_name + '| is not supported'
```

```
          );
          throw error;
        }
      }
    }
  };
  // End Public method /setConfigMap/

  return {
    makeError    : makeError,
    setConfigMap : setConfigMap
  };
}());
```

Finally, we can tie all of these changes together by modifying our browser document to load the new JavaScript and CSS files. First we'll load our stylesheets and then our JavaScript. JavaScript library inclusion order *is* important: third-party libraries should be loaded first as they're often a prerequisite, and this practice also helps overcome occasional bone-headed third-party namespace snafus (see the sidebar "Why our libraries are loaded last"). Our libraries come next, and must be ordered by namespace hierarchy—for example, modules that supply the namespaces of `spa`, `spa.model`, and `spa.model.user` must be loaded in that order. Any ordering beyond that is convention and isn't a requirement. We like this convention: root -> core utilities -> Model -> browser utilities -> Shell -> feature modules.

> **Why our libraries are loaded last**
>
> We like our libraries to have final claim on namespaces, and so we load them last. If some rogue third-party library claims the `spa.model` namespace, our libraries will "take it back" when they load. If this happens, our SPA has a good chance to continue functioning, although the third-party feature probably wouldn't work. If the library order were reversed, our SPA would almost certainly be *completely* hosed. We'd rather fix a problem with, say, a third-party comments feature than explain to the CEO why our website *completely stopped working* at midnight.

Let's update our browser document as shown in listing 4.7. Changes from chapter 3 are shown in **bold**:

Listing 4.7 Changes to the browser document—spa/spa.html

```
<!doctype html>
<!--
  spa.html
  spa browser document
-->

<html>
<head>
  <!-- ie9+ rendering support for latest standards -->
```

Add headers to allow IE9+ to work.

```
    <meta http-equiv="Content-Type" content="text/html; charset=ISO-8859-1">
    <meta http-equiv="X-UA-Compatible" content="IE=edge" />
    <title>SPA Chapter 4</title>

    <!-- third-party stylesheets -->

    <!-- our stylesheets -->
    <link rel="stylesheet" href="css/spa.css"       type="text/css"/>
    <link rel="stylesheet" href="css/spa.chat.css" type="text/css"/>
    <link rel="stylesheet" href="css/spa.shell.css" type="text/css"/>

    <!-- third-party javascript -->
    <script src="js/jq/jquery-1.9.1.js"></script>
    <script src="js/jq/jquery.uriAnchor-1.1.3.js"></script>

    <!-- our javascript -->
    <script src="js/spa.js"      ></script>
    <script src="js/spa.util.js" ></script>
    <script src="js/spa.model.js"></script>
    <script src="js/spa.shell.js"></script>
    <script src="js/spa.chat.js" ></script>
    <script>
      $(function () { spa.initModule( $('#spa') ); });
    </script>

  </head>
  <body>
  <div id="spa"></div>
  </body>
  </html>
```

Add a third-party stylesheet section.

Change title to reflect new chapter. Sorry Toto, we're not in chapter 3 anymore.

Include our stylesheets. Mirror the JavaScript inclusion order to ease maintenance.

Include third-party JavaScript first. See the sidebar on why this is a good practice.

Include our libraries in the order of namespace. At minimum, the spa namespace must be loaded first.

Include our utility library, which shares routines with all modules.

Include the browser Model, which is currently a stub.

Load feature modules after the Shell.

Now let's have the Shell configure and initialize Chat as shown in listing 4.8. All changes are shown in **bold**:

Listing 4.8 Shell revision—spa/js/spa.shell.js

```
...
    // configure uriAnchor to use our schema
    $.uriAnchor.configModule({
    schema_map : configMap.anchor_schema_map
    });

    // configure and initialize feature modules
    spa.chat.configModule( {} );
    spa.chat.initModule( jqueryMap.$chat );

    // Handle URI anchor change events
...
```

We're now finished with our first pass. Although this is a fair amount of work, many of these steps won't be needed for future feature modules. Now let's take a look at what we've created.

4.2.3 *What we've wrought*

When we load our browser document (spa/spa.html), the chat slider should look like figure 4.8.

Figure 4.8 Our updated browser document—spa/spa.html

The `Say hello to chat` text shows that Chat was configured and initiated properly and that it has provided the chat slider content. But this presentation is far from impressive. In the next section, we'll significantly improve the chat interface.

4.3 Design method APIs

According to our architecture, the Shell can call any subordinate module in the SPA. Feature modules should only call shared utility modules; calls *between* feature modules are *not* allowed. The only other source of data or capabilities for the feature module should come from the Shell in the form of arguments provided to the module's public methods, like during configuration or initialization. Figure 4.9 illustrates this layering.

This isolation is deliberate as it helps prevent feature-specific flaws from propagating to the application level or to other features.[5]

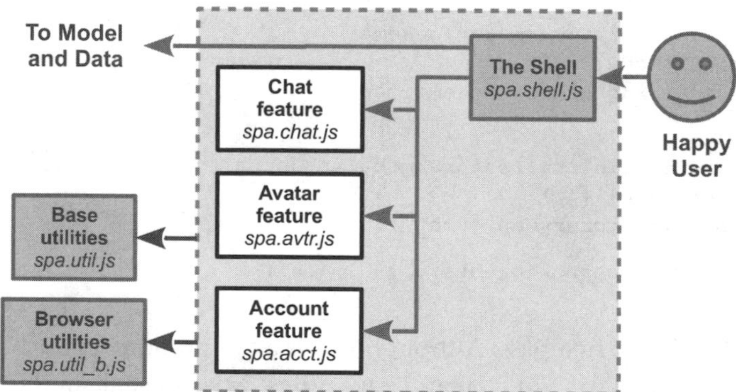

Figure 4.9 Feature modules close up—allowable calls

[5] Communication between feature modules should always be coordinated by the Shell or the Model.

4.3.1 The anchor interface pattern

Recall in chapter 3 that we want the URI anchor to always drive page state, and not the other way around. Sometimes the execution path can seem hard to follow, as the Shell is responsible for the URI anchor management, yet Chat is responsible for the slider presentation. We rely on the *anchor interface pattern* to support URI anchor *and* user-event-driven states *using the same jQuery* `hashchange` *event* in both cases. This single path to change application state ensures history-safe URLs,[6] consistent behavior, and helps accelerate development because there is only one state change mechanism. The pattern is shown in figure 4.10.

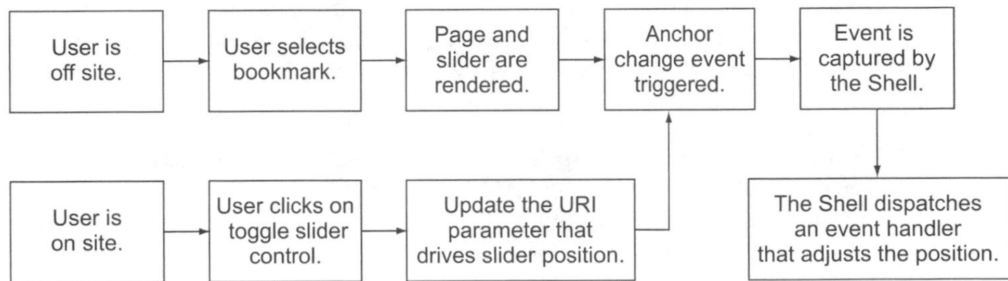

Figure 4.10 The anchor interface pattern for Chat

We already implemented much of the behavior of Chat in the last chapter. Now let's move the remaining chat code to its own module. Let's also specify the APIs that both Chat and the Shell will use to communicate. This will benefit us immediately and also make code reuse much simpler. The API specifications need to detail which resources are required and which capabilities will be provided. They should be considered "living documents" and be updated whenever an API is changed.

One common public method that we want Chat to provide is `configModule`, which we'll use to change settings prior to initialization. Chat, like every feature module, should usually have an initialization method, `initModule`, that we'll then use to direct the module to offer its capability to the user. We also want Chat to provide a `setSliderPosition` method so the Shell may request a slider position. We'll design the APIs for these methods in the following sections.

4.3.2 Chat configuration APIs

When we *configure* a module, we adjust settings that we don't expect to change during a user session. With Chat the following settings fit that criteria:

- A function that provides the capability to adjust the `chat` URI anchor parameter.
- An object that provides methods for sending and receiving messages (from the Model).

[6] "History-safe" means the browser history controls, like the Forward, Back, bookmarks, and browser history, all work as the user expects.

- An object that provides methods to interact with a list of users (from the Model).
- Any number of behavior settings such as slider opened height, slider open time, and slider close time.

The dirt on JavaScript arguments

Remember that only simple values—strings, numbers, and booleans—are passed directly to functions. All complex data types in JavaScript (like objects, arrays, and functions) are *passed by reference*. This means they are *never* copied as they can be in some other languages. Instead, a memory location value is passed. This is usually much faster than copying, but the downside is that it's easy to accidentally change an object or array that has been passed in by reference.

When a function expects a reference to a function as an argument, the reference is commonly called a *callback*. Callbacks are powerful, but they can become difficult to manage. We show how one can reduce the use of callbacks in chapters 5 and 6 by using jQuery global custom events instead.

Based on these expectations, we can devise the Chat `configModule` API specification shown in listing 4.9. This documentation isn't used by JavaScript:

Listing 4.9 Chat API specification for `configModule`—spa/js/spa.chat.js

```
// Begin public method /configModule/
// Example    : spa.chat.configModule({ slider_open_em : 18 });
// Purpose    : Configure the module prior to initialization
// Arguments :
//   * set_chat_anchor - a callback to modify the URI anchor to
//     indicate opened or closed state. This callback must return
//     false if the requested state cannot be met
//   * chat_model - the chat model object provides methods
//       to interact with our instant messaging
//   * people_model - the people model object which provides
//       methods to manage the list of people the model maintains
//   * slider_* settings. All these are optional scalars.
//       See mapConfig.settable_map for a full list
//       Example: slider_open_em is the open height in em's
// Action     :
//   The internal configuration data structure (configMap) is
//   updated with provided arguments. No other actions are taken.
// Returns    : true
// Throws     : JavaScript error object and stack trace on
//              unacceptable or missing arguments
//
```

Now that we have an API for our Chat configuration, let's work on a specification for the `setChatAnchor` callback in the Shell. Listing 4.10 is a good start. This documentation isn't used by JavaScript:

Listing 4.10 Shell API specification for `setChatAnchor` callback—spa/js/spa.shell.js

```
// Begin callback method /setChatAnchor/
// Example  : setChatAnchor( 'closed' );
// Purpose  : Change the chat component of the anchor
// Arguments:
//   * position_type - may be 'closed' or 'opened'
// Action   :
//   Changes the URI anchor parameter 'chat' to the requested
//   value if possible.
// Returns  :
//   * true  - requested anchor part was updated
//   * false - requested anchor part was not updated
// Throws   : none
//
```

Now that we've completed designing the Chat configuration API and the Shell callback API, let's move on to Chat initialization.

4.3.3 The Chat initialization API

When we *initialize* one of our feature modules, we ask it to render HTML and begin offering its capabilities to the user. Unlike configuration, we expect that a feature module may be initialized many times during a user session. In the case of Chat, we want to send a single jQuery collection as the argument. The jQuery collection will contain one element—the one to which we want to append the chat slider. Let's sketch the API as shown in listing 4.11. This documentation isn't used by JavaScript:

Listing 4.11 Chat API specification for `initModule`—spa/js/spa.chat.js

```
// Begin public method /initModule/
// Example    : spa.chat.initModule( $('#div_id') );
// Purpose    :
//   Directs Chat to offer its capability to the user
// Arguments  :
//   * $append_target (example: $('#div_id')).
//     A jQuery collection that should represent
//     a single DOM container
// Action     :
//   Appends the chat slider to the provided container and fills
//   it with HTML content.  It then initializes elements,
//   events, and handlers to provide the user with a chat-room
//   interface
// Returns    : true on success, false on failure
// Throws     : none
//
```

The last API we'll specify in this chapter will be for the Chat `setSliderPosition` method. This will be used to open and close the chat slider. We'll work on this in the next section.

4.3.4 The Chat setSliderPosition API

We've decided to have Chat provide a public method, `setSliderPosition`, that will enable the Shell to request a slider position. Our decision to tie the slider position into the URI anchor raises some interesting issues we need to address:

- Chat may not always be able to adjust the slider to the requested position. For example, it may decide that the slider can't be opened because the user isn't signed in. We'll have `setSliderPosition` return `true` or `false` so the Shell will know if the request succeeded.
- If the Shell invokes a `setSliderPosition` callback, and the callback can't honor the request (in other words, it returns `false`), the Shell will need to revert the URI anchor `chat` parameter to the value prior to the request.

Let's specify an API, as shown in listing 4.12, that meets these requirements. This documentation isn't used by JavaScript:

Listing 4.12 Chat API specification for `setSliderPosition`—spa/js/spa.chat.js

```
// Begin public method /setSliderPosition/
//
// Example   : spa.chat.setSliderPosition( 'closed' );
// Purpose   : Ensure chat slider is in the requested state
// Arguments:
//   * position_type - enum('closed', 'opened', or 'hidden')
//   * callback - optional callback at end of animation.
//     (callback receives slider DOM element as argument)
// Action    :
//   Leaves slider in current state if it matches requested,
//   otherwise animate to requested state.
// Returns   :
//   * true  - requested state achieved
//   * false - requested state not achieved
// Throws    : none
//
```

With this API defined, we're almost ready to write some code. But before we do, let's look at how configuration and initialization will cascade through our application.

4.3.5 Configuration and initialization cascade

Our configuration and initialization follow a common pattern. First, a script tag in our browser document configures and initializes our *root namespace* module, `spa.js`. Then our root module then configures and initializes the Shell module, `spa.shell.js`. The Shell module then configures and initializes our feature module, `spa.chat.js`. This cascade of configuration and initialization is shown in figure 4.11.

All of our modules provide a public `initModule` method. We provide a `configModule` method only if we need to support settings. At this stage of development, only Chat can be configured.

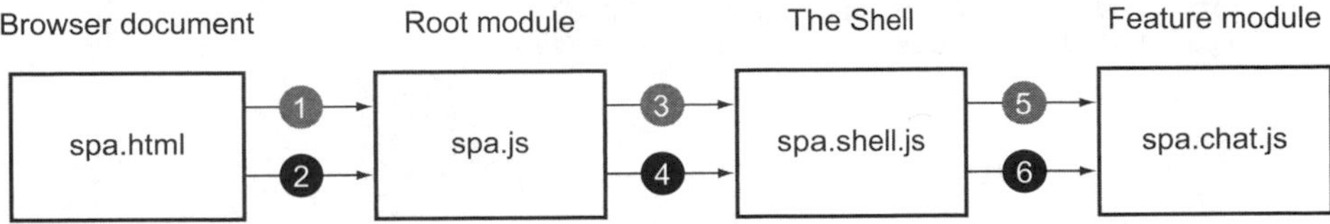

Figure 4.11 Configuration and initialization cascade

When we load the browser document (spa/spa.html), it loads all our CSS and JavaScript files. Next a script in the page does the initial housekeeping and initializes the root namespace module (spa/js/spa.js), presenting it a page element (the `spa div`) for it to use:

```
$(function (){
  // housekeeping here ...
  // if we needed to configure the root module,
  // we would invoke spa.configModule first
  spa.initModule( $('#spa' ) );
}());
```

When initialized, the root namespace module (spa/js/spa.js) does any root-level housekeeping, then configures and initializes the Shell (spa/js/spa.shell.js), providing it with a page element (`$container`) for it to use:

```
var initModule = function ( $container ){
  // housekeeping here ...
  // if we needed to configure the Shell,
  // we would invoke spa.shell.configModule first
  spa.shell.initModule( $container );
};
```

The Shell (spa/js/spa.shell.js) then does any Shell-level housekeeping and configures and initializes all its feature modules, like Chat (spa/js/spa.chat.js), providing it with a page element (`jqueryMap.$chat`) for it to use:

```
initModule = function ( $container ) {
  // housekeeping here ...
  // configure and initialize feature modules
```

```
  spa.chat.configModule( {} );
  spa.chat.initModule( jqueryMap.$chat );

  // ...

};
```

It's important that we're comfortable with this cascade because it's the same for all feature modules. We may, for example, wish to split some function of Chat (spa/js/spa.chat.js) into a subordinate module that handles the online user list—we'll call it the Roster—and create its file at spa/js/spa.chat.roster.js. We'd then have Chat use the `spa.chat.roster.configModule` method to configure the module, and the `spa.chat.roster.initModule` method to initialize it. Chat would also provide a jQuery container to the Roster, where it would show the list of users.

Now that we have reviewed the cascade of configuration and initialization, we're ready to update our application to the APIs we've designed. We're going to make some changes that will break things for a bit, so if you're playing along at home don't panic—we'll get things fixed soon enough.

4.4 Implement the feature API

Our primary goal in this section is to implement the API we've defined. And, because we'll have the "code up on blocks" as they say, we'd like to take care of a few secondary objectives as well:

- Complete moving Chat configuration and implementation to its own module. The only aspect of Chat that the Shell should have to worry about is the URI anchor management.
- Update the chat feature to look more, well, *chatty*.

The files we'll need to update and a summary of how they'll need to change are presented in listing 4.13.

Listing 4.13 Files we'll be changing during our API implementation

```
spa
+-- css
|   +-- spa.chat.css  # Move chat styles from spa.shell.css, enhance
|   `-- spa.shell.css # Remove chat styles
`-- js
    +-- spa.chat.js   # Move capabilities from the Shell, implement APIs
    `-- spa.shell.js  # Removed Chat capabilities
                      # and add setSliderPosition callback per API
```

We'll modify these files in exactly the order presented.

4.4.1 The stylesheets

We want to move all our Chat styles to their own stylesheet (spa/css/spa.chat.css) and improve our layout as we do so. Our local CSS layout specialist has provided a nice plan, as shown in figure 4.12.

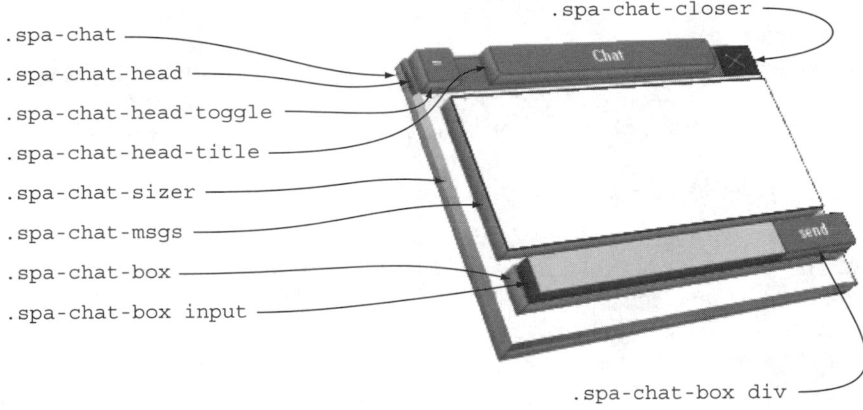

Figure 4.12 3D view of elements and selectors—spa/css/spa.chat.css

Note how we namespaced our CSS as we did with our JavaScript. This has numerous advantages:

- We don't need to worry about collisions with our other modules because we're guaranteeing a unique prefix for all class names: `spa-chat`.
- Collisions with third-party packages are almost always avoided. And even if by some odd chance they aren't, the fix (changing a prefix) is trivial.
- It helps debugging a great deal, because when we inspect an element controlled by Chat, its class name points us to the originating feature module, `spa.chat`.
- The names indicate what contains (and therefore controls) what. For example, note how `spa-chat-head-toggle` is contained within `spa-chat-head`, which is contained within `spa-chat`.

Most of this styling is boilerplate stuff (sorry, CSS-layout-specialist-guy). But we have a few points that will make our work special. First, the `spa-chat-sizer` element needs to have a fixed height. This will provide room for the chat and message areas even when the slider retracts. If this element isn't included, the slider contents get "scrunched" when the slider is retracted, and this is at best confusing to the user. Second, our layout guy wants us to remove all references to absolute pixels in favor of relative measurements such as `ems` and percentages. This will enable our SPA to present equally well on low-density and high-density displays.

Pixels versus relative units

HTML gurus often go through serious contortions to use relative measurements when developing CSS, eschewing the use of *px* units altogether so that their creation can work well on any size display. We've observed a phenomenon that's making us reconsider the value of such an effort: browsers lie about their pixel dimensions.

(continued)

Consider the latest ultra-high resolution displays on laptops, tablets, and smartphones. The browsers on these devices don't correlate *px* in the browser directly with the physical screen pixels available. Instead, they normalize the *px* unit so the viewing experience approximates a traditional desktop monitor with a pixel density somewhere between 96 and 120 pixels per inch.

The result is that a *10 px* square box rendered on a smart phone browser may actually be 15 or 20 physical pixels on each side. This means *px* has become a relative unit as well, and compared to all the other units (*%, in, cm, mm, em, ex, pt, pc*) it's often more reliable. We have, among other devices, a 10.1-inch and 7-inch tablet with the exact same resolution of 1280 by 800 and the same OS. A *400 px* square box fits onto the 10.1-inch tablet screen; it doesn't on the 7-inch tablet though. Why? Because the amount of physical pixels used per *px* is higher on the smaller tablet. It appears the scaling is 1.5 pixels per *px* for the larger tablet, and 2 pixels per *px* for the smaller tablet.

We don't know what the future holds, but we've recently felt a lot less guilty when using the *px* unit.

With all that planning behind us, we can now add the CSS that meets the specifications into spa.chat.css, as shown in listing 4.14:

Listing 4.14 Adding enhanced Chat styles—spa/css/spa.chat.css

```
/*
 * spa.chat.css
 * Chat feature styles
*/

.spa-chat {
  position      : absolute;
  bottom        : 0;
  right         : 0;
  width         : 25em;
  height        : 2em;
  background    : #fff;
  border-radius : 0.5em 0 0 0;
  border-style  : solid;
  border-width  : thin 0 0 thin;
  border-color  : #888;
  box-shadow    : 0 0 0.75em 0 #888;
  z-index       : 1;
}

.spa-chat-head, .spa-chat-closer {
  position      : absolute;
  top           : 0;
  height        : 2em;
  line-height   : 1.8em;
  border-bottom : thin solid #888;
```

Define `spa-chat` class for the chat slider. We include subtle drop shadows. Like all other Chat selectors, we've converted to relative units.

Add common rules for both the `spa-chat-head` and `spa-chat-closer` classes. Doing this helps us employ the DRY (Don't Repeat Yourself) maxim. But if we've said it once we've said it a thousand times: we hate that acronym.

```
  cursor          : pointer;
  background      : #888;
  color           : white;
  font-family     : arial, helvetica, sans-serif;
  font-weight     : 800;
  text-align      : center;
}

.spa-chat-head {
  left           : 0;
  right          : 2em;
  border-radius  : 0.3em 0 0 0;
}

.spa-chat-closer {
  right : 0;
  width : 2em;
}
  .spa-chat-closer:hover {
    background : #800;
  }

.spa-chat-head-toggle {
  position       : absolute;
  top            : 0;
  left           : 0;
  width          : 2em;
  bottom         : 0;
  border-radius  : 0.3em 0 0 0;
}

.spa-chat-head-title {
  position     : absolute;
  left         : 50%;
  width        : 16em;
  margin-left  : -8em;
}

.spa-chat-sizer {
  position : absolute;
  top      : 2em;
  left     : 0;
  right    : 0;
}

.spa-chat-msgs {
  position : absolute;
  top      : 1em;
  left     : 1em;
  right    : 1em;
  bottom   : 4em;
  padding  : 0.5em;
  border   : thin solid #888;
  overflow-x : hidden;
  overflow-y : scroll;
}

.spa-chat-box {
```

Add the unique rules for the `spa-chat-head` class. We expect the element with this class will contain the `spa-chat-head-toggle` and `spa-chat-head-title` class elements.

Define a `spa-chat-closer` class to provide a little [x] on the top-right corner. Note that this isn't contained in the header, as we want the header to be a hotspot for opening and closing the slider, and the closer has a different function. We've also added a derived `:hover` pseudo-class here to highlight the element when the cursor is over it.

Create the `spa-chat-head-toggle` class for the toggle button. As the name suggests, we plan that an element with this style will be contained within an element of the `spa-chat-head` class.

Create the `spa-chat-head-title` class. Again, as the name suggests, we expect that an element with this style will be contained within an element of the `spa-chat-head` class. We employ the standard "negative margin" trick to center the element (see Google for details).

Define the `spa-chat-sizer` class so we can provide a fixed-size element to contain slider contents.

Add the `spa-chat-messages` class to be used by an element where we expect chat messages to be displayed. We hide the overflow on the x-axis and provide a vertical scrollbar always (we could use `overflow-y: auto` but that causes a jarring text flow problem when the scrollbar appears).

Create the `spa-chat-box` class for an element that we expect to contain an input field and the Send button.

```
    position : absolute;
    height   : 2em;
    left     : 1em;
    right    : 1em;
    bottom   : 1em;
    border   : thin solid #888;
    background : #888;
  }

  .spa-chat-box input[type=text] {
    float      : left;
    width      : 75%;
    height     : 100%;
    padding    : 0.5em;
    border     : 0;
    background : #ddd;
    color      : #404040;
  }
    .spa-chat-box input[type=text]:focus {
       background : #fff;
    }

  .spa-chat-box div {
    float       : left;
    width       : 25%;
    height      : 2em;
    line-height : 1.9em;
    text-align  : center;
    color       : #fff;
    font-weight : 800;
    cursor      : pointer;
  }
    .spa-chat-box div:hover {
      background-color: #444;
      color       : #ff0;
    }

  .spa-chat-head:hover .spa-chat-head-toggle {
    background : #aaa;
  }
```

Define a rule that styles "any text input inside of any element with the `.spa-chat-box` class." This will be our chat input field.

Create a derived `:focus` pseudo-class so that when a user selects the input, contrast is increased.

Define a rule that styles "any div element inside of the `.spa-chat-box` class." This will be our Send button.

Create a derived `:hover` pseudo-class that will highlight the Send button when the user hovers the mouse over it.

Define a selector that highlights the element styled with the `spa-chat-head-toggle` whenever the cursor hovers anywhere over an element of the `spa-chat-head` class.

Now that we have the stylesheet for Chat, we can remove prior definitions in the Shell's stylesheet at spa/css/spa.shell.css. First, let's remove `.spa-shell-chat` from the list of absolute position selectors. The change should look like the following (we can omit the comment):

```
.spa-shell-head, .spa-shell-head-logo, .spa-shell-head-acct,
.spa-shell-head-search, .spa-shell-main, .spa-shell-main-nav,
.spa-shell-main-content, .spa-shell-foot, /* .spa-shell-chat */
 .spa-shell-modal {
  position : absolute;
}
```

We also want to remove any `.spa-shell-chat` classes in spa/css/spa.shell.css. There are two to delete, as the following shows:

```
/* delete these from spa/css/spa.shell.css
 .spa-shell-chat {
  bottom  : 0;
  right   : 0;
  width   : 300px;
  height  : 15px;
  cursor  : pointer;
  background : red;
  border-radius : 5px 0 0 0;
  z-index : 1;
}
  .spa-shell-chat:hover {
    background : #a00;
  } */
```

Finally, let's hide the modal container so it doesn't get in the way of our chat slider:

```
...
.spa-shell-modal {
...
  display: none;
}
...
```

At this point, we should be able to open our browser document (spa/spa.html) and not see any errors in the Chrome Developer Tools JavaScript console. But the chat slider will no longer be visible. Stay calm and carry on—we'll fix this when we finish modifying Chat in the next section.

4.4.2 Modify Chat

We'll now modify Chat to implement the APIs we designed earlier. Here are the changes we have planned:

- Add the HTML for our more detailed chat slider.
- Expand the configuration to include settings like slider height and retract time.
- Create the `getEmSize` utility that converts `em` units to `px` (pixels).
- Update `setJqueryMap` to cache many of the new elements of the updated chat slider.
- Add the `setPxSizes` method that sets the slider dimensions using pixel units.
- Implement the `setSliderPosition` public method to match our API.
- Create the `onClickToggle` event handler to change the URI anchor and promptly return.
- Update the `configModule` public method documentation to match our API.
- Update the `initModule` public method to match our API.

Let's update Chat to implement these changes as shown in listing 4.15. The API specifications we designed earlier were copied into this file and used as a guideline during implementation. This accelerated development *and* ensured accurate documentation for future maintenance. All changes are shown in **bold**:

Listing 4.15 Modify Chat to meet API specifications—spa/js/spa.chat.js

```
/*
 * spa.chat.js
 * Chat feature module for SPA
*/

/*jslint         browser : true, continue : true,
  devel  : true, indent  : 2,    maxerr   : 50,
  newcap : true, nomen   : true, plusplus : true,
  regexp : true, sloppy  : true, vars     : false,
  white  : true
*/

/*global $, spa, getComputedStyle */

spa.chat = (function () {
  //---------------- BEGIN MODULE SCOPE VARIABLES --------------
  var
    configMap = {
      main_html : String()
        + '<div class="spa-chat">'
          + '<div class="spa-chat-head">'
            + '<div class="spa-chat-head-toggle">+</div>'
            + '<div class="spa-chat-head-title">'
              + 'Chat'
            + '</div>'
          + '</div>'
          + '<div class="spa-chat-closer">x</div>'
          + '<div class="spa-chat-sizer">'
            + '<div class="spa-chat-msgs"></div>'
            + '<div class="spa-chat-box">'
              + '<input type="text"/>'
              + '<div>send</div>'
            + '</div>'
          + '</div>'
        + '</div>',

      settable_map : {
        slider_open_time    : true,
        slider_close_time   : true,
        slider_opened_em    : true,
        slider_closed_em    : true,
        slider_opened_title : true,
        slider_closed_title : true,

        chat_model      : true,
        people_model    : true,
        set_chat_anchor : true
      },

      slider_open_time    : 250,
      slider_close_time   : 250,
      slider_opened_em    : 16,
```

Use the feature module template from appendix A.

Use an HTML template to fill the chat slider container.

Move all chat settings to this module.

```
    slider_closed_em    : 2,
    slider_opened_title : 'Click to close',
    slider_closed_title : 'Click to open',

    chat_model       : null,
    people_model     : null,
    set_chat_anchor  : null
  },
  stateMap  = {
    $append_target    : null,
    position_type     : 'closed',
    px_per_em         : 0,
    slider_hidden_px  : 0,
    slider_closed_px  : 0,
    slider_opened_px  : 0
  },
  jqueryMap = {},

  setJqueryMap, getEmSize, setPxSizes, setSliderPosition,
  onClickToggle, configModule, initModule
  ;
//----------------- END MODULE SCOPE VARIABLES ---------------

//------------------- BEGIN UTILITY METHODS ------------------
getEmSize = function ( elem ) {
  return Number(
    getComputedStyle( elem, '' ).fontSize.match(/\d*\.?\d*/)[0]
  );
};
//-------------------- END UTILITY METHODS -------------------
```

Add the `getEmSize` method to convert the em display unit to pixels so we can use measurements in jQuery.

Update `setJqueryMap` to cache a larger number of jQuery collections. We prefer to use classes instead of IDs because it allows us to add more than one chat slider to a page without refactoring.

```
//--------------------- BEGIN DOM METHODS --------------------
// Begin DOM method /setJqueryMap/
setJqueryMap = function () {
var
  $append_target = stateMap.$append_target,
  $slider = $append_target.find( '.spa-chat' );

jqueryMap = {
  $slider : $slider,
  $head   : $slider.find( '.spa-chat-head' ),
  $toggle : $slider.find( '.spa-chat-head-toggle' ),
  $title  : $slider.find( '.spa-chat-head-title' ),
  $sizer  : $slider.find( '.spa-chat-sizer' ),
  $msgs   : $slider.find( '.spa-chat-msgs' ),
  $box    : $slider.find( '.spa-chat-box' ),
  $input  : $slider.find( '.spa-chat-input input[type=text]') };
};
// End DOM method /setJqueryMap/

// Begin DOM method /setPxSizes/
setPxSizes = function () {
  var px_per_em, opened_height_em;
```

Add the `setPxSize` method to calculate the pixel sizes for elements managed by this module.

```
  px_per_em = getEmSize( jqueryMap.$slider.get(0) );

  opened_height_em = configMap.slider_opened_em;

  stateMap.px_per_em = px_per_em;
  stateMap.slider_closed_px = configMap.slider_closed_em * px_per_em;
  stateMap.slider_opened_px = opened_height_em * px_per_em;
  jqueryMap.$sizer.css({
    height : ( opened_height_em - 2 ) * px_per_em
  });
};
// End DOM method /setPxSizes/

// Begin public method /setSliderPosition/
// Example : spa.chat.setSliderPosition( 'closed' );
// Purpose : Move the chat slider to the requested position
// Arguments : // * position_type - enum('closed', 'opened', or 'hidden')
// * callback - optional callback to be run end at the end
// of slider animation. The callback receives a jQuery
// collection representing the slider div as its single
// argument
// Action :
// This method moves the slider into the requested position.
// If the requested position is the current position, it
// returns true without taking further action
// Returns :
// * true - The requested position was achieved
// * false - The requested position was not achieved
// Throws : none
//
setSliderPosition = function ( position_type, callback ) {
  var
    height_px, animate_time, slider_title, toggle_text;

// return true if slider already in requested position
if ( stateMap.position_type === position_type ){
  return true;
}

// prepare animate parameters
switch ( position_type ){
  case 'opened' :
    height_px = stateMap.slider_opened_px;
    animate_time = configMap.slider_open_time;
    slider_title = configMap.slider_opened_title;
    toggle_text = '=';
  break;

  case 'hidden' :
    height_px = 0;
    animate_time = configMap.slider_open_time;
    slider_title = '';
    toggle_text = '+';
  break;

  case 'closed' :
    height_px = stateMap.slider_closed_px;
    animate_time = configMap.slider_close_time;
```

Add the `setSliderPosition` method as detailed earlier in this chapter.

```
      slider_title = configMap.slider_closed_title;
      toggle_text = '+';
    break;
    // bail for unknown position_type
    default : return false;
  }

  // animate slider position change
  stateMap.position_type = '';
  jqueryMap.$slider.animate(
    { height : height_px },
    animate_time,
    function () {
      jqueryMap.$toggle.prop( 'title', slider_title );
      jqueryMap.$toggle.text( toggle_text );
      stateMap.position_type = position_type;
      if ( callback ) { callback( jqueryMap.$slider ); }
    }
  );
  return true;
};
// End public DOM method /setSliderPosition/
//---------------------- END DOM METHODS ---------------------

//------------------- BEGIN EVENT HANDLERS -------------------
onClickToggle = function ( event ){
  var set_chat_anchor = configMap.set_chat_anchor;
  if ( stateMap.position_type === 'opened' ) {
    set_chat_anchor( 'closed' );
  }
  else if ( stateMap.position_type === 'closed' ){
    set_chat_anchor( 'opened' );
  } return false;
};
//------------------- END EVENT HANDLERS ---------------------
```

Update the `onClick` event handler to make a call to change the URI anchor and then promptly exit, leaving the `hashchange` event handler in the Shell to pick up the change.

Update our `configModule` method to meet our API specification. Use the `spa.util.setConfigMap` utility, as we do with all our feature modules that can be configured.

```
//------------------- BEGIN PUBLIC METHODS -------------------
// Begin public method /configModule/
// Example   : spa.chat.configModule({ slider_open_em : 18 });
// Purpose   : Configure the module prior to initialization
// Arguments :
//   * set_chat_anchor - a callback to modify the URI anchor to
//     indicate opened or closed state. This callback must return
//     false if the requested state cannot be met
//   * chat_model - the chat model object provides methods
//       to interact with our instant messaging
//   * people_model - the people model object which provides
//       methods to manage the list of people the model maintains
//   * slider_* settings. All these are optional scalars.
//       See mapConfig.settable_map for a full list
//       Example: slider_open_em is the open height in em's
// Action    :
```

```
//   The internal configuration data structure (configMap) is
//   updated with provided arguments. No other actions are taken.
// Returns    : true
// Throws     : JavaScript error object and stack trace on
//              unacceptable or missing arguments
//
configModule = function ( input_map ) {
  spa.util.setConfigMap({
    input_map    : input_map,
    settable_map : configMap.settable_map,
    config_map   : configMap
  });
  return true;
};
// End public method /configModule/

// Begin public method /initModule/
// Example     : spa.chat.initModule( $('#div_id') );
// Purpose     : Directs Chat to offer its capability to the user
// Arguments   :
//   * $append_target (example: $('#div_id')).
//     A jQuery collection that should represent
//     a single DOM container
// Action      :
//   Appends the chat slider to the provided container and fills
//   it with HTML content. It then initializes elements,
//   events, and handlers to provide the user with a chat-room
//   interface
// Returns     : true on success, false on failure
// Throws      : none
//
initModule = function ( $append_target ) {
  $append_target.append( configMap.main_html );
  stateMap.$append_target = $append_target;
  setJqueryMap();
  setPxSizes();

  // initialize chat slider to default title and state
  jqueryMap.$toggle.prop( 'title', configMap.slider_closed_title );
  jqueryMap.$head.click( onClickToggle );
  stateMap.position_type = 'closed';

  return true;
};
// End public method /initModule/

// return public methods
return {
  setSliderPosition : setSliderPosition,
  configModule      : configModule,
  initModule        : initModule
};
//------------------- END PUBLIC METHODS ---------------------
}());
```

Update our `initModule` method to meet the API specification. As with the Shell, this routine generally has three parts: (1) fill the feature container with HTML, (2) cache jQuery collections, and (3) initialize event handlers.

Neatly export our public methods: `configModule`, `initModule`, and `setSliderPosition`.

At this point we should be able to load our browser document (spa/spa.html) and not see any errors in the Chrome Developer Tools JavaScript console. We should see the top portion of the chat slider. But if we click on it we should see an error message like "`set_chat_anchor` *is not a function*" in the console. We'll fix that next when we clean up the Shell.

4.4.3 Clean up the Shell

We'll now finish our changes with an update to the Shell. Here's what we want to do:

- Remove most chat slider settings and capabilities, as these have been moved to Chat.
- Revise the `onHashchange` event handler to fall back to a valid position if it can't set a requested slider position.
- Add the `setChatAnchor` method to meet the API we designed earlier.
- Improve the `initModule` documentation.
- Update `initModule` to configure Chat using the API we designed earlier.

Let's modify the Shell as shown in listing 4.16. Note how any new API specifications we developed earlier were placed directly in this file and used as a guideline during implementation. All changes are shown in **bold**:

Listing 4.16 Clean up the Shell—spa/js/spa.shell.js

```
/*
 * spa.shell.js
 * Shell module for SPA
*/

/*jslint         browser : true, continue : true,
  devel  : true, indent  : 2,    maxerr   : 50,
  newcap : true, nomen   : true, plusplus : true,
  regexp : true, sloppy  : true, vars     : false,
  white  : true
*/
/*global $, spa */

spa.shell = (function () {
  //---------------- BEGIN MODULE SCOPE VARIABLES --------------
  var
    configMap = {
      anchor_schema_map : {
        chat  : { opened : true, closed : true }
      },
      main_html : String()
        + '<div class="spa-shell-head">'
          + '<div class="spa-shell-head-logo"></div>'
          + '<div class="spa-shell-head-acct"></div>'
          + '<div class="spa-shell-head-search"></div>'
        + '</div>'
        + '<div class="spa-shell-main">'
          + '<div class="spa-shell-main-nav"></div>'
          + '<div class="spa-shell-main-content"></div>'
        + '</div>'
        + '<div class="spa-shell-foot"></div>'
        + '<div class="spa-shell-modal"></div>'
```

Change our anchor states to be `opened` and `closed` consistently in both Chat and the Shell.

Remove chat slider HTML and settings.

```
    },

  stateMap  = { anchor_map : {} },
  jqueryMap = {},

  copyAnchorMap,    setJqueryMap,
  changeAnchorPart, onHashchange,
  setChatAnchor,    initModule;
//----------------- END MODULE SCOPE VARIABLES ---------------

//------------------- BEGIN UTILITY METHODS ------------------
// Returns copy of stored anchor map; minimizes overhead
copyAnchorMap = function () {
  return $.extend( true, {}, stateMap.anchor_map );
};
//-------------------- END UTILITY METHODS -------------------

//--------------------- BEGIN DOM METHODS --------------------
// Begin DOM method /setJqueryMap/
setJqueryMap = function () {
  var $container = stateMap.$container;
  jqueryMap = { $container : $container };
};
// End DOM method /setJqueryMap/

// Begin DOM method /changeAnchorPart/
// Purpose    : Changes part of the URI anchor component
// Arguments  :
//   * arg_map - The map describing what part of the URI anchor
//     we want changed.
// Returns    :
//   * true  - the Anchor portion of the URI was updated
//   * false - the Anchor portion of the URI could not be updated
// Actions    :
//   The current anchor rep stored in stateMap.anchor_map.
//   See uriAnchor for a discussion of encoding.
//   This method
//     * Creates a copy of this map using copyAnchorMap().
//     * Modifies the key-values using arg_map.
//     * Manages the distinction between independent
//       and dependent values in the encoding.
//     * Attempts to change the URI using uriAnchor.
//     * Returns true on success, and false on failure.
//
changeAnchorPart = function ( arg_map ) {
  var
    anchor_map_revise = copyAnchorMap(),
    bool_return       = true,
    key_name, key_name_dep;

  // Begin merge changes into anchor map
  KEYVAL:
  for ( key_name in arg_map ) {
    if ( arg_map.hasOwnProperty( key_name ) ) {

      // skip dependent keys during iteration
      if ( key_name.indexOf( '_' ) === 0 ) { continue KEYVAL; }

      // update independent key value
```

Remove `toggleChat` from list of module-scope variables.

Remove the `toggleChat` method. Remove Chat element from `jqueryMap`.

```
      anchor_map_revise[key_name] = arg_map[key_name];

      // update matching dependent key
      key_name_dep = '_' + key_name;
      if ( arg_map[key_name_dep] ) {
        anchor_map_revise[key_name_dep] = arg_map[key_name_dep];
      }
      else {
        delete anchor_map_revise[key_name_dep];
        delete anchor_map_revise['_s' + key_name_dep];
      }
    }
  }
  // End merge changes into anchor map

  // Begin attempt to update URI; revert if not successful
  try {
    $.uriAnchor.setAnchor( anchor_map_revise );
  }
  catch ( error ) {
    // replace URI with existing state
    $.uriAnchor.setAnchor( stateMap.anchor_map,null,true );
    bool_return = false;
  }
  // End attempt to update URI...

  return bool_return;
};
// End DOM method /changeAnchorPart/
//--------------------- END DOM METHODS ----------------------

//------------------- BEGIN EVENT HANDLERS -------------------
// Begin Event handler /onHashchange/
// Purpose    : Handles the hashchange event
// Arguments  :
//   * event - jQuery event object.
// Settings   : none
// Returns    : false
// Actions    :
//   * Parses the URI anchor component
//   * Compares proposed application state with current
//   * Adjust the application only where proposed state
//     differs from existing and is allowed by anchor schema
//
onHashchange = function ( event ) {
  var
    _s_chat_previous, _s_chat_proposed, s_chat_proposed,
    anchor_map_proposed,
    is_ok = true,
    anchor_map_previous = copyAnchorMap();

  // attempt to parse anchor
  try { anchor_map_proposed = $.uriAnchor.makeAnchorMap(); }
  catch ( error ) {
    $.uriAnchor.setAnchor( anchor_map_previous, null, true );
    return false;
  }
```

```
stateMap.anchor_map = anchor_map_proposed;

// convenience vars
_s_chat_previous = anchor_map_previous._s_chat;
_s_chat_proposed = anchor_map_proposed._s_chat;

// Begin adjust chat component if changed
if ( ! anchor_map_previous
 || _s_chat_previous !== _s_chat_proposed
) {
  s_chat_proposed = anchor_map_proposed.chat;
  switch ( s_chat_proposed ) {
    case 'opened' :
      is_ok = spa.chat.setSliderPosition( 'opened' );
    break;
    case 'closed' :
      is_ok = spa.chat.setSliderPosition( 'closed' );
    break;
    default :
      spa.chat.setSliderPosition( 'closed' );
      delete anchor_map_proposed.chat;
      $.uriAnchor.setAnchor( anchor_map_proposed, null, true );
  }
}
// End adjust chat component if changed

// Begin revert anchor if slider change denied
if ( ! is_ok ){
  if ( anchor_map_previous ){
    $.uriAnchor.setAnchor( anchor_map_previous, null, true );
    stateMap.anchor_map = anchor_map_previous;
  } else {
      delete anchor_map_proposed.chat;
      $.uriAnchor.setAnchor( anchor_map_proposed, null, true );
  }
}
// End revert anchor if slider change denied

return false;
};
// End Event handler /onHashchange/
//-------------------- END EVENT HANDLERS --------------------

//--------------------- BEGIN CALLBACKS ---------------------
// Begin callback method /setChatAnchor/
// Example  : setChatAnchor( 'closed' );
// Purpose  : Change the chat component of the anchor
// Arguments:
//   * position_type - may be 'closed' or 'opened'
// Action   :
//   Changes the URI anchor parameter 'chat' to the requested
//   value if possible.
// Returns  :
//   * true  - requested anchor part was updated
//   * false - requested anchor part was not updated
// Throws   : none
//
```

Clear the URI anchor parameter Chat if the provided position isn't allowed by the `uriAnchor` settings and revert to the default position. We can test this by typing `#!chat=fred` as the URI anchor.

Use the public method Chat method, `setSliderPosition`.

React properly when `setSliderPosition` returns a false value (which means the change in position request was denied). Either revert to the prior position anchor value, or, if that doesn't exist, employ the default.

Create the callback `setChatAnchor`. It's provided to Chat as a safe way to request a URI change.

```
setChatAnchor = function ( position_type ){
  return changeAnchorPart({ chat : position_type });
};
// End callback method /setChatAnchor/
//----------------------- END CALLBACKS ---------------------

//------------------- BEGIN PUBLIC METHODS -------------------
// Begin Public method /initModule/
// Example   : spa.shell.initModule( $('#app_div_id') );
// Purpose   :
// Directs the Shell to offer its capability to the user
// Arguments :
//   * $container (example: $('#app_div_id')).
//     A jQuery collection that should represent
//     a single DOM container
// Action    :
//   Populates $container with the shell of the UI
//   and then configures and initializes feature modules.
//   The Shell is also responsible for browser-wide issues
//   such as URI anchor and cookie management.
// Returns   : none
// Throws    : none
//
initModule = function ( $container ) {
  // load HTML and map jQuery collections
  stateMap.$container = $container;
  $container.html( configMap.main_html );
  setJqueryMap();

  // configure uriAnchor to use our schema
  $.uriAnchor.configModule({
    schema_map : configMap.anchor_schema_map
  });

  // configure and initialize feature modules
  spa.chat.configModule({
    set_chat_anchor : setChatAnchor,
    chat_model      : spa.model.chat,
    people_model    : spa.model.people
  });
  spa.chat.initModule( jqueryMap.$container );

  // Handle URI anchor change events.
  // This is done /after/ all feature modules are configured
  // and initialized, otherwise they will not be ready to handle
  // the trigger event, which is used to ensure the anchor
  // is considered on-load
  //
  $(window)
    .bind( 'hashchange', onHashchange )
    .trigger( 'hashchange' );

};
// End PUBLIC method /initModule/

return { initModule : initModule };
//------------------- END PUBLIC METHODS --------------------
}());
```

Document the initModule routine.

Replace the chat slider click binding with Chat configuration and initialization.

Figure 4.13 Our more dashing Chat slider

When we open the browser document (spa/spa.html) we should now see something similar to figure 4.13. We think this revised chat slider is significantly more dashing. It doesn't display messages yet—we'll get to that capability in chapter 6.

Now that the code is working nicely, let's analyze some key revisions by walking through the execution of our application.

4.4.4 Walk through the execution

This section highlights the revisions we made to our application in the last section. We look at how the application is configured and initialized, and then explore what happens when a user clicks on the chat slider.

When we load our browser document (spa/spa.html), a script initializes our root namespace (spa/js/spa.js), presenting it with a page element (the `#spa` `div`) for it to use:

```
$(function (){ spa.initModule( $('#spa') ); });
```

The root namespace module (spa/js/spa.js) then initializes the Shell (spa/js/spa.shell.js), presenting it with a page element (`$container`) for it to use:

```
var initModule = function ( $container ){
  spa.shell.initModule( $container );
};
```

The Shell (spa/js/spa.shell.js) then configures and initializes Chat (spa/js/spa.chat.js). But this time both steps are a bit different. The configuration now matches the API we defined earlier. The `set_chat_anchor` configuration is the callback that follows the specification we created earlier:

```
...
// configure and initialize feature modules
spa.chat.configModule({
  set_chat_anchor : setChatAnchor,
  chat_model      : spa.model.chat,
  people_model    : spa.model.people
});
spa.chat.initModule(jqueryMap.$container);
...
```

Chat initialization is also subtly different: instead of providing a container to use, the Shell now provides a container to which Chat will *append* a chat slider. This is a good arrangement if you trust the module author. And we do.

```
...
  //    * set_chat_anchor - a method modify to modify the URI anchor to
  //      indicate opened or closed state.  Return false if requested
  //      state cannot be met.
...
```

When the user clicks on the slider toggle button, Chat uses the `set_chat_anchor` callback to request that the URI anchor `chat` parameter be changed to *opened* or *closed*, and then returns. The Shell still handles `hashchange` events, as we see in spa/js/spa.shell.js:

```
initModule = function ( $container ){
  ...
  $(window)
    .bind( 'hashchange', onHashchange )
  ...
```

So when the user clicks on the slider, the `hashchange` event is caught by the Shell, which dispatches to the `onHashchange` event handler. If the chat component of the URI anchor has changed, this routine calls `spa.chat.setSliderPosition` to request the new position:

```
// Begin adjust chat component if changed
   if ( ! anchor_map_previous
    || _s_chat_previous !== _s_chat_proposed
   ) {
     s_chat_proposed = anchor_map_proposed.chat;
     switch ( s_chat_proposed ) {
       case 'opened' :
         is_ok = spa.chat.setSliderPosition( 'opened' );
       break;
       case 'closed' :
         is_ok = spa.chat.setSliderPosition( 'closed' );
       break;
       ...
     }
   }
   // End adjust chat component if changed
```

If the position is valid, the slider moves to the requested position and the URI anchor `chat` parameter is changed.

The changes we've made result in an implementation that meets our design goals. The URI controls the chat slider state, and we've also moved all Chat UI logic and code to our new feature module. The slider also looks and works better. Now let's add some other public methods that are commonly found in many feature models.

4.5 Add frequently needed methods

A few public methods are needed frequently enough in feature modules that they're worth discussing in their own right. The first is a reset method (removeSlider); the second is a window resize method (handleResize). We're going to implement both. First, let's declare these method names in Chat at the bottom of the Module Scope Variables section, and also export them as public methods at the end of the module, as shown in listing 4.17. Changes are shown in **bold**:

Listing 4.17 Declare method function names—spa/js/spa.chat.js

```
...
    jqueryMap = {},

    setJqueryMap, getEmSize, setPxSizes, setSliderPosition,
    onClickToggle, configModule, initModule,
    removeSlider, handleResize
    ;
  //----------------- END MODULE SCOPE VARIABLES ---------------
  ...

  // return public methods
  return {
    setSliderPosition : setSliderPosition,
    configModule      : configModule,
    initModule        : initModule,
    removeSlider      : removeSlider,
    handleResize      : handleResize
  };
  //------------------- END PUBLIC METHODS ---------------------
}());
```

Now with the method names declared, we'll implement them in the following sections, starting with the remove method.

4.5.1 The removeSlider method

We find that we want a remove method for many of our feature modules. If we implement authentication, for example, we may want to completely remove the chat slider when a user signs out. Usually, this sort of action is taken either to improve performance or enhance security—assuming the remove method does a good job of deleting obsolete data structures.

Our method will need to delete the DOM container that Chat has appended and otherwise *unwind* our initialization and configuration, in that order. Listing 4.18 contains the code changes for the removeSlider method. Changes are shown in **bold**:

Listing 4.18 removeSlider method—spa/js/spa.chat.js

```
...
  // End public method /initModule/

  // Begin public method /removeSlider/
```

```
// Purpose :
//   * Removes chatSlider DOM element
//   * Reverts to initial state
//   * Removes pointers to callbacks and other data
// Arguments : none
// Returns   : true
// Throws    : none
//
removeSlider = function () {
  // unwind initialization and state
  // remove DOM container; this removes event bindings too
  if ( jqueryMap.$slider ) {
    jqueryMap.$slider.remove();
    jqueryMap = {};
  }
  stateMap.$append_target = null;
  stateMap.position_type  = 'closed';

  // unwind key configurations
  configMap.chat_model      = null;
  configMap.people_model    = null;
  configMap.set_chat_anchor = null;

  return true;
};
// End public method /removeSlider/

// return public methods
...
```

We don't try to get too clever with any remove method. The point is to lay waste to any prior configuration and initialization, and that's it. We carefully ensure that data pointers are removed. This is important so that reference counts to data structures can drop to 0, which allows garbage collection to do its job. *This is one reason why we always list potential configMap and stateMap keys at the top of the module*—so we can see what we need to clean up.

We can test the removeSlider method by opening the Chrome Developer Tools JavaScript console and entering the following (don't forget to press Return!):

```
spa.chat.removeSlider();
```

When we inspect the browser window we can see the chat slider has been removed. If we want to get it back, we can enter the following lines into the JavaScript console:

```
spa.chat.configModule({ set_chat_anchor: function (){ return true; } });
spa.chat.initModule( $( '#spa') );
```

The chat slider we "restored" with the JavaScript console isn't fully functional, as we have provided a null function for the set_chat_anchor callback. In real use, we would always reenable the chat module from the Shell where we have access to the required callback.

We could do a lot more with this method—like having the slider disappear gracefully—but we'll leave that as an exercise for the reader. Let's now implement another method which is commonly required by feature modules, `handleResize`.

4.5.2 The handleResize method

The second method common to many feature modules is `handleResize`. With good use of CSS, most content in an SPA can be made to work within a window that's a reasonable size. But there are some cases where *most* doesn't work and some recalculation is required. Let's first implement the `handleResize` method as shown in listing 4.19 and then discuss its use. Changes are shown in **bold**:

Listing 4.19 Add the `handleResize` method—spa/js/spa.chat.js

```
...
   configMap = {
     ...
     slider_opened_em      : 18,
      ...
     slider_opened_min_em : 10,
     window_height_min_em : 20,
     ...
   },
  ...
  // Begin DOM method /setPxSizes/
  setPxSizes = function () {
    var px_per_em, window_height_em, opened_height_em;

    px_per_em = getEmSize( jqueryMap.$slider.get(0) );
    window_height_em = Math.floor(
      ( $(window).height() / px_per_em ) + 0.5
    );

    opened_height_em
      = window_height_em > configMap.window_height_min_em
      ? configMap.slider_opened_em
      : configMap.slider_opened_min_em;

    stateMap.px_per_em        = px_per_em;
    stateMap.slider_closed_px = configMap.slider_closed_em * px_per_em;
    stateMap.slider_opened_px = opened_height_em * px_per_em;
    jqueryMap.$sizer.css({
      height : ( opened_height_em - 2 ) * px_per_em
    });
  };
  // End DOM method /setPxSizes/

  ...

  // Begin public method /handleResize/
  // Purpose    :
  //   Given a window resize event, adjust the presentation
  //   provided by this module if needed
  // Actions    :
```

Increase the height of the opened slider a bit.

Add configuration for a minimum opened slider height.

Add configuration for the threshold widow height. If the window height is less than the threshold, we want to set the slider to the minimized height. If the height is greater than or equal to the threshold, we want to set the slider to the normal height.

Calculate window height in em units.

Here is the "secret sauce" where we determine the slider opened height by comparing the current window height to the threshold.

Add the `handleResize` documentation and method.

```
//   If the window height or width falls below
//   a given threshold, resize the chat slider for the
//   reduced window size.
// Returns    : Boolean
//   * false - resize not considered
//   * true  - resize considered
// Throws     : none
//
handleResize = function () {
  // don't do anything if we don't have a slider container
  if ( ! jqueryMap.$slider ) { return false; }

  setPxSizes();
  if ( stateMap.position_type === 'opened' ){
    jqueryMap.$slider.css({ height : stateMap.slider_opened_px });
  }
  return true;
};
// End public method /handleResize/

// return public methods
...
```

Recalculate the pixel sizes each time the `handleResize` method is called.

Ensure the slider height is set to the value calculated in `setPxSizes` if it's extended during resize.

The `handleResize` event doesn't call itself. Now we might be tempted to implement a `window.resize` event handler for every feature module, but that would be a *bad idea*. The trouble is that the frequency at which a `window.resize` event fires varies wildly by browser. Let's say we have five feature modules, all of which have `window.resize` event handlers, and our user decided to resize the browser. If the `window.resize` event fires every 10 milliseconds, and the resulting graphical changes are sufficiently complex, this can easily bring an SPA—and possibly the entire browser and OS it's running on—to its knees.

A better approach is to have a Shell event handler capture resize events and then have it call all subordinate feature module `handleResize` methods. This allows us to throttle the resize handling and dispatch from one event handler. Let's implement this strategy in the Shell as shown in listing 4.20. Changes are shown in **bold**:

Listing 4.20 Add the `onResize` event handler—spa/js/spa.shell.js

```
...
  //---------------- BEGIN MODULE SCOPE VARIABLES --------------
  var
    configMap = {
      ...
      resize_interval : 200,
      ...
    },
    stateMap = {
      $container  : undefined,
      anchor_map  : {},
      resize_idto : undefined
    },
    jqueryMap = {},
```

Create a 200-millisecond interval in our settings to consider resize events.

Set up a state variable to retain the resize timeout ID (see more later in this section).

```
    copyAnchorMap,     setJqueryMap,
    changeAnchorPart, onHashchange, onResize,
    setChatAnchor,     initModule;
  //----------------- END MODULE SCOPE VARIABLES ---------------
    ...
  //------------------- BEGIN EVENT HANDLERS -------------------
    ...
  // Begin Event handler /onResize/
  onResize = function (){
    if ( stateMap.resize_idto ){ return true; }

    spa.chat.handleResize();
    stateMap.resize_idto = setTimeout(
      function (){ stateMap.resize_idto = undefined; },
      configMap.resize_interval
    );

    return true;
  };
  // End Event handler /onResize/
  //-------------------- END EVENT HANDLERS --------------------

  ...

  initModule = function (){
  ...
    $(window)
      .bind( 'resize', onResize )
      .bind( 'hashchange', onHashchange )
      .trigger( 'hashchange' );
  };
  // End PUBLIC method /initModule/
  ...
```

Run the `onResize` logic only if no resize timer is currently running.

The timeout function clears its own timeout ID, so once every 200 milliseconds during a resize, `stateMap.resize_idto` will be undefined, and the full `onResize` logic will run.

Return true from the `window.resize` event handler so that jQuery doesn't `preventDefault()` or `stopPropagation()`.

Bind the `window.resize` event.

We want to adjust our stylesheet so we can better see the fruits of our labor. In listing 4.21 we adjust spa.css to decrease the minimal window size, move to relative units, and remove the gratuitous border around the content. Changes are shown in **bold**:

Listing 4.21 Style changes to emphasize `onResize`—spa/css/spa.css

```
...

/** Begin reset */
  * {
    margin  : 0;
    padding : 0;
    -webkit-box-sizing : border-box;
    -moz-box-sizing    : border-box;
    box-sizing         : border-box;
  }
  h1,h2,h3,h4,h5,h6,p { margin-bottom : 6pt; }
  ol,ul,dl { list-style-position : inside;}
/** End reset */

/** Begin standard selectors */
  body {
```

Move to relative units for margin (points).

Move to relative units on font size (points).

```
    font : 10pt 'Trebuchet MS', Verdana, Helvetica, Arial, sans-serif;
  ...

/** End standard selectors */

/** Begin spa namespace selectors */
  #spa {
    position   : absolute;
    top        : 0;
    left       : 0;
    bottom     : 0;
    right      : 0;
    background : #fff;
    min-height : 15em;
    min-width  : 35em;
    overflow   : hidden;
  }
/** End spa namespace selectors */

/** Begin utility selectors */

...
```

Remove the 8-pixel offset from the #spa div. This makes it flush with the window on all sides.

Significantly reduce minimum width and height of the #spa div. Convert measurements to relative units (ems).

Remove the border rounding as it's no longer needed.

We can now watch the resize event work by opening our browser document (spa/spa.html) and then increasing or decreasing the browser window height. Figure 4.14 compares the slider presentation before and after the threshold has been reached:

Of course, there's always room for more flourish. A nice enhancement would be to have the slider maintain a minimum distance from the top border. For example, if the window were 0.5 em over the threshold, the slider could be made to be precisely 0.5 em shorter than normal. This would provide a better user experience with optimal chat space and a smoother adjustment during resizing. The implementation isn't hard and is left as an exercise for the reader.

4.6 Summary

This chapter showed how feature modules can be employed to take advantage of the good aspects of third-party modules without all of their disadvantages. We defined what feature modules are, compared them to third-party modules, and discussed how they fit into our architecture. We explored how our application—and that of most websites—

Figure 4.14 A comparison of chat slider sizes before and after threshold

contains a fractal repetition of MVC patterns, and how this manifests itself in feature modules. We then created a feature module starting with the code we developed in chapter 3. In our first pass, we added all the files we needed and added basic capabilities. Then we designed our APIs and implemented them during a second pass. Finally, we added some frequently needed feature module methods and detailed their use.

Now it's time to centralize our business logic into the Model. In the next few chapters we develop the Model and show how to embody the business logic for the user, people, and chat. We use jQuery events to trigger DOM changes instead of relying on fragile callbacks, and we simulate a "live" chat session. Stick with us—this is where we take our SPA from a fancy demo to a near-complete client application.

5 Build the Model

This chapter covers

- Defining the Model and how it fits into our architecture
- The relationship between the Model, Data, and Fake modules
- Setting up files for the Model
- Enabling touch devices
- Designing the `people` object
- Building the `people` object and testing the API
- Updating the Shell so users may sign in and sign out

This chapter builds on code we've written in chapters 3 and 4 of this book. Before starting, you should have the project files from chapter 4, as we'll be adding to them. We recommend you copy the entire directory structure you created in chapter 4 into a new "chapter_5" directory and update it there.

In this chapter we design and build the `people` object portion of the Model. The Model provides the business logic and data to the Shell and feature modules. The Model is independent of the user interface (UI) and isolates it from logic and data management. The Model is itself isolated from the web server through the use of a *Data* module.

We want our SPA to use the `people` object to manage a list of people, which includes the user as well as people with whom they're chatting. After we modify and test the Model, we update the Shell so that a user may sign in and sign out. Along the way, we add touch controls so we can use our SPA on a smart phone or tablet. Let's get started by getting a better understanding of what the Model does and how it fits into our architecture.

5.1 Understand the Model

In chapter 3 we introduced the Shell module, which is responsible for application-wide tasks like URI anchor management and application layout. The Shell dispatches feature-specific tasks to carefully isolated feature modules that we introduced in chapter 4. These modules have their own View, Controller, and a slice of the Model that the Shell shares with them. An overview of the architecture is shown in figure 5.1.[1]

The Model consolidates all business logic and data in one namespace. The Shell or feature modules never communicate with the web server directly, but instead interact with the Model. The Model is itself isolated from the web server through the use of the Data module. This isolation results in faster development *and* higher quality, as we shall soon see.

This chapter begins the development and use of the Model. In chapter 6, we'll complete this work. Let's look at what we'll accomplish over these two chapters and the corresponding capabilities the Model will need to have.

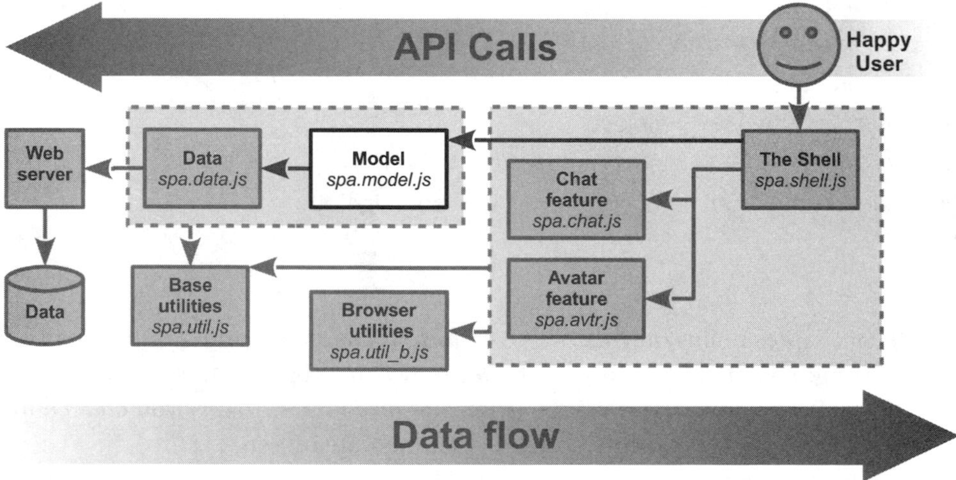

Figure 5.1 The Model in our SPA architecture

[1] Groups of modules that use shared utilities are surrounded by a dashed-line box. For example, the Chat, Avatar, and Shell modules all use the "Browser utilities" and the "Base utilities," whereas the Data and Model modules use only the "Base utilities."

5.1.1 What we're going to build

Before we discuss the Model, it's useful to refer to an example application. Figure 5.2 illustrates the capabilities we plan to add to our SPA by the end of chapter 6. The Shell will manage the sign-in process—we can see the signed-in user in the top right. The Chat feature module will manage the chat window, which is shown at bottom right. And the *Avatar* feature module will manage the colored boxes representing people shown on the left. Let's consider the business logic and data we'll need per module:

- The Shell will need a representation of the current user to manage the sign-in and sign-out process. It'll need methods to determine who the current user is, and to change the user if desired.
- The Chat feature module will also need to be able to inspect the current user ("Josh" in this example), and determine if he is authorized to send or receive messages. It'll need to determine the person with whom the user is chatting—if any. It'll need to inquire about the list of online people so it may show them on the left of the chat slider. Finally, it'll need methods to send messages and to select a person to chat with.
- The Avatar feature module will also need to inspect the current user ("Josh"), and determine if he is authorized to see and interact with the avatars. It'll also need the current user identification so it may outline the associated avatar in blue. It'll also need to determine the person with whom the user is chatting ("Betty") so it may outline this person's avatar in green. Finally, it'll need methods to set and retrieve avatar details (such as color and position) for all people currently online.

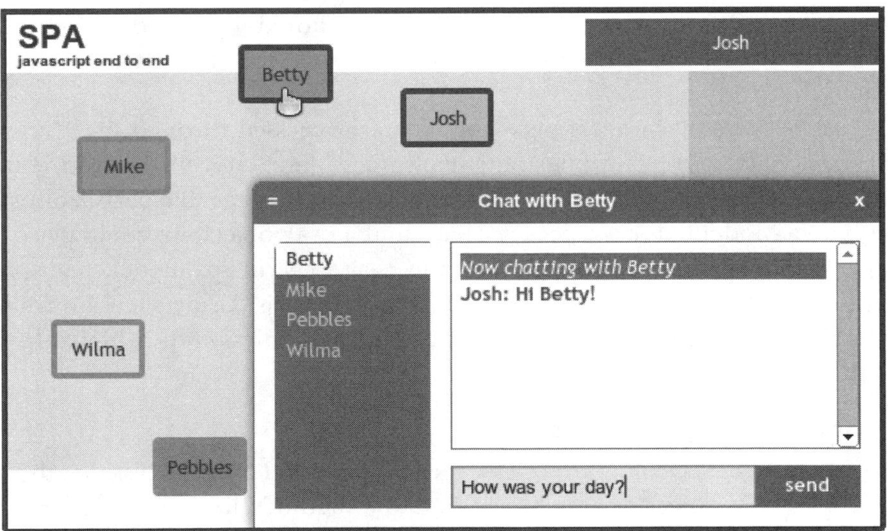

Figure 5.2 A vision of the our SPA in the near future

We have a lot of overlap in the business logic and data our modules require. For example, we know the current user object is required by the Shell as well as the Chat and Avatar modules. We also know we'll need to provide a roster of online users to both Chat and Avatar. A few strategies come to mind on how we might manage this overlap:

- Build the required logic and data in every feature module.
- Build parts of the logic and data in different feature modules. For example, we might consider Chat to be the owner of the `people` object, and the Avatar to be the owner of the `chat` object. We would then make calls between our modules to share information.
- Build a central Model to consolidate our logic and data.

The first option of maintaining parallel data and methods in different modules is amusingly error-prone and labor intensive. If we do this, we might rather seek an exciting career flipping burgers. And yes, I *would* like fries with that.

The second option works better, but only for a while. Once logic and data reach a moderate level of complexity, the amount of cross-module dependencies results in the dreaded "SPA-ghetti" code.

The final option, using a Model, is by far the best option in our experience, and also provides benefits which aren't immediately obvious. Let's take a look at what a well-written Model should do.

5.1.2 What the Model does

The Model is where the Shell and all of our feature modules access data and business logic in our SPA. If we need to sign in, we invoke a method provided by the Model. If we want to get a list of people, we get it from the Model. If we want to get avatar information… well, you get the idea. Any data or logic that we want to share between feature modules, or is central to the application, should go into the Model. If you're comfortable with Model-View-Controller (MVC) architecture, you should be comfortable with the Model.

Just because all business logic and data are accessed through the Model doesn't mean we have to use only one (potentially huge) JavaScript file to provide it. We can use namespacing to break up our Model into more manageable parts. For example, if we have a Model that has a `people` object and a `chat` object, we could place the `people` logic in spa.model.people.js, and the `chat` logic in spa.model.chat.js, and then consolidate them in our main Model file, spa.model.js. Using such a technique, the interface presented to the Shell doesn't change, regardless of the number of files used by the Model.

5.1.3 What the Model does not do

The Model doesn't require a browser. This means the Model must not assume the presence of a `document` object or that browser-specific methods like `document.location` are available. It's good MVC hygiene to have the Shell and (especially) the feature modules render the representation of Model data. And this separation makes automated unit and regression testing much simpler. We've found that as you get into browser interaction, the value of automated testing diminishes greatly as the cost of implementation rises. But by avoiding the DOM, we can test everything up to the UI without having to run a browser.

Unit and regression testing

Development teams must decide when to invest in automated testing. Automating the tests of Model API is almost always a good investment because the tests can be isolated to use the same data for each API call. Automating the tests of a UI is much more expensive due to the many variables that aren't easily controlled or predicted. For example, it can be difficult and expensive to simulate how quickly a user might click on one button and then another, or to foresee how data will propagate through the system when a user is involved, or to know how fast a network will perform. For these reasons, web page testing is often performed manually, with the help of a few tools like HTML validators and link checkers.

A well designed SPA has independent Data, Model, and feature module (View + Controller) layers. We ensure our Data and Model have well-defined APIs and are isolated from the feature modules, and as a result we don't have to use a browser to test these layers. Instead we can inexpensively employ automated unit and regression testing using a JavaScript execution environment like Node.js or Java's Rhino. In our experience, the View and Controller layers are still best tested manually by real people.

The Model doesn't provide general purpose utilities. Instead, we use a general utility library (spa/js/spa.util.js) that doesn't require the DOM. We package these utilities separately because we'll use them with multiple SPAs. The Model, on the other hand, is often tailored for a specific SPA.

The Model doesn't communicate directly with the server. We have a separate module for that called Data. The Data module is responsible for getting all the data the Model requires from the server.

Now that we have a better understanding of the Model's role in our architecture, let's set up the files we'll need in this chapter.

5.2 Set up the Model and other files

We need to add and modify a number of files to support building our Model. We also want to add the Avatar feature module files now, as we'll need them soon enough.

5.2.1 Plan the file structure

We recommend you copy the whole directory structure you created in chapter 4 into a new "chapter_5" directory so we can update them there. Let's review our file structure as we left it in chapter 4, as shown in listing 5.1:

Listing 5.1 File structure from chapter 4

```
spa
+-- css
|   +-- spa.chat.css
|   +-- spa.css
|   `-- spa.shell.css
+-- js
|   +-- jq
|   |   +-- jquery-1.9.1.js
|   |   `-- jquery.uriAnchor-1.1.3.js
|   +-- spa.js
|   +-- spa.chat.js
|   +-- spa.model.js
|   +-- spa.shell.js
|   `-- spa.util.js
`-- spa.html
```

Here are the modifications we plan to make:

- *Create* our namespaced CSS stylesheet for Avatar.
- *Modify* our namespaced CSS stylesheet for the Shell to support user sign-in.
- *Include* the jQuery plugin for unified touch and mouse input.
- *Include* the jQuery plugin for global custom events.
- *Include* the JavaScript library for the browser database.
- *Create* our namespaced Avatar module. This is a placeholder for chapter 6.
- *Create* our namespaced Data module. This will provide an interface to "real" data from the server.
- *Create* our namespaced Fake module. This will provide an interface to "fake" data that we use for testing.
- *Create* our namespaced browser utilities modules so we can share common routines that require a browser.
- *Modify* our namespaced Shell module to support user sign-in.
- *Modify* our browser document to include the new CSS and JavaScript files.

Our updated files and directories should look like listing 5.2. We show all files we'll have to create or modify in **bold**:

Listing 5.2 Updated file structure

```
spa
+-- css
|   +-- spa.avtr.css          <-- Create the Avatar stylesheet.
|   +-- spa.chat.css
|   +-- spa.css
|   `-- spa.shell.css         <-- Modify the Shell stylesheet for sign-in.
+-- js
|   +-- jq
|   |   +-- jquery-1.9.1.js
|   |   +-- jquery.event.ue-0.3.2.js   <-- Include the jQuery plugin for unified touch and mouse input.
```

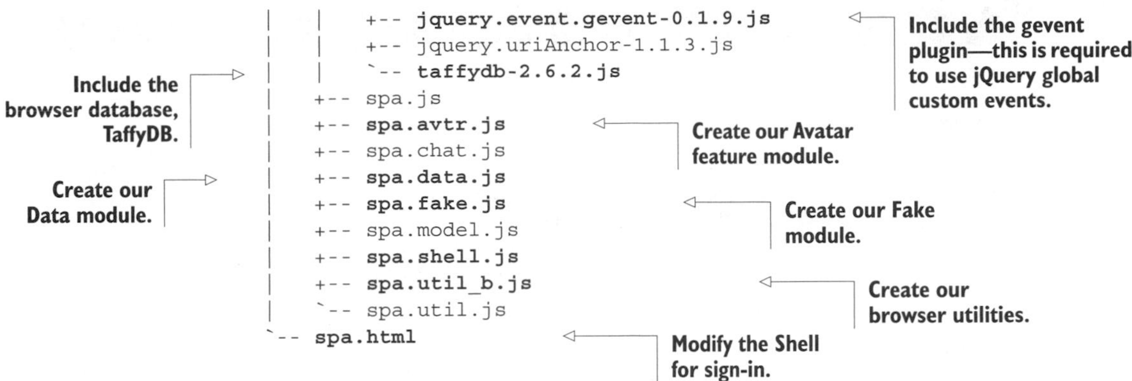

Now that we've identified the files we want to add or modify, let's fire up our trusty text editor and get the job done. It turns out the best order to consider each file in is exactly the order presented. If you're playing along at home, you can build the files as we walk through the code.

5.2.2 Populate the files

Our first file to consider is spa/css/spa.avtr.css. We'll create the file and populate it with the contents shown in listing 5.3. Initially, it'll be a *stub*:

Listing 5.3 Our *Avatar* stylesheet (stub) — spa/css/spa.avtr.css

```
/*
 * spa.avtr.css
 * Avatar feature styles
*/
```

The next three files are libraries. Let's download them into the spa/js/jq directory.

- The spa/js/jq/jquery.event.ue-0.3.2.js file is available at https://github.com/mmikowski/jquery.event.ue. It provides unified touch and mouse input.
- The spa/js/jq/jquery.event.gevent-0.1.9.js file is available at https://github.com/mmikowski/jquery.event.gevent and is required to use global custom events.
- The spa/js/jq/taffydb-2.6.2.js file provides our client database. It may be found at https://github.com/typicaljoe/taffydb. It's not a jQuery plugin, and if we were dealing with a larger project we'd place this in a separate spa/js/lib directory.

The next three JavaScript files—spa/js/spa.avtr.js, spa/js/spa.data.js, and spa/js/spa.fake.js—will be stubs. Their contents are shown in listings 5.4, 5.5, and 5.6. They're mostly identical—each has a header, followed by our JSLint options, and then a namespace declaration that is congruent with the file name. We've shown the unique parts in **bold**:

Listing 5.4 Create the Avatar feature module—spa/js/spa.avtr.js

```
/*
 * spa.avtr.js
 * Avatar feature module
*/

/*jslint         browser : true, continue : true,
  devel  : true, indent  : 2,    maxerr   : 50,
  newcap : true, nomen   : true, plusplus : true,
  regexp : true, sloppy  : true, vars     : false,
  white  : true
*/
/*global $, spa */
spa.avtr = (function () { return {}; }());
```

Listing 5.5 Create the Data module—spa/js/spa.data.js

```
/*
 * spa.data.js
 * Data module
*/

/*jslint         browser : true, continue : true,
  devel  : true, indent  : 2,    maxerr   : 50,
  newcap : true, nomen   : true, plusplus : true,
  regexp : true, sloppy  : true, vars     : false,
  white  : true
*/
/*global $, spa */
spa.data = (function () { return {}; }());
```

Listing 5.6 Create the Fake data module—spa/js/spa.fake.js

```
/*
 * spa.fake.js
 * Fake module
*/

/*jslint         browser : true, continue : true,
  devel  : true, indent  : 2,    maxerr   : 50,
  newcap : true, nomen   : true, plusplus : true,
  regexp : true, sloppy  : true, vars     : false,
  white  : true
*/
/*global $, spa */
spa.fake = (function () { return {}; }());
```

Recall that the `/*jslint ...*/` and `/*global ...*/` sections are used when we run JSLint to check our code for common errors. The `/*jslint ...*/` section sets preferences for validation. For example, `browser : true` tells the JSLint validator to assume that we'll run this JavaScript in a browser, and therefore we'll have a `document` object (among other things). The `/*global $, spa */` section tells the JSLint validator that the variables `$` and `spa` are defined outside of this module. Without this information,

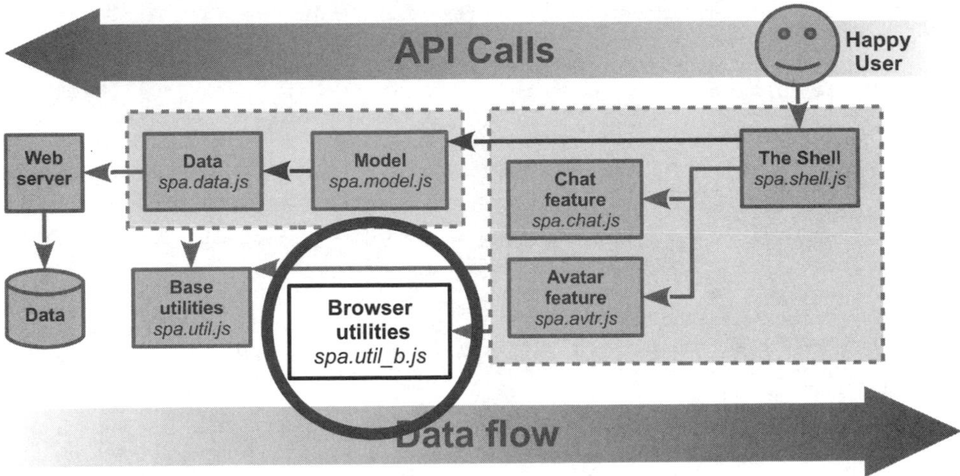

Figure 5.3 The browser utilities module provides utilities that require a browser to run

the validator would complain that these variables aren't defined before being used. See appendix A for a full discussion of our JSLint settings.

Next we can add our browser utilities file, spa/js/spa.util_b.js. This module provides common routines that work only in a browser environment. In other words, the browser utilities won't normally work with Node.js, whereas our standard utilities (spa/js/spa.util.js) will. Figure 5.3 shows this module in our architecture.

Our browser utilities will provides the `encodeHtml` and `decodeHtml` utilities which, not surprisingly, can be used to encode and decode special characters used in HTML like `&` or `<`.[2] It'll also provide the `getEmSize` utility, which can calculate the number of pixels for the `em` unit in the browser. Sharing these utilities ensures they're implemented consistently and also minimizes the amount of code we need to write. Let's fire up our text editor and create the file as shown in listing 5.7. The methods are shown in **bold**:

Listing 5.7 Create the browser utilities module—spa/js/spa.util_b.js

```
/**
 * spa.util_b.js
 * JavaScript browser utilities
 *
 * Compiled by Michael S. Mikowski
 * These are routines I have created and updated
 * since 1998, with inspiration from around the web.
 * MIT License
*/

/*jslint         browser : true, continue : true,
```

2 These methods are important to prevent cross-site-scripting attacks when we present data that comes from user input.

```
  devel  : true, indent  : 2,    maxerr   : 50,
  newcap : true, nomen   : true, plusplus : true,
  regexp : true, sloppy  : true, vars     : false,
  white  : true
*/
/*global $, spa, getComputedStyle */

spa.util_b = (function () {
  'use strict';
  //--------------- BEGIN MODULE SCOPE VARIABLES --------------
  var
    configMap = {
      regex_encode_html  : /[&"'><]/g,
      regex_encode_noamp : /["'><]/g,
      html_encode_map    : {
        '&' : '&#38;',
        '"' : '&#34;',
        "'" : '&#39;',
        '>' : '&#62;',
        '<' : '&#60;'
      }
    },

    decodeHtml,  encodeHtml, getEmSize;

  configMap.encode_noamp_map = $.extend(
    {}, configMap.html_encode_map
  );
  delete configMap.encode_noamp_map['&'];
  //----------------- END MODULE SCOPE VARIABLES ---------------

  //------------------ BEGIN UTILITY METHODS ------------------
  // Begin decodeHtml
  // Decodes HTML entities in a browser-friendly way
  // See http://stackoverflow.com/questions/1912501/\
  //   unescape-html-entities-in-javascript
  //
  decodeHtml = function ( str ) {
    return $('<div/>').html(str || '').text();
  };
  // End decodeHtml


  // Begin encodeHtml
  // This is single pass encoder for html entities and handles
  // an arbitrary number of characters
  //
  encodeHtml = function ( input_arg_str, exclude_amp ) {
    var
      input_str = String( input_arg_str ),
      regex, lookup_map
      ;

    if ( exclude_amp ) {
      lookup_map = configMap.encode_noamp_map;
      regex      = configMap.regex_encode_noamp;
    }
```

Annotations:

- Use `strict` pragma (we'll talk about this in a bit).
- Use `configMap` to store module configurations.
- Create a modified copy of the configuration used to encode entities ...
- ... but remove the ampersand.
- Create the `decodeHtml` method to convert browser entities like & into a displayed character like &.
- Create the `encodeHtml` method to convert special characters like & into an HTML encoded value like `&`.

```
    else {
      lookup_map = configMap.html_encode_map;
      regex      = configMap.regex_encode_html;
    }
    return input_str.replace(regex,
      function ( match, name ) {
        return lookup_map[ match ] || '';
      }
    );
  };
  // End encodeHtml

  // Begin getEmSize
  // returns size of ems in pixels
  //
  getEmSize = function ( elem ) {
    return Number(
      getComputedStyle( elem, '' ).fontSize.match(/\d*\.?\d*/)[0]
    );
  };
  // End getEmSize

  // export methods
  return {
    decodeHtml : decodeHtml,
    encodeHtml : encodeHtml,
    getEmSize  : getEmSize
  };
  //------------------- END PUBLIC METHODS ---------------------
}());
```

Create the `getEmSize` method to calculate the pixel size of the `em` unit.

Neatly export all public methods.

The final file to consider is the browser document. We'll update it to use all our new CSS and JavaScript files, as shown in listing 5.8. The changes from chapter 4 are shown in **bold**:

Listing 5.8 Update the browser document—spa/spa.html

```
<!doctype html>
<!--
  spa.html
  spa browser document
-->

<html>
<head>
  <!-- ie9+ rendering support for latest standards -->
  <meta http-equiv="Content-Type" content="text/html;
    charset=ISO-8859-1">
  <meta http-equiv="X-UA-Compatible" content="IE=edge"/>
  <title>SPA Chapters 5-6</title>

  <!-- third-party stylesheets -->

  <!-- our stylesheets -->
  <link rel="stylesheet" href="css/spa.css"       type="text/css"/>
  <link rel="stylesheet" href="css/spa.shell.css" type="text/css"/>
```

Change the title. We're not in Kansas or chapter 4 anymore, Toto.

```
  <link rel="stylesheet" href="css/spa.chat.css"  type="text/css"/>
  <link rel="stylesheet" href="css/spa.avtr.css"  type="text/css"/>

  <!-- third-party javascript -->
  <script src="js/jq/taffydb-2.6.2.js" ></script>
  <script src="js/jq/jquery-1.9.1.js"            ></script>
  <script src="js/jq/jquery.uriAnchor-1.1.3.js"  ></script>
  <script src="js/jq/jquery.event.gevent-0.1.9.js"></script>
  <script src="js/jq/jquery.event.ue-0.3.2.js" ></script>

  <!-- our javascript -->
  <script src="js/spa.js"       ></script>
  <script src="js/spa.util.js"  ></script>
  <script src="js/spa.data.js"  ></script>
  <script src="js/spa.fake.js"  ></script>
  <script src="js/spa.model.js" ></script>
  <script src="js/spa.util_b.js"></script>
  <script src="js/spa.shell.js" ></script>
  <script src="js/spa.chat.js"  ></script>
  <script src="js/spa.avtr.js"  ></script>
  <script>
    $(function () { spa.initModule( $('#spa') ); });
  </script>

</head>
<body>
<div id="spa"></div>
</body>
</html>
```

Include the client-side database library.

Include our Avatar stylesheet.

Include the gevent events library. This is required to use global custom events.

Include the unified input event plugin.

Include our Data module.

Include our Fake module.

Include our browser utilities.

Include our Avatar feature module.

Now that everything is in place, let's talk about adding touch controls to our SPA.

5.2.3 Use the unified touch-mouse library

Smartphones and tablets are currently outselling traditional laptops and desktops worldwide. We expect the mobile device sales to continue to exceed traditional computing devices and grow as a percentage of active SPA-capable devices. Soon the majority of potential customers who wish to use our site may be using a touch device.

We recognize this trend and have included the unified touch-mouse interface library—`jquery.event.ue-0.3.2.js`—in this chapter. This library, although not perfect, does a lot of magic in making an application work seamlessly across touch and pointer interfaces; it handles multi-touch, pinch-to-zoom, drag-and-drop, and long-press along with the more pedestrian events. We'll detail its use as we update our UI in this and future chapters.

We've now readied our files for the changes we'll be applying. When we load our browser document (spa/spa.html), we should see the same page as we left it in chapter 4 without any errors. Now let's start building our Model.

5.3 Design the people object

In this chapter we'll build the `people` object portion of the Model, as shown in figure 5.4.

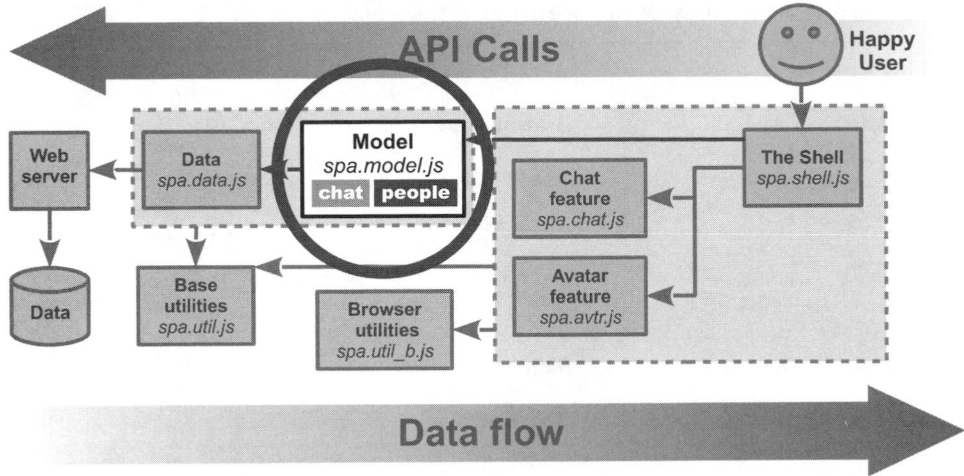

Figure 5.4 In this section we start the design of our Model with the `people` object

We expect our model to be split into two sections: a `chat` object and a `people` object. Here is the specification we first sketched in chapter 4:

```
...
  //   * chat_model - the chat model object provides methods
  //       to interact with our instant messaging
  //   * people_model - the people model object which provides methods
  //       to interact with the list of people the model maintains
...
```

The description provided for the `people` object—"an object that provides methods to interact with the list of people the Model maintains"—is a good start, but it's not detailed enough for implementation. Let's design the `people` object starting with the objects we will use to represent each person in our list.

5.3.1 Design the person objects

We've decided that the `people` object should manage a list of persons. Experience has shown us that a person is well represented by an object. Therefore our `people` object will manage many `person` objects. Here are the minimal properties we think each `person` object should have:

- `id`—The server ID. This will be defined for all objects sent from the backend.
- `cid`—The client ID. This should always be defined, and usually will be the same as the ID; but if we create a new `person` object on the client and the backend has not yet been updated, the server ID will be undefined.
- `name`—The name of the person.
- `css_map`—A map of display properties. We'll need this to support avatars.

A UML class diagram of a `person` object is shown in table 5.1:

Table 5.1 A UML class diagram of a `person` object

`person`	
Attribute name	**Attribute type**
`id`	`string`
`cid`	`string`
`name`	`string`
`css_map`	`map`
Method name	**Return type**
`get_is_user()`	`boolean`
`get_is_anon()`	`boolean`

Doing without a client ID property

These days, we rarely use a separate property for client ID. Instead we use a single ID property and apply a unique prefix for IDs that are client-generated. For example, a client ID might look like `x23`, whereas an ID that originated from the backend might look like `50a04142c692d1fd18000003` (especially if you're using MongoDB). Because the backend-generated ID can never start with an `x`, it's easy to determine where any ID was generated. Most of the application logic doesn't need to worry about where an ID originated. The only time it becomes important is when we sync to the backend.

Before we consider what methods a `person` object should have, let's consider the types of persons our `people` object might need to manage. Figure 5.5 shows a mockup of what we'd like our user to see, with some notes about people.

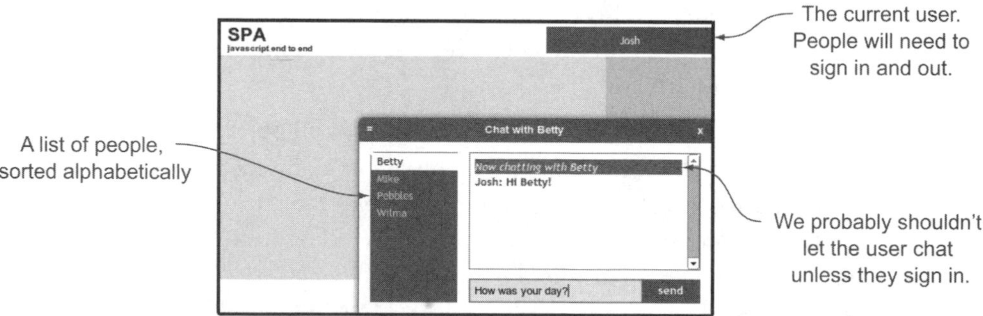

Figure 5.5 A mockup of our SPA with notes about people

It appears the `people` object will need to identify four types of persons:

1. The current user person
2. The anonymous person
3. The person with whom the user is chatting
4. Other online persons

At present we're only concerned with the current user person and the anonymous person—we'll worry about online persons in the next chapter. We should like to have methods to help us identify these types of users:

- `get_is_user()`—Return `true` if the `person` object is the current user.
- `get_is_anon()`—Return `true` if the `person` object is anonymous.

Now that we've detailed `person` objects, let's consider how the `people` object will manage them.

5.3.2 Design the people object API

The `people` object API will consist of methods and jQuery global custom events. We'll consider method calls first.

DESIGN PEOPLE METHOD CALLS

We want our Model to always have a current user object available. If a person isn't signed in, the user object should be the *anonymous* `person` object. Of course, this implies we should provide a means for a person to sign in and sign out. The list of people on the left column of the chat slider indicates we'd like to maintain a list of online people with whom we can chat, and that we'd like them returned in alphabetical order. Given these requirements, this list of methods seems about right:

- `get_user()`—Return the current user `person` object. If the current user isn't signed in, return the anonymous `person` object.
- `get_db()`—Get the collection of all the `person` objects including the current user. We'd like the person list to always be in alphabetical order.
- `get_by_cid( <client_id> )`—Get the `person` object associated with a unique client ID. Though the same could be accomplished by getting the collection and searching for the `person` object by client ID, we expect this capability to be used often enough that a dedicated method can help avoid errors and provide opportunity for optimization.
- `login( <user_name> )`—Sign in as the user with the specified user name. We'll avoid the complexity of sign-in authentication as it's outside the scope of this book, and there are many examples to be had elsewhere. When a user signs in, the current user object should change to reflect the new identity. We should also publish an event called `spa-login` with the current user object as data.
- `logout()`—Revert the current user object to the anonymous person. We should publish an event called `spa-logout` with the former user object as data.

Both the `login()` and `logout()` method descriptions state that we'll publish events as part of their response. The next section discusses what these events are and why we use them.

DESIGN PEOPLE EVENTS

We use events to publish data asynchronously. For example, if the people list changes, the Model may want to publish a `spa-listchange` event which shares an updated list of people.[3] Methods in our feature modules or the Shell that are interested in this event may register with the Model to receive it—this is often called *subscribing to an event*. When the `spa-listchange` event occurs, the subscribing methods are notified and receive the data that the Model publishes. For example, we may have a method in Avatar to add a new graphical avatar, and a method in Chat to add to the list of persons shown in the chat slider. Figure 5.6 shows how events are broadcast to subscribing feature modules and the Shell.

We'd like the Model to publish at least two event types as part of the `people` object API:[4]

- `spa-login` should be published when the sign-in process is complete. This won't happen right away, as the sign-in process usually requires a round-trip to the backend. The updated current user object should be supplied as the event data.
- `spa-logout` should be published when the sign-out process is complete. The previous user object should be supplied as the event data.

Events are often a preferable manner to distribute asynchronous data. The classic JavaScript implementation uses callbacks, and this results in a tangle of code that's hard to debug and keep modular. Events allow module code to remain independent

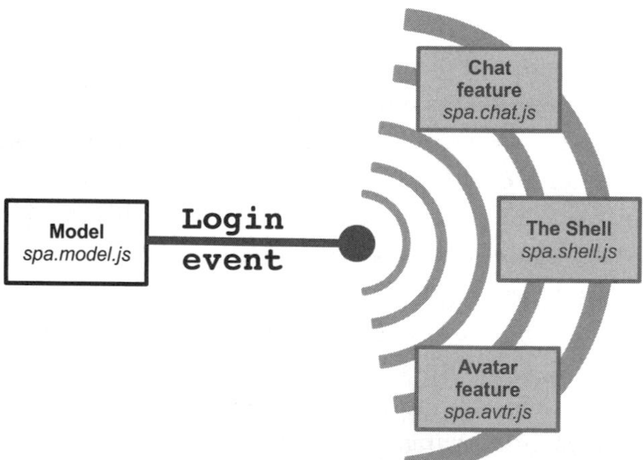

Figure 5.6 Events are broadcast from our Model and can be received by subscribed methods in our feature modules or the Shell

[3] Other names for the event mechanism include *push communications*, or *pub-sub* (short for *publish-subscribe*).

[4] We use a namespace prefix (`spa-`) for all published event names. This helps avoid potential conflicts with third-party JavaScript and libraries.

yet use the same data. For these reasons, we strongly prefer events when distributing asynchronous data from the Model.

Since we're already using jQuery, it's a wise choice to use jQuery global custom events as our publishing mechanism. We have created a global custom event plugin to provide this capability.[5] jQuery global custom events perform well and have the same familiar interface as other jQuery events. Any jQuery collection may subscribe to a specific global custom event and invoke a function when it occurs. An event often has data associated with it. A `spa-login` event, for example, may pass along the freshly updated user object. When an element is removed from the document, any function that is subscribed "on" that deleted element is automatically removed. Listing 5.9 illustrates these concepts. We can open the browser document (spa/spa.html), open the JavaScript console, and test:

Listing 5.9 Use of jQuery global custom events

```
$( 'body' ).append( '<div id="spa-chat-list-box"/>' );
var $listbox = $( '#spa-chat-list-box' );
$listbox.css({
  position: 'absolute', 'z-index' : 3,
  top : 50, left : 50, width : 50, height :50,
  border : '2px solid black', background : '#fff'
});
var onListChange = function ( event, update_map ) {
  $( this ).html( update_map.list_text );
  alert( 'onListChange ran' );
};

$.gevent.subscribe(
  $listbox,
  'spa-listchange',
  onListChange
);

$.gevent.publish(
  'spa-listchange',
  [ { list_text : 'the list is here' } ]
);

$listbox.remove();
$.gevent.publish( 'spa-listchange', [ {} ] );
```

Append a `<div>` to the page body.

Create a `$listbox` jQuery collection. Style it so we can see it.

Define a handler we plan to use for the `spa-listchange` jQuery global custom event. This method expects an event object and a map detailing a user list update as arguments. Have the handler open an alert box so we can verify when it is invoked.

Have the `$listbox` jQuery collection subscribe to the `spa-listchange` custom global event with the `onListChange` function. When the `spa-listchange` event occurs, `onListChange` is invoked with the event object as the first argument, followed by any other arguments published by the event. The value of `this` in `onListChange` will be the DOM element used by `$listbox`.

The `onListChange` function subscribed on the `$listbox` jQuery collection is invoked by this event. The `alert` box should appear. We can close the `alert` box.

When we remove the `$listbox` collection elements from the DOM, the subscription is no longer valid and the subscription to `onListChange` is removed.

The `onListChange` function bound on `$listbox` will not be invoked, and we should not see the `alert` box.

If you're already comfortable with jQuery event handling, this is probably all old news, and that's good news. If not, don't worry about it too much. Just be glad that this

[5] Prior to version 1.9.0, jQuery supported this natively. Of course, they removed it shortly before we went to press just to make our lives more, um, interesting.

behavior is consistent with all other jQuery events. It's also powerful, exceedingly well tested, and leverages the same code as jQuery internal methods. *Why learn two event mechanisms when you can use just one?* That's a strong argument for using jQuery global custom events—and a strong argument against using a "framework" library that introduces a redundant and subtly different event mechanism.

5.3.3 Document the people object API

Let's now consolidate all of this thinking to a relatively terse format that we can put into our Model module for reference. The Listing 5.10 is a good first attempt:

Listing 5.10 The `people` object API

```
// The people object API
// ---------------------
// The people object is available at spa.model.people.
// The people object provides methods and events to manage
// a collection of person objects. Its public methods include:
//   * get_user() - return the current user person object.
//     If the current user is not signed-in, an anonymous person
//     object is returned.
//   * get_db() - return the TaffyDB database of all the person
//     objects - including the current user - pre-sorted.
//   * get_by_cid( <client_id> ) - return a person object with
//     provided unique id.
//   * login( <user_name> ) - login as the user with the provided
//     user name. The current user object is changed to reflect
//     the new identity.
//   * logout()- revert the current user object to anonymous.
//
// jQuery global custom events published by the object include:
//   * 'spa-login' is published when a user login process
//     completes. The updated user object is provided as data.
//   * 'spa-logout' is published when a logout completes.
//     The former user object is provided as data.
//
// Each person is represented by a person object.
// Person objects provide the following methods:
//   * get_is_user() - return true if object is the current user
//   * get_is_anon() - return true if object is anonymous
//
// The attributes for a person object include:
//   * cid - string client id. This is always defined, and
//     is only different from the id attribute
//     if the client data is not synced with the backend.
//   * id - the unique id. This may be undefined if the
//     object is not synced with the backend.
//   * name - the string name of the user.
//   * css_map - a map of attributes used for avatar
//     presentation.
//
```

Now that we've completed a specification for the `people` object, let's build it and test the API. After that, we'll adjust the Shell to use the API so a user may sign in and sign out.

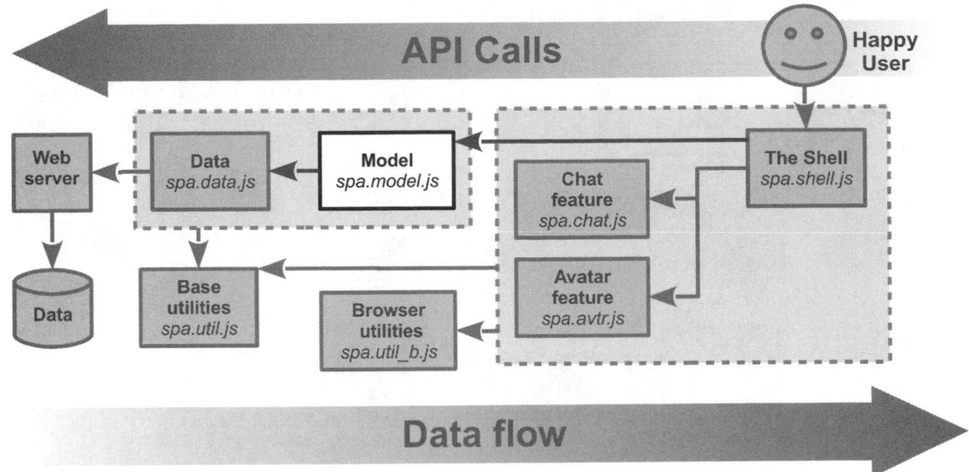

Figure 5.7 The Model in our SPA architecture

5.4 Build the people object

Now that we've designed the `people` object, we can build it. We're going to use a Fake module to provide mock data to the Model. This will allow us to proceed without having a server or feature module in place. Fake is a key enabler of rapid development, and we're going to fake it until we make it.

Let's revisit our architecture and see how Fake can help improve development. Our fully implemented architecture is shown in figure 5.7.

Well, that's *nice*, but we can't get there in one pass. We'd rather develop without requiring a web server or a UI. We want to focus on the Model at this stage and not be distracted by other modules. We can use the Fake module to emulate Data and the server connection, and we can use the JavaScript console to make API calls directly instead of using the browser window. Figure 5.8 illustrates what modules we need when we develop in this manner.

Let's sweep away all the unused code and see what modules are left, as shown in figure 5.9.

Through the use of the Fake module and the JavaScript console, we're able to focus solely on the development and testing of the Model. This is especially beneficial for a module as important as the Model. *As we progress, we should keep in mind that the "backend" is emulated by the Fake module in this chapter.* Now that we've outlined a development strategy, let's start work on the Fake module.

5.4.1 Create a fake people list

What we call "real" data is usually sent from the web server to the browser. But what if we're tired and had a long day at work, and don't have the energy for "real" data? That's all right—sometimes it's OK to fake it. We discuss how to fake data openly and

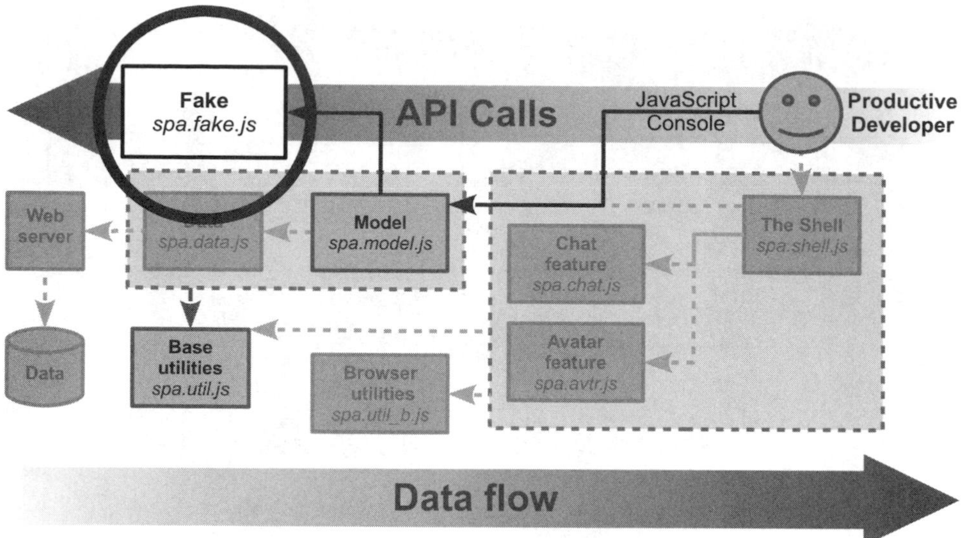

Figure 5.8 We use a mock data module called Fake during development

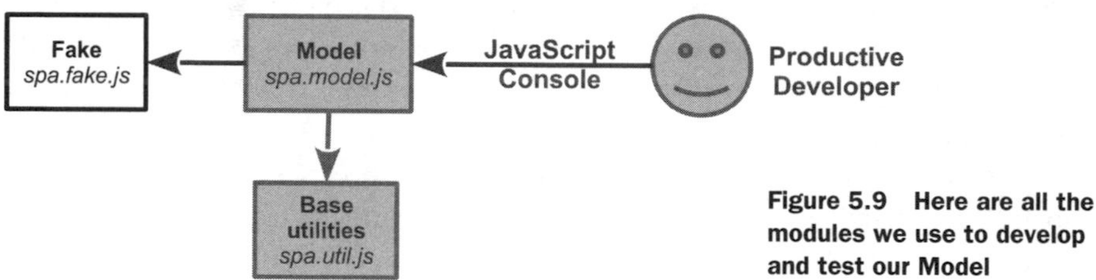

Figure 5.9 Here are all the modules we use to develop and test our Model

honestly in this section. We hope we'll provide everything you ever wanted to know about fake data but may have been to afraid to ask.

We'll use a module called Fake during development to provide mock data and methods to the application. We'll set an `isFakeData` flag in our Model to instruct it to use the Fake module instead of using "real" web server data and methods from the Data module. This enables rapid, focused development that's independent of the server. Because we've done a good job outlining how `person` objects are going to behave, we should be able to fake our data pretty easily. First we'd like to create a method that returns data for a list of fake persons. Let's fire up our text editor and create `spa.fake.getPeopleList` as shown in listing 5.11:

Listing 5.11 Add a mock user list to Fake—spa/js/spa.fake.js

```
/*
 * spa.fake.js
 * Fake module
*/
```

```
/*jslint         browser : true, continue : true,
  devel  : true, indent  : 2,    maxerr   : 50,
  newcap : true, nomen   : true, plusplus : true,
  regexp : true, sloppy  : true, vars     : false,
  white  : true
*/
/*global $, spa */

spa.fake = (function () {
  'use strict';
  var getPeopleList;

  getPeopleList = function () {
    return [
      { name : 'Betty', _id : 'id_01',
        css_map : { top: 20, left: 20,
          'background-color' : 'rgb( 128, 128, 128)'
        }
      },
      { name : 'Mike', _id : 'id_02',
        css_map : { top: 60, left: 20,
          'background-color' : 'rgb( 128, 255, 128)'
        }
      },
      { name : 'Pebbles', _id : 'id_03',
        css_map : { top: 100, left: 20,
          'background-color' : 'rgb( 128, 192, 192)'
        }
      },
      { name : 'Wilma', _id : 'id_04',
        css_map : { top: 140, left: 20,
          'background-color' : 'rgb( 192, 128, 128)'
        }
      }
    ];
  };

  return { getPeopleList : getPeopleList };
}());
```

We introduced the `'use strict'` pragma in this module as shown in **bold**. If you're serious about large-scale JavaScript projects—and we know you are—we encourage you to consider using the strict pragma *within a namespace function scope*. When in strict mode, JavaScript is more likely to throw exceptions when unsafe actions are taken, such as using undeclared global variables. It also disables confusing or poorly considered features. Though it's tempting, *don't* use the strict pragma in the global scope, as it can break the JavaScript of other, lesser third-party developers who aren't as enlightened as you. Now let's use this fake person list in our Model.

5.4.2 Start the people object

We'll now start building the `people` object in the Model. When it's initialized (using the `spa.model.initModule()` method), we'll first create the anonymous `person` object using the same makePerson constructor as we used to create other person objects. This ensures that this object has the same methods and attributes of other person objects regardless of future changes to the constructor.

Next we'll use the fake people list provided by spa.fake.getPeopleList() to create a TaffyDB collection of person objects. TaffyDB is a JavaScript data store designed for use in a browser. It provides many database-style capabilities, like selecting an array of objects by matching properties. For example, if we have a TaffyDB collection of person objects named people_db, we might select an array of persons with the name of Pebbles like so:

```
found_list = people_db({ name : 'Pebbles' }).get();
```

Why we like TaffyDB

We like TaffyDB because it's focused on providing rich data management capabilities in the browser, and it doesn't try to do anything else (like introducing a subtly different event model that's redundant with jQuery). We like to use optimal, focused tools like TaffyDB. If, for some reason, we need different data management capabilities, we can swap it out with another tool (or write our own) without having to refactor our entire application. Please see http://www.taffydb.com for thorough documentation on this handy tool.

Finally, we'll export the people object so that we can test our API. At this time we'll provide two methods to interact with person objects: spa.model.people.get_db() will return the TaffyDB people collection, and spa.model.people.get_cid_map() will return a map with the client IDs as the keys. Let's fire up the trusty text editor and start our Model as shown in listing 5.12. This is just our first pass, so don't feel you have to understand everything yet:

Listing 5.12 Start building the Model—spa/js/spa.model.js

```
/*
 * spa.model.js
 * Model module
*/

/*jslint         browser : true, continue : true,
  devel  : true, indent  : 2,    maxerr   : 50,
  newcap : true, nomen   : true, plusplus : true,
  regexp : true, sloppy  : true, vars     : false,
  white  : true
*/
/*global TAFFY, $, spa */

spa.model = (function () {
  'use strict';
  var
    configMap = { anon_id : 'a0' },
```

Reserve a special ID for the "anonymous" person.

```
stateMap  = {
  anon_user      : null,
  people_cid_map : {},
  people_db      : TAFFY()
},

isFakeData = true,

personProto, makePerson, people, initModule;

personProto = {
  get_is_user : function () {
    return this.cid === stateMap.user.cid;
  },
  get_is_anon : function () {
    return this.cid === stateMap.anon_user.cid;
  }
};

makePerson = function ( person_map ) {
  var person,
    cid     = person_map.cid,
    css_map = person_map.css_map,
    id      = person_map.id,
    name    = person_map.name;

  if ( cid === undefined || ! name ) {
    throw 'client id and name required';
  }

  person         = Object.create( personProto );
  person.cid     = cid;
  person.name    = name;
  person.css_map = css_map;

  if ( id ) { person.id = id; }

  stateMap.people_cid_map[ cid ] = person;

  stateMap.people_db.insert( person );
  return person;
};

people = {
  get_db      : function () { return stateMap.people_db; },
  get_cid_map : function () { return stateMap.people_cid_map; }
};

initModule = function () {
  var i, people_list, person_map;

  // initialize anonymous person
  stateMap.anon_user = makePerson({
    cid    : configMap.anon_id,
    id     : configMap.anon_id,
    name   : 'anonymous'
  });
  stateMap.user = stateMap.anon_user;

  if ( isFakeData ) {
```

Reserve the `anon_user` key in our state map to store the anonymous `person` object.

Reserve the `people_cid_map` key in our state map to store a map of `person` objects keyed by client ID.

Reserve the `people_db` key in our state map to store a TaffyDB collection of `person` objects. Initialize it as an empty collection.

Set `isFakeData` to true. This flag tells the Model to use the example data, objects, and methods from the Fake module instead of actual data from the Data module.

Create a prototype for `person` objects. Use of a prototype usually reduces memory requirements and improves the performance of objects.

Add a `makePerson` method that creates a `person` object and stores it in a TaffyDB collection. Ensure it also updates the index in the `people_cid_map`.

Use `Object.create ( <prototype> )` to create our object from a prototype and then add instance-specific properties.

Add the `get_db` method to return the TaffyDB collection of `person` objects.

Define the `people` object.

Add the `get_cid_map` method to return a map of `person` objects keyed by client ID.

Make the `anonymous person` object in `initModule` to ensure it has the same methods and attributes of other `person` objects regardless of future changes. This is an example of “design for quality.”

Get the list of online people from the Fake module and add them to the `people_db` TaffyDB collection.

```
          people_list = spa.fake.getPeopleList();
          for ( i = 0; i < people_list.length; i++ ) {
            person_map = people_list[ i ];
            makePerson({
              cid     : person_map._id,
              css_map : person_map.css_map,
              id      : person_map._id,
              name    : person_map.name
            });
          }
        }
      };

      return {
        initModule : initModule,
        people     : people
      };
    }());
```

Of course, nothing calls `spa.model.initModule()` yet. Let's fix that by updating our root namespace module, spa/js/spa.js, as shown in listing 5.13:

Listing 5.13 Add Model initialization to root namespace module—spa/js/spa.js

```
...
var spa = (function () {
  'use strict';
  var initModule = function ( $container ) {
    spa.model.initModule();
    spa.shell.initModule( $container );
  };

  return { initModule: initModule };
}());
```

Add the `use strict` pragma.

Initialize the Model before the Shell.

Now let's load our browser document (spa/spa.html) to make sure that the page works as before—if it does *not* or there are errors in the console, we did something wrong and should retrace our steps to here. Although it might look the same, under the hood the code is working differently. Let's open the Chrome Developer Tools JavaScript console to test the `people` API. We can get the people collection and explore some of the benefits of TaffyDB as shown in listing 5.14. Typed input is shown in **bold**; output is shown in *italics*:

Listing 5.14 Playing with fake people and liking it

```
// get the people collection
var peopleDb = spa.model.people.get_db();

// get list of all people
var peopleList = peopleDb().get();

// show our list of people
peopleList;
>> [ >Object, >Object, >Object, >Object, >Object ]
```

Use the TaffyDB `get()` method to extract an array from the collection

Get the TaffyDB collection populated with `person` objects.

Inspect the list of users. The `>Object` presented is expandable. We can click on the > symbol to see its properties.

```
// show the names of all people in our list
peopleDb().each(function(person, idx){console.log(person.name);});
>> anonymous
>> Betty
>> Mike
>> Pebbles
>> Wilma

// get the person with the id of 'id_03':
var person = peopleDb({ cid : 'id_03' }).first();

// inspect the name attribute
person.name;
>> "Pebbles"

// inspect the css_map attribute
JSON.stringify( person.css_map );
>> "{"top":100,"left":20,"background-color":"rgb( 128, 192, 192)"}""

// try an inherited method
person.get_is_anon();
>> false

// the anonymous person should have an id of 'a0'
person = peopleDb({ id : 'a0' }).first();

// use the same method
person.get_is_anon();
>> true

person.name;
>> "anonymous"

// check our person_cid_map too...
var personCidMap = spa.model.people.get_cid_map();

personCidMap[ 'a0' ].name;
>> "anonymous"
```

Iterate over all person objects and print the name. We use the each method provided by the TaffyDB collection. This method takes a function as its argument, which receives a person object and index number as arguments.

Filter the TaffyDB collection using peopleDb(<match_map>) and then extract the first object of the returned array using the first() method.

Ensure our person object has the name property we expect.

Display another expected property, css_map.

Ensure our person object has the get_is_anon method and provides the correct results—Pebbles isn't the anonymous person.

Get the anonymous person object by its ID.

Ensure this person object has the get_is_anon method and works as expected.

Check the name of the anonymous person object.

Test getting a person object by client ID.

This testing shows that we've been successful in building part of the `people` object. In the next section we'll finish the job.

5.4.3 Finish the people object

We need to update both the Model and the Fake modules to ensure the `people` object API meets the specifications we wrote earlier. Let's update the Model first.

UPDATE THE MODEL

We want our `people` object to fully support the concept of a `user`. Let's consider the new methods we'll need to add:

- `login( <user_name> )` will start the sign-in process. We'll need to create a new `person` object and add it to the people list. When the sign-in process is complete, we'll emit an `spa-login` event that publishes the current user object as data.

- logout() will start the sign-out process. When a user signs out, we'll delete the user person object from the people list. When the sign-out process is complete, we'll emit an spa-logout event with the prior user object as data.
- get_user() will return the current user person object. If someone has not signed in, the user object will be the anonymous person object. We'll use a module state variable (stateMap.user) to store the current user person object.

We need to add a number of other capabilities to support these methods:

- Because we'll be using a Socket.IO connection to send and receive messages to the Fake module, we'll use a mock sio object in the login(<user_name>) method.
- Because we'll be creating a new person object with login(<username>), we'll use the makeCid() method to create a client ID for the signed-in user. We'll use a module state variable (stateMap.cid_serial) to store a serial number used to create this ID.
- Because we'll be removing the user person object from the people list, we'll need a method to remove a user. We'll use a removePerson(<client_id>) method to do this.
- Because the sign-in process is asynchronous (it only completes when the Fake module returns a userupdate message), we'll use a completeLogin method to finish the process.

Let's update the Model with these changes as shown in listing 5.15. All changes are shown in **bold**:

Listing 5.15 Finish the people object of the Model—spa/js/spa.model.js

```
/*
 * spa.model.js
 * Model module
*/

/*jslint         browser : true, continue : true,
  devel  : true, indent  : 2,    maxerr   : 50,
  newcap : true, nomen   : true, plusplus : true,
  regexp : true, sloppy  : true, vars     : false,
  white  : true
*/
/*global TAFFY, $, spa */

spa.model = (function () {
  'use strict';
  var
    configMap = { anon_id : 'a0' },
    stateMap  = {
      anon_user      : null,
      cid_serial     : 0,
      people_cid_map : {},
      people_db      : TAFFY(),
```

```
      user            : null
    },

    isFakeData = true,

    personProto, makeCid, clearPeopleDb, completeLogin,
    makePerson, removePerson, people, initModule;

  // The people object API
  // ---------------------
  // The people object is available at spa.model.people.
  // The people object provides methods and events to manage
  // a collection of person objects. Its public methods include:
  //   * get_user() - return the current user person object.
  //     If the current user is not signed-in, an anonymous person
  //     object is returned.
  //   * get_db() - return the TaffyDB database of all the person
  //     objects - including the current user - presorted.
  //   * get_by_cid( <client_id> ) - return a person object with
  //     provided unique id.
  //   * login( <user_name> ) - login as the user with the provided
  //     user name. The current user object is changed to reflect
  //     the new identity. Successful completion of login
  //     publishes a 'spa-login' global custom event.
  //   * logout()- revert the current user object to anonymous.
  //     This method publishes a 'spa-logout' global custom event.
  //
  // jQuery global custom events published by the object include:
  //   * spa-login - This is published when a user login process
  //     completes. The updated user object is provided as data.
  //   * spa-logout - This is published when a logout completes.
  //     The former user object is provided as data.
  //
  // Each person is represented by a person object.
  // Person objects provide the following methods:
  //   * get_is_user() - return true if object is the current user
  //   * get_is_anon() - return true if object is anonymous
  //
  // The attributes for a person object include:
  //   * cid - string client id. This is always defined, and
  //     is only different from the id attribute
  //     if the client data is not synced with the backend.
  //   * id - the unique id. This may be undefined if the
  //     object is not synced with the backend.
  //   * name - the string name of the user.
  //   * css_map - a map of attributes used for avatar
  //     presentation.
  //
  personProto = {
    get_is_user : function () {
      return this.cid === stateMap.user.cid;
    },
    get_is_anon : function () {
      return this.cid === stateMap.anon_user.cid;
    }
  };
```

Include the API documentation we previously developed.

Add a client ID generator. Usually the client ID of a `person` object is the same as the server ID. But those created on the client and not yet saved to the backend don't yet have a server ID.

Add a method to remove all `person` objects except the anonymous person, and, if a user is signed in, the current user object.

Add a method to complete user sign-in when the backend sends confirmation and data for the user. This routine updates the current user information, and then publishes the success of the sign-in using an `spa-login` event.

Create a method to remove a `person` object from the people list. We add a few checks to avoid logical inconsistencies—for example, we won't remove the current user or anonymous `person` objects.

```
makeCid = function () {
  return 'c' + String( stateMap.cid_serial++ );
};

clearPeopleDb = function () {
  var user = stateMap.user;
  stateMap.people_db      = TAFFY();
  stateMap.people_cid_map = {};
  if ( user ) {
    stateMap.people_db.insert( user );
    stateMap.people_cid_map[ user.cid ] = user;
  }
};

completeLogin = function ( user_list ) {
  var user_map = user_list[ 0 ];
  delete stateMap.people_cid_map[ user_map.cid ];
  stateMap.user.cid     = user_map._id;
  stateMap.user.id      = user_map._id;
  stateMap.user.css_map = user_map.css_map;
  stateMap.people_cid_map[ user_map._id ] = stateMap.user;

  // When we add chat, we should join here
  $.gevent.publish( 'spa-login', [ stateMap.user ] );
};

makePerson = function ( person_map ) {
  var person,
    cid     = person_map.cid,
    css_map = person_map.css_map,
    id      = person_map.id,
    name    = person_map.name;

  if ( cid === undefined || ! name ) {
    throw 'client id and name required';
  }

  person          = Object.create( personProto );
  person.cid      = cid;
  person.name     = name;
  person.css_map  = css_map;

  if ( id ) { person.id = id; }

  stateMap.people_cid_map[ cid ] = person;

  stateMap.people_db.insert( person );
  return person;
};

removePerson = function ( person ) {
  if ( ! person ) { return false; }
  // can't remove anonymous person
  if ( person.id === configMap.anon_id ) {
    return false;
  }

  stateMap.people_db({ cid : person.cid }).remove();
  if ( person.cid ) {
```

```
    delete stateMap.people_cid_map[ person.cid ];
  }
  return true;
};

people = (function () {
  var get_by_cid, get_db, get_user, login, logout;

  get_by_cid = function ( cid ) {
    return stateMap.people_cid_map[ cid ];
  };

  get_db = function () { return stateMap.people_db; };

  get_user = function () { return stateMap.user; };

  login = function ( name ) {
    var sio = isFakeData ? spa.fake.mockSio : spa.data.getSio();

    stateMap.user = makePerson({
      cid     : makeCid(),
      css_map : {top : 25, left : 25, 'background-color':'#8f8'},
      name    : name
    });

    sio.on( 'userupdate', completeLogin );

    sio.emit( 'adduser', {
      cid     : stateMap.user.cid,
      css_map : stateMap.user.css_map,
      name    : stateMap.user.name
    });
  };

  logout = function () {
    var is_removed, user = stateMap.user;
    // when we add chat, we should leave the chatroom here

    is_removed    = removePerson( user );
    stateMap.user = stateMap.anon_user;

    $.gevent.publish( 'spa-logout', [ user ] );
    return is_removed;
  };

  return {
    get_by_cid : get_by_cid,
    get_db     : get_db,
    get_user   : get_user,
    login      : login,
    logout     : logout
  };
}());

initModule = function () {
  var i, people_list, person_map;

  // initialize anonymous person
  stateMap.anon_user = makePerson({
    cid   : configMap.anon_id,
    id    : configMap.anon_id,
```

Define the `people` closure. This allows us to share only the methods we want.

Define the `get_by_cid` method in the `people` closure. This is a convenience method that's easy to implement.

Define the `get_user` method in the `people` closure. This returns the current user `person` object.

Define the `get_db` method in the `people` closure. This returns the TaffyDB collection of `person` objects.

Define the `login` method in the `people` closure. We don't do any fancy credential checking here.

Send an `adduser` message to the backend along with all the user details. Adding a user and signing in are the same thing in this context.

Register a callback to complete sign-in when the backend publishes a `userupdate` message.

Define the `logout` method in the `people` closure. This publishes an `spa-logout` event.

Neatly export all of our public `people` methods.

```
      name   : 'anonymous'
    });
    stateMap.user = stateMap.anon_user;

    if ( isFakeData ) {
      people_list = spa.fake.getPeopleList();
      for ( i = 0; i < people_list.length; i++ ) {
        person_map = people_list[ i ];
        makePerson({
          cid     : person_map._id,
          css_map : person_map.css_map,
          id      : person_map._id,
          name    : person_map.name
        });
      }
    }
  };

  return {
    initModule : initModule,
    people     : people
  };
}());
```

Now that we've updated the Model, we can proceed with the Fake module.

UPDATE THE FAKE MODULE

Our Fake module needs to be updated to provide a mock Socket.IO connection object, `sio`. We want this to emulate the capabilities we need to sign in and sign out:

- The mock `sio` object must provide the ability to register callbacks for a message. We only need to support a callback for a single message, `userupdate`, to test sign-in and sign-out. In the Model we register the `completeLogin` method for this message.
- When a user signs in, the mock `sio` object will receive an `adduser` message from the Model along with the a map of user data as its argument. We emulate a server response by waiting three seconds and then executing the `userupdate` callback. We purposely delay this response so we might spot any race conditions in the sign-in process.
- We don't need to worry about sign-out with the mock `sio` object just yet, as the Model currently handles that condition.

Let's update the Fake module with these changes as shown in listing 5.16. All changes are shown in **bold**:

Listing 5.16 Add a mock socket object with latency to Fake—spa/js/spa.fake.js

```
...

spa.fake = (function () {
  'use strict';
  var getPeopleList, fakeIdSerial, makeFakeId, mockSio;    // Add new module-scope variables.
```

```
fakeIdSerial = 5;

makeFakeId = function () {
  return 'id_' + String( fakeIdSerial++ );
};

getPeopleList = function () {
  return [
    { name : 'Betty', _id : 'id_01',
      css_map : { top: 20, left: 20,
        'background-color' : 'rgb( 128, 128, 128)'
      }
    },
    { name : 'Mike', _id : 'id_02',
      css_map : { top: 60, left: 20,
        'background-color' : 'rgb( 128, 255, 128)'
      }
    },
    { name : 'Pebbles', _id : 'id_03',
      css_map : { top: 100, left: 20,
        'background-color' : 'rgb( 128, 192, 192)'
      }
    },
    { name : 'Wilma', _id : 'id_04',
      css_map : { top: 140, left: 20,
        'background-color' : 'rgb( 192, 128, 128)'
      }
    }
  ];
};

mockSio = (function () {
  var on_sio, emit_sio, callback_map = {};

  on_sio = function ( msg_type, callback ) {
    callback_map[ msg_type ] = callback;
  };

  emit_sio = function ( msg_type, data ) {

    // respond to 'adduser' event with 'userupdate'
    // callback after a 3s delay
    //
    if ( msg_type === 'adduser' && callback_map.userupdate ) {
      setTimeout( function () {
        callback_map.userupdate(
          [{ _id     : makeFakeId(),
             name    : data.name,
             css_map : data.css_map
          }]
        );
      }, 3000 );
    }
  };

  return { emit : emit_sio, on : on_sio };
}());
```

Add a mock server ID serial number counter.

Create a method to make a mock server ID string.

Define the `mockSio` object closure. This has two public methods: on and `emit`.

Create the `on_sio` method for the `mockSio` closure. This method registers a callback for a message type. For example, `on_sio( 'updateuser,' onUpdateuser );` would register an `onUpdateuser` function as a callback for the `updateuser` message type. The callback will receive message data as arguments.

Create the `emit_sio` method for the `mockSio` closure. The method emulates sending a message to the server. In this first pass, we'll only handle the `adduser` message type. When received, we wait 3 seconds to simulate network latency and then invoke the `updateuser` callback.

Export the public methods for our mock `mockSio` object. We export `on_sio` as on and `emit_sio` as `emit` so we can emulate a real SocketIO object.

```
  return {
    getPeopleList : getPeopleList,
    mockSio : mockSio
  };
}());
```

Add the mockSio object to the public Fake API.

Now that we've completed updating the Model and Fake, we can test sign-in and sign-out.

5.4.4 Test the people object API

As we planned, isolating the Model allows us to test the sign-in and sign-out process without the time and expense of setting up a server or preparing a UI. Beyond the saved expense, it ensures higher quality because our test results aren't distorted by interface or data bugs, and we're testing a known data set. This method also allows us to proceed without needing other development groups to complete their components.

Let's load our browser document (spa/spa.html) to ensure the application works as before. We can then open the JavaScript console and test the `login`, `logout`, and other methods as shown in listing 5.17. Typed input is shown in **bold**; output is shown in *italics*:

Listing 5.17 Test sign-in and sign-out using the JavaScript console

```
// create a jQuery collection
$t = $('<div/>');

// Have $t subscribe to global custom events with test functions
$.gevent.subscribe( $t, 'spa-login', function () {
  console.log( 'Hello!', arguments ); });

$.gevent.subscribe( $t, 'spa-logout', function () {
  console.log('!Goodbye', arguments ); });

// get the current user object
var currentUser = spa.model.people.get_user();

// confirm it is anonymous
currentUser.get_is_anon();
>> true

// get the people collection
var peopleDb = spa.model.people.get_db();

// show the names of all people in our list
peopleDb().each(function(person, idx){console.log(person.name);});
>> anonymous
>> Betty
>> Mike
>> Pebbles
>> Wilma

// sign-in as 'Alfred'; get current user within 3s!
```

Create a jQuery collection ($t) that isn't attached to the browser document. We'll use this for event testing.

Have the $t jQuery collection subscribe to the spa-login event with a function that prints "Hello!" and the list of arguments to the console.

Have the $t jQuery collection subscribe to the spa-logout event with a function that prints "!Goodbye" and the list of arguments to the console.

Confirm the user object is the anonymous person object.

Confirm the user list is as expected.

```
spa.model.people.login( 'Alfred' );
currentUser = spa.model.people.get_user();

// confirm the current user is no longer anonymous
currentUser.get_is_anon();
>> false

// inspect the current user id and cid
currentUser.id;
>> undefined

currentUser.cid;
>> "c0"

// wait 3s ...
>> Hello! > [jQuery.Event, Object]

// revisit the people collection
peopleDb().each(function(person, idx){console.log(person.name);});
>> anonymous
>> Betty
>> Mike
>> Pebbles
>> Wilma
>> Alfred

// sign-out and watch for the event
spa.model.people.logout();
>> !Goodbye [jQuery.Event, Object]

// look at the people collection and current user
peopleDb().each(function(person, idx){console.log(person.name);});
>> anonymous
>> Betty
>> Mike
>> Pebbles
>> Wilma

currentUser = spa.model.people.get_user();
currentUser.get_is_anon();
>> true
```

Log in as Alfred.

Ensure the user object is no longer the anonymous `person` object. Even though the backend has yet to respond, the user has been set and so `get_is_anon()` returns false.

Inspect the user object `id`. We can see that Alfred is added to the client but `id` is undefined. This means the Model has yet to respond to the login request.

Wait 3 seconds and the `spa-login` event will publish. This invokes the function we subscribed on the `$t` jQuery collection to the `spa-login` event, and so we see the "Hello!" message along with the list of arguments.

List each person in the people collection and ensure we see "Alfred."

Invoke the `logout()` method. This does a bit of house cleaning and publishes the `spa-logout` event almost immediately. This invokes the function we subscribed on the `$t` jQuery collection to `spa-logout` event, and so we see the "!Goodbye" message along with a list of arguments.

Confirm the list of people no longer contains Alfred.

Confirm the current user object is the anonymous `person` object.

This testing is reassuring. We've shown that the `people` object does a good job of meeting its goals. We can sign in and sign out and the Model behaves as defined. And because the Model doesn't require a UI or a server, it's easy to create a test suite to ensure all methods meet their design specification. This suite can be run without a browser by using jQuery with Node.js. See appendix B for a review of how this can be accomplished.

This might be a good time to take a break. In the next section we'll update our interface so the user may sign in and sign out.

5.5 Enable sign-in and sign-out in the Shell

Up to this point we've isolated our Model development from the UI as shown in figure 5.10:

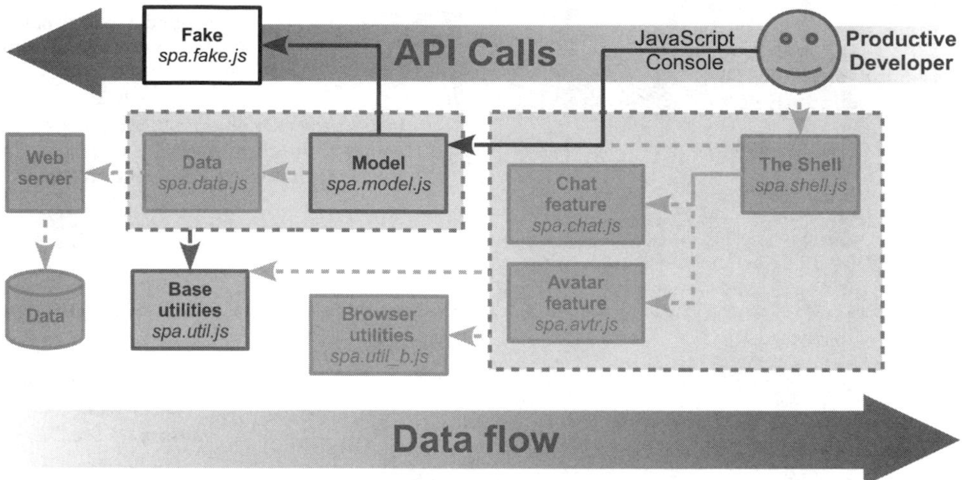

Figure 5.10 Testing the Model using the JavaScript console

Now that we've tested the Model thoroughly, we want a user to sign in and sign out through the UI instead of the JavaScript console. We'll now employ the Shell to do just that, as shown in figure 5.11.

Of course, before we can build the UI, we must agree on how it should work. We'll do that next.

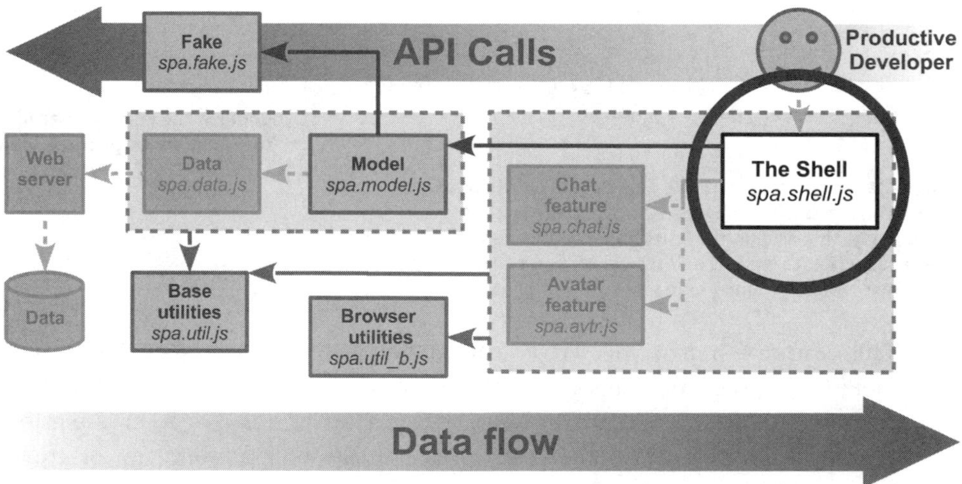

Figure 5.11 In this section we add a graphical sign-in capability to the Shell

5.5.1 *Design the user sign-in experience*

We'd like to keep the user experience simple and familiar. As is the popular convention, we'd like the user to click on the top-right of the page to begin the sign-in process. The steps we envision are illustrated in figure 5.12.

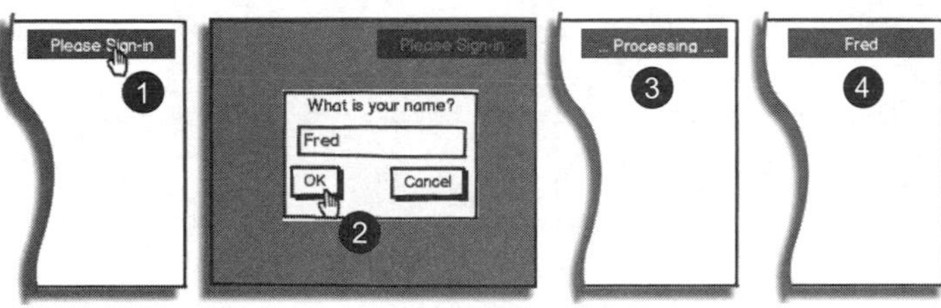

Figure 5.12 The sign-in process as seen by the user

1. If the user isn't signed in, the top-right area (the "user area") will prompt *Please Sign-in*. When the user clicks on this text, a sign-in dialog will appear.
2. Once the user completes the dialog form and clicks on the OK button, the sign-in processing begins.
3. The sign-in dialog is removed, and the user area shows ... *processing* ... while the sign-in is underway (our Fake module always takes three seconds for this step).
4. Once the sign-in process is complete, the user area shows the name of the signed-in user.

A signed-in user may sign out by clicking on the user area. This will revert the text back to *Please Sign-in*.

Now that we have the user experience designed, we can update the Shell to make it happen.

5.5.2 *Update the Shell JavaScript*

Because we put all of our data handling and logic into our Model, we can have the Shell handle the view and control roles only. While we're under the hood, as they say, we can also easily add support for touch devices (such as tablets and mobile phones). Let's modify the Shell as shown in listing 5.18. Changes are shown in **bold**:

Listing 5.18 Update the Shell to add sign-in—spa/js/spa.shell.js

```
...
spa.shell = (function () {
  'use strict';
  //---------------- BEGIN MODULE SCOPE VARIABLES --------------
  var
    configMap = {
      anchor_schema_map : {
        chat  : { opened : true, closed : true }
      },
      resize_interval : 200,
      main_html : String()
```

Use the `strict` pragma.

```
      + '<div class="spa-shell-head">'
        + '<div class="spa-shell-head-logo">'
          + '<h1>SPA</h1>'
          + '<p>javascript end to end</p>'
        + '</div>'
        + '<div class="spa-shell-head-acct"></div>'
      + '</div>'
      + '<div class="spa-shell-main">'
        + '<div class="spa-shell-main-nav"></div>'
        + '<div class="spa-shell-main-content"></div>'
      + '</div>'
      + '<div class="spa-shell-foot"></div>'
      + '<div class="spa-shell-modal"></div>'
  },
...
  copyAnchorMap,    setJqueryMap,   changeAnchorPart,
  onResize,         onHashchange,
    onTapAcct,        onLogin,        onLogout,
    setChatAnchor,    initModule;
  ...
  // Begin DOM method /setJqueryMap/
  setJqueryMap = function () {
    var $container = stateMap.$container;

    jqueryMap = {
      $container : $container,
      $acct      : $container.find('.spa-shell-head-acct'),
      $nav       : $container.find('.spa-shell-main-nav')
    };
  };
  // End DOM method /setJqueryMap/

  ...
  onTapAcct = function ( event ) {
    var acct_text, user_name, user = spa.model.people.get_user();
    if ( user.get_is_anon() ) {
      user_name = prompt( 'Please sign-in' );
      spa.model.people.login( user_name );
      jqueryMap.$acct.text( '... processing ...' );
    }
    else {
      spa.model.people.logout();
    }
    return false;
  };

  onLogin = function ( event, login_user ) {
    jqueryMap.$acct.text( login_user.name );
  };

  onLogout = function ( event, logout_user ) {
    jqueryMap.$acct.text( 'Please sign-in' );
  };

  //------------------- END EVENT HANDLERS -------------------

  ...
```

Give the header a nicer look and provide an element for account name.

Declare the `onTapAcct`, `onLogin`, and `onLogout` event handlers.

Add to our jQuery cache map.

Add the `onTapAcct` method. When the account element is tapped, if the user is anonymous (in other words, not logged in), then we prompt for a user name and then invoke `spa.model.people.login( <user_name> )`. If the user is already signed in, we invoke the `spa.model.people.logout()` method.

Create the `onLogin` event handler. This updates the user area (in the top-right corner) by replacing the "Please Sign-in" text with the user name. This is provided by the `login_user` object that's distributed by the `spa-login` event.

Create the `onLogout` event handler. This reverts the user area text back to "Please Sign-in."

```
initModule = function ( $container ) {
  ...
  $.gevent.subscribe( $container, 'spa-login', onLogin );
  $.gevent.subscribe( $container, 'spa-logout', onLogout );

  jqueryMap.$acct
    .text( 'Please sign-in')
    .bind( 'utap', onTapAcct );
  };
  // End PUBLIC method /initModule/

  return { initModule : initModule };
  //------------------- END PUBLIC METHODS --------------------
}());
```

Have the `$container` jQuery collection subscribe the `onLogin` and `onLogout` event handlers to the `spa-login` and `spa-logout` events respectively.

Initialize the user area text. Bind a touch or mouse click on the user area to the `onTapAcct` event handler.

The changes we made are easy to understand once we're comfortable with the publish-subscribe nature of jQuery global custom events. Now let's tweak the CSS to show our user area correctly.

5.5.3 Update the Shell stylesheet

Our stylesheet changes aren't anything fancy. We add or modify a few selectors to make the user area look nice, and we clean up some cruft along the way. Listing 5.19 shows the changes we need in **bold**:

Listing 5.19 Add styles for user area in the Shell stylesheet—spa/css/spa.shell.css

```
...
.spa-shell-head-logo {
  top    : 4px;
  left   : 8px;
  height : 32px;
  width  : 128px;
}
  .spa-shell-head-logo h1 {
    font : 800 22px/22px Arial, Helvetica, sans-serif;
    margin : 0;
  }
  .spa-shell-head-logo p {
    font : 800 10px/10px Arial, Helvetica, sans-serif;
    margin : 0;
  }

.spa-shell-head-acct {
  top           : 4px;
  right         : 0;
  width         : 210px;
  height        : 32px;
  line-height   : 32px;
  background    : #888;
  color         : #fff;
  text-align    : center;
  cursor        : pointer;
  overflow      : hidden;
```

Update the `spa-shell-head-logo` class to move our logo area away from the edge a bit.

Create and indent the `.spa-shell-head-logo h1` derived selector. This modifies the headerl (`h1`) style inside the logo div.

Create and indent the `.spa-shell-head-logo p` derived selector. This modifies the paragraph (`p`) inside the logo `div`.

Delete the `.spa-shell-head-search` selector.

Modify the `.spa-shell-head-acct` selector so the user area text will be more legible.

```
    text-overflow : ellipsis;
  }
  ...
  .spa-shell-main-nav {
    width       : 400px;
    background  : #eee;
    z-index     : 1;
  }
  ...
  .spa-shell-main-content {
    left        : 400px;
    right       : 0;
    background  : #ddd;
  }
  ...
```

Modify the `.spa-shell-main-nav` selector to make it wider and ensure its z-index is "above" any `spa-shell-main-content` class container.

Modify the `.spa-shell-main-content` selector to accommodate the increased width of any adjacent `spa-shell-main-nav` class container.

Now with our CSS in place, let's test the changes.

5.5.4 Test sign-in and sign-out using the UI

When we load our browser document (spa/spa.html), we should see a page with "Please sign in" in the user area in the top-right of the window. When we click on this, we should be presented with a dialog as shown in figure 5.13.

Once we enter a user name and click OK, the dialog should close and we should see "... processing ..."[6] for three seconds in the user area, after which the `spa-login` event should be published. The handler in the Shell subscribed to this event should then update the user name in the upper-right of the window, as shown in figure 5.14.

We ensure a good experience by keeping the user apprised of what's happening throughout the process. This is a hallmark of good design—consistently providing

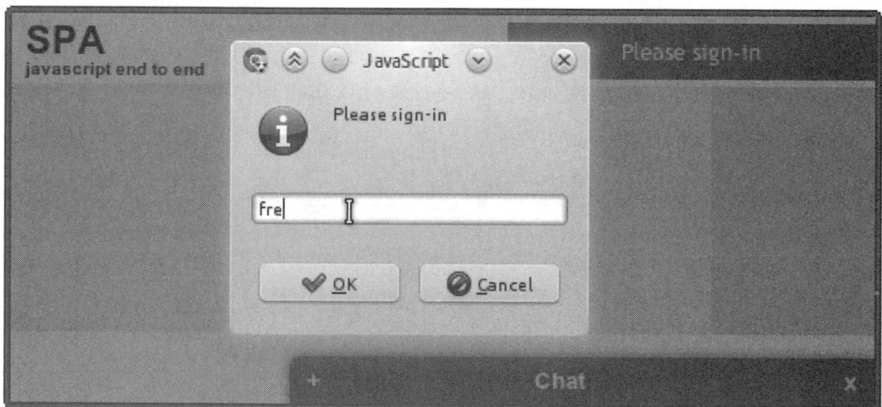

Figure 5.13 Screenshot of sign-in dialog

[6] Before we went public with the site, we'd probably use a nice "in-progress" animated graphic instead of the text. A number of web sites provide quality custom in-progress graphics for free.

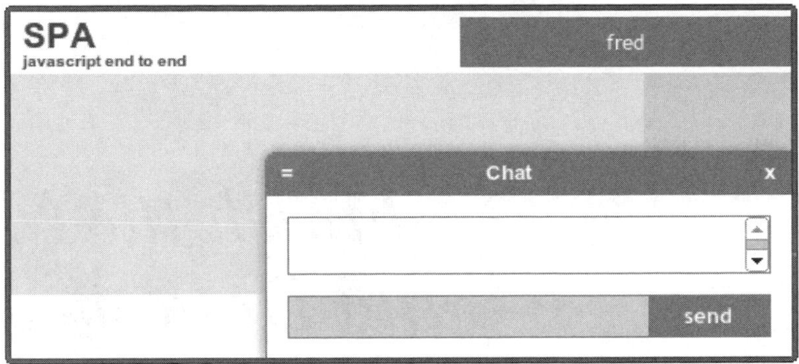

Figure 5.14 Screenshot after completion of sign-in

immediate feedback can make even a relatively slow application seem snappy and responsive.

5.6 Summary

In this chapter we introduced the Model and discussed how it fits into our architecture. We outlined what the Model should and should *not* do. We then set up the files required to build and test the Model.

We designed, specified, developed, and tested one part of the Model—the `people` object. We used a Fake module to provide a controlled data set to the Model, and we used the JavaScript console to test the `people` object API. Isolating the Model in this way resulted in faster development and more controlled testing. We also modified our SPA to use a mouse-touch plugin so that mobile users may use it.

In the final section we modified the Shell to present the sign-in and sign-out capabilities to the user. We used the API provided by the `people` object to provide this capability. We also ensured a positive user experience by having our SPA provide feedback immediately after user input.

In the next chapter, we'll add the `chat` object to the Model. This will allow us to complete the Chat feature module and create an Avatar feature module. Then we'll prepare the client to work with a real web server.

6 Finish the Model and Data modules

This chapter covers

- Designing the `chat` object portion of the Model
- Implementing the `chat` object and testing its API
- Completing the Chat feature module
- Creating a new Avatar feature module
- Using jQuery for data binding
- Communicating with the server using the Data module

This chapter concludes the work on the Model and feature modules begun in chapter 5. Before starting, you should have the project files from chapter 5, as we'll be adding to them. We recommend you copy the entire directory structure you created in chapter 5 into a "chapter_6" directory and update them there.

In this chapter we design and build the `chat` object portion of the Model. We then complete the Chat slider UI by having it use and respond to the `chat` object API. We also add an Avatar feature module which also uses the `chat` object API to display on-screen representations of online people. We discuss how we accomplish data

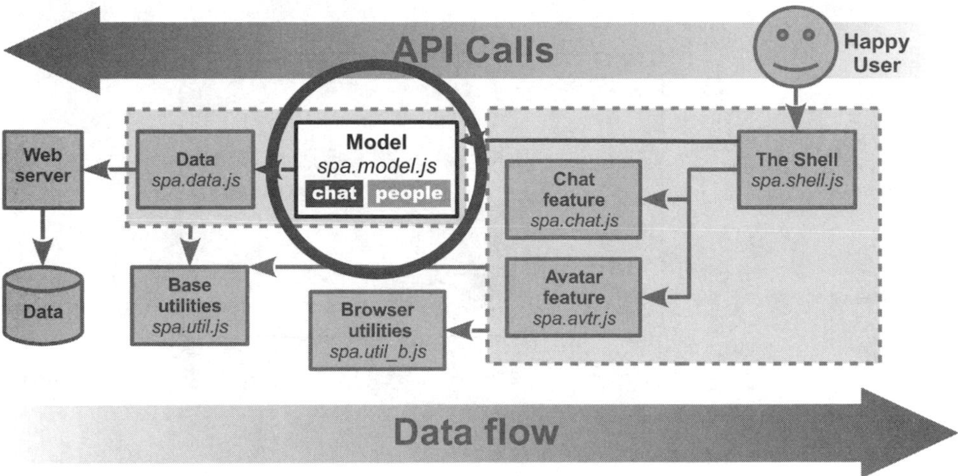

Figure 6.1 We'll work the Model's `chat` object in this chapter

binding using jQuery. Finally, we complete the client portion of the SPA with the addition of the Data module.

Let's start by designing the `chat` object.

6.1 Design the chat object

In this chapter we will build the `chat` object portion of the Model as shown in figure 6.1.

In the last chapter we designed, built, and tested the `people` object portion of the Model. In this chapter we'll design, build, and test the `chat` object. Let's revisit the API specification we first presented in chapter 4:

```
...
  //    * chat_model - the chat model object provides methods
  //        to interact with our instant messaging
  //    * people_model - the people model object which provides methods
  //        to interact with the list of people the model maintains
...
```

The description provided for the `chat` object—"an object that provides methods to interact with our instant messaging"—is a good start but too broad for implementation. Let's design the `chat` object by first analyzing what we'd like it to accomplish.

6.1.1 Design methods and events

We know we want the `chat` object to provide instant messaging capabilities, but we need to determine what those capabilities are in detail. Let's consider figure 6.2, which shows a mockup of the SPA with some notes about our chat interface.

We know from experience that we'll probably need to initialize a chat room. We also expect that the user may change the *chatee* (the person with whom they're chatting), and

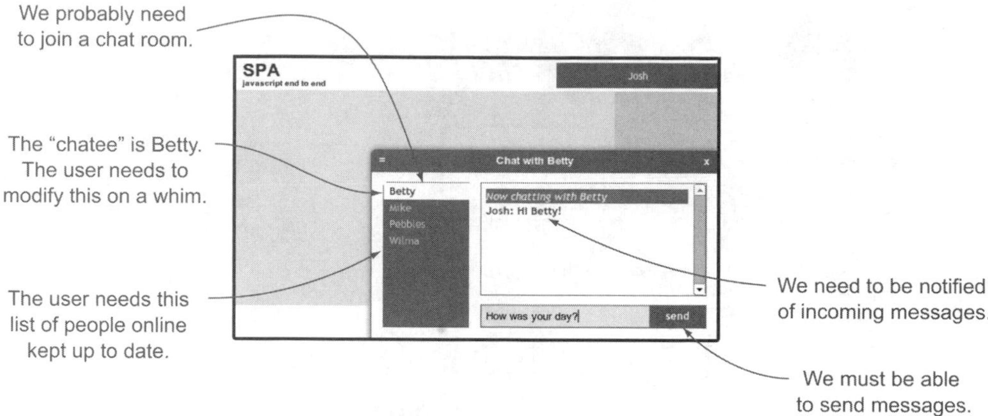
We probably need to join a chat room.
SPA
javascript end to end
Josh
The "chatee" is Betty. The user needs to modify this on a whim.
Chat with Betty
Betty
Mike
Pebbles
Wilma
Now chatting with Betty
Josh: Hi Betty!
The user needs this list of people online kept up to date.
We need to be notified of incoming messages.
How was your day?
send
We must be able to send messages.

Figure 6.2 A mockup of our SPA—chat focus

may send messages to this person. And from our discussion about avatars, we know the user may update avatar information. The user won't be the only source driving the UI, as we expect other people to join and leave the chat room, send and receive messages, and change avatar information. Based on this analysis, we can list the capabilities that we need to be exposed by the `chat` object API:

- Provide methods to join or leave a chat room.
- Provide a method to change the chatee.
- Provide a method to send messages to other people.
- Provide a method to tell the server that an avatar has been updated by the user.
- Publish an event if the chatee is changed for any reason. For example, if the chatee goes offline or a new chatee is selected by the user.
- Publish an event when the message pane needs to change for any reason. For example, if the user sends or receives a message.
- Publish an event if the list of online persons changes for any reason. For example, if a person joins or leaves the chat room, or if an avatar is moved by any user.

Our `chat` object API will use two channels of communication. One channel is the classic method-return-value mechanism. This channel is *synchronous*—the data transfer happens in a known sequence. The `chat` object may invoke external methods and receive information as return values. And other code may invoke the `chat` object's public methods and receive information from the return values.

The other channel of communication that will be used by the chat object is the event mechanism. This channel is *asynchronous*—events may happen at any time regardless of the actions of the `chat` object. The `chat` object will receive events (like messages from the server) and publish events for use by the UI.

Let's start designing the `chat` object by first considering the synchronous methods we will provide.

DESIGN CHAT METHODS

As we discussed in chapter 5, a method is a publicly exposed function, like `spa.model`**`.chat.get_chatee`**, which can be used to perform an action and return data synchronously. Given our requirements, this list of methods seems about right:

- `join()`—Join the chat. If the user is anonymous, this method should abort and return `false`.
- `get_chatee()`—Return the `person` object of the user with whom we're chatting. If there's no chatee, return `null`.
- `set_chatee( <person_id> )`—Set the chatee to the `person` object uniquely identified by `person_id`. This method should publish an `spa-setchatee` event with chatee information provided as data. If a matching `person` object can't be found in the collection of online people, set the chatee to `null`. If the requested person is already the chatee, return `false`.
- `send_message( <msg_text> )`—Send a message to the chatee. We should publish an `spa-updatechat` event with message information provided as data. If the user is anonymous or the chatee is `null`, this method should take no action and return `false`.
- `update_avatar( <update_avatar_map> )`—Adjust avatar information for a `person` object. The argument (`update_avatar_map`) should include the properties `person_id` and `css_map`.

These methods appear to meet our requirements. Now let's consider in more detail the events that the `chat` object should publish.

DESIGN CHAT EVENTS

As we discussed earlier, events are used to publish data asynchronously. For example, if a message is received, the `chat` object will need to notify subscribed jQuery collections of the change and provide the data necessary to update the presentation.

We expect that the collection of online people, and the chatee, will change often. These changes won't always be due to the user's actions—for example, a chatee may send a message at any time. Here are the events that should communicate these changes to the feature modules:

- `spa-listchange` should be published when the list of online people changes. An updated people collection should be provided as data.
- `spa-setchatee` should be published when the chatee changes. A map of the old and new chatee should be provided as data
- `spa-updatechat` should be published when a new message is sent or received. A map of message information should be provided as data.

As we did in chapter 5, we'll use jQuery global events as our publishing mechanism. Now that we've thought through the methods and events we will need, let's proceed to documentation and implementation.

6.1.2 Document the chat object API

Let's consolidate our plans into an API specification that we can place into the Model code for reference.

Listing 6.1 The chat object API—spa/js/spa.model.js

```
// The chat object API
// -------------------
// The chat object is available at spa.model.chat.
// The chat object provides methods and events to manage
// chat messaging. Its public methods include:
//  * join() - joins the chat room. This routine sets up
//    the chat protocol with the backend including publishers
//    for 'spa-listchange' and 'spa-updatechat' global
//    custom events. If the current user is anonymous,
//    join() aborts and returns false.
//  * get_chatee() - return the person object with whom the user
//    is chatting. If there is no chatee, null is returned.
//  * set_chatee( <person_id> ) - set the chatee to the person
//    identified by person_id. If the person_id does not exist
//    in the people list, the chatee is set to null. If the
//    person requested is already the chatee, it returns false.
//    It publishes a 'spa-setchatee' global custom event.
//  * send_msg( <msg_text> ) - send a message to the chatee.
//    It publishes a 'spa-updatechat' global custom event.
//    If the user is anonymous or the chatee is null, it
//    aborts and returns false.
//  * update_avatar( <update_avtr_map> ) - send the
//    update_avtr_map to the backend. This results in an
//    'spa-listchange' event which publishes the updated
//    people list and avatar information (the css_map in the
//    person objects). The update_avtr_map must have the form
//    { person_id : person_id, css_map : css_map }.
//
// jQuery global custom events published by the object include:
//  * spa-setchatee - This is published when a new chatee is
//    set. A map of the form:
//      { old_chatee : <old_chatee_person_object>,
//        new_chatee : <new_chatee_person_object>
//      }
//    is provided as data.
//  * spa-listchange - This is published when the list of
//    online people changes in length (i.e. when a person
//    joins or leaves a chat) or when their contents change
//    (i.e. when a person's avatar details change).
//    A subscriber to this event should get the people_db
//    from the people model for the updated data.
//  * spa-updatechat - This is published when a new message
//    is received or sent. A map of the form:
//      { dest_id   : <chatee_id>,
//        dest_name : <chatee_name>,
//        sender_id : <sender_id>,
```

```
//        msg_text   : <message_content>
//      }
//    is provided as data.
//
```

Now that we've completed a specification for the `chat` object, let's implement it and test the API. After that, we'll adjust the Shell and the feature modules to use the `chat` object API to provide new capabilities.

6.2 Build the chat object

Now that we've designed the `chat` object API we can build it. As in chapter 5, we're going to use the Fake module and the JavaScript console to avoid the use of a web server or a UI. *As we progress, we should keep in mind that the "backend" is emulated by the Fake module in this chapter.*

6.2.1 Start the chat object with the join method

In this section we'll create the `chat` object in the Model so that we may:

- Sign in using the `spa.model.people.login(<username>)` method.
- Join the chat room using the `spa.model.chat.join()` method.
- Register a callback to publish an `spa-listchange` event whenever the Model receives a `listchange` message from the backend. This indicates the list of users has changed.

Our `chat` object will rely on the `people` object to handle the sign-in and to maintain the list of online people. It won't allow an anonymous user to `join` a chat room. Let's start building the `chat` object in the Model as shown in listing 6.2. Changes are shown in **bold**:

Listing 6.2 Start our `chat` object—spa/js/spa.model.js

```
spa.model = (function () {
  ...
    stateMap  = {
      ...
      is_connected : false,
      ...
    },
  ...
    personProto, makeCid, clearPeopleDb, completeLogin,
    makePerson, removePerson, people, chat, initModule;
  ...
  // The chat object API
  // -------------------
  // The chat object is available at spa.model.chat.
  // The chat object provides methods and events to manage
  // chat messaging. Its public methods include:
  // * join() - joins the chat room. This routine sets up
  //   the chat protocol with the backend including publishers
  //   for 'spa-listchange' and 'spa-updatechat' global
```

Create the `stateMap.is_connected` flag to indicate if the user is currently in the chat room.

```
//   custom events. If the current user is anonymous,
//   join() aborts and returns false.
// ...
//
// jQuery global custom events published by the object include:
// ...
// * spa-listchange - This is published when the list of
//   online people changes in length (i.e. when a person
//   joins or leaves a chat) or when their contents change
//   (i.e. when a person's avatar details change).
//   A subscriber to this event should get the people_db
//   from the people model for the updated data.
// ...
//
chat = (function () {
  var
    _publish_listchange,
    _update_list, _leave_chat, join_chat;

  // Begin internal methods
  _update_list = function( arg_list ) {
    var i, person_map, make_person_map,
      people_list = arg_list[ 0 ];

    clearPeopleDb();

    PERSON:
    for ( i = 0; i < people_list.length; i++ ) {
      person_map = people_list[ i ];

      if ( ! person_map.name ) { continue PERSON; }

      // if user defined, update css_map and skip remainder
      if ( stateMap.user && stateMap.user.id === person_map._id ) {
        stateMap.user.css_map = person_map.css_map;
        continue PERSON;
      }

      make_person_map = {
        cid     : person_map._id,
        css_map : person_map.css_map,
        id      : person_map._id,
        name    : person_map.name
      };

      makePerson( make_person_map );
    }

    stateMap.people_db.sort( 'name' );
  };

  _publish_listchange = function ( arg_list ) {
    _update_list( arg_list );
    $.gevent.publish( 'spa-listchange', [ arg_list ] );
  };
  // End internal methods

  _leave_chat = function () {
    var sio = isFakeData ? spa.fake.mockSio : spa.data.getSio();
```

Create a `chat` namespace.

Create the `_update_list` method to refresh the `people` object when a new people list is received.

Create the `_publish_listchange` method to publish an `spa-listchange` global jQuery event with an updated people list as its data. We expect to use this method whenever a `listchange` message is received from the backend.

Create the `_leave_chat` method, which sends a `leavechat` message to the backend and cleans up state variables.

Create the `join_chat` method so we may join the chat room. This checks if the user has already joined the chat (`stateMap.is_connected`) so that it doesn't register the `listchange` callback more than once.

Neatly export all public `chat` methods.

Remove the code that inserts the mock people list into the `people` object, as this is now provided when the user joins the chat.

Add `chat` as a public object.

```
      stateMap.is_connected = false;
      if ( sio ) { sio.emit( 'leavechat' ); }
    };

    join_chat = function () {
      var sio;

      if ( stateMap.is_connected ) { return false; }

      if ( stateMap.user.get_is_anon() ) {
        console.warn( 'User must be defined before joining chat');
        return false;
      }

      sio = isFakeData ? spa.fake.mockSio : spa.data.getSio();
      sio.on( 'listchange', _publish_listchange );
      stateMap.is_connected = true;
      return true;
    };

    return {
      _leave : _leave_chat,
      join : join_chat

    };
  }());

  initModule = function () {
    // initialize anonymous person
    stateMap.anon_user = makePerson({
      cid   : configMap.anon_id,
      id    : configMap.anon_id,
      name  : 'anonymous'
    });
    stateMap.user = stateMap.anon_user;
  };

  return {
    initModule : initModule,
    chat       : chat,
    people     : people
  };
}());
```

This is our first pass implementation of the `chat` object. Instead of adding more methods, we want to test the ones we've created so far. In the next section we'll update the Fake module to emulate the server interaction we need for testing.

6.2.2 Update Fake to respond to chat.join

Now we need to update the Fake module so it can emulate the server responses we need to test the `join` method. The changes we need include:

- Include the signed-in user in the mock people list.
- Emulate the receipt of a `listchange` message from the server.

The first step is simple: we create a person map and push it into the people list that Fake manages. The second step is trickier, so stick with me here: the chat object registers a handler for a listchange message from the backend *only after the user has signed in and joined a chat.* Therefore, we can add a private send_listchange function that will send a mock people list only once this handler is registered. Let's employ these changes as shown in listing 6.3. Changes are shown in **bold**:

Listing 6.3 Update Fake to simulate join server messages—spa/js/spa.fake.js

```
...
spa.fake = (function () {
  'use strict';
  var peopleList, fakeIdSerial, makeFakeId, mockSio;

  fakeIdSerial = 5;

  makeFakeId = function () {
    return 'id_' + String( fakeIdSerial++ );
  };

  peopleList = [
    { name : 'Betty', _id : 'id_01',
      css_map : { top: 20, left: 20,
        'background-color' : 'rgb( 128, 128, 128)'
      }
    },
    { name : 'Mike', _id : 'id_02',
      css_map : { top: 60, left: 20,
        'background-color' : 'rgb( 128, 255, 128)'
      }
    },
    { name : 'Pebbles', _id : 'id_03',
      css_map : { top: 100, left: 20,
        'background-color' : 'rgb( 128, 192, 192)'
      }
    },
    { name : 'Wilma', _id : 'id_04',
      css_map : { top: 140, left: 20,
        'background-color' : 'rgb( 192, 128, 128)'
      }
    }
  ];

  mockSio = (function () {
    var
      on_sio, emit_sio,
      send_listchange, listchange_idto,
      callback_map = {};

    on_sio = function ( msg_type, callback ) {
      callback_map[ msg_type ] = callback;
    };

    emit_sio = function ( msg_type, data ) {
      var person_map;
```

Create peopleList to store the mock people list as an array of maps.

Revise the response to an adduser message (which occurs when the user signs in) to push the user definition into the mock people list.

```
    // Respond to 'adduser' event with 'userupdate'
    // callback after a 3s delay.
    if ( msg_type === 'adduser' && callback_map.userupdate ) {
      setTimeout( function () {
        person_map = {
          _id     : makeFakeId(),
          name    : data.name,
          css_map : data.css_map
        };
        peopleList.push( person_map );
        callback_map.userupdate([ person_map ]);
      }, 3000 );
    }
  };

  // Try once per second to use listchange callback.
  // Stop trying after first success.
  send_listchange = function () {
    listchange_idto = setTimeout( function () {
      if ( callback_map.listchange ) {
        callback_map.listchange([ peopleList ]);
        listchange_idto = undefined;
      }
      else { send_listchange(); }
    }, 1000 );
  };

  // We have to start the process ...
  send_listchange();

  return { emit : emit_sio, on : on_sio };
}());

return { mockSio : mockSio };
}());
```

Add a send_listchange function that emulates the receipt of a listchange message from the backend. Once per second, this method looks for the listchange callback (which the chat object registers only after a user has signed in and joined the chat room). If the callback is found, it is executed using the mock peopleList as its argument, and send_listchange stops polling.

Add this line to start the send_listchange function.

Remove the getPeopleList method since the desired data is now provided by the listchange handler.

Now that we've completed part of the chat object, let's test it as we did with the people object in chapter 5.

6.2.3 Test the chat.join method

Before we continue building our chat object, we should ensure the capabilities we have implemented so far work as expected. First let's load our browser document (spa/spa.html), open the JavaScript console, and ensure that the SPA shows no JavaScript errors. Then, using the console, we may test our methods as shown in listing 6.4. Typed input is shown in **bold**; output is shown in *italics*:

Listing 6.4 Test spa.model.chat.join() without a UI or server

Create a jQuery collection ($t) that isn't attached to the browser document. We'll use this for event testing.

Have the $t jQuery collection subscribe to the spa-login event with a function that prints "Hello!" and the list of arguments to the console.

```
// create a jQuery collection
var $t = $('<div/>');

// Have $t subscribe to global custom events with test functions
```

```
$.gevent.subscribe( $t, 'spa-login', function () {
  console.log( 'Hello!', arguments ); });

$.gevent.subscribe( $t, 'spa-listchange', function () {
  console.log( '*Listchange', arguments ); });

// get the current user object
var currentUser = spa.model.people.get_user();

// confirm this is not yet signed-in
currentUser.get_is_anon();
>> true

// try to join chat without being signed-in
spa.model.chat.join();
>> User must be defined before joining chat

// sign-in, wait 3s. The UI updates too!
spa.model.people.login( 'Fred' );
>> Hello! > [jQuery.Event, Object]

// get the people collection
var peopleDb = spa.model.people.get_db();

// show the names of all people in the collection.
peopleDb().each(function(person, idx){console.log(person.name);});
>> anonymous
>> Fred

// join the chat
spa.model.chat.join();
>> true
// the spa-listchange event should fire almost immediately.
>> *Listchange > [jQuery.Event, Array[1]]

// inspect the user list again. We see the people list has
// been updated to show all online people.
var peopleDb = spa.model.people.get_db();
peopleDb().each(function(person, idx){console.log(person.name);});
>> Betty
>> Fred
>> Mike
>> Pebbles
>> Wilma
```

Have the `$t` jQuery collection subscribe to the `spa-listchange` event with a function that prints "*Listchange" and the list of arguments to the console.

Get the current user object from the `people` object.

Confirm the user isn't yet signed in using the `get_is_anon()` method.

Try to join the chat without signing in. Per our API specification, we're denied.

Sign in as Fred. In the user area in the top-right corner of the browser, you'll see the text proceed from "Please sign-in" to "... processing ..." to "Fred." At the end of sign-in, the `spa-login` event will publish. This invokes the function we subscribed to the `spa-login` event on the `$t` jQuery collection, so we see the "Hello!" message and the list of arguments.

Get the TaffyDB people collection from the `people` object.

Confirm that only Fred and anonymous are in the people collection. This makes sense, as we haven't yet joined the chat.

Join the chat.

Confirm we see a Socket.IO-style array of arguments returned. An updated user list is the first in the argument array.

Less than one second after `join()`, the `spa-listchange` event should publish. This invokes the function we subscribed to the `spa-listchange` event on the `$t` jQuery collection, and so we see the "Hello!" message along with the list of arguments.

Get the updated people list.

Confirm the people list now contains our mock chat-party along with our user, Fred.

We've completed and tested the first installment of the chat object, where we may sign in, join a chat, and inspect the people list. Now we want the chat object to handle sending and receiving messages.

6.2.4 Add messaging to the chat object

Sending and receiving messages aren't quite as simple as they seem. As FedEx will tell you, we have to deal with *logistics*—the management of the transfer and receipt of the message. We'll need to:

- Maintain a record of the *chatee*—the person with whom the user is chatting.

- Send metadata such as the sender ID, name, and the recipient ID along with the message.
- Gracefully handle the condition where a latent connection might result in our user sending a message to an offline person.
- Publish jQuery custom global events when messages are received from the backend so that our jQuery collections may subscribe to these events and have functions act upon them.

First let's update our Model as shown in listing 6.5. Changes are shown in **bold**:

Listing 6.5 Add messaging to the Model–spa/js/spa.model.js

```
...
completeLogin = function ( user_list ) {
  ...
  stateMap.people_cid_map[ user_map._id ] = stateMap.user;
  chat.join();
  $.gevent.publish( 'spa-login', [ stateMap.user ] );
};
...

people = (function () {
  ...
  logout = function () {
    var is_removed, user = stateMap.user;

    chat._leave();
    is_removed    = removePerson( user );
    stateMap.user = stateMap.anon_user;

    $.gevent.publish( 'spa-logout', [ user ] );
    return is_removed;
  };
  ...
}());

// The chat object API
// -------------------
// The chat object is available at spa.model.chat.
// The chat object provides methods and events to manage
// chat messaging. Its public methods include:
//  * join() - joins the chat room. This routine sets up
//    the chat protocol with the backend including publishers
//    for 'spa-listchange' and 'spa-updatechat' global
//    custom events. If the current user is anonymous,
//    join() aborts and returns false.
//  * get_chatee() - return the person object with whom the user
//    is chatting with. If there is no chatee, null is returned.
//  * set_chatee( <person_id> ) - set the chatee to the person
//    identified by person_id. If the person_id does not exist
//    in the people list, the chatee is set to null. If the
//    person requested is already the chatee, it returns false.
```

Have completeLogin method invoke chat.join() so a user will automatically join the chat room once sign-in is complete.

Have the people._logout method invoke chat._leave() so a user will automatically exit the chat room once sign-out is complete.

Add the API docs for get_chatee(), set_chatee(), and send_msg().

Add the API docs for spa-setchatee and spa-updatechat events.

```
//    It publishes a 'spa-setchatee' global custom event.
//  * send_msg( <msg_text> ) - send a message to the chatee.
//    It publishes a 'spa-updatechat' global custom event.
//    If the user is anonymous or the chatee is null, it
//    aborts and returns false.
// ...
//
// jQuery global custom events published by the object include:
// * spa-setchatee - This is published when a new chatee is
//   set. A map of the form:
//     { old_chatee : <old_chatee_person_object>,
//       new_chatee : <new_chatee_person_object>
//     }
//   is provided as data.
//  * spa-listchange - This is published when the list of
//    online people changes in length (i.e. when a person
//    joins or leaves a chat) or when their contents change
//    (i.e. when a person's avatar details change).
//    A subscriber to this event should get the people_db
//    from the people model for the updated data.
// * spa-updatechat - This is published when a new message
//   is received or sent. A map of the form:
//     { dest_id : <chatee_id>,
//       dest_name : <chatee_name>,
//       sender_id : <sender_id>,
//       msg_text : <message_content>
//     }
//   is provided as data.
//
chat = (function () {
  var
    _publish_listchange, _publish_updatechat,
    _update_list, _leave_chat,

    get_chatee, join_chat, send_msg, set_chatee,

    chatee = null;

  // Begin internal methods
  _update_list = function( arg_list ) {
    var i, person_map, make_person_map,
      people_list      = arg_list[ 0 ],
      is_chatee_online = false;

    clearPeopleDb();

    PERSON:
    for ( i = 0; i < people_list.length; i++ ) {
      person_map = people_list[ i ];

      if ( ! person_map.name ) { continue PERSON; }

      // if user defined, update css_map and skip remainder
      if ( stateMap.user && stateMap.user.id === person_map._id ) {
        stateMap.user.css_map = person_map.css_map;
        continue PERSON;
      }
```

Add the is_chatee_online flag.

```
    make_person_map = {
      cid      : person_map._id,
      css_map  : person_map.css_map,
      id       : person_map._id,
      name     : person_map.name
    };

    if ( chatee && chatee.id === make_person_map.id ) {
      is_chatee_online = true;
    }
    makePerson( make_person_map );
  }

  stateMap.people_db.sort( 'name' );
  // If chatee is no longer online, we unset the chatee
  // which triggers the 'spa-setchatee' global event
  if ( chatee && ! is_chatee_online ) { set_chatee('');   }
};

_publish_listchange = function ( arg_list ) {
  _update_list( arg_list );
  $.gevent.publish( 'spa-listchange', [ arg_list ] );
};

_publish_updatechat = function ( arg_list ) {
  var msg_map = arg_list[ 0 ];

  if ( ! chatee ) { set_chatee( msg_map.sender_id ); }
  else if ( msg_map.sender_id !== stateMap.user.id
    && msg_map.sender_id !== chatee.id
  ) { set_chatee( msg_map.sender_id ); }

  $.gevent.publish( 'spa-updatechat', [ msg_map ] );
};
// End internal methods

_leave_chat = function () {
  var sio = isFakeData ? spa.fake.mockSio : spa.data.getSio();
  chatee = null;
  stateMap.is_connected = false;
  if ( sio ) { sio.emit( 'leavechat' ); }
};

get_chatee = function () { return chatee; };

join_chat  = function () {
  var sio;

  if ( stateMap.is_connected ) { return false; }

  if ( stateMap.user.get_is_anon() ) {
    console.warn( 'User must be defined before joining chat');
    return false;
  }

  sio = isFakeData ? spa.fake.mockSio : spa.data.getSio();
  sio.on( 'listchange', _publish_listchange );
  sio.on( 'updatechat', _publish_updatechat );
  stateMap.is_connected = true;
```

Add code to set is_chatee_online flag to true if the chatee person object is found in the updated user list.

Add code to set the chatee person object to null if it's not found in the updated user list.

Create the _publish_updatechat convenience method. This will publish the spa-updatechat event with a map of message details as the data.

Create the get_chatee method to return the chatee person object.

Bind _publish_update chat to handle updatechat messages received from the backend. As a result, an spa-updatechat event is published whenever a message is received.

```
    return true;
  };
  send_msg = function ( msg_text ) {
    var msg_map,
      sio = isFakeData ? spa.fake.mockSio : spa.data.getSio();

    if ( ! sio ) { return false; }
    if ( ! ( stateMap.user && chatee ) ) { return false; }

    msg_map = {
      dest_id   : chatee.id,
      dest_name : chatee.name,
      sender_id : stateMap.user.id,
      msg_text  : msg_text
    };

    // we published updatechat so we can show our outgoing messages
    _publish_updatechat( [ msg_map ] );
    sio.emit( 'updatechat', msg_map );
    return true;
  };

  set_chatee = function ( person_id ) {
    var new_chatee;
    new_chatee = stateMap.people_cid_map[ person_id ];
    if ( new_chatee ) {
      if ( chatee && chatee.id === new_chatee.id ) {
        return false;
      }
    }
    else {
      new_chatee = null;
    }

    $.gevent.publish( 'spa-setchatee',
      { old_chatee : chatee, new_chatee : new_chatee }
    );
    chatee = new_chatee;
    return true;
  };

  return {
    _leave       : _leave_chat,
    get_chatee   : get_chatee,
    join         : join_chat,
    send_msg     : send_msg,
    set_chatee   : set_chatee
  };
}());

initModule = function () {  ...
};

return {
  initModule : initModule,
  chat       : chat,
  people     : people
};
}());
```

Add code to abort sending a message if there's no connection. The logic also aborts if either the user or chatee isn't set.

Create the `send_msg` method to send a text message and associated details.

Add code to construct a map of message and associated details.

Add code to publish `spa-updatechat` events so the user may see their messages in the chat window.

Create the `set_chatee` method to change the `chatee` object to the one provided. If the provided `chatee` is the same as the current one, the code does nothing and returns false.

Add code to publish an `spa-setchattee` event with a map of the `old_chatee` and `new_chatee` as data.

Neatly export our new public methods: `get_chatee`, `send_msg`, and `set_chatee`.

We've completed our second-pass implementation of the chat object, where we added messaging capabilities. As before, we want to check our work before adding more capabilities. In the next section we'll update the Fake module to emulate the server interaction we need.

6.2.5 Update Fake to emulate messaging

Now we need to update the Fake module so it can emulate the server responses we need to test the messaging methods. The changes we need include:

- Emulate the response to an outgoing updatechat message by responding with an incoming updatechat message from the current chatee.
- Emulate an unsolicited incoming updatechat message coming from the Wilma person.
- Emulate the response to an outgoing leavechat message. This message is sent when the user signs out. We can unbind chat message callbacks at this point.

Let's update Fake to employ these changes as shown in listing 6.6. Changes are shown in **bold**:

Listing 6.6 Add mock messages to Fake—spa/js/spa.fake.js

```
...
  mockSio = (function () {
    var
      on_sio, emit_sio, emit_mock_msg,
      send_listchange, listchange_idto,
      callback_map = {};

    on_sio = function ( msg_type, callback ) {
      callback_map[ msg_type ] = callback;
    };

    emit_sio = function ( msg_type, data ) {
      var person_map;

      // Respond to 'adduser' event with 'userupdate'
      // callback after a 3s delay.
      if ( msg_type === 'adduser' && callback_map.userupdate ) {
        setTimeout( function () {
          person_map = {
            _id     : makeFakeId(),
            name    : data.name,
            css_map : data.css_map
          };
          peopleList.push( person_map );
          callback_map.userupdate([ person_map ]);
        }, 3000 );
      }

      // Respond to 'updatechat' event with an 'updatechat'
      // callback after a 2s delay. Echo back user info.
      if ( msg_type === 'updatechat' && callback_map.updatechat ) {
        setTimeout( function () {
```

Add declaration for mock message function, emit_mock_msg.

Create code to respond to a sent message with a mock response after a 2 second delay.

```
          var user = spa.model.people.get_user();
          callback_map.updatechat([{
            dest_id : user.id,
            dest_name : user.name,
            sender_id : data.dest_id,
            msg_text : 'Thanks for the note, ' + user.name
          }]);
        }, 2000);
      }

      if ( msg_type === 'leavechat' ) {
        // reset login status
        delete callback_map.listchange;
        delete callback_map.updatechat;

        if ( listchange_idto ) {
          clearTimeout( listchange_idto );
          listchange_idto = undefined;
        }
        send_listchange();
      }
    };

    emit_mock_msg = function () {
      setTimeout( function () {
        var user = spa.model.people.get_user();
        if ( callback_map.updatechat ) {
          callback_map.updatechat([{
            dest_id : user.id,
            dest_name : user.name,
            sender_id : 'id_04',
            msg_text : 'Hi there ' + user.name + '! Wilma here.'
          }]);
        }
        else { emit_mock_msg(); }
      }, 8000 );
    };

    // Try once per second to use listchange callback.
    // Stop trying after first success.
    send_listchange = function () {
      listchange_idto = setTimeout( function () {
        if ( callback_map.listchange ) {
          callback_map.listchange([ peopleList ]);
          emit_mock_msg();
          listchange_idto = undefined;
        }
        else { send_listchange(); }
      }, 1000 );
    };

    // We have to start the process ...
    send_listchange();

    return { emit : emit_sio, on : on_sio };
  }());

  return { mockSio : mockSio };
}());
```

Create code to clear the callbacks used by chat if `leavechat` message is received. This means the user has signed out.

Add code to try to send a mock message to the signed-in user once every 8 seconds. This will succeed only after a user is signed in when the `updatechat` callback is set. On success, the routine does not call itself again and therefore no further attempts to send a mock message will be made.

Add the code to start trying to send a mock message after the user signs in.

Now that we have the chat object and Fake updated, we can test messaging.

6.2.6 Test chat messaging

Now we can test setting the chatee, sending messages, and receiving them. Let's load our browser document (spa/spa.html) and open the JavaScript console and ensure there are no errors. We can then test as shown in listing 6.7. Typed input is shown in **bold**; output is shown in *italics*:

Listing 6.7 Test the exchange of messages

```
// create a jQuery collection
var $t = $('<div/>');

// bind functions to test global events
$.gevent.subscribe( $t, 'spa-login', function( event, user ) {
  console.log('Hello!', user.name); });

$.gevent.subscribe( $t, 'spa-updatechat', function( event, chat_map ) {
  console.log( 'Chat message:', chat_map);
});

$.gevent.subscribe( $t, 'spa-setchatee',
  function( event, chatee_map ) {
  console.log( 'Chatee change:', chatee_map);
});

$.gevent.subscribe( $t, 'spa-listchange',
  function( event, changed_list ) {
  console.log( '*Listchange:', changed_list );
});

// sign-in, wait 3s
spa.model.people.login( 'Fanny' );
>> Hello! Fanny
>> *Listchange: [Array[5]]

// try to send a message without setting chatee
spa.model.chat.send_msg( 'Hi Pebbles!' );
>> false

// wait about 8 seconds for a test message to come in
>> Chatee change: Object {old_chatee: null, new_chatee: Object}
>> Chat message: Object {dest_id: "id_5", dest_name: "Fanny",
>> sender_id: "id_04", msg_text: "Hi there Fanny! Wilma here."}
```

Create a jQuery collection ($t) that isn't attached to the browser document. We'll use this for event testing.

Have the $t jQuery collection subscribe to the spa-login event with a function that prints "Hello!" and the user name to the console.

Have the $t jQuery collection subscribe to the spa-updatechat event with a function that prints "Chat message:" and the chat_map.

Have the $t jQuery collection subscribe to the spa-setchatee event with a function that prints "Chatee change:" and the chatee_map.

Have the $t jQuery collection subscribe to the spa-listchange event with a function that prints "*Listchange:" and the changed_list.

Sign in as Fanny.

Three seconds later an spa-login event is published and this invokes the function subscribed on $t for the event.

An spa-listchange event is also published and this invokes the function subscribed on $t for the event.

This method returns false because a we haven't set a recipient yet.

Try to send a message without setting a chatee. Do this within 8 seconds, before we receive a message from Wilma.

In a few seconds an spa-setchatee event is published and this invokes the function subscribed on $t for the event.

```
// receipt of a message sets the chatee
spa.model.chat.send_msg( 'What is up, tricks?' );
>> Chat message: Object {dest_id: "id_04", dest_name: "Wilma",
>>   sender_id: "id_5", msg_text: "What is up tricks?"}
>> true

>> Chat message: Object {dest_id: "id_5", dest_name: "Fanny",
>> sender_id: "id_04", msg_text: "Thanks for the note, Fanny"}

// Set the chatee to Pebbles
spa.model.chat.set_chatee( 'id_03' );
>> Chatee change: Object {old_chatee: Object, new_chatee: Object}

>> true

// Send a message
spa.model.chat.send_msg( 'Hi Pebbles!' )
>> Chat message: Object {dest_id: "id_03", dest_name: "Pebbles",
>>   sender_id: "id_5", msg_text: "Hi Pebbles!"}
>> true
>> Chat message: Object {dest_id: "id_5", dest_nam: "Fanny",
>>   sender_id: "id_03", msg_text: "Thanks for the note, Fanny"}
```

An spa-updatechat event is published, which invokes the function subscribed on $t for the event.

Send a "What is up, tricks?" message to the chatee. This is the last person who sent to the user.

This method returns true on success.

We see a response to our message and an spa-updatechat event is published and this invokes the function subscribed on $t for the event.

Set the chatee to the person with ID id_03.

Confirm the set_chatee method returns true on success.

The spa-setchatee event is published.

Send a "Hi Pebbles!" message to our current chatee, Pebbles.

This method returns true on success.

Another automated response is received.

The spa-updatechat message is published, which invokes the function subscribed on $t.

Our chat object is nearly complete. All we need now is to add the Avatar support. Once we have accomplished that, we'll update the user interface.

6.3 Add Avatar support to the Model

The Avatar capability is relatively easy to add because we can build on the messaging infrastructure of the chat object. The primary reason we present this capability is to show other uses for near-real-time messaging. The fact that it shows well at conferences is just icing on the cake. First we'll update the Model.

6.3.1 Add Avatar support to the chat object

The changes we require for the chat object to support avatars are relatively modest. We only need to add the update_avatar method, which will send an updateavatar message to the backend with a map describing which avatar changed and how. We expect the backend to send a listchange message when an avatar is updated, and the code to handle *that* message is already written and tested.

Let's update the Model as shown in listing 6.8. Changes are shown in **bold**:

Listing 6.8 Update the Model to support avatars—spa/js/spa.model.js

```
...
  //      If the user is anonymous or the chatee is null, it
  //      aborts and returns false.
  //    * update_avatar( <update_avtr_map> ) - send the
  //      update_avtr_map to the backend. This results in an
  //      an 'spa-listchange' event which publishes the updated
  //      people list and avatar information (the css_map in the
  //      person objects). The update_avtr_map must
  //      have the form { person_id : person_id, css_map : css_map }
  //
  // jQuery global custom events published by the object include:

...
  chat = (function () {
    var
      _publish_listchange, _publish_updatechat,
      _update_list, _leave_chat,

      get_chatee, join_chat, send_msg,
      set_chatee, update_avatar,

      chatee = null;
...

// avatar_update_map should have the form:
// { person_id : <string>, css_map : {
//   top : <int>, left : <int>,
//   'background-color' : <string>
// }};
//
update_avatar = function ( avatar_update_map ) {
  var sio = isFakeData ? spa.fake.mockSio : spa.data.getSio();
  if ( sio ) {
    sio.emit( 'updateavatar', avatar_update_map );
  }
};

    return {
      _leave        : _leave_chat,
      get_chatee    : get_chatee,
      join          : join_chat,
      send_msg      : send_msg,
      set_chatee    : set_chatee,
      update_avatar : update_avatar
    };
  }());

...
```

Annotations: **Add documentation from our API specification.** (points to the `update_avatar` documentation lines) **Declare the `update_avatar` method variable.** **Create the `update_avatar` method. We send an `updateavatar` message to the backend with a map as data.** **Add `update_avatar` to the list of exported public methods.**

We've completed adding all the methods and events we designed for the `chat` object. In the next section we'll update the Fake module to emulate the server interaction to support avatars.

6.3.2 Modify Fake to emulate avatars

Our next step is to modify the Fake module to support sending an `updateavatar` message to the backend whenever the user drops an avatar to a new location or clicks on the avatar to change its color. When Fake receives this message, it should:

- Simulate sending an `updateavatar` message to the server.
- Simulate receiving a `listchange` message from the server with an updated people list.
- Execute the callback registered for the `listchange` message, providing it the updated people list.

These three steps can be accomplished as shown in listing 6.9. Changes are shown in **bold**:

Listing 6.9 Modify Fake to support avatars—spa/js/spa.fake.js

```
...
  emit_sio = function ( msg_type, data ) {
    var person_map, i;
...
    if ( msg_type === 'leavechat' ) {
      // reset login status
      delete callback_map.listchange;
      delete callback_map.updatechat;

      if ( listchange_idto ) {
        clearTimeout( listchange_idto );
        listchange_idto = undefined;
      }
      send_listchange();
    }

    // simulate send of 'updateavatar' message and data to server
    if ( msg_type === 'updateavatar' && callback_map.listchange ) {
      // simulate receipt of 'listchange' message
      for ( i = 0; i < peopleList.length; i++ ) {
        if ( peopleList[ i ]._id === data.person_id ) {
          peopleList[ i ].css_map = data.css_map;
          break;
        }
      }
      // execute callback for the 'listchange' message
      callback_map.listchange([ peopleList ]);
    }
  };
...
```

Annotations:
- Declare the `i` loop variable.
- Create a handler for receipt of an `updateavatar` message.
- Find the `person` object specified by the data from the `updateavatar` message and change its `css_map` property.
- Execute the callback registered for the `listchange` message.

Now that we have the `chat` object and Fake updated, we can test avatars.

6.3.3 Test avatar support

This is our final bit of Model testing. Again, let's load our browser document (spa/spa.html) and ensure the SPA works as before. We'll open the JavaScript console and test our `update_avatar` method as shown in listing 6.10. Typed input is shown in **bold**; output is shown in *italics*:

Listing 6.10 Test the `update_avatar` method

```
// create a jQuery collection
var $t = $('<div/>');

// bind functions to test global events
$.gevent.subscribe( $t, 'spa-login', function( event, user ) {
  console.log('Hello!', user.name); });

$.gevent.subscribe( $t, 'spa-listchange',
  function( event, changed_list ) {
  console.log( '*Listchange:', changed_list );
});

// sign-in, wait 3s
spa.model.people.login( 'Jessy' );
>> Hello! Jessy
>> *Listchange: [Array[5]]

// get the Pebbles person
var person = spa.model.people.get_by_cid( 'id_03' );

// inspect avatar information
JSON.stringify( person.css_map );
>> "{"top":100,"left":20,
>> "background-color":"rgb( 128, 192, 192)"}"

// update the avatar information
spa.model.chat.update_avatar({
  person_id : 'id_03', css_map : {} });
>> *Listchange: [Array[5]]

// get Pebbles again
person = spa.model.people.get_by_cid( 'id_03' );

// and now inspect
JSON.stringify( person.css_map );
>> {}
```

Annotations:

- Create a jQuery collection (`$t`) that isn't attached to the browser document. We'll use this for event testing.
- Have the `$t` jQuery collection subscribe to the `spa-login` event with a function that prints to the console.
- Have the `$t` jQuery collection subscribe to the `spa-listchange` event with a function that prints "*Listchange:" and the `changed_list`.
- Sign in as Jessy.
- Three seconds later an `spa-login` event is published and this invokes the function subscribed on `$t` for the event.
- An `spa-listchange` event is also published, which invokes the associated function subscribed on `$t` for the event.
- Get the `person` object for ID `id_03`, Pebbles.
- Inspect the avatar information for the Pebbles person.
- Use the `update_avatar` method to change the `css_map` for the Pebbles `person` object.
- Confirm the `update_avatar` method publishes an `spa-listchange` event, which invokes the function subscribed on `$t` for the event.
- The updated `css_map` for the Pebbles `person` object.

We've completed the `chat` object. As with the `people` object from chapter 5, the testing is reassuring, and we can add to a test suite for use without a server or browser.

6.3.4 Test-driven development

All those test-driven development (TDD) freaks out there are probably looking at all this manual testing and thinking "Gosh, why not just put this into a test suite that can run automatically?" Being aspiring freaks ourselves, we can—and we did. Check out appendix B to see how one can use Node.js to automate this process.

We actually found a few issues as the result of the test suite. Most were specific to testing, so we will leave *those* to the appendix. But there were two bona fide bugs we needed to fix: our sign-out mechanism wasn't quite right, as it wasn't clearing the user list properly, and the `chatee` object wasn't being updated properly after an `spa.model.chat.update_avatar` method call. Let's fix both of those now as shown in listing 6.11. Changes are shown in **bold**:

Listing 6.11 Fix sign-out and chatee object update—spa/js/spa.model.js

```
...
  people = (function () {
    ...
    logout = function () {
      var user = stateMap.user;

      chat._leave();
      stateMap.user = stateMap.anon_user;
      clearPeopleDb();

      $.gevent.publish( 'spa-logout', [ user ] );
    };
    ...
  }());

  chat = (function () {
    ...
    // Begin internal methods
    _update_list = function( arg_list ) {
      var i, person_map, make_person_map, person,
        people_list      = arg_list[ 0 ],
        is_chatee_online = false;

      clearPeopleDb();

      PERSON:
      for ( i = 0; i < people_list.length; i++ ) {
        person_map = people_list[ i ];

        if ( ! person_map.name ) { continue PERSON; }

        // if user defined, update css_map and skip remainder
        if ( stateMap.user && stateMap.user.id === person_map._id ) {
          stateMap.user.css_map = person_map.css_map;
          continue PERSON;
        }

        make_person_map = {
          cid     : person_map._id,
          css_map : person_map.css_map,
          id      : person_map._id,
          name    : person_map.name
        };
        person = makePerson( make_person_map );
```

Remove the `is_removed` variable.

Clear the people Taffy collection on logout.

Declare the `person` object.

Assign the results of `makePerson` to the `person` object.

```
      if ( chatee && chatee.id === make_person_map.id ) {
        is_chatee_online = true;
        chatee = person;
      }
    }

    stateMap.people_db.sort( 'name' );

    // If chatee is no longer online, we unset the chatee
    // which triggers the 'spa-setchatee' global event
    if ( chatee && ! is_chatee_online ) { set_chatee(''); }
  };
  ...
}());
...
```

If we find the chatee, update it to the new `person` object.

This is a good point to take a break. In the remainder of the chapter we'll return to the UI and finish the Chat feature module using the `chat` and `people` object APIs provided by the Model. We'll also create an Avatar feature module.

6.4 Complete the Chat feature module

In this section we'll update the Chat feature module shown in figure 6.3. We can now take advantage of the Model's `chat` and `people` objects to provide a simulated chat experience. Let's revisit the Chat UI we mocked up earlier and decide how to modify it to work with the `chat` object. Figure 6.4 shows what we'd like to accomplish. We can distill this mockup into a list of capabilities that we'd like to add to the Chat feature module. These include:

- Change the design of the chat slider to include the people list.
- When the user signs in, perform the following actions: join the chat, open the chat slider, change the chat slider title, and display the list of online people.

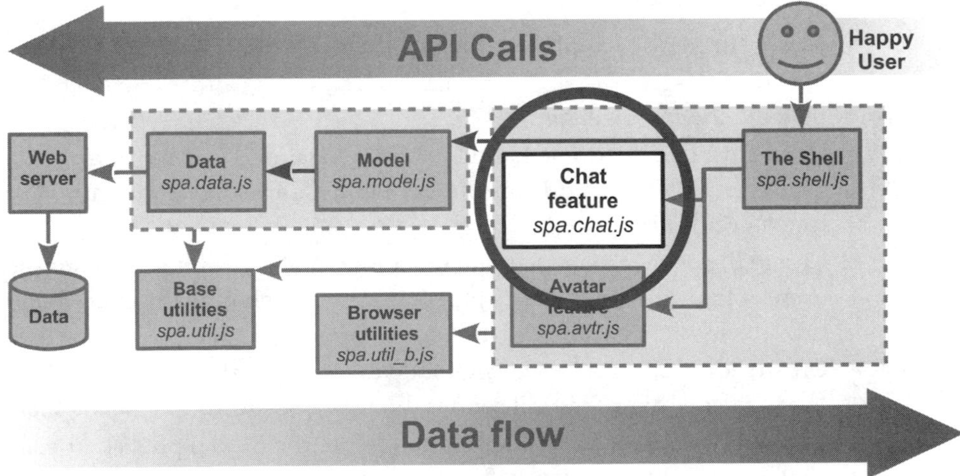

Figure 6.3 The Chat feature module in our SPA architecture

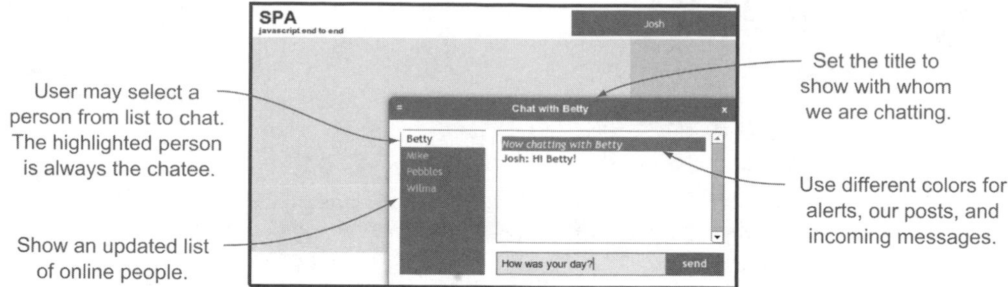

Figure 6.4 What we want in the Chat UI

- Update the online people list whenever it changes.
- Highlight the chatee in the online people list and update the display whenever the list changes.
- Empower the user to send a message and select a chatee from the online people list.
- Display messages from the user, other people, and the system in the message log. These messages should all look different, and the message log should scroll smoothly from the bottom up.
- Revise the interface to support touch controls.
- When the user signs out, perform the following actions: change the title of the chat slider, erase the message log, and retract the slider.

Let's start by updating the JavaScript.

6.4.1 *Update the Chat JavaScript*

We need to update the Chat JavaScript to add the capabilities we just discussed. The primary changes include:

- Revise the HTML template to include the people list.
- Create the `scrollChat`, `writeChat`, `writeAlert`, and `clearChat` methods to manage the message log.
- Create user input event handlers, `onTapList` and `onSubmitMsg`, to allow the user to select a chatee from the people list and send a message. Ensure that touch events are supported.
- Create the `onSetchatee` method to handle the Model-published `spa-setchatee` event. This will change the display of the chatee, change the chat slider title, and provide a system alert in the message window.
- Create the `onListchange` method to handle the Model-published `spa-listchange` event. This will render the people list with the chatee highlighted.
- Create the `onUpdatechat` method to handle the Model-published `spa-updatechat` event. This will display new messages sent by the user, the server, or other people.

- Create the onLogin and onLogout methods to handle the Model-published spa-login and spa-logout events. The onLogin handler will open the chat slider when a user signs in. The onLogout handler will clear the message log, reset the title, and close the chat slider.
- Subscribe to all Model-published events and then bind all user input events.

> **About those event handler names**
>
> We know some of you out there are thinking "Is there a reason why the method name onSetchatee isn't onSetChatee?" Well, there is.
>
> Our naming convention for event handlers is on<Event>[<Modifier>], where the *Modifier* is an option. This usually works great, as most events are single syllables. Examples include onTap or onTapAvatar. This convention is handy so we can trace the handler precisely to the *event* that it's handling.
>
> Like all conventions, there are edge cases that can get confusing. In the case of onListchange, for example, we've followed our convention: the event name is listchange, *not* listChange. Thus onListchange is correct, whereas onListChange is not. The same holds true for onSetchatee and onUpdatechat.

Let's update the JavaScript file as shown in listing 6.12. Changes are shown in **bold**:

Listing 6.12 Update the Chat JavaScript file—spa/js/spa.chat.js

```
...
/*global $, spa */
spa.chat = (function () {
  'use strict';
  //---------------- BEGIN MODULE SCOPE VARIABLES --------------
  var
    configMap = {
      main_html : String()
        + '<div class="spa-chat">'
          + '<div class="spa-chat-head">'
            + '<div class="spa-chat-head-toggle">+</div>'
            + '<div class="spa-chat-head-title">'
              + 'Chat'
            + '</div>'
          + '</div>'
          + '<div class="spa-chat-closer">x</div>'
          + '<div class="spa-chat-sizer">'
            + '<div class="spa-chat-list">'
              + '<div class="spa-chat-list-box"></div>'
            + '</div>'
            + '<div class="spa-chat-msg">'
              + '<div class="spa-chat-msg-log"></div>'
              + '<div class="spa-chat-msg-in">'
                + '<form class="spa-chat-msg-form">'
```

Add the use strict pragma.

Removed getComputedStyle from the global symbol list. This was used by getEmSize, which has been moved to our browser utilities module.

Update the slider template to include the people list and other refinements.

```
                + '<input type="text"/>'
                + '<input type="submit" style="display:none"/>'
                + '<div class="spa-chat-msg-send">'
                  + 'send'
                + '</div>'
              + '</form>'
            + '</div>'
          + '</div>'
        + '</div>'
      + '</div>',
    ...
    slider_closed_em     : 2,
    slider_opened_title  : 'Tap to close',
    slider_closed_title  : 'Tap to open',
    slider_opened_min_em : 10,
    ...
  },
  ...
  setJqueryMap,  setPxSizes,   scrollChat,
  writeChat,     writeAlert,   clearChat,
  setSliderPosition,
  onTapToggle,   onSubmitMsg,  onTapList,
  onSetchatee,   onUpdatechat, onListchange,
  onLogin,       onLogout,
  configModule,  initModule,
  removeSlider,  handleResize;
//----------------- END MODULE SCOPE VARIABLES ---------------

//------------------- BEGIN UTILITY METHODS ------------------
//-------------------- END UTILITY METHODS -------------------

//--------------------- BEGIN DOM METHODS --------------------
// Begin DOM method /setJqueryMap/
setJqueryMap = function () {
  var
    $append_target = stateMap.$append_target,
    $slider        = $append_target.find( '.spa-chat' );

  jqueryMap = {
    $slider   : $slider,
    $head     : $slider.find( '.spa-chat-head' ),
    $toggle   : $slider.find( '.spa-chat-head-toggle' ),
    $title    : $slider.find( '.spa-chat-head-title' ),
    $sizer    : $slider.find( '.spa-chat-sizer' ),
    $list_box : $slider.find( '.spa-chat-list-box' ),
    $msg_log  : $slider.find( '.spa-chat-msg-log' ),
    $msg_in   : $slider.find( '.spa-chat-msg-in' ),
    $input    : $slider.find( '.spa-chat-msg-in input[type=text]'),
    $send     : $slider.find( '.spa-chat-msg-send' ),
    $form     : $slider.find( '.spa-chat-msg-form' ),
    $window   : $(window)
  };
};
// End DOM method /setJqueryMap/

// Begin DOM method /setPxSizes/
setPxSizes = function () {
```

Change the `click` to `tap` so that those with touch devices understand.

Declare the new methods to handle user and Model events.

Remove the `getEmSize` method, as it's now available from our browser utilities (`spa.util_b.js`)

Update the jQuery collection cache for the modified chat slider.

```
  var px_per_em, window_height_em, opened_height_em;

  px_per_em = spa.util_b.getEmSize( jqueryMap.$slider.get(0) );
  window_height_em = Math.floor(
    ( jqueryMap.$window.height() / px_per_em ) + 0.5
  );
  ...
}
...
// Begin public method /setSliderPosition/
...
setSliderPosition = function ( position_type, callback ) {
  var
    height_px, animate_time, slider_title, toggle_text;

  // position type of 'opened' is not allowed for anon user;
  // therefore we simply return false; the shell will fix the
  // uri and try again.
  if ( position_type === 'opened'
    && configMap.people_model.get_user().get_is_anon()
  ){ return false; }

  // return true if slider already in requested position
  if ( stateMap.position_type === position_type ){
    if ( position_type === 'opened' ) {
      jqueryMap.$input.focus();
    }
    return true;
  }

  // prepare animate parameters
  switch ( position_type ){
    case 'opened' :
      ...
      jqueryMap.$input.focus();
    break;
    ...
  }
  ...
};
// End public DOM method /setSliderPosition/

// Begin private DOM methods to manage chat message
scrollChat = function() {
  var $msg_log = jqueryMap.$msg_log;
  $msg_log.animate(
    { scrollTop : $msg_log.prop( 'scrollHeight' )
      - $msg_log.height()
    },
    150
  );
};

writeChat = function ( person_name, text, is_user ) {
  var msg_class = is_user
    ? 'spa-chat-msg-log-me' : 'spa-chat-msg-log-msg';

  jqueryMap.$msg_log.append(
```

Annotations:

- Use `getEmSize` from the browser utilities.
- Get the jQuery collection for the `window` from the `jqueryMap` cache.
- Add code to refuse to open the slider if user is anonymous. The Shell callback will adjust the URI accordingly.
- Add code to focus on the input box when the slider is opened.
- Begin the section for all DOM methods used to manipulate the message log.
- Create the `scrollChat` method to provide smooth scrolling of the message log as text appears.
- Create the `writeChat` method to append to the message log. If the originator is the user, use a different style. Be sure to encode the HTML output.

```
      '<div class="' + msg_class + '">'
      + spa.util_b.encodeHtml(person_name) + ': '
      + spa.util_b.encodeHtml(text) + '</div>'
    );

    scrollChat();

  };

  writeAlert = function ( alert_text ) {
    jqueryMap.$msg_log.append(
      '<div class="spa-chat-msg-log-alert">'
        + spa.util_b.encodeHtml(alert_text)
      + '</div>'
    );
    scrollChat();
  };

  clearChat = function () { jqueryMap.$msg_log.empty(); };
  // End private DOM methods to manage chat message
  //--------------------- END DOM METHODS --------------------

  //------------------- BEGIN EVENT HANDLERS -------------------
  onTapToggle = function ( event ) {
    ...
  };

  onSubmitMsg = function ( event ) {
    var msg_text = jqueryMap.$input.val();
    if ( msg_text.trim() === '' ) { return false; }
    configMap.chat_model.send_msg( msg_text );
    jqueryMap.$input.focus();
    jqueryMap.$send.addClass( 'spa-x-select' );
    setTimeout(
      function () { jqueryMap.$send.removeClass( 'spa-x-select' ); },
      250
    );
    return false;
  };

  onTapList = function ( event ) {
    var $tapped = $( event.elem_target ), chatee_id;
    if ( ! $tapped.hasClass('spa-chat-list-name') ) { return false; }

    chatee_id = $tapped.attr( 'data-id' );
    if ( ! chatee_id ) { return false; }

    configMap.chat_model.set_chatee( chatee_id );
    return false;
  };

  onSetchatee = function ( event, arg_map ) {
    var
      new_chatee = arg_map.new_chatee,
      old_chatee = arg_map.old_chatee;

    jqueryMap.$input.focus();
    if ( ! new_chatee ) {
      if ( old_chatee ) {
```

Create the `writeAlert` method to append system alerts to the message log. Be sure to encode the HTML output.

End the section for all DOM methods used to manipulate the message log.

Create the `clearChat` method to clear the message log.

Place user event handlers at the top of this section and place the Model event handlers at the bottom.

Rename `onClickToggle` event handler to `onTapToggle`.

Create the `onSubmitMsg` event handler for a user-generated event when submitting a message to send. Use the `model.chat.send_msg` method to send the message.

Create the `onTapList` handler for a user-generated event when they click or tap on a person name. Use the `model.chat.set_chatee` method to set the chatee.

Create the `onSetchatee` event handler for the Model-published event `spa-setchatee`. This handler selects the new chatee and deselects the old one. It also changes the chat slider title and notifies the user that the chatee has changed.

```
      writeAlert( old_chatee.name + ' has left the chat' );
    }
    else {
      writeAlert( 'Your friend has left the chat' );
    }
    jqueryMap.$title.text( 'Chat' );
    return false;
  }

  jqueryMap.$list_box
    .find( '.spa-chat-list-name' )
    .removeClass( 'spa-x-select' )
    .end()
    .find( '[data-id=' + arg_map.new_chatee.id + ']' )
    .addClass( 'spa-x-select' );

  writeAlert( 'Now chatting with ' + arg_map.new_chatee.name );
  jqueryMap.$title.text( 'Chat with ' + arg_map.new_chatee.name );
  return true;
};

onListchange = function ( event ) {
  var
    vlist_html = String(),
    people_db = configMap.people_model.get_db(),
    chatee = configMap.chat_model.get_chatee();

  people_db().each( function ( person, idx ) {
    var select_class = '';

    if ( person.get_is_anon() || person.get_is_user()
    ) { return true;}

    if ( chatee && chatee.id === person.id ) {
      select_class=' spa-x-select';
    }
    list_html
      += '<div class="spa-chat-list-name'
      + select_class + '" data-id="' + person.id + '">'
      + spa.util_b.encodeHtml( person.name ) + '</div>';
  });

  if ( ! list_html ) {
    list_html = String()
      + '<div class="spa-chat-list-note">'
      + 'To chat alone is the fate of all great souls...<br><br>'
      + 'No one is online'
      + '</div>';
    clearChat();
  }
  // jqueryMap.$list_box.html( list_html );
  jqueryMap.$list_box.html( list_html );
};

onUpdatechat = function ( event, msg_map ) {
  var
    is_user,
    sender_id = msg_map.sender_id,
```

Create the `onListchange` event handler for the Model-published event `spa-listchange`. This handler gets the current people collection and renders the people list, making sure the chatee is highlighted if defined.

Create the `onUpdatechat` event handler for the Model-published event `spa-updatechat`. This handler updates the display of the message log. If the originator of the message is the user, it clears the input area and refocus. It also sets the chatee to the sender of the message.

```
      msg_text = msg_map.msg_text,
      chatee = configMap.chat_model.get_chatee() || {},
      sender = configMap.people_model.get_by_cid( sender_id );

    if ( ! sender ) {
      writeAlert( msg_text );
      return false;
    }

    is_user = sender.get_is_user();

    if ( ! ( is_user || sender_id === chatee.id ) ) {
      configMap.chat_model.set_chatee( sender_id );
    }

    writeChat( sender.name, msg_text, is_user );

    if ( is_user ) {
      jqueryMap.$input.val( '' );
      jqueryMap.$input.focus();
    }
  };

  onLogin = function ( event, login_user ) {
    configMap.set_chat_anchor( 'opened' );
  };

  onLogout = function ( event, logout_user ) {
    configMap.set_chat_anchor( 'closed' );
    jqueryMap.$title.text( 'Chat' );
    clearChat();
  };

  //------------------- END EVENT HANDLERS ------------------
...
  initModule = function ( $append_target ) {
    var $list_box;

    // load chat slider html and jquery cache
    stateMap.$append_target = $append_target;
    $append_target.append( configMap.main_html );
    setJqueryMap();
    setPxSizes();

    // initialize chat slider to default title and state
    jqueryMap.$toggle.prop( 'title', configMap.slider_closed_title );
    stateMap.position_type = 'closed';

    // Have $list_box subscribe to jQuery global events
    $list_box = jqueryMap.$list_box;
    $.gevent.subscribe( $list_box, 'spa-listchange', onListchange );
    $.gevent.subscribe( $list_box, 'spa-setchatee',   onSetchatee );
    $.gevent.subscribe( $list_box, 'spa-updatechat', onUpdatechat );
    $.gevent.subscribe( $list_box, 'spa-login',           onLogin );
    $.gevent.subscribe( $list_box, 'spa-logout',         onLogout );

    // bind user input events
    jqueryMap.$head.bind(     'utap', onTapToggle );
    jqueryMap.$list_box.bind( 'utap', onTapList   );
    jqueryMap.$send.bind(     'utap', onSubmitMsg );
```

Create the `onLogin` event handler for the Model-published event `spa-login`. This handler opens the chat slider.

Create the `onLogout` event handler for the Model-published event `spa-logout`. This handler clears the chat slider message log, resets the chat slider title, and closes the chat slider.

Modify `initModule` to append the updated slider template to the container specified by the caller.

Subscribe to all Model-published events first.

Bind all user input events next. Binding before subscribing could result in a race condition

```
    jqueryMap.$form.bind(    'submit', onSubmitMsg );
  };
  // End public method /initModule/
  ...
```

Template systems and you

Our SPA uses simple string concatenation to generate HTML, which is perfectly acceptable for our purposes. But there comes a time when we require more sophisticated HTML generation. That's when it's time to consider a template system.

Template systems convert data into display elements. We can divide template systems broadly by the language the developer uses to direct element generation. The *Embedded style* allows us to embed the host language—in our case, JavaScript—directly in the template. The *Toolkit style* provides a domain-specific template language (DSL) independent of the host language.

We don't recommend use of any *Embedded style* systems because they make it far too easy to intermingle business logic with display logic. The most popular JavaScript *Embedded style* system is probably provided by *underscore.js*'s *template* method, but there are many others.

We've noticed that *Toolkit style* systems in other languages have tended to become preferred over time. This is probably because these systems tend to encourage clean segregation of display and business logic. Many good *Toolkit style* template systems are available for SPAs. At the time of this writing, popular and well-tested Toolkit style template systems include *Handlebars*, *Dust*, and *Mustache*. We feel they're all worthy of your consideration.

Now that we have the JavaScript in place, let's revise the stylesheets to match.

6.4.2 *Update the stylesheets*

We now will update the stylesheets for our enhanced interface. First we wish to update our root stylesheet to prevent selection of text on most elements. This removes an annoying user experience that's especially noticeable on touch devices. The update is shown in listing 6.13. Changes are shown in **bold**:

Listing 6.13 Update the root stylesheet—spa/css/spa.css

```
...
/** Begin reset */
  ...
  h1,h2,h3,h4,h5,h6,p { margin-bottom : 6pt; }
  ol,ul,dl { list-style-position : inside;}

  * {
    -webkit-user-select : none;
    -khtml-user-select  : none;
    -moz-user-select    : -moz-none;
```

Add a selector that prevents text selection for all elements. We really look forward to the day when we can drop all these vendor prefixes like `-moz` or `-ms` or `-webkit`. This change would be one-sixth the size if we could!

```
    -o-user-select      : none;
    -ms-user-select     : none;
    user-select         : none;

    -webkit-user-drag : none;
    -moz-user-drag    : none;
    user-drag         : none;

    -webkit-tap-highlight-color : transparent;
    -webkit-touch-callout       : none;
  }

  input, textarea, .spa-x-user-select {
    -webkit-user-select : text;
    -khtml-user-select  : text;
    -moz-user-select    : text;
    -o-user-select      : text;
    -ms-user-select     : text;
    user-select         : text;
  }
/** End reset */
...
```

Add a selector that makes an exception for input fields, text areas, or any element that has an `spa-x-user-select` class.

We now need to update our Chat stylesheet. The primary changes include:

- Style an online people list to be shown on the left side of the slider.
- Make the slider wider to accommodate the people list.
- Style the message window.
- Remove all `spa-chat-box*` and `spa-chat-msgs*` selectors.
- Add styles for messages received from the user, the chatee, and the system.

These updates are shown in listing 6.14. Changes are shown in **bold**:

Listing 6.14 Update the Chat stylesheet—spa/css/spa.chat.css

```
...
.spa-chat {
  ...
  right         : 0;
  width         : 32em;
  height        : 2em;
  ...
}
...
.spa-chat-sizer {
  position : absolute;
  top      : 2em;
  left     : 0;
  right    : 0;
}
.spa-chat-list {
  position : absolute;
  top      : 0;
  left     : 0;
  bottom   : 0;
```

Make the chat slider class 10em wider to accommodate the people list.

Create a class to style the people list container on the left one-third of the chat slider.

```
  width : 10em;
}

.spa-chat-msg {
  position : absolute;
  top      : 0;
  left     : 10em;
  bottom   : 0;
  right    : 0;
}

.spa-chat-msg-log,
.spa-chat-list-box {
  position   : absolute;
  top        : 1em;
  overflow-x : hidden;
}

.spa-chat-msg-log {
  left       : 0em;
  right      : 1em;
  bottom     : 4em;
  padding    : 0.5em;
  border     : thin solid #888;
  overflow-y : scroll;
}

.spa-chat-msg-log-msg {
  background-color : #eee;
}

.spa-chat-msg-log-me {
  font-weight : 800;
  color       : #484;
}

.spa-chat-msg-log-alert {
  font-style : italic;
  background : #a88;
  color      : #fff;
}

.spa-chat-list-box {
  left             : 1em;
  right            : 1em;
  bottom           : 1em;
  overflow-y       : auto;
  border-width     : thin 0 thin thin;
  border-style     : solid;
  border-color     : #888;
  background-color : #888;
  color            : #ddd;
  border-radius    : 0.5em 0 0 0;
}

.spa-chat-list-name, .spa-chat-list-note {
  width   : 100%;
  padding : 0.1em 0.5em;
```

Create a class to style the message container on the right two-thirds of the chat slider. (`.spa-chat-msg`)

Create common rules to style both the message log container and the people list container. (`.spa-chat-msg-log, .spa-chat-list-box`)

Add rules to style the message log container. (`.spa-chat-msg-log`)

Create a class to style normal messages. (`.spa-chat-msg-log-msg`)

Create a class to style messages sent by the user. (`.spa-chat-msg-log-me`)

Create a class to style system-alert messages. (`.spa-chat-msg-log-alert`)

Add rules to the style-people-list container. (`.spa-chat-list-box`)

Create common rules to style both a person name and a single notification shown in the people list. (`.spa-chat-list-name, .spa-chat-list-note`)

```
}

.spa-chat-list-name {
  cursor : pointer;
}

  .spa-chat-list-name:hover {
    background-color : #aaa;
    color            : #888;
  }

  .spa-chat-list-name.spa-x-select {
    background-color : #fff;
    color            : #444;
  }

.spa-chat-msg-in {
  position   : absolute;
  height     : 2em;
  left       : 0em;
  right      : 1em;
  bottom     : 1em;
  border     : thin solid #888;
  background : #888;
}

.spa-chat-msg-in input[type=text] {
  position    : absolute;
  width       : 75%;
  height      : 100%;
  line-height : 100%;
  padding     : 0 0.5em;
  border      : 0;
  background  : #ddd;
  color       : #666;
}

  .spa-chat-msg-in input[type=text]:focus {
    background : #ff8;
    color      : #222;
  }

.spa-chat-msg-send {
  position    : absolute;
  top         : 0;
  right       : 0;
  width       : 25%;
  height      : 100%;
  line-height : 1.9em;
  text-align  : center;
  color       : #fff;
  font-weight : 800;
  cursor      : pointer;
}

  .spa-chat-msg-send:hover,
  .spa-chat-msg-send.spa-x-select {
    background : #444;
```

Add rules to style a person name shown in the people list.

Create a class to style the user input area.

Create a selector to style the input field within the the user input area.

Create a dependent selector that turns the input field background yellow when it is in focus.

Create a class to style the send button.

```
    color        : #ff0;
  }
.spa-chat-head:hover .spa-chat-head-toggle {
  background : #aaa;
}
```

Now with our stylesheet in place, let's see how well our updated Chat UI works.

6.4.3 Test the Chat UI

When we load our browser document (spa/spa.html), we should now see a page with "Please sign in" in the user area on the upper-right. When we click on this, we can sign in as before. The user area will present "... processing ..." for 3 seconds, and then show the user name in the user area. At that time, the chat slider should open and the interface should look like that shown in Figure 6.5.

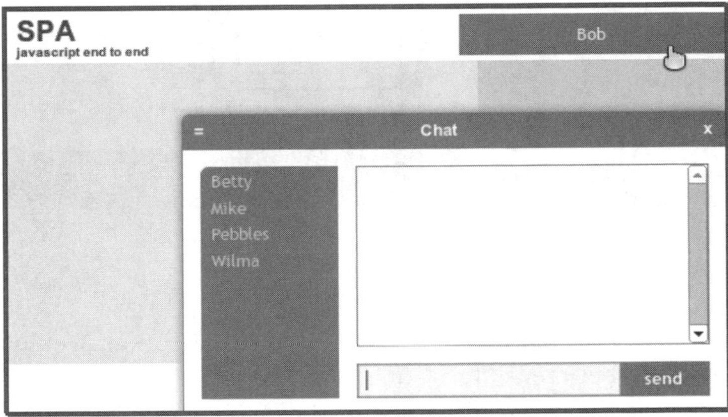

Figure 6.5 Our updated chat interface after sign-in

After a few seconds, we'll receive our first message from Wilma. We can respond, and then select Pebbles and send her a message. The chat interface should look similar to figure 6.6.

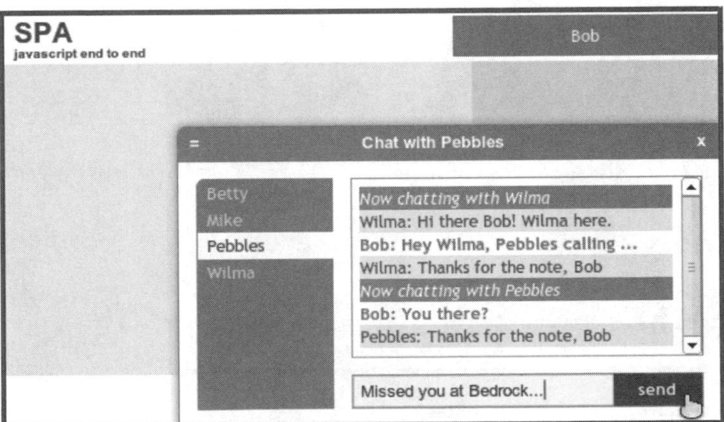

Figure 6.6 The chat slider after a bit of use

We have now used the Model's `chat` and `people` APIs to provide all the capabilities we want in our Chat feature module. Now we'd like to add the Avatar feature module.

6.5 Create the Avatar feature module

In this section we create the Avatar feature module as shown in figure 6.7.

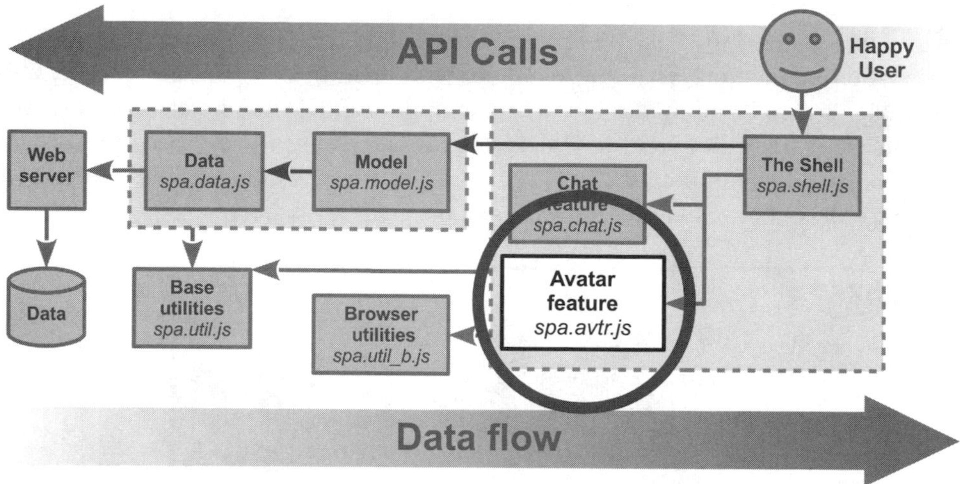

Figure 6.7 The Avatar feature module in our SPA architecture

The `chat` object already provides for managing avatar information. We just need to decide on some details. Let's revisit the Avatar UI as shown in figure 6.8.

Each online person has an avatar that's shaped like a box with a thick border and with their name displayed in the center. The avatar that represents the user should have a blue border. The avatar for the chatee should have a green border. When we

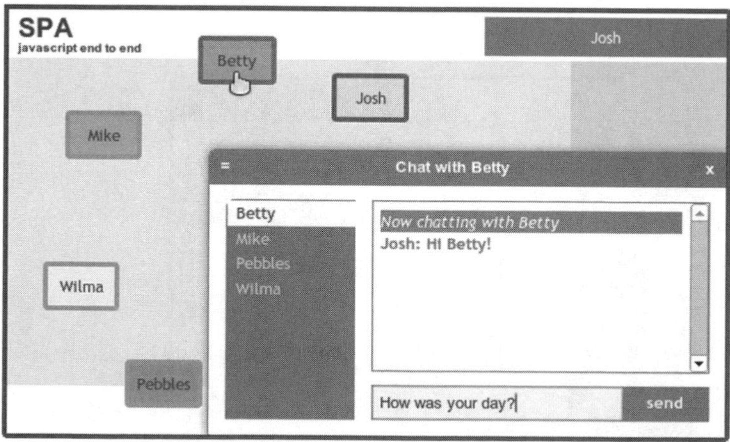

Figure 6.8 Avatars as we'd like them presented

tap or click on an avatar, it should change color. After a long press or touch on an avatar, its appearance should change and we should be able to drag it to a new location.

We will develop our Avatar module using the typical process for feature modules:

- Create a JavaScript file for the feature module using an isolated namespace.
- Create the stylesheet file for the feature module with classes prefixed by the namespace.
- Update the browser document to include the new JavaScript and stylesheet files.
- Adjust the Shell to configure and initialize the new module.

We'll follow these steps in the following sections.

6.5.1 Create the Avatar JavaScript

Our first step in adding the Avatar feature module is to create the JavaScript file. Since the module uses many of the same events as the Chat module, we can copy spa/js/spa.chat.js to spa/js/spa.avtr.js and then adjust accordingly. Listing 6.15 is our freshly minted feature module file. Because this is so similar to Chat, we don't offer an in-depth discussion. But the interesting parts have been annotated:

Listing 6.15 Create the Avatar JavaScript—spa/js/spa.avtr.js

```
/*
 * spa.avtr.js
 * Avatar feature module
*/

/*jslint         browser : true, continue : true,
  devel  : true, indent  : 2,    maxerr   : 50,
  newcap : true, nomen   : true, plusplus : true,
  regexp : true, sloppy  : true, vars     : false,
  white  : true
*/
/*global $, spa */

spa.avtr = (function () {
  'use strict';                                     // Employ the use strict pragma.
  //---------------- BEGIN MODULE SCOPE VARIABLES --------------
  var
    configMap = {
      chat_model   : null,                          // Declare configuration properties for
      people_model : null,                          // the people and chat objects.

      settable_map : {
        chat_model   : true,
        people_model : true
      }
    },

    stateMap  = {                                   // Declare state properties to
      drag_map     : null,                          // allow us to track a dragged
      $drag_target : null,                          // avatar between event handlers.
```

```
      drag_bg_color: undefined
    },

    jqueryMap = {},

    getRandRgb,
    setJqueryMap,
    updateAvatar,
    onTapNav,          onHeldstartNav,
    onHeldmoveNav,     onHeldendNav,
    onSetchatee,       onListchange,
    onLogout,
    configModule,      initModule;
  //----------------- END MODULE SCOPE VARIABLES ---------------

  //------------------- BEGIN UTILITY METHODS ------------------
  getRandRgb = function (){
    var i, rgb_list = [];
    for ( i = 0; i < 3; i++ ){
      rgb_list.push( Math.floor( Math.random() * 128 ) + 128 );
    }
    return 'rgb(' + rgb_list.join(',') + ')';
  };
  //-------------------- END UTILITY METHODS -------------------

  //--------------------- BEGIN DOM METHODS --------------------
  setJqueryMap = function ( $container ) {
    jqueryMap = { $container : $container };
  };

  updateAvatar = function ( $target ){
    var css_map, person_id;

    css_map = {
      top  : parseInt( $target.css( 'top'  ), 10 ),
      left : parseInt( $target.css( 'left' ), 10 ),
      'background-color' : $target.css('background-color')
    };
    person_id = $target.attr( 'data-id' );

    configMap.chat_model.update_avatar({
      person_id : person_id, css_map : css_map
    });
  };
  //---------------------- END DOM METHODS ---------------------

  //------------------- BEGIN EVENT HANDLERS -------------------
  onTapNav = function ( event ){
    var css_map,
      $target = $( event.elem_target ).closest('.spa-avtr-box');

    if ( $target.length === 0 ){ return false; }
    $target.css({ 'background-color' : getRandRgb() });
    updateAvatar( $target );
  };

  onHeldstartNav = function ( event ){
    var offset_target_map, offset_nav_map,
      $target = $( event.elem_target ).closest('.spa-avtr-box');
```

Create a utility to generate a random RGB color string.

Create the `updateAvatar` method to read the `css` values from the provided `$target` avatar, and then invoke the `model.chat.update_avatar` method.

Create the `onTapNav` event handler, which is triggered when a user clicks or taps on the navigation area. This handler uses event delegation, as it only reacts if the element beneath the tap target is an avatar. Otherwise, it ignores the event.

Create the `OnHeldstartNav` event handler. This is triggered when the user starts a dragging motion in the navigation area.

```
  if ( $target.length === 0 ){ return false; }

  stateMap.$drag_target = $target;
  offset_target_map = $target.offset();
  offset_nav_map    = jqueryMap.$container.offset();

  offset_target_map.top  -= offset_nav_map.top;
  offset_target_map.left -= offset_nav_map.left;

  stateMap.drag_map      = offset_target_map;
  stateMap.drag_bg_color = $target.css('background-color');

  $target
    .addClass('spa-x-is-drag')
    .css('background-color','');
};

onHeldmoveNav = function ( event ){
  var drag_map = stateMap.drag_map;
  if ( ! drag_map ){ return false; }

  drag_map.top  += event.px_delta_y;
  drag_map.left += event.px_delta_x;

  stateMap.$drag_target.css({
    top : drag_map.top, left : drag_map.left
  });
};

onHeldendNav = function ( event ) {
  var $drag_target = stateMap.$drag_target;
  if ( ! $drag_target ){ return false; }

  $drag_target
    .removeClass('spa-x-is-drag')
    .css('background-color',stateMap.drag_bg_color);

  stateMap.drag_bg_color= undefined;
  stateMap.$drag_target = null;
  stateMap.drag_map     = null;
  updateAvatar( $drag_target );
};

onSetchatee = function ( event, arg_map ) {
  var
    $nav       = $(this),
    new_chatee = arg_map.new_chatee,
    old_chatee = arg_map.old_chatee;

  // Use this to highlight avatar of user in nav area
  // See new_chatee.name, old_chatee.name, etc.

  // remove highlight from old_chatee avatar here
  if ( old_chatee ){
    $nav
      .find( '.spa-avtr-box[data-id=' + old_chatee.cid + ']' )
      .removeClass( 'spa-x-is-chatee' );
  }

  // add highlight to new_chatee avatar here
  if ( new_chatee ){
```

Create the `onHeldmoveNav` event handler, which is triggered when the user is in the process of dragging an avatar. This is executed frequently, so calculations are kept to a minimum.

Create the `onHeldendNav` event handler. This is triggered when the user releases an avatar after a drag. The handler returns the dragged avatar back to its original color. It then invokes the `updateAvatar` method to read the avatar details and invoke the `model.chat.update_avatar ( <update_map> )` method.

Create the `onSetchatee` event handler. This is invoked when the Model publishes an `spa-setchatee` event. In this module, we set the outline of the chatee avatar to green.

```
    $nav
      .find( '.spa-avtr-box[data-id=' + new_chatee.cid + ']' )
      .addClass('spa-x-is-chatee');
  }
};

onListchange = function ( event ){
  var
    $nav      = $(this),
    people_db = configMap.people_model.get_db(),
    user      = configMap.people_model.get_user(),
    chatee    = configMap.chat_model.get_chatee() || {},
    $box;

  $nav.empty();
  // if the user is logged out, do not render
  if ( user.get_is_anon() ){ return false;}

  people_db().each( function ( person, idx ){
    var class_list;
    if ( person.get_is_anon() ){ return true; }
    class_list = [ 'spa-avtr-box' ];

    if ( person.id === chatee.id ){
      class_list.push( 'spa-x-is-chatee' );
    }
    if ( person.get_is_user() ){
      class_list.push( 'spa-x-is-user');
    }

    $box = $('<div/>')
      .addClass( class_list.join(' '))
      .css( person.css_map )
      .attr( 'data-id', String( person.id ) )
      .prop( 'title', spa.util_b.encodeHtml( person.name ))
      .text( person.name )
      .appendTo( $nav );
  });
};

onLogout = function (){
  jqueryMap.$container.empty();
};
//-------------------- END EVENT HANDLERS --------------------

//------------------- BEGIN PUBLIC METHODS -------------------
// Begin public method /configModule/
// Example  : spa.avtr.configModule({...});
// Purpose  : Configure the module prior to initialization,
//   values we do not expect to change during a user session.
// Action   :
//   The internal configuration data structure (configMap)
//   is updated  with provided arguments. No other actions
//   are taken.
// Returns  : none
// Throws   : JavaScript error object and stack trace on
//            unacceptable or missing arguments
//
```

Create the `onListchange` event handler. This is invoked when the Model publishes an `spa-listchange` event. In this module, we redraw the avatars.

Create the `onLogout` event handler. This is invoked when the Model publishes an `spa-logout` event. In this module, we remove all avatars.

```
  configModule = function ( input_map ) {
    spa.util.setConfigMap({
      input_map    : input_map,
      settable_map : configMap.settable_map,
      config_map   : configMap
    });
    return true;
  };
  // End public method /configModule/

  // Begin public method /initModule/
  // Example    : spa.avtr.initModule( $container );
  // Purpose    : Directs the module to begin offering its feature
  // Arguments  : $container - container to use
  // Action     : Provides avatar interface for chat users
  // Returns    : none
  // Throws     : none
  //
  initModule = function ( $container ) {
    setJqueryMap( $container );

    // bind model global events
    $.gevent.subscribe( $container, 'spa-setchatee',  onSetchatee  );
    $.gevent.subscribe( $container, 'spa-listchange', onListchange );
    $.gevent.subscribe( $container, 'spa-logout',     onLogout     );

    // bind actions
    $container
      .bind( 'utap',        onTapNav       )
      .bind( 'uheldstart', onHeldstartNav )
      .bind( 'uheldmove',  onHeldmoveNav  )
      .bind( 'uheldend',   onHeldendNav   );

    return true;
  };
  // End public method /initModule/

  // return public methods
  return {
    configModule : configModule,
    initModule   : initModule
  };
  //------------------- END PUBLIC METHODS ---------------------
}());
```

Create the code to bind Model-published events first.

Create the code to bind browser events next. Doing this before the Model events could result in a race condition.

Now that we have the JavaScript portion of the module complete, we can create the associated stylesheet.

6.5.2 Create the Avatar stylesheet

Our Avatar module draws boxes to graphically represent a user. We can define a single class (`spa-avtr-box`) to style the box. This class can then be modified to highlight the user (`spa-x-is-user`), highlight the chatee (`spa-x-is-chatee`), or highlight a box that's being dragged (`spa-x-is-drag`). These selectors are shown in listing 6.16:

Listing 6.16 Create the Avatar stylesheet—spa/css/spa.avtr.css

```
/*
 * spa.avtr.css
 * Avatar feature styles
*/

.spa-avtr-box {
  position      : absolute;
  width         : 62px;
  padding       : 0 4px;
  height        : 40px;
  line-height   : 32px;
  border        : 4px solid #aaa;
  cursor        : pointer;
  text-align    : left;
  overflow      : hidden;
  text-overflow : ellipsis;
  border-radius : 4px;
  text-align    : center;
}
  .spa-avtr-box.spa-x-is-user {
    border-color : #44f;
  }

  .spa-avtr-box.spa-x-is-chatee {
    border-color : #080;
  }
  .spa-avtr-box.spa-x-is-drag {
    cursor           : move;
    color            : #fff;
    background-color : #000;
    border-color     : #800;
  }
```

Create the class used to style the avatars.

Add a `text-overflow: ellipsis` rule to elegantly truncate long text. We have to set the `overflow:hidden` rule as well or this won't work.

Create a derived selector to style the avatar that represents the user.

Create a derived selector to style the avatar that represents the chatee.

Create a derived selector to style an avatar that is being moved by the user.

With the module files complete, we now need to adjust two additional files: the Shell and the browser document.

6.5.3 Update the Shell and the browser document

If we want to use the newly created feature module, we need to update the Shell to configure and initialize it, as shown in listing 6.17:

Listing 6.17 Update the Shell to configure and initialize Avatar—spa/js/spa.shell.js

```
...
  initModule = function ( $container ) {
  ...
    // configure and initialize feature modules
    spa.chat.configModule({
      set_chat_anchor : setChatAnchor,
      chat_model      : spa.model.chat,
      people_model    : spa.model.people
```

```
    });
    spa.chat.initModule( jqueryMap.$container );

    spa.avtr.configModule({                                  First configure the
      chat_model   : spa.model.chat,                          feature module . . .
      people_model : spa.model.people
    });
    spa.avtr.initModule( jqueryMap.$nav );                   . . . then
                                                              initialize it.
    // Handle URI anchor change events.
    ...
  };
...
```

The last step when creating a feature module is to update the browser document to include the JavaScript and stylesheet files. This step was already accomplished in chapter 5, but for the sake of completeness, the changes are shown again in listing 6.18:

Listing 6.18 Update the browser document for avatars—spa/spa.html

```
...
  <!-- our stylesheets -->
  <link rel="stylesheet" href="css/spa.css"       type="text/css"/>
  <link rel="stylesheet" href="css/spa.shell.css" type="text/css"/>
  <link rel="stylesheet" href="css/spa.chat.css"  type="text/css"/>
  <link rel="stylesheet" href="css/spa.avtr.css"  type="text/css"/>
...
  <!-- our javascript -->
...
  <script src="js/spa.shell.js" ></script>
  <script src="js/spa.chat.js"  ></script>
  <script src="js/spa.avtr.js"  ></script>
...
```

The creation and integration of the Avatar feature module is complete. Now let's test it out.

6.5.4 Test the Avatar feature module

When we load our browser document (spa/spa.html), we should see a page with "Please sign in" in the user area on the upper-right. When we click on this, we can sign in as before. Once the chat slider opens, we should see an interface that looks like figure 6.9.

We can now drag the avatars around (they all start in the top-left corner) by hold-dragging them. A tap on an avatar will result in a color change. After a little tapping and dragging, we should see the interface look something like figure 6.10. The user avatar has a blue border, the chatee has a green border, and any avatar that is being dragged has a black-white-red color scheme:

We've implemented all the features we discussed at the beginning of this chapter. Now let's look at how we accomplished one facet of our work that is a popular topic these days—data binding.

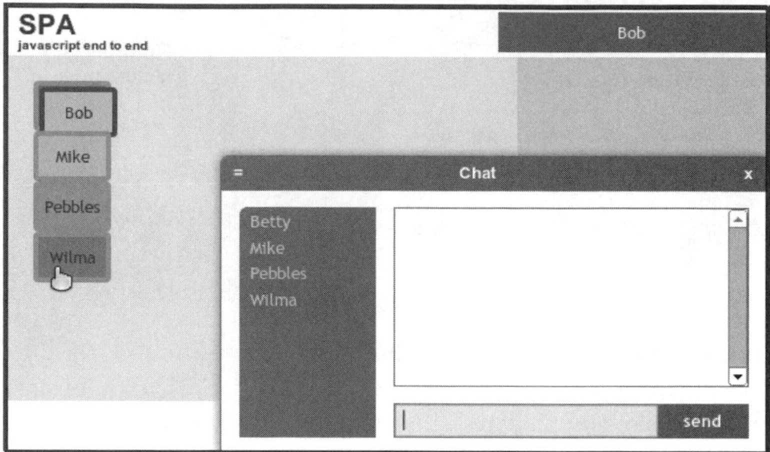

Figure 6.9 Avatars shown after sign-in

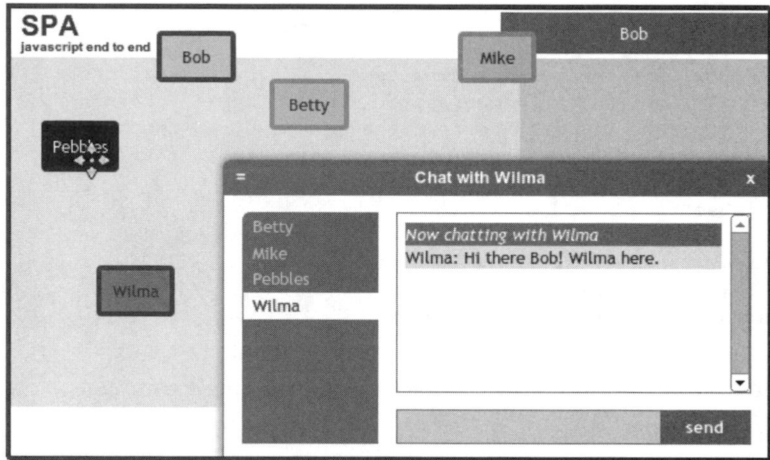

Figure 6.10 Avatars at play

6.6 Data binding and jQuery

Data binding is a mechanism to ensure that when Model data changes, the interface is changed to reflect it; and, conversely, when the user changes the interface, the Model data is updated accordingly. This is nothing new—if you've ever worked on a UI you've implemented data binding as a matter of course.

We implemented data binding in this chapter using jQuery methods. When the Model data changes in our SPA, we publish jQuery global custom events. Our jQuery collections subscribe to specific custom global events and invoke functions to update their presentation when the events occur. And when the users modify data on-screen, they trigger event handlers that invoke methods to update the Model. It's simple and provides a good deal of flexibility in how and when the data and presentation are updated. Data binding using jQuery isn't hard, and it isn't mysteriously magical either—which is a good thing.

Beware SPA "framework" libraries bearing gifts

Some SPA "framework" libraries promise "automatic two-way data binding" which certainly sounds good. But we've learned a few points of caution about such promises in spite of the impressive canned demos:

- We'll need to learn the language of the library—its API and terminology to make it do the things a well-groomed presenter can do. This can be a significant investment.
- The library author often has a vision of how an SPA is supposed to be structured. If our SPA *doesn't* meet that vision, retrofitting can get expensive.
- Libraries can be big, buggy, and offer another layer of complexity where things can go wrong.
- The library's data binding may often not meet our SPA requirements.

Let's focus on that last point. Perhaps we'd like a user to be able to edit a row in a table, and when finished, either accept the entire row or cancel (in which case the row should revert back to old values). And, when the user is done editing rows, we'd like to have the user accept or cancel the entire edited table. And only then would we even consider saving the table to the backend.

The probability of a framework library supporting this kind of reasonable interaction "out-of-the-box" is low. So if we go with a library, we'll need to create a custom override method to circumvent the default behavior. If we have to do that just a few times, we can easily end up with *more* code, *more* layers, *more* files, and *more* complexity than if we'd written the damn thing ourselves in the first place.

After a few well-intended attempts, we've learned to approach framework libraries with caution. We've found they can add complexity to an SPA rather than making development better, faster, or easier to understand. That doesn't mean we should never use framework libraries—they have their place. But our example SPAs (and quite a few in production) work fine with just jQuery, some plugins, and a few specialized tools like TaffyDb. Often, simpler is better.

Now let's finish the client portion of the SPA by adding the Data module and making a few minor tweaks.

6.7 Create the Data module

In this section we create the Data module as shown in figure 6.11.

This will prepare the client to use "real" data and services from the server instead of our Fake module. The application will *not* work after we have completed this section, as the required server capabilities aren't yet in place. That will come in chapters 7 and 8.

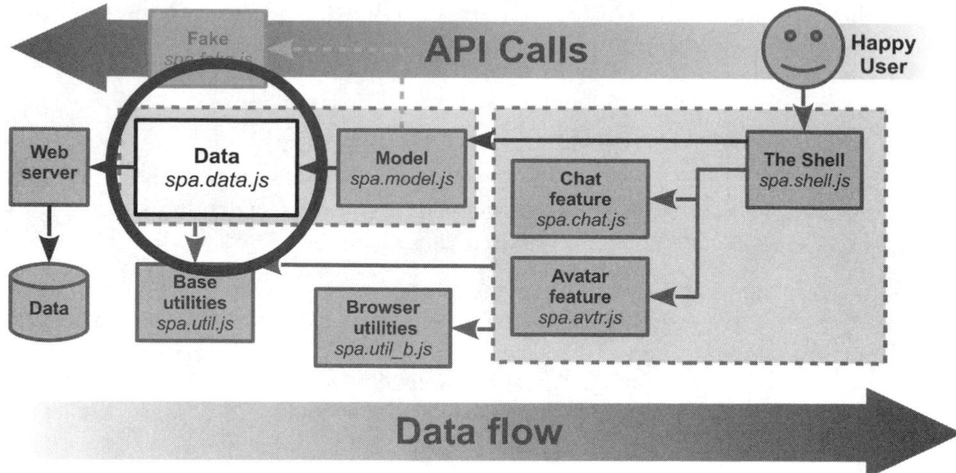

Figure 6.11 The Data model in our SPA architecture

We'll need to add the Socket.IO library to the list of libraries we load, as this will be our message transport mechanism. This is accomplished as shown in listing 6.19. Changes are shown in **bold**:

Listing 6.19 Include the Socket.IO library in the browser document—spa/spa.html

```
...
  <!-- third-party javascript -->
  <script src="socket.io/socket.io.js"        ></script>
  <script src="js/jq/taffydb-2.6.2.js"        ></script>
...
```

We wish to ensure that the Data module is initialized prior to the Model or the Shell, as shown in listing 6.20. Changes are shown in **bold**:

Listing 6.20 Initialize Data in the root namespace module—spa/js/spa.js

```
...
var spa = (function () {
  'use strict';
  var initModule = function ( $container ) {
    spa.data.initModule();
    spa.model.initModule();
    spa.shell.initModule( $container );
  };

  return { initModule: initModule };
}());
```

Ensure Data is initialized before the Model and the Shell.

Next we update the Data module as shown in listing 6.21. This module manages *all* the connections to the server in our architecture, and *all* data communicated between the client and server flows through this module. All that this module does may not be clear at present, but don't worry—we'll cover Socket.IO in further detail in the next chapter. Changes are shown in **bold**:

Listing 6.21 Update the Data module—spa/js/spa.data.js

```
...
/*global $, io, spa */

spa.data = (function () {
  'use strict';
  var
    stateMap = { sio : null },
    makeSio, getSio, initModule;

  makeSio = function (){
    var socket = io.connect( '/chat' );

    return {
      emit : function ( event_name, data ) {
        socket.emit( event_name, data );
      },
      on : function ( event_name, callback ) {
        socket.on( event_name, function (){
          callback( arguments );
        });
      }
    };
  };

  getSio = function (){
    if ( ! stateMap.sio ) { stateMap.sio = makeSio(); }
    return stateMap.sio;
  };

  initModule = function (){};

  return {
    getSio     : getSio,
    initModule : initModule
  };
}());
```

Create the socket connection using the `/chat` namespace.

Write the code to return our methods for an `sio` object

Ensure the `emit` method sends data associated with a given event name to the server.

Ensure the `on` method registers a callback for a given event name. Any event data received from the server will be passed back to the callback.

Create a `getSio` method, which tries to always return a valid `sio` object.

Create an `initModule` method. This doesn't do anything yet, but we always want to ensure it's available and that our root namespace module (`spa/js/spa.js`) invokes it before the initialization of the Model or the Shell.

Neatly export all public data methods.

Our final step in preparation to use server data is to tell the Model to stop using fake data, as shown in listing 6.22. Changes are shown in **bold**:

Listing 6.22 Update the Model to use "real" data—spa/js/spa.model.js

```
...
spa.model = (function () {
  'use strict';
  var
    configMap = { anon_id : 'a0' },
    stateMap  = {
      ...
    },
    isFakeData = false,
...
```

After this last change, when we load our browser document (spa/spa.html) we'll find our SPA won't function as before, and we'll see errors in the console. If we want to continue development without the server, we can easily "flip the switch" and revert the `isFakeData` assignment to `true`.[1] Now we're ready to add the server to our SPA.

6.8 Summary

In this chapter we concluded our work on the Model. We methodically designed, specified, developed, and tested the `chat` object. As in chapter 5, we used mock data from a Fake module to speed development. We then updated the Chat feature module to use the `chat` and `people` object APIs provided by the Model. We also created the Avatar feature module, which also used the same APIs. We then discussed data binding using jQuery. Finally, we added a Data module that will communicate with the Node.js server using Socket.IO. In chapter 8 we'll set up the server to work with the Data module. In the next chapter, we'll get familiar with Node.js.

---

[1] Our browser may complain about not being able to find the Socket.IO library, but this should be harmless.

Part 3

The SPA server

When a user navigates through a traditional website, the server burns lots of processing power to generate and send page after page of content to the browser. The SPA server is quite different. Most of the business logic—and all of the HTML templating and presentation logic—is moved to the client. The server remains important, but it becomes leaner and more focused on services like persistent data storage, data validation, user authentication, and data synchronization.

Historically, web developers had to spend a good deal of time developing logic to transform one data format to another, much like shoveling dirt from one giant, musty dirt pile to another—and just about as productive. Web developers have also had to master many different languages and toolkits. A traditional website stack might require detailed knowledge of SQL, Apache2, mod_rewrite, mod_perl2, Perl, DBI, HTML, CSS, and JavaScript. Learning all these languages and switching between them is expensive and annoying. Even worse, if we need to move some logic from one part of the application to the other, we get to rewrite it in a completely different language. In part 3 we learn:

- The fundamentals of Node.js and MongoDB
- How to stop wasting server cycles on data transformations and instead use the JSON data format throughout the SPA stack
- How to build an HTTP server application and interact with the database using only one language—JavaScript
- The challenges of SPA deployment and how we can resolve them

We use JSON and JavaScript end-to-end in our stack. This *eliminates* the overhead of data transformations. And it *significantly reduces* the number of languages and development environments we need to master. The result is a better product that's significantly less expensive to develop, deliver, and maintain.

7 The web server

This chapter covers

- The role of the web server when supporting an SPA
- Using JavaScript as the web server language with Node.js
- Using Connect middleware
- Using the Express framework
- Configuring Express to support an SPA architecture
- Routing and CRUD
- Messaging using Socket.IO and why we care

This chapter discusses the logic and code a server needs to support an SPA. It also provides a good introduction to Node.js. If after reading this chapter you're really excited and want to build out a fully production-ready application using Node.js, we suggest checking out the book *Node.js in Action* (Manning 2013).

7.1 The role of the server

An SPA moves much of the business logic found on the server in a traditional website to the browser. But we still need some server Ying to match the browser client Yang. There are areas where the web server must be involved to achieve a desired effect—for example, security—or where the server is better suited to the task than the client. The most common responsibilities of an SPA web server include *authentication and authorization*, *data validation*, and *data storage and synchronization*.

7.1.1 Authentication and authorization

Authentication is the process of making sure that someone is who they say they are. The server is needed because we should never rely solely on data provided from the client. If authentication was handled solely on the client side, a malicious hacker could reverse-engineer the authentication mechanism and create the necessary credentials to impersonate a user and steal their account. Authentication is often initiated by the user entering a user name and password.

Increasingly, developers are turning to third-party authentication services, such as those provided by Facebook or Yahoo. When authenticating with a third party, the user is required to provide credentials—typically a username and password—*for* the third-party service. If, for example, we use Facebook authentication, the user will be expected to provide the username and password for their Facebook account to the Facebook server. The third-party server then communicates with our server to authenticate the user. The advantage to users is they can reuse a username and password they've already memorized. The advantage to developers is they get to outsource most of the tedious details of implementation and get access to the third party's user population.

Authorization is the processes of ensuring that only people and systems that are supposed to have access to data are able to receive it. This can be accomplished by tying permissions to a user, so that when the user signs in there's a record of what they're permitted to see. It's important that authorization be handled on the server so that no unauthorized data is ever sent to the client. Otherwise, our malicious hacker could again reverse-engineer our application and access sensitive information they're not supposed to see. A side benefit of authorization is that because it only sends data that a user is authorized to see, it minimizes the amount of data sent to the client, potentially making the transaction much quicker.

7.1.2 Validation

Validation is a quality control process, ensuring that only accurate and reasonable data can be saved. Validation helps prevent errors from being saved and propagated to other users or systems. For example, an airline might validate that when a user selects a flight date for purchasing a ticket, they're selecting a date in the future that has available seats. Without this validation, the airline could overbook flights, book seats on flights that don't exist, or book seats on flights that have already departed.

It's important that validation occur on both the client side and the server: it should be implemented on the client for a speedy response, and it should be validated on the server because it should never trust code from the client to be valid. All sorts of issues could result in the server receiving invalid data:

- A programming error could damage or omit client validation from the SPA.
- A different client may lack validation—web server applications often have multiple clients accessing the same server.
- A once-valid option could become invalid by the time the data is submitted (say, the seat was booked by someone else just after the user clicked Submit).
- Our malicious hacker might again appear and attempt to hijack or break the site by stuffing our data store with corrupt data.

The classic example of improper server validation is the SQL-injection attacks which have embarrassed many notable organizations that really should have known better. We don't want to join that club, do we?

7.1.3 Preservation and synchronization of data

Although an SPA can save data in the client, that data is transitory and is easily modified or deleted outside of control of the SPA. In most cases, the client should be used only for temporary storage, with the server being responsible for long-term storage.

Data may also need to be synchronized between multiple clients, like when a person's online status needs to be shared with everyone who's viewing their home page. The simplest way to accomplish this is to have the client send the status to the server, have the server save it, and then broadcast the status to all authenticated clients. Synchronizing may also be used with transient data; for example, when we use a chat server to dispatch messages to an authenticated client: though the server doesn't store the data, it has the critical task of routing the messages to the correct authenticated clients.

7.2 Node.js

Node.js is a platform that uses JavaScript as its control language. When we use it as an HTTP server, it's philosophically similar to Twisted, Tornado, or mod_perl. Many other popular web server platforms, in contrast, are split into two components: the HTTP server and the application process container. Examples include Apache/PHP, Passenger/Ruby, or Tomcat/Java.

Writing the HTTP server and application together enables us to easily complete some tasks that are difficult on platforms with separate HTTP and application components. If, for example, we want to write our logs to an in-memory database, we can do so without having to worry about where the HTTP server stops and the application server begins.

7.2.1 Why Node.js?

We've selected Node.js as our server platform because it has capabilities that make it a great choice for a modern SPA:

- The server is the application. The result is not having to worry about setting up and interfacing with a separate application server. Everything is controlled in one place, by one process.

- The server application language is JavaScript, meaning we can eliminate the cognitive load of writing the server application in one language and the SPA in another. It also means we can share code between the client and server, which has many advantages. For example, we might use the same data validation libraries on both the SPA and the server.
- Node.js is non-blocking and event-driven. In a nutshell, this means a single Node.js instance on modest hardware can handle tens or hundreds of thousands of concurrent open connections, such as those used in real-time messaging, which is often a highly desired feature of modern SPAs.
- Node.js is fast, well supported, and has a rapidly growing body of modules and developers.

Node.js handles network requests differently than most other server platforms. Most HTTP servers maintain a pool of processes or threads that are kept ready to service incoming requests. Node.js, in contrast, only has one event queue that processes each incoming request as it happens, and even splits up the processing of parts of an incoming request into separate events in the main event queue. What this means in practice is that Node.js doesn't tend to wait around for a long event to finish before processing other events. If a particular database query is taking a long time, Node.js goes right on processing other events. When the database query does finish, an event is placed in the queue so that the controlling routine may use the results.

Without further ado, let's get into Node.js and see how to create a web server application with it.

7.2.2 Create 'Hello World' using Node.js

Let's go to the Node.js site (http://nodejs.org/#download) and download and install Node.js. There are many ways to download and install it; the simplest, if you're not familiar with the command line, is probably to use the installer for your operating system.

The Node Package Manager, `npm`, is installed along with Node.js. It is similar to Perl's `CPAN`, Ruby's `gem`, or Python's `pip`. On our command, it downloads and installs packages, resolving dependencies along the way. It's much easier than manually doing this ourselves. Now that we have Node.js and `npm` installed, let's create our first server. The Node.js website (http://nodejs.org) has an example of a simple Node web server, so we'll use that. Let's create a directory called webapp and make it our working directory. Then we can create a file in it called app.js with the code in listing 7.1:

Listing 7.1 Create a simple node server application—`webapp/app.js`

```
/*
 * app.js - Hello World
*/

/*jslint         node    : true, continue : true,
  devel  : true, indent  : 2,    maxerr   : 50,
  newcap : true, nomen   : true, plusplus : true,
  regexp : true, sloppy  : true, vars     : false,
```

```
  white   : true
*/
/*global */

var http, server;

http   = require( 'http' );
server = http.createServer( function ( request, response ) {
  response.writeHead( 200, { 'Content-Type': 'text/plain' } );
  response.end( 'Hello World' );
}).listen( 3000 );

console.log( 'Listening on port %d', server.address().port );
```

Open a terminal, navigate to the directory where we saved our app.js file, and start the server with the following command:

```
node app.js
```

You should see `Listening on port 3000`. When we open a web browser (on the same computer) and go to `http://localhost:3000`, we should see `Hello World` appear in the browser. Wow, that was simple! A server in only seven lines of code. I don't know how you feel right about now, but I was delighted to have a web server application written and running in minutes. Now let's walk through what the code means.

Our first section is our standard heading with JSLint settings. It allows us to validate our server JavaScript just like we do with our client:

```
/*
 * app.js - Hello World
*/

/*jslint         node    : true, continue : true,
  devel  : true, indent  : 2,    maxerr   : 50,
  newcap : true, nomen   : true, plusplus : true,
  regexp : true, sloppy  : true, vars     : false,
  white  : true
*/
/*global */
```

The next line declares the module-scope variable we will be using:

```
var http, server;
```

The next line tells Node.js to include the `http` module for use in this server application. It's similar to using HTML `script` tags to include JavaScript files for use by the browser. The `http` module is a core Node.js module used to create an HTTP server, and we store the module in the variable `http`:

```
http   = require( 'http' );
```

Next we use the `http.createServer` method to create an HTTP server. We provide it an anonymous function that will be called whenever the Node.js server receives a request event. The function receives a `request` object and a `response` object as arguments. The `request` object is the HTTP request sent by the client:

```
server = http.createServer( function ( request, response ) {
```

Inside our anonymous function, we begin defining the response to the HTTP request. The next line creates the HTTP headers using the `response` argument. We provide a `200` HTTP response code to indicate success, and we provide an anonymous object with the property `Content-Type` and the value `text/plain`. This tells the browser what sort of content to expect in the message:

```
response.writeHead( 200, { 'Content-Type': 'text/plain' } );
```

The next line uses the `response.end` method to send the string `'Hello World'` to the client and let Node.js know that we're done with this response:

```
response.end( 'Hello World' );
```

We then close the anonymous function and the call to the `createServer` method. The code then chains a call to the `listen` method on the `http` object. The `listen` method instructs the `http` object to listen on port 3000:

```
}).listen( 3000 );
```

Our last line prints to the console when this server application is started. We are able to use an attribute from the `server` object we created earlier to report the port that is being used:

```
console.log( 'Listening on port %d', server.address().port );
```

We've used Node.js to create a very basic server. It's worth spending some time playing around with the `request` and `response` arguments passed to the anonymous function in the `http.createServer` method. Let's start by logging the `request` argument in listing 7.2. The new line is shown in **bold**:

Listing 7.2 Add simple logging to a node server application—`webapp/app.js`

```
/*
 * app.js - Basic logging
*/
...
var http, server;

http   = require( 'http' );
server = http.createServer( function ( request, response ) {
  console.log( request );
  response.writeHead( 200, { 'Content-Type': 'text/plain' } );
  response.end( 'Hello World' );
}).listen( 3000 );

console.log( 'Listening on port %d', server.address().port );
```

When we restart the web application, we'll see the object logged, shown in listing 7.3, in the terminal where the Node.js application is running. Don't worry too much about the structure of the object right now; we'll go over the parts we need to know later.

Listing 7.3 The request object

```
{ output: [],
  outputEncodings: [],
  writable: true,
  _last: false,
  chunkedEncoding: false,
  shouldKeepAlive: true,
  useChunkedEncodingByDefault: true,
  sendDate: true,
  _hasBody: true,
  _trailer: '',
  finished: false,

...  // down another 100 or so lines of code
```

Some notable properties of the `request` object include:

- `ondata`—A method that gets called when the server starts receiving data from the client, for example when `POST` variables are set. This is a substantially different method of getting arguments from the client than most frameworks. We'll abstract this away so that the full list of parameters is available in a variable.
- `headers`—All of the headers from the request.
- `url`—The page that was requested without the host. For example, http://www.singlepagewebapp.com/test will have a `url` of `/test`.
- `method`—The method used to make the request: `GET` or `POST`.

Armed with the knowledge of these attributes, we can start to write a rudimentary router in listing 7.4. Changes are shown in **bold**:

Listing 7.4 Add simple routing to a node server application—`webapp/app.js`

```
/*
 * app.js - Basic routing
*/
...
var http, server;

http   = require( 'http' );
server = http.createServer( function ( request, response ) {
  var response_text = request.url === '/test'
    ? 'you have hit the test page'
    : 'Hello World';
  response.writeHead( 200, { 'Content-Type': 'text/plain' } );
  response.end( response_text );
}).listen( 3000 );

console.log( 'Listening on port %d', server.address().port );
```

Check the request object for the URL of the requesting page.

We could continue to write our own router, and for simple applications that is a reasonable choice. We have larger aspirations for our server application, however, and we'd like to use a framework that the Node.js community has developed and tested. The first framework we will consider is Connect.

7.2.3 Install and use Connect

Connect is an extensible *middleware* framework that adds capabilities like basic authentication, session management, static file serving, and form handling to a Node.js web server. It's not the only framework available, but it's simple and relatively standard. Connect allows us to inject *middleware* functions between the receipt of a request and the final response. Generally, a middleware function takes an incoming request, performs some actions on it, and then hands the request to the next middleware function or ends the response using the `response.end` method.

The best way to become familiar with Connect and the middleware pattern is to use it. Let's ensure webapp is our working directory, and install connect. Type the following at the command line:

```
npm install connect
```

This will create a folder called node_modules and install the Connect framework inside of it. The node_modules directory is the folder that all of the modules for your Node.js application go in. `npm` will install modules in this directory, and when we write our own modules, this is where they'll go. We can modify our server application as shown in listing 7.5. Changes are shown in **bold**:

Listing 7.5 Modify the node server application to use Connect—webapp/app.js

```
/*
 * app.js - Simple connect server
*/
...
var
  connectHello, server,
  http     = require( 'http'    ),
  connect  = require( 'connect' ),
  app      = connect(),
  bodyText = 'Hello Connect';

connectHello = function ( request, response, next ) {
  response.setHeader( 'content-length', bodyText.length );
  response.end( bodyText );
};

app.use( connectHello );
server = http.createServer( app );

server.listen( 3000 );
console.log( 'Listening on port %d', server.address().port );
```

This Connect server behaves very much like our first node server in the previous section. We define our first middleware function, `connectHello`, and then tell the Connect object, `app`, to use this method as its one and only middleware function. Since the `connectHello` function invokes the `response.end` method, it concludes the server response. Let's build on this by adding more middleware.

7.2.4 *Add Connect middleware*

Let's say that we want to log every time someone accesses a page. We do that using a built-in middleware function that Connect provides. Listing 7.6 shows the addition of the `connect.logger()` middleware function. Changes are shown in **bold**:

Listing 7.6 Add logging to a node server application using Connect—`webapp/app.js`

```
/*
 * app.js - Simple connect server with logging
*/
...
var
  connectHello, server,
  http     = require( 'http'    ),
  connect  = require( 'connect' ),

  app      = connect(),
  bodyText = 'Hello Connect';

connectHello = function ( request, response, next ) {
  response.setHeader( 'content-length', bodyText.length );
  response.end( bodyText );
};

app
  .use( connect.logger() )
  .use( connectHello     );
server = http.createServer( app );

server.listen( 3000 );
console.log( 'Listening on port %d', server.address().port );
```

All we did was add `connect.logger()` as middleware before our `connectHello` middleware. Now every time a client issues an HTTP request to the server application, the first middleware function that gets invoked is `connect.logger()`, which prints out log information to the console. The *next* middleware function that gets called is the one we defined, `connectHello`, which, as before, sends `Hello Connect` to the client and ends the response. When we point our browser to http://localhost:3000, we should see something like the following in the Node.js console log:

```
Listening on port 3000
127.0.0.1 - - [Wed, 01 May 2013 19:27:12 GMT] "GET / HTTP/1.1" 200 \
13 "-" "Mozilla/5.0 (X11; Linux x86_64) AppleWebKit/537.31 \
(KHTML, like Gecko) Chrome/26.0.1410.63 Safari/537.31"
```

Even though Connect is a higher-level abstraction than Node.js, we would like even more capability. It's time to upgrade to Express.

7.2.5 *Install and use Express*

Express is a lightweight web framework designed after Sinatra, a lightweight Ruby web framework. In an SPA we don't need to take full advantage of every feature that Express offers, but it does provide a richer feature set than Connect—in fact, it is built on top of Connect.

Let's ensure webapp is our working directory and install Express. Instead of using the command line like we did with Connect, we'll use a manifest file called package.json to tell npm what modules and versions our application needs to run correctly. This comes in handy when installing the application on a remote server or when someone downloads and installs our application on their machine. Let's create package.json to install Express as shown in listing 7.7:

Listing 7.7 Create a manifest for npm install—webapp/package.json

```
{
  "name"    : "SPA",
  "version" : "0.0.3",
  "private" : true,
  "dependencies" : {
    "express"    : "3.2.x"
  }
}
```

The name attribute is the name of our application; it can be whatever we want it to be. The version attribute is the version of your application, and it should use a major, minor, and patch version scheme (<major>.<minor>.<patch>). Setting the private attribute to true tells npm not to publish your application. Finally, the dependencies attribute describes the modules and versions we want npm to install. In this case we only have one module, express. Let's first remove the existing webapp/node_modules directory and then use npm to install Express:

```
npm install
```

When adding new modules with the npm command, we can use the --save option to automatically update package.json to contain the new module. This is handy during development. Notice also how we specified the version we wanted for Express as "3.2.x" which means we want Express version 3.2, with the latest patch. This is a recommended version declaration, as patches rarely break APIs but instead fix bugs or help ensure backward capability.

Now let's edit app.js to use Express. We'll be a little stricter in this implementation by using the 'use strict' pragma and putting in a few section delimiters, as shown in listing 7.8. Changes are shown in **bold**:

Listing 7.8 Create a node server application using Express—webapp/app.js

```
/*
 * app.js - Simple express server
*/
...
// ------------ BEGIN MODULE SCOPE VARIABLES --------------
'use strict';
var
  http    = require( 'http'    ),
  express = require( 'express' ),

  app     = express(),
```

```
  server   = http.createServer( app );
// ------------- END MODULE SCOPE VARIABLES ---------------

// ------------- BEGIN SERVER CONFIGURATION ---------------
app.get( '/', function ( request, response ) {
  response.send( 'Hello Express' );
});
// -------------- END SERVER CONFIGURATION ----------------

// ----------------- BEGIN START SERVER -------------------
server.listen( 3000 );
console.log(
  'Express server listening on port %d in %s mode',
   server.address().port, app.settings.env
);
// ------------------ END START SERVER --------------------
```

When looking at this small example, it might not be immediately apparent why Express is simpler to use, so let's walk through the lines and see. First, we load the express and http modules (shown in **bold**):

```
// ------------ BEGIN MODULE SCOPE VARIABLES --------------
'use strict';
var
  http = require( 'http' ),
  express = require( 'express' ),

  app     = express(),
  server  = http.createServer( app );
// ------------- END MODULE SCOPE VARIABLES ---------------
```

We then create an app object using express. This object has methods for setting the routes and other properties of the application. We also create the HTTP server object, which we will use later (shown in **bold**):

```
// ------------ BEGIN MODULE SCOPE VARIABLES --------------
'use strict';
var
  http    = require( 'http'    ),
  express = require( 'express' ),
  app = express(),
  server = http.createServer( app );
// ------------- END MODULE SCOPE VARIABLES ---------------
```

Next we define the routing for our application by using the app.get method:

```
// ------------- BEGIN SERVER CONFIGURATION ---------------
app.get( '/', function ( request, response ) {
  response.send( 'Hello Express' );
});
// -------------- END SERVER CONFIGURATION ----------------
```

Express makes routing in Node.js simple thanks to a rich set of methods like get. The first argument to app.get is a pattern to compare with the request URL. For example, if a browser on our development box makes a request to http://localhost:3000 or http://localhost:3000/, the GET request string will be '/' which matches the pattern.

The second argument is a callback function that's executed when a match occurs. The `request` and `response` objects are arguments provided to the callback function. Query string parameters can be found in `request.params`.

Our third and final section starts the server and logs to the console:

```
// ----------------- BEGIN START SERVER -------------------
server.listen( 3000 );
console.log(
  'Express server listening on port %d in %s mode',
  server.address().port, app.settings.env
);
```

Now that we have a working Express application, let's add some middleware.

7.2.6 Add Express middleware

Since Express is built on top of Connect, we can also call and pass along middleware using similar syntax. Let's add the logging middleware for our app, as shown in 7.9. The changes are shown in **bold**.

Listing 7.9 Add Express logging middleware to our application—webapp/app.js

```
/*
 * app.js - Simple express server with logging
*/
...
// ------------- BEGIN SERVER CONFIGURATION ---------------
app.use( express.logger() );
app.get( '/', function ( request, response ) {
  response.send( 'Hello Express' );
});
// ------------- END SERVER CONFIGURATION ----------------
```

Express provides all of the Connect middleware methods so that we don't have to require Connect in the page. Running the preceding code will result in the app logging requests to the console, just like `connect.logger` did in the last section.

We can organize our middleware using the Express `app.configure` method, as in listing 7.10. Changes are shown in **bold**.

Listing 7.10 Use `configure` to organize our Express middleware—webapp/app.js

```
/*
 * app.js - Express server with middleware
*/
...
// ------------- BEGIN SERVER CONFIGURATION ---------------
app.configure( function () {
  app.use( express.logger() );
  app.use( express.bodyParser() );
  app.use( express.methodOverride() );
});
app.get( '/', function ( request, response ) {
  response.send( 'Hello Express' );
```

```
});
// -------------- END SERVER CONFIGURATION ----------------
...
```

This configuration adds two new middleware methods: `bodyParser` and `methodOverride`. `bodyParser` decodes forms and will be used extensively later. `methodOverride` is used for creating RESTful services. The `configure` method also lets us change our configuration depending on the Node.js environment in which the application is running.

7.2.7 Use environments with Express

Express supports the concept of switching configurations based on an environment setting. Example environments include `development`, `testing`, `staging`, and `production`. Express can determine which environment is being used by reading the `NODE_ENV` environment variable and will then respond by setting its configuration accordingly. If you're using Windows, you would start the server application like this:

```
SET NODE_ENV=production node app.js
```

Using a Mac or Linux, set it like this:

```
NODE_ENV=production node app.js
```

If you're using something else, we have every confidence that you can figure it out.

We can use any string for an environment name when we run an Express server application. If no `NODE_ENV` variable is set, it uses `development` by default.

Let's adjust our application to adjust itself to the environment being provided. We want to use the `bodyParser` and `methodOverride` middleware in every environment. In the `development` environment we would like the application to log HTTP requests and detailed errors. In the `production` environment we only want to log error summaries, as shown in listing 7.11. Changes are shown in **bold**:

Listing 7.11 Support different environments with Express—webapp/app.js

```
...
// ------------- BEGIN SERVER CONFIGURATION ---------------
app.configure( function () {
  app.use( express.bodyParser() );
  app.use( express.methodOverride() );
});

app.configure( 'development', function () {
  app.use( express.logger() );
  app.use( express.errorHandler({
    dumpExceptions : true,
    showStack      : true
  }) );
});

app.configure( 'production', function () {
  app.use( express.errorHandler() );
});

app.get( '/', function ( request, response ) {
```

Add `bodyParser` and `methodOverride` middleware to every environment.

For the development environment, add the logger and configure the `errorHandler` method to dump exceptions and show the stack trace.

For the production environment, add the `errorHandler` middleware using the default options.

```
  response.send( 'Hello Express' );
});
// -------------- END SERVER CONFIGURATION ----------------
...
```

We can test these configurations by running the application in development mode (`node app.js`) and loading the page in a browser. You should see the log output in the Node.js console. Next, we can stop the server and run it in production mode (`NODE_ENV=production node app.js`). When we reload the page in the browser, there should be no entry in the log.

Now that we have a good understanding of some of the fundamentals of Node.js, Connect, and Express, let's move on to more advanced routing methods.

7.2.8 Serving static files with Express

As you might expect, serving static files with Express requires adding a bit of middleware and a little redirection. Let's copy the contents of the spa directory from chapter 6 into a public directory as shown in listing 7.12.

Listing 7.12 Add the public directory for static files

```
webapp
  +-- app.js
  +-- node_modules/...
  +-- package.json
  `-- public # contents of 'spa' copied here
      +-- css/...
      +-- js/...
      `-- spa.html
```

Now we can adjust the application to serve the static files, as shown in listing 7.13. Changes are shown in **bold**.

Listing 7.13 Serve static files with Express—webapp/app.js

```
/*
 * app.js - Express server static files
*/
...
// ------------- BEGIN SERVER CONFIGURATION ---------------
app.configure( function () {
  app.use( express.bodyParser() );
  app.use( express.methodOverride() );
  app.use( express.static( __dirname + '/public' ) );
  app.use( app.router );
});

app.configure( 'development', function () {
  app.use( express.logger() );
  app.use( express.errorHandler({
    dumpExceptions : true,
    showStack      : true
  }) );
});
```

Define the root directory for static files as <current_directory>/public.

Add the router middleware after the static files.

```
app.configure( 'production', function () {
  app.use( express.errorHandler() );
});

app.get( '/', function ( request, response ) {
  response.redirect( '/spa.html' );
});
// ------------- END SERVER CONFIGURATION ----------------
...
```

Redirect requests to the root directory to our browser document, `/spa.html`.

Now when we run the application (`node app.js`) and point our browser to http://localhost:3000, we should see our SPA as we left it in chapter 6. We can't sign in yet, though, as the backend isn't ready for that yet.

Now that we have a good feel for Express middleware, let's look at advanced routing, which we will need for web data services.

7.3 Advanced routing

Until now, all our application has done is provide a route for the root of the web application and returned some text to the browser. In this section we'll:

- Use the Express framework to provide CRUD routes for managing `user` objects.
- Set response properties, such as content type, for all routes used for CRUD.
- Make the code generic so that it works for all CRUD routes.
- Place the routing logic into a separate module.

7.3.1 User CRUD routes

CRUD operations *(Create, Read, Update, Delete)* are the major operations often required for persistent storage of data. Wikipedia has a great in-depth discussion if you need a refresher or are hearing about CRUD for the first time. One common design pattern in web applications used to implement CRUD is known as *REST*, or *Representational State Transfer*. REST uses strict and well-defined semantics to define what the verbs `GET`, `POST`, `PUT`, `PATCH`, and `DELETE` do. If you know and love REST, by all means feel free to implement it; it's a perfectly valid method of exchanging data between distributed systems, and Node.js even has many modules intended to help out with that.

We've implement basic CRUD routes for our user object and have opted not to implement REST in this example for a few reasons. One challenge is that many browsers have yet to implement native REST verbs, so `PUT`, `PATCH`, and `DELETE` are often implemented by passing extra form parameters or a header in a `POST`. This means a developer can't easily tell what verb is being used in a request, but instead must hunt through the headers of the data being sent. REST is also not a perfect mapping to CRUD, even though the REST verbs look similar to the CRUD operations. Finally, the web browser can get in the way when processing status codes. For example, instead of passing a 302 status code to the client SPA, the browser may intercept the code and try to do "the right thing" and redirect to a different resource. This may not always be the behavior we want.

We can get started by listing all of our users.

MAKE A ROUTE TO GET A USER LIST

We can make a simple route to provide a list of users. Notice that we set the `contentType` of the response object to `json`. This sets the HTTP headers to let the browser know the response is in the JSON format, as shown in listing 7.14. Changes are shown in **bold**:

Listing 7.14 Make a route to get a user list—webapp/app.js

```
/*
 * app.js - Express server with advanced routing
*/
...
// ------------ BEGIN SERVER CONFIGURATION --------------
...
// all configurations below are for routes
app.get( '/', function ( request, response ) {
  response.redirect( '/spa.html' );
});

app.get( '/user/list', function ( request, response ) {
  response.contentType( 'json' );
  response.send({ title: 'user list' });
});
// ------------- END SERVER CONFIGURATION ---------------
...
```

The user-list route expects an HTTP `GET` request. This is just fine if we are retrieving data. In our next route, we will use a `POST` so that we can send copious amounts of data to the server.

MAKE A ROUTE TO CREATE A USER OBJECT

When we make a route to create a user object, we need to process `POST` data from the client. Express provides a shortcut method, `app.post`, which handles `POST` requests that match a provided pattern. We can add the following to our server application, as shown in listing 7.15. Changes are shown in **bold**:

Listing 7.15 Make a route to create a user object—webapp/app.js

```
/*
 * app.js - Express server with advanced routing
*/
...
// ------------ BEGIN SERVER CONFIGURATION --------------
...

app.get( '/user/list', function ( request, response ) {
  response.contentType( 'json' );
  response.send({ title: 'user list' });
});

app.post( '/user/create', function ( request, response ) {
  response.contentType( 'json' );
  response.send({ title: 'user created' });
});
// ------------- END SERVER CONFIGURATION ---------------
...
```

We haven't done anything with the posted data yet; we'll cover that in the next chapter. If we navigate to http://localhost:3000/user/create with our browser, we'll see a 404 error and the message `Cannot GET /user/create`. This is because the browser is sending a `GET` request and this route only handles `POST`s. Instead we can use the command line to create a user:

```
curl http://localhost:3000/user/create -d {}
```

and the server should respond with:

```
{"title":"User created"}
```

CURLing and WGETing

If you're using a Mac or Linux box, you can use `curl` to test out your API and skip the browser. We can test the URL we just created by doing a `POST` to user/create:

```
curl http://localhost:3000/user/create -d {}
{"title":"User created"}
```

The `-d` is used to send data and the empty object literal sends no data over. Instead of opening a browser to test a route, using `curl` can dramatically speed up your development time. To discover more about `curl`'s capabilities, type `curl -h` at the command prompt.

One can get similar results with `wget`:

```
wget http://localhost:3000/user/create --post-data='{}' -O -
```

To discover more about `wget`'s capabilities, type `wget -h` at the command prompt.

Now that we have a route to create a user object, we want to create a route to read a user object.

MAKE A ROUTE TO READ A USER OBJECT

The route to read a user object is similar to the create route, but uses the `GET` method and has an additional argument passed in through the URL: the ID of the user. This route is created by using a colon to define a parameter in the route path, as shown in listing 7.16. Changes are shown in **bold**:

Listing 7.16 Make a route to read a user object—webapp/app.js

```
/*
 * app.js - Express server with advanced routing
*/
...
// ------------- BEGIN SERVER CONFIGURATION ---------------
...

app.post( '/user/create', function ( request, response ) {
  response.contentType( 'json' );
  response.send({ title: 'user created' });
```

```
});

app.get( '/user/read/:id', function ( request, response ) {
  response.contentType( 'json' );
  response.send({
    title: 'user with id ' + request.params.id + ' found'
  });
});
// -------------- END SERVER CONFIGURATION ----------------
...
```

The user `:id` parameter at the end of the route is accessible through the `request.params` object. The route of `/user/read/:id` makes the user ID accessible at `request.params['id']` or `request.params.id`. If the requested URL was http://localhost:3000/user/read/12 then the value of `request.params.id` would be 12. Give it a try, and also notice that this route works no matter what the value of `id` is—it accepts just about anything as long as there's a valid value. There are more examples in table 7.1.

Table 7.1 Routes and their results

Try these in the browser	Output in Node.js terminal
/user/read/19	{"title":"User with id 19 found"}
/user/read/spa	{"title":"User with id spa found"}
/user/read/	Cannot GET /user/read/
/user/read/?	Cannot GET /user/read/?

It's good that the routes with anything are caught, but what if our ID will always be a number? We don't want the router to intercept a path that doesn't have a number as the ID. Express provides the capability to only accept routes that contain numbers by adding a regular expression pattern, `[(0-9)]+`, into the route definition, as shown in listing 7.17. Changes are shown in **bold**:

Listing 7.17 Constrain the route to only numeric IDs—webapp/app.js

```
/*
 * app.js - Express server with advanced routing
*/
...
// ------------- BEGIN SERVER CONFIGURATION ---------------
...

app.get( '/user/read/:id([0-9]+)', function ( request, response ) {
  response.contentType( 'json' );
  response.send({
    title: 'user with id ' + request.params.id + ' found'
  });
});
// -------------- END SERVER CONFIGURATION ----------------
...
```

Table 7.2 shows that the route will now only accept numbered IDs.

Table 7.2 Routes and their results

Try these in the browser	Result
/user/read/19	{"title":"User with id 19 found"}
/user/read/spa	Cannot GET /user/read/spa

MAKE ROUTES TO UPDATE OR DELETE A USER

The routes for updating and deleting a user are much the same as those for reading a user at this point, though in the next chapter the actions they take on the user object will be much different. We add the routes for updating and deleting a user in listing 5.18. Changes are shown in **bold**:

Listing 7.18 Define routes for CRUD—webapp/app.js

```
/*
 * app.js - Express server with advanced routing
*/
...
// ------------ BEGIN SERVER CONFIGURATION --------------
...

app.get( '/user/read/:id([0-9]+)', function ( request, response ) {
  response.contentType( 'json' );
  response.send({
    title: 'user with id ' + request.params.id + ' found'
  });
});

app.post( '/user/update/:id([0-9]+)',
  function ( request, response ) {
    response.contentType( 'json' );
    response.send({
      title: 'user with id ' + request.params.id + ' updated'
    });
  }
);

app.get( '/user/delete/:id([0-9]+)',
  function ( request, response ) {
    response.contentType( 'json' );
    response.send({
      title: 'user with id ' + request.params.id + ' deleted'
    });
  }
);
// ------------- END SERVER CONFIGURATION ---------------
...
```

Creating these basic routes was easy, but you may have noticed that we're having to set the contentType for every response. That's error-prone and inefficient—a better way would be if we could set the contentType for all responses to these user CRUD operations. Ideally, we'd like to create a route that intercepts all incoming user routes and sets the response contentType to json. Two complications stand in our way:

1 Some of the requests are using the GET method, and others are using POST.
2 After setting the response's contentType, we want the router to work as before.

Fortunately, Express again delivers. In addition to the app.get and app.post methods, there's an app.all method that will intercept routes regardless of their method type. Express also lets us pass control back to the router to see if any other routes match the request by setting and calling a third argument in the router callback method. The third argument is called next by convention, and immediately passes control to the next middleware or route. We add the app.all method in listing 7.19. Changes are shown in **bold**:

Listing 7.19 Using app.all() to set common attributes—webapp/app.js

```
/*
 * app.js - Express server with advanced routing
*/
...
// ------------ BEGIN SERVER CONFIGURATION --------------
...
// all configurations below are for routes
app.get( '/', function ( request, response ) {
  response.redirect( '/spa.html' );
});

app.all( '/user/*?', function ( request, response, next ) {
  response.contentType( 'json' );
  next();
});

app.get( '/user/list', function ( request, response ) {
  // REMOVE response.contentType( 'json' );
  response.send({ title: 'user list' });
});

app.post( '/user/create', function ( request, response ) {
  // REMOVE response.contentType( 'json' );
  response.send({ title: 'user created' });
});

app.get( '/user/read/:id([0-9]+)',
  function ( request, response ) {
    // REMOVE response.contentType( 'json' );
    response.send({
      title: 'user with id ' + request.params.id + ' found'
    });
  }
);

app.post( '/user/update/:id([0-9]+)',
  function ( request, response ) {
```

```
    // REMOVE response.contentType( 'json' );
    response.send({
      title: 'user with id ' + request.params.id + ' updated'
    });
  }
);

app.get( '/user/delete/:id([0-9]+)',
  function ( request, response ) {
    // REMOVE response.contentType( 'json' );
    response.send({
      title: 'user with id ' + request.params.id + ' deleted'
    });
  }
);
// -------------- END SERVER CONFIGURATION ----------------
...
```

In the route pattern, /user/*?, the * will match anything and the ? makes it optional. /user/*? will match any of the following routes:

- /user
- /user/
- /user/12
- /user/spa
- /user/create
- /user/delete/12

Now that our user routing is in place, it's easy to imagine the number of routes exploding as we add object types. Do we really need to define five new routes for every type of object? Fortunately, no. We can make these routes generic and place them in their own module.

7.3.2 Generic CRUD routing

We already know that we can use route parameters to accept arguments from the client, but we can also use them to make our routes generic. We just need to tell Express to use a portion of the URI as a parameter. This will do the trick:

```
app.get( '/:obj_type/read/:id([0-9]+)',
  function ( request, response ) {
    response.send({
      title: request.params.obj_type + ' with id '
       + request.params.id + ' found'
    });
  }
);
```

Now when we request /horse/read/12 we will get the object type (horse) in the request parameter, request.params.obj_type, and the response JSON will be { title: "horse with id 12 found" }. Applying that logic to the rest of our methods, we end up with the code in listing 7.20. All changes are shown in **bold**.

Listing 7.20 Complete generic CRUD routes—webapp/app.js

```
/*
 * app.js - Express server with generic routing
*/
...
// ------------ BEGIN SERVER CONFIGURATION --------------
...
// all configurations below are for routes
app.get( '/', function ( request, response ) {
  response.redirect( '/spa.html' );
});

app.all( '/:obj_type/*?', function ( request, response, next ) {
  response.contentType( 'json' );
  next();
});

app.get( '/:obj_type/list', function ( request, response ) {
  response.send({ title: request.params.obj_type + ' list' });
});

app.post( '/:obj_type/create', function ( request, response ) {
  response.send({ title: request.params.obj_type + ' created' });
});

app.get( '/:obj_type/read/:id([0-9]+)',
  function ( request, response ) {
    response.send({
      title: request.params.obj_type
        + ' with id ' + request.params.id + ' found'
    });
  }
);

app.post( '/:obj_type/update/:id([0-9]+)',
  function ( request, response ) {
    response.send({
      title: request.params.obj_type
        + ' with id ' + request.params.id + ' updated'
    });
  }
);

app.get( '/:obj_type/delete/:id([0-9]+)',
  function ( request, response ) {
    response.send({
      title: request.params.obj_type
        + ' with id ' + request.params.id + ' deleted'
    });
  }
);
// ------------- END SERVER CONFIGURATION ---------------
...
```

Now when we start up the application (`node app.js`) and point our browser to http://localhost:3000, we will see our familiar SPA, as shown in figure 7.1:

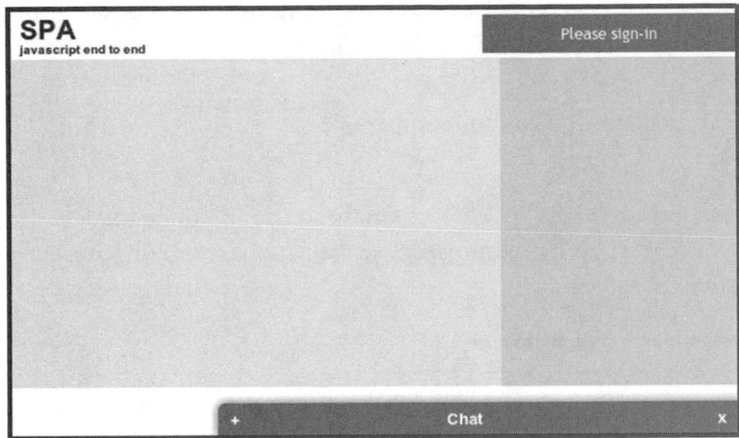

Figure 7.1 Our SPA in the browser—http://localhost:3000

This shows that our static file configuration allowed the browser to read all the HTML, JavaScript, and CSS files. But we still also have access to our CRUD API. If we point our browser to http://localhost:3000/user/read/12, we should see something like:

```
{
  title: "user with id 12 found"
}
```

What if we were to have a file at <root_directory>/user/read/12 (don't laugh, you *know* this stuff happens)? In our case, the file would be returned instead of a CRUD response. This is because the `express.static` middleware is added before the router, as shown next:

```
...
app.configure( function () {
  app.use( express.bodyParser() );
  app.use( express.methodOverride() );
  app.use( express.static( __dirname + '/public' ) );
  app.use( app.router );
});
...
```

If, however, we reversed the order and put the router first, the CRUD response would be returned instead of the static file. The benefit of this arrangement might be faster response to a CRUD request; the downside is slower and more complicated file access. The *smart* thing to do is to place all the CRUD requests under a single root name like /api/1.0.0/ so that dynamic and static content are neatly separated.

Now we have the basics of a clean, generic router to manage any object type. Obviously, this doesn't take into account authorization issues, but we'll get to that logic a little later. First, let's first move all the routing logic into a separate module.

7.3.3 Place routing in a separate Node.js module

Keeping all of your routes defined in the main app.js file is rather like writing client-side JavaScript in the HTML page—it clutters up your app and doesn't maintain a clean separation of responsibilities. Let's start by looking a little closer at the Node.js module system, which is Node.js's way of including modular code.

NODE MODULES

Node modules are loaded with the function `require`.

```
var spa = require( './routes' );
```

The string passed in to `require` specifies the path to the file to be loaded. There are a few different syntax rules to be memorized, so have patience. For your convenience, these are described in table 7.3.

Table 7.3 Node search path logic for *require*

Syntax	Search paths, in order of precedence
`require( './routes.js' );`	`app/routes.js`

`require( './routes' );`	`app/routes.js`
	`app/routes.json`
	`app/routes.node`

`require( '../routes.js' );`	`../routes.js`

`require( 'routes' );`	`app/node_modules/routes.js`
	`app/node_modules/routes/index.js`
	`<system_install>/node_modules/routes.js`
	`<system_install>/node_modules/routes/index.js`
	This syntax is also used to refer to core node.js modules, such as the http module.

Inside of a node module, variables scoped with `var` are constrained to the module and don't need a self-executing anonymous function to keep the variable out of the global scope like the client side requires. Instead, there's the `module` object. The value assigned to the `module.exports` attribute is provided as the return value of the `require` method. Let's create the routes module, as shown in listing 7.21:

Listing 7.21 Create the routes module—`webapp/routes.js`

```
module.exports = function () {
  console.log( 'You have included the routes module.' );
};
```

The `module.exports` value can be any data type such as a function, object, array, string, number, or boolean. In this case, routes.js sets the value of `module.exports` to an anonymous function. Let's `require` routes.js in app.js and store the return value in the `routes` variable. We can then invoke the returned function as shown in listing 7.22. Changes are shown in **bold**:

Listing 7.22 Include a module and use the return value—webapp/app.js

```
/*
 * app.js - Express server with sample module
*/
...
// ------------ BEGIN MODULE SCOPE VARIABLES --------------
'use strict';
var
  http    = require( 'http'     ),
  express = require( 'express'  ),
  routes  = require( './routes' ),
  app     = express(),
  server  = http.createServer( app );

routes();
// ------------- END MODULE SCOPE VARIABLES ---------------
...
```

When we type node app.js at the command prompt, we should see the following:

```
You have included the routes module.
 Express server listening on port 3000 in development mode
```

Now that we have added our routes module, let's move our router configuration to it.

MOVE ROUTING TO A MODULE

When we create a non-trivial application we like to define our routing in a single file in the main application folder. In a larger application with lots of routes, we can define them in a routes folder with as many files as we need.

Since our next app will be non-trivial, let's create a file in the root spa directory called routes.js and copy the existing routes into the module.exports function. It should look like listing 7.23.

Listing 7.23 Place routes in a separate module—webapp/routes.js

```
/*
 * routes.js - module to provide routing
*/
/*jslint         node    : true, continue : true,
  devel  : true, indent  : 2,    maxerr   : 50,
  newcap : true, nomen   : true, plusplus : true,
  regexp : true, sloppy  : true, vars     : false,
  white  : true
*/
/*global */

// ------------ BEGIN MODULE SCOPE VARIABLES --------------
'use strict';
var configRoutes;
// ------------- END MODULE SCOPE VARIABLES ---------------

// --------------- BEGIN PUBLIC METHODS ------------------
configRoutes = function ( app, server ) {
  app.get( '/', function ( request, response ) {
```

The app and server variables aren't global so they must be passed into the function. Node.js goes to great lengths to not let variables defined in one module or in the main application have an impact on variables in other modules.

```
    response.redirect( '/spa.html' );
  });

  app.all( '/:obj_type/*?', function ( request, response, next ) {
    response.contentType( 'json' );
    next();
  });

  app.get( '/:obj_type/list', function ( request, response ) {
    response.send({ title: request.params.obj_type + ' list' });
  });

  app.post( '/:obj_type/create', function ( request, response ) {
    response.send({ title: request.params.obj_type + ' created' });
  });

  app.get( '/:obj_type/read/:id([0-9]+)',
    function ( request, response ) {
      response.send({
        title: request.params.obj_type
          + ' with id ' + request.params.id + ' found'
      });
    }
  );

  app.post( '/:obj_type/update/:id([0-9]+)',
    function ( request, response ) {
      response.send({
        title: request.params.obj_type
          + ' with id ' + request.params.id + ' updated'
      });
    }
  );

  app.get( '/:obj_type/delete/:id([0-9]+)',
    function ( request, response ) {
      response.send({
        title: request.params.obj_type
          + ' with id ' + request.params.id + ' deleted'
      });
    }
  );
};
module.exports = { configRoutes : configRoutes };
// ----------------- END PUBLIC METHODS -------------------
```

Set the content type of `json`.

We export a method that can be invoked when `webapp/app.js` is read to use it.

Now we can adjust `webapp/app.js` to use the routing module, as shown in listing 7.24. Changes are shown in **bold**.

Listing 7.24 Update server application to use external routes—`webapp/app.js`

```
/*
 * app.js - Express server with routes module
*/
...
// ------------ BEGIN MODULE SCOPE VARIABLES --------------
'use strict';
```

```
var
  http    = require( 'http'     ),
  express = require( 'express'  ),
  routes = require( './routes' ),

  app     = express(),
  server  = http.createServer( app );
// ------------- END MODULE SCOPE VARIABLES ---------------

// ------------- BEGIN SERVER CONFIGURATION ---------------
app.configure( function () {
  app.use( express.bodyParser() );
  app.use( express.methodOverride() );
  app.use( express.static( __dirname + '/public' ) );
  app.use( app.router );
});

app.configure( 'development', function () {
  app.use( express.logger() );
  app.use( express.errorHandler({
    dumpExceptions : true,
    showStack      : true
  }) );
});

app.configure( 'production', function () {
  app.use( express.errorHandler() );
});

routes.configRoutes( app, server );
// -------------- END SERVER CONFIGURATION ----------------

// ----------------- BEGIN START SERVER -------------------
server.listen( 3000 );
console.log(
  'Express server listening on port %d in %s mode',
   server.address().port, app.settings.env
);
// ------------------ END START SERVER --------------------
```

Load the routes module.

Use the `configRoutes` method to set up the routes.

This leaves us with a pretty clean app.js: it loads the needed library modules, creates our Express application, configures our middleware, adds our routes, and starts the server. What it doesn't do is persist your data to a database by actually performing any of the requested actions. We'll hook that up in the next chapter after setting up MongoDB and connecting it to our Node.js application. Before doing that, let's take a look at some other things we might need first.

7.4 Adding authentication and authorization

Now that we've created the routes for performing CRUD actions on our objects, we should add authentication. We can do this the hard way and code it ourselves, or do it the easy way and take advantage of another Express middleware. Hmm. Think... think, which to choose?

7.4.1 Basic Authentication

Basic Authentication is an HTTP/1.0 and 1.1 standard for how a client provides a username and password when making a request; it's commonly referred to as *basic auth*. Remember that middleware is called in the order it's added to the application, so if you want the application to authorize access to the routes, the middleware needs to be added before the router middleware. That's easy enough to do as shown in listing 7.25. Changes are shown in **bold**:

Listing 7.25 Add basic auth to our server application—webapp/app.js

```
/*
 * app.js - Express server with basic auth
*/
...
// ------------ BEGIN SERVER CONFIGURATION --------------
app.configure( function () {
  app.use( express.bodyParser() );
  app.use( express.methodOverride() );
  app.use( express.basicAuth( 'user', 'spa' ) );
  app.use( express.static( __dirname + '/public' ) );
  app.use( app.router );
});
...
```

In this case, we've hard-coded the app to expect the user to be `user` and the password to be `spa`. `basicAuth` also accepts a function as the third parameter, which can be used to provide more advanced mechanisms, like looking up user details in a database. That function should return `true` if the user is valid, and `false` when the user is not. When we restart the server and reload the browser, it should open an alert dialog that looks like figure 7.2, requiring a valid User Name and Password before allowing access.

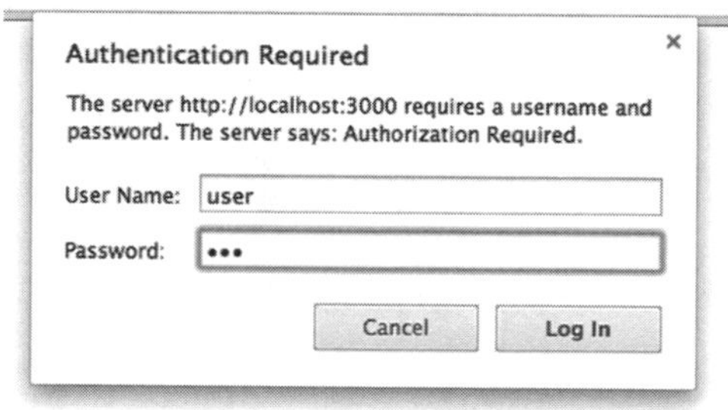

Figure 7.2 Chrome's authentication dialog

If we enter the wrong password, it'll keep prompting until we get it right. Pressing the Cancel button will bring us to a page that says `Unauthorized`.

Basic authentication is *not* recommended for use in a production app. It sends the credentials for every request in plain text—security experts call this a *large attack vector.* And even if we use SSL (HTTPS) to encrypt the transmission, we only have one layer of security between the client and server.

Rolling your own authentication mechanism is getting passé these days. Many startups and even larger more established companies are using third-party authentication from the likes of Facebook or Google. There are many online tutorials showing how to integrate with these services; the Node.js middleware Passport can get you started.

7.5 Web sockets and Socket.IO

Web sockets are an exciting technology that's gaining widespread browser support. Web sockets allow the client and server to maintain a persistent, lightweight, and bi-directional communication channel over a single TCP connection. This lets the client or server push messages in real-time without the overhead and latency of an HTTP request-response cycle. Prior to web sockets, developers had employed alternate—but less efficient—techniques to provide similar capabilities. These techniques included using Flash sockets; long-polling, where the browser opens a request to a server and then reinitializes the request when there's a response or when the request times out; and server polling at close intervals (say, once per second).

The trouble with web sockets is that the specifications haven't yet been finalized and older browsers will never support it. Socket.IO is a Node.js module that gracefully resolves the latter concern, as it provides browser-to-server messaging over web sockets if available, but will degrade to use other techniques if sockets aren't available.

7.5.1 Simple Socket.IO

Let's create a simple Socket.IO application that updates a counter on the server every second and pushes the current count to connected clients. We can install Socket.IO by updating our package.json as shown in listing 7.26. Changes are shown in **bold**:

Listing 7.26 Installing Socket.IO—webapp/package.json

```
{
  "name"    : "SPA",
  "version" : "0.0.3",
  "private" : true,
  "dependencies" : {
    "express"   : "3.2.x",
    "socket.io" : "0.9.x"
  }
}
```

Now we can run `npm install` to ensure both Express and Socket.IO are installed.

Let's add two files, a server application named webapp/socket.js and browser document named webapp/socket.html. Let's start by building a server application that can serve static files and that has a timer that increments once per second. Since we know we are going to use Socket.IO, we will include that library too. Listing 7.27 shows our new socket.js server application:

Listing 7.27 Begin the server application—webapp/socket.js

```
/*
 * socket.js - simple socket.io example
*/

/*jslint         node    : true, continue : true,
  devel  : true, indent  : 2,    maxerr   : 50,
  newcap : true, nomen   : true, plusplus : true,
```

```
  regexp : true, sloppy  : true, vars     : false,
  white  : true
*/
/*global */

// ------------ BEGIN MODULE SCOPE VARIABLES --------------
'use strict';
var
  countUp,

  http     = require( 'http'      ),
  express  = require( 'express'   ),
  socketIo = require( 'socket.io' ),

  app      = express(),
  server   = http.createServer( app ),
  countIdx = 0
  ;
// ------------- END MODULE SCOPE VARIABLES ---------------

// --------------- BEGIN UTILITY METHODS ------------------
countUp = function () {
  countIdx++;
  console.log( countIdx );
};
// ---------------- END UTILITY METHODS -------------------

// ------------- BEGIN SERVER CONFIGURATION ---------------
app.configure( function () {
  app.use( express.static( __dirname + '/' ) );
});

app.get( '/', function ( request, response ) {
  response.redirect( '/socket.html' );
});
// -------------- END SERVER CONFIGURATION ----------------

// ----------------- BEGIN START SERVER -------------------
server.listen( 3000 );
console.log(
  'Express server listening on port %d in %s mode',
   server.address().port, app.settings.env
);

setInterval( countUp, 1000 );
 // ------------------ END START SERVER -------------------
```

Create a module-scope count variable.

Create a utility to increment the count and log it.

Direct the application to serve static files from the current working directory.

Use the JavaScript `setInterval` function to call the `countUp` function every 1000 milliseconds.

When we start the server—`node socket.js`—we see it logging a constantly incrementing number in the terminal. Now, let's create the `webapp/socket.html` shown in listing 7.28 to display this number. We'll include jQuery because it makes grabbing the body tag simple:

Listing 7.28 Create the browser document—webapp/socket.html

```
<!doctype html>
<!-- socket.html - simple socket example -->
<html>
<head>
```

```
  <script type="text/javascript"
src="http://ajax.googleapis.com/ajax/libs/jquery/1.9.1/jquery.min.js"
  ></script>
</head>
<body>
  Loading...
</body>
</html>
```

We should now be able to load `http://localhost:3000` and see the nearly blank page. Getting Socket.IO to send this information to the client takes just two additional lines in our server application, as shown in listing 7.29. Changes are shown in **bold**:

Listing 7.29 Add web sockets to the server application—webapp/socket.js

```
...
  server     = http.createServer( app ),
  io         = socketIo.listen( server ),    // Instruct Socket.IO to listen using our HTTP server.
  countIdx   = 0
  ;
// ------------- END MODULE SCOPE VARIABLES ---------------

// --------------- BEGIN UTILITY METHODS ------------------
countUp = function () {
  countIdx++;
  console.log( countIdx );
  io.sockets.send( countIdx );    // Send the count to all listening sockets.
};
// ---------------- END UTILITY METHODS -------------------

// ------------- BEGIN SERVER CONFIGURATION ---------------
...
```

The browser document requires just an additional six lines to enable Socket.IO, as shown in listing 7.30. Changes are shown in **bold**:

Listing 7.30 Add web sockets to the browser document—webapp/socket.html

```
<!doctype html>
<!-- socket.html - simple socket example -->
<html>
<head>
  <script type="text/javascript"
src="http://ajax.googleapis.com/ajax/libs/jquery/1.9.1/jquery.min.js"
  ></script>
  <script src="/socket.io/socket.io.js"></script>
  <script>
    io.connect().on('message', function ( count ) {
      $('body').html( count );
    });
  </script>
</head>
<body>
  Loading...
</body>
</html>
```

The JavaScript file `/socket.io/socket.io.js` is provided by the Socket.IO installation so there's no need to create one; it's also a "magical" file that doesn't actually exist on the server, so don't go looking for it. `io.connect()` returns a Socket.IO connection and the `on` method is similar to the `bind` method in jQuery, in that it tells it to watch for a certain kind of Socket.IO event. In this case, the event we're looking for is any message coming over the connection. Then we use jQuery to update the body with the new count. You went looking for the socket.io.js file on the server, didn't you?

If we open `http://localhost:3000/` in a browser we should see the counter incrementing. When we open another tab to the same location we should see another counter incrementing at the same number and rate because `countIdx` is a module-scope variable in the server application.

7.5.2 Socket.IO and messaging servers

When we use Socket.IO to route messages between clients and servers, we're creating a messaging server. An example of another messaging server is *Openfire*, which serves messages using XMPP, the protocol used by Google Chat and Jabber. A messaging server must maintain connections to all clients so they can receive and respond to messages quickly. They should also minimize the size of the message by avoiding unnecessary data.

Traditional web servers such as Apache2 are poor messaging servers because they create and assign a process (or thread) for every connection, *and each process must live for as long as its connection persists.* As you might guess, after a few hundred or thousand connections, a web server will have all its resources consumed by all the processes used to service the connections. Apache2 was never designed for this; it was written as a content server, where the idea is to push data out as fast as possible in response to a request and then close the connection as fast as possible. For these types of uses, Apache2 is a great choice—just ask YouTube.

Node.js, by comparison, is an excellent messaging server. Thanks to its event model, it *doesn't* create a process for every connection. Instead it does some bookkeeping when a connection is opened or closed, and some maintenance in between. Therefore it can handle tens or hundreds of thousands of concurrent connections on modest hardware. Node.js doesn't do any significant work until a messaging event—like a request or a response—occurs on one or more of its open connections.

The number of messaging clients Node.js can handle depends on the actual workload the server encounters. If the clients are relatively quiet and the server tasks are lightweight, the server can handle *lots* of clients. If the clients are chatty and the server tasks are heavier, the server can handle *a lot less.* It's conceivable in a high-volume environment that a load balancer would route traffic between a cluster of Node.js servers that provides messaging, another cluster of Node.js servers that provides dynamic web content, and a cluster of Apache2 servers that provides static content.

There are many benefits of using Node.js over other messaging protocols such as XMPP. Here are just a few:

- Socket.IO makes cross-browser messaging in a web app almost trivial. We've used XMPP before for a production application. Trust us: it's a *lot* more work just for the software.
- We can avoid maintaining a separate server and configuration. Again, another big win.
- We can work with native JSON protocol instead of a different language. XMPP is XML and requires sophisticated software to encode and decode.
- We don't have to worry (at least initially) about the dreaded "same domain" policy that plagues other messaging platforms. This browser policy prevents content from loading into browsers if it doesn't come from the same server as the JavaScript that's using it.

Now let's look at a use of Socket.IO that's sure to impress: dynamically updating our SPA.

7.5.3 Updating JavaScript with Socket.IO

One challenge with an SPA is ensuring the client software matches the server application. Imagine if Bobbie loaded our SPA into her browser, and five minutes later we update our server application. Now Bobbie has a problem, because our updated server communicates in a new data format, yet Bobbie's SPA still expects the old. One way to resolve this situation is to force Bobbie to reload the entire SPA when it recognizes it's out of date—say after we sent it a message announcing the server update. But we can get even fancier—we can selectively update only the JavaScript that has changed in the SPA without forcing the entire application to reload.

So how do we do this magical update? There are three parts to consider:

1 Watching the JavaScript files to detect when they're modified.
2 Notifying the client the file has been updated.
3 Updating the client side JavaScript when it's notified of the change.

The first part, detecting when the file is modified, can be accomplished using the native node file system module `fs`. The second is a matter of sending a Socket.IO notification to the browser as described in the previous section, and updating the client can be accomplished through injecting a new script tag when receiving a notification. We can update our server application from the last example as shown in listing 7.31. Changes are shown in **bold**:

Listing 7.31 Update the server application to watch files—webapp/socket.js

```
/*
 * socket.js - dynamic JS loading example
*/

/*jslint         node    : true, continue : true,
  devel  : true, indent  : 2,    maxerr   : 50,
  newcap : true, nomen   : true, plusplus : true,
  regexp : true, sloppy  : true, vars     : false,
  white  : true
```

```
*/
/*global */

// ------------ BEGIN MODULE SCOPE VARIABLES --------------
'use strict';
var
  setWatch,

  http      = require( 'http'      ),
  express   = require( 'express'   ),
  socketIo  = require( 'socket.io' ),
  fsHandle  = require( 'fs'        ),

  app       = express(),
  server    = http.createServer( app ),
  io        = socketIo.listen( server ),
  watchMap  = {}
  ;
// ------------- END MODULE SCOPE VARIABLES ---------------

// --------------- BEGIN UTILITY METHODS ------------------
setWatch = function ( url_path, file_type ) {
  console.log( 'setWatch called on ' + url_path );

  if ( ! watchMap[ url_path ] ) {
    console.log( 'setting watch on ' + url_path );

    fsHandle.watchFile(

      url_path.slice(1),
      function ( current, previous ) {

        console.log( 'file accessed' );
        if ( current.mtime !== previous.mtime ) {
          console.log( 'file changed' );
          io.sockets.emit( file_type, url_path );
        }
      }
    );
    watchMap[ url_path ] = true;
  }
};
// ---------------- END UTILITY METHODS -------------------

// ------------- BEGIN SERVER CONFIGURATION ---------------
app.configure( function () {
  app.use( function ( request, response, next ) {
    if ( request.url.indexOf( '/js/' ) >= 0 ) {
      setWatch( request.url, 'script' );
    }
    else if ( request.url.indexOf( '/css/' ) >= 0 ) {
      setWatch( request.url, 'stylesheet' );
    }
    next();
  });
  app.use( express.static( __dirname + '/' ) );
});

app.get( '/', function ( request, response ) {
```

Load the file system module into `fsHandle`.

Compare the modified timestamps (`mtime`) of the current state of the file with the previous state of the file to see if it has been modified.

Instruct the file system module to watch the file for changes.

Trim the / from `url_path`, as the file system module needs the relative path from the current directory.

Emit a `script` or `stylesheet` event to the client containing the path of the file that changed.

Use custom middleware to set a watch for any statically served files.

If the requested file is in the `js` folder, consider it a `script` file.

If the requested file is in the `css` folder, consider it a `stylesheet` file.

```
  response.redirect( '/socket.html' );
});
// -------------- END SERVER CONFIGURATION ----------------

// ----------------- BEGIN START SERVER -------------------
server.listen( 3000 );
console.log(
  'Express server listening on port %d in %s mode',
  server.address().port, app.settings.env
);
// ------------------ END START SERVER --------------------
```

Now that we've prepared the server application, let's look at the client, starting with the JavaScript file we'll be updating and then the index page. Our data file, webapp/js/data.js, consists of one line assigning some text to a variable, as shown in listing 7.32:

Listing 7.32 Create a data file—webapp/js/data.js

```
var b = 'SPA';
```

Changes to our browser document need to be a little more substantial, as shown in listing 7.33. Changes are shown in **bold**:

Listing 7.33 Update the browser document—webapp/socket.html

```
<!doctype html>
<!-- socket.html - dynamic JS loading example -->
<html>
<head>
  <script type="text/javascript"
src="http://ajax.googleapis.com/ajax/libs/jquery/1.9.1/jquery.min.js"
  ></script>
  <script src="/socket.io/socket.io.js"></script>
  <script id="script_a" src="/js/data.js"></script>
  <script>
    $(function () {
      $( 'body' ).html( b );
    });
    io.connect('http://localhost').on( 'script', function ( path ) {
      $( '#script_a' ).remove();
      $( 'head' ).append(
        '<script id="script_a" src="'
        + path +
        '"></scr' + 'ipt>'
      );
      $( 'body' ).html( b );
    });
  </script>
</head>
<body>
  Loading...
</body>
</html>
```

Include the JavaScript file we'll be updating.

When the page first loads, set the HTML body to the value of the b variable set in the data.js file.

When we receive a script event emitted from the server, execute this function.

Remove the old script tag and inject a new one pointing to the updated JavaScript file. This will execute the JavaScript in that file and, in the case of webapp/js/data.js, reload the b variable.

Replace the HTML body with the update value of the b variable.

Now we can make the magic happen. First, let's start our server application (type `node socket.js` on the command line). Next, let's open our browser document (webapp/socket.html). We should see `SPA` in our browser body. Let's then edit the webapp/js/data.js file and change the value of `SPA` to `the meaning of life is a rutabaga` or some other equally pithy comment. When we return to the browser, we should see the display change (without reloading the browser) from `SPA` to the aforementioned pithy comment. There may be a delay of a few seconds because the `watchFile` command can take that long to notice a file change.[1]

7.6 Summary

In this chapter, we've seen that although much of the logic of an SPA has been moved to the client, the server is still responsible for authentication, data validation, and data storage. We've set up a Node.js server and used the Connect and Express middleware to make routing, logging, and authentication easier.

Separating the routing and configuration logic into different files makes it easier to comprehend, and Express gives us the capability to define different configurations for different environments. Express provided us the tools to easily create CRUD routes that work for all our object types.

We haven't yet tackled how to validate and store data—that comes in the next chapter, when we bring the application and the data together.

---

1 In a production setting we generally want to keep file polling (`fstats`) to a minimum, as it can be a real drag on performance. The `fileWatch` method can have options set so that files are polled less frequently. For example, we might poll once every 30,000 milliseconds (30 seconds) instead of the default of 0 (which we can only assume means "check really, really often").

8 The server database

This chapter covers

- The role of the database in an SPA
- Using JavaScript as the database language with MongoDB
- Understanding the Node.js MongoDB driver
- Implementing CRUD operations
- Using JSV for data validation
- Pushing data changes to the client with Socket.IO

This chapter builds on code we've written in chapter 7. We recommend copying the entire directory structure for that chapter into a new "chapter_8" directory and updating the files there.

In this chapter, we add the database to our SPA for persistent data storage. This completes our vision of using JavaScript end-to-end—on the database, the server, and the browser. When we're finished, we'll be able to start our Node.js server application and invite our friends to sign in to the SPA with their computer or touch device. They can then chat with each other or make changes to avatars that everyone can see in near-real time. Let's get started by looking more closely at the role of the database.

8.1 The role of the database

We use the database server to provide reliable, persistent storage of data. We rely on the server for this role because data stored on the client is transitory and prone to application errors, user error, and user tampering. Client-side data is also difficult to share peer-to-peer and is available only when the client is online.

8.1.1 Select the data store

We have many options to consider when selecting a server storage solution: relational databases, key/value stores, and NoSQL databases to name a few. But what's the best option? Like many questions in life, the answer is "it depends." We've worked with web applications where many of these solutions were used concurrently for different purposes. Many people have written volumes on the merits of various data stores such as relational databases (like *MySQL*), key-value stores (like *memcached*), graph databases (like *Neo4J*), or document databases (like *Cassandra* or *MongoDB*). Discussion of the relative merits of these solutions is outside of the scope of this book, though the authors tend to be agnostic and think that each of these has its place.

Let's envision that we've created an SPA that's a word processor. We might use a round-robin file system data store for the bulk files, but index them using a MySQL database. In addition, we may store authentication objects in MongoDB. In any case, the user will almost certainly expect to save their documents to the server for long-term storage. Sometimes the user may want to read from or save to a file on their local disk, and we almost certainly should provide that option. But the use case for local storage continues to diminish as the value and reliability of networks, remote storage, and accessibility continue to improve.

We've selected MongoDB as our data store for a number of reasons: it has proven reliable, it's scalable, it has good performance, and—unlike some other NoSQL options—it's positioned to be a general purpose database. We find it well-suited for SPAs because it enables us to use JavaScript and JSON from one end of the SPA to the other. Its command-line interface uses JavaScript as its query language, so we can easily test JavaScript constructs while exploring a database, or manipulate data using the exact same expressions as we do in our server or browser environment. It uses JSON as its storage format and its data management tools are purpose-built for JSON.

8.1.2 Eliminate data transformations

Consider the traditional web application written in MySQL/Ruby on Rails (or mod_perl, PHP, ASP, Java, or Python) and JavaScript: the developer must write code to convert from SQL -> Active Record -> JSON on the way to the client, and then JSON -> Active Record -> SQL on the way back (see figure 8.1). That's three languages (SQL, Ruby, JavaScript), three data formats (SQL, Active Record, JSON), and four data transformations. At best, this wastes a great deal of server power that could be better used elsewhere. At worst, each transformation provides an opportunity to introduce bugs, and it can require a great deal of effort to implement *and* maintain.

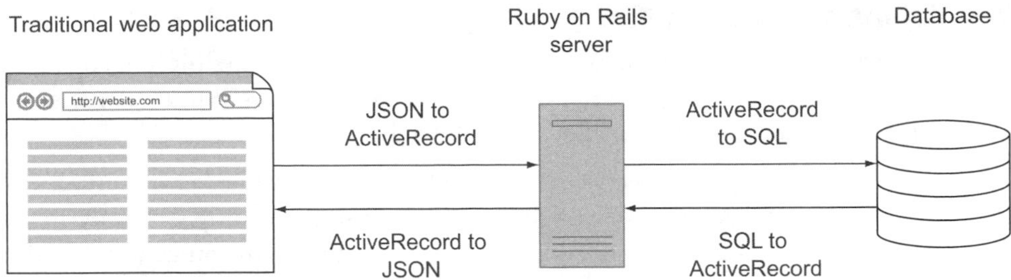

Figure 8.1 Data transformations in a web application

We use MongoDB, Node.js, and a native JavaScript SPA, so our data mapping looks like this: JSON -> JSON -> JSON on the way to the client, and then JSON -> JSON -> JSON on the way back (see figure 8.2). We work with one language (JavaScript), one data format (JSON), and no data transformations. This brings powerful simplicity to a once complex system.

The simplicity of this setup also enables us to be flexible when deciding where to place our application logic.

8.1.3 Move the logic where you need it

In our traditional web application example, consider how we choose where to place some application logic. Perhaps we should place it in a stored SQL procedure? Or perhaps we should embed the logic in the server application? Maybe we should put the logic on the client? If we need to move from one layer to another, it usually requires a great deal of effort because the layers use different languages and data formats. In other words, it was often enormously expensive to be wrong (imagine rewriting logic from Java to JavaScript, for example). That leads to compromised "safe" choices that limit the capability of the application.

The use of a single language and data format greatly reduces the expense of changing our minds. This allows us to be much more inventive during development because *the cost of being wrong is minimal.* If we need to move some logic from the server to the client, we can use the same JavaScript with little or no or alteration.

Now let's take a deeper look at our database of choice, MongoDB.

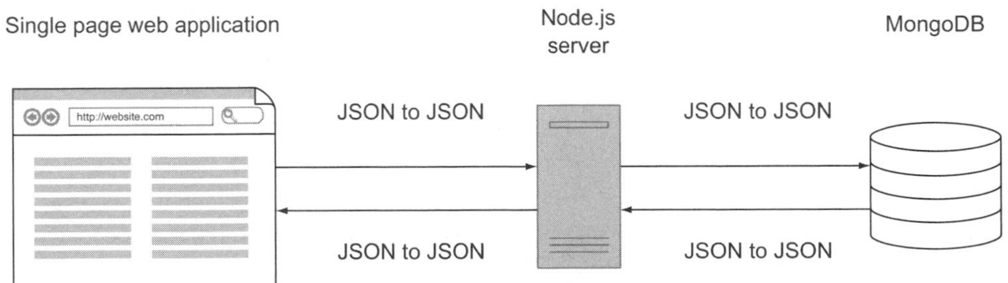

Figure 8.2 With MongoDB, Node.js, and an SPA there's no data transformation

8.2 An introduction to MongoDB

According to the MongoDB website, MongoDB is "a scalable, high-performance, open source NoSQL database" using document-oriented storage with dynamic schemas that offer "simplicity and power." Let's step through what that means:

- *Scalable, high performance*—MongoDB is designed to scale horizontally, using less-expensive servers. With relational databases, the only easy way to scale your database is to buy better hardware.[1] With MongoDB you can easily add another server to provide more capacity or performance.
- *Document-oriented storage*—MongoDB stores data in the JSON document format instead of in tables with columns and rows. Documents, which are roughly equivalent to SQL rows, are stored in collections, which are similar to SQL tables.
- *Dynamic schemas*—Whereas relational databases require a schema to define what data can be stored in what tables, MongoDB doesn't. You can store any JSON document in a collection. Individual documents within the same collection can have completely different structures, and a document structure may be completely changed during a document update.

The first point about performance will appeal to everyone, especially operations managers. The second two points are of particular interest to SPA developers and are worth exploring in detail. If you are already familiar with MongoDB, feel free to skip to section 8.3, where we hook it up to our Node.js application.

8.2.1 Document-oriented storage

MongoDB stores data in JSON documents, which makes it a great match for most SPAs. JSON documents from our SPA can be stored and retrieved without transformation.[2] This is compelling because we don't have to spend development or processing time transforming data back and forth from our native format. When we find a problem in the data on the client side, it's simple to check whether it's found in the database because the formats are identical.

Not only does this result in a simpler development and a simpler application, but it also provides performance benefits. Instead of the server having to manipulate data from format to format, it passes it along. This has an impact on the cost of hosting and scaling the application as well, as the servers have to perform less work. In this case, the work isn't offloaded onto the client; it's just *gone* because of the single data format. This doesn't necessarily mean that Node.js + MongoDB is faster than Java + PostgreSQL—many other factors impact overall speed of the application—but

---

1 Yes, you can create relational database clusters and replicas, but they typically require a good deal of expertise to configure and maintain. Buying a faster server is a lot easier.

2 Compare this with a relational database, where we first have to convert to SQL to store the documents, and then convert it back to JSON on retrieval.

it does mean that everything else being equal, a single data format should provide better performance.

8.2.2 Dynamic document structure

MongoDB doesn't constrain the structure of documents. Instead of defining a structure, we can just start adding documents to collections. We don't even have to `create` a collection first—inserting data into a non-existent collection creates it. Compare this to a relational database, where you must define tables and schemas explicitly, and any change in data structure requires a change in schema. Having a database that doesn't require a schema has some interesting benefits:

- *Document structure is flexible.* MongoDB will store the documents regardless of structure. If the document structure changes frequently or is unstructured, MongoDB will store them without need for adjustment.
- *Application changes often don't require database changes.* When we update a document to have new or different attributes, we can deploy the application and it'll start storing the new document structure immediately. On the other hand, we may need to adjust the code to account for document attributes that don't exist in previously saved documents.
- *No schema changes to cause downtime and delays.* We don't have to lock parts of the database to accommodate a document structure change. But as before, we may need to adjust our application.
- *Specialized knowledge of schema design isn't needed.* Being schema-less means there's an entire sphere of knowledge that doesn't need to be mastered to build an application. That means the applications are easier for generalists to build and may require less planning to get up and running.

But there are downsides to not having a schema:

- *No document structure enforcement.* Document structure isn't enforced at the database level, and any changes to their structure aren't automatically propagated to existing documents. This can be especially painful when multiple applications are using the same collection.
- *No document structure definition.* There's no place in the database for a database engineer or the application to determine what structure the data *should* have. It's more difficult to determine the purpose of a collection by inspecting the documents because there's no guarantee the structure is the same from document to document.
- *Not well-defined.* Document databases aren't well-defined mathematically. When storing data in a relational database, there are often mathematically proven best practices to follow to make the data access as flexible and fast as possible. Optimizations aren't nearly as well-defined for MongoDB, although some traditional methods, such as creating indexes, are supported.

Now that we have a feel for how MongoDB stores data, let's start using it.

8.2.3 Get started with MongoDB

A good way to start with MongoDB is to install it and then interact with collections and documents using the MongoDB shell. First, let's install MongoDB from the MongoDB website, http://www.mongodb.org/downloads, and then start the server `mongodb` process. The startup procedure varies by OS, so please consult the documentation for details (http://docs.mongodb.org/manual/tutorial/manage-mongodb-processes/). Once we've started the database, let's open a terminal and start the shell by typing `mongo` (`mongo.exe` on Windows). You should see something like this:

```
MongoDB shell version: 2.4.3
connecting to: test
>
```

One important concept to take into account when interacting with MongoDB is that you don't manually create databases or collections: they're created when they're needed. In order to "create" a new database, issue the command to use that database. In order to "create" a collection, insert a document into the collection. If you reference a collection that doesn't exist in a query, the query won't fail; it'll act like the collection exists but won't actually create it until you insert a document. Table 8.11 shows some common operations. We recommend you try them out in order using "spa" as the *database_name*.

Table 8.1 Basic MongoDB shell commands

Command	Description
`show dbs`	Show a list of all the databases in this MongoDB instance.
`use database_name`	Switch the current database to the *database_name*. If the database doesn't exist yet, it'll create it the first time a document is inserted into a collection on that database.
`db`	Current database.
`help`	Get general help. `db.help()` will provide help on db methods.
`db.getCollectionNames()`	Get a list of all collections available in the current database.
`db.collection_name`	A collection in the current database.
`db.collection_name.insert({ 'name': 'Josh Powell' })`	Insert a document with the field *name* with a value of "Josh Powell" into the *collection_name* collection.
`db.collection_name.find()`	Return all documents in the *collection_name* collection.

Table 8.1 Basic MongoDB shell commands *(continued)*

Command	Description
`db.collection_name.find({ 'name' : 'Josh Powell' })`	Return all documents in the *collection_name* collection that have the field *name* with a value of "Josh Powell."
`db.collection_name.update({ 'name': 'Josh Powell' }, {'name': 'Mr. Joshua C. Powell'})`	Find all documents with a *name* of "Josh Powell" and *replace* them with `{'name': 'Mr. Joshua C. Powell'}`.
`db.collection_name.update({ 'name': 'Mr. Joshua C. Powell' }, {$set: {'job': 'Author'} })`	Find all documents with a *name* of "Mr. Joshua C. Powell" and *add or modify* the attributes provided by the `$set` attribute.
`db.collection_name.remove({ 'name': 'Mr. Joshua C. Powell' })`	Remove all documents with the field *name* with a value of "Mr. Joshua C. Powell" from the *collection_name* collection.
`exit`	Exit the MongoDB shell.

Of course, MongoDB has many more capabilities than presented in the table. For example, there are methods to sort, return a subset of the existing fields, upsert documents, increment or otherwise modify an attribute, manipulate arrays, add an index, and much, much more. For a more in-depth examination of all that MongoDB offers, check out *MongoDB in Action* (Manning 2011), the online MongoDB manual (http://docs.mongodb.org/manual/), or the *Little MongoDB Book* (http://openmymind.net/mongodb.pdf). We've now run through some basic MongoDB commands, so let's hook our application up to MongoDB. First, we'll need to prepare the project files.

8.3 Use the MongoDB driver

An application in a given language requires a database driver to efficiently interface with MongoDB. Without a driver, the only way to interact with MongoDB would be through the shell. A number of MongoDB drivers have been written in various languages, including one for JavaScript in Node.js. A good driver handles many low-level tasks around interacting with a database without troubling the developer. Some examples include reconnecting to the database in case of a lost connection, managing the connections to replica sets, buffer pooling, and cursor support.

8.3.1 Prepare the project files

In this chapter, we build on the work we completed in chapter 7. We'll copy our entire file structure from chapter 7 into a new "chapter_8" directory where we'll continue our work. Listing 8.1 shows our file structure after we have completed the copy. Files and directories we will be removing are shown in **bold**:

Listing 8.1 Copy files from chapter 7

```
chapter_8
`-- webapp
    |-- app.js
    |-- js
    |   `-- data.js
    |-- node_modules
    |-- package.json
    |-- public
    |   |-- css/
    |   |-- js/
    |   `-- spa.html
    |-- routes.js
    |-- socket.html
    `-- socket.js
```

Let's remove the js directory, the socket.html file, and the socket.js file. We should also remove the node_modules directory, as that will be regenerated during module installation. Our updated structure should then look like listing 8.2:

Listing 8.2 Remove some files and directories we no longer need

```
chapter_8
`-- webapp
    |-- app.js
    |-- package.json
    |-- public
    |   |-- css/
    |   |-- js/
    |   `-- spa.html
    `-- routes.js
```

Now with our directory copied and tidied up, we're ready to attach MongoDB to our application. Our first step is to install the MongoDB driver.

8.3.2 Install and connect to MongoDB

We find that the MongoDB driver is a good solution for many applications. It's simple, fast, and easy to understand. If we need more capability we might consider using an *Object Document Mapper (ODM)*. An ODM is analogous to an *Object Relational Mapper (ORM)* frequently used for relational databases. There are a few options available: *Mongoskin*, *Mongoose*, and *Mongolia* to name a few.

We'll be using the basic MongoDB driver for our application because most of our associations and higher-level data modelling are handled on the client. We don't want any ODM validation features, as we'll be validating our document structure using a general purpose JSON schema validator. We've made that choice because the JSON schema validator is standards-compliant and works on both the client and the server, whereas the ODM validations only work on the server at this time.

We can use our `package.json` to install the MongoDB driver. As before, we'll specify the major and minor versions of the module, but request the latest patch version, as shown in listing 8.3. Changes are shown in **bold**:

Listing 8.3 Update the manifest for `npm install`—webapp/package.json

```
{ "name"    : "SPA",
  "version" : "0.0.3",
  "private" : true,
  "dependencies" : {
    "express"   : "3.2.x",
    "mongodb"   : "1.3.x",
    "socket.io" : "0.9.x"
  }
}
```

We can run `npm install` to install all the modules in the manifest, including the MongoDB driver. Let's edit the routes.js file to include `mongodb` and start a connection, as shown in listing 8.4. Changes are shown in **bold**:

Listing 8.4 Open a MongoDB connection—webapp/routes.js

```
/*
 * routes.js - module to provide routing
*/
...
// ------------ BEGIN MODULE SCOPE VARIABLES --------------
'use strict';
var
  configRoutes,
  mongodb     = require( 'mongodb' ),

  mongoServer = new mongodb.Server(
    'localhost',
    mongodb.Connection.DEFAULT_PORT
  ),
  dbHandle    = new mongodb.Db(
    'spa', mongoServer, { safe : true }
  );

dbHandle.open( function () {
  console.log( '** Connected to MongoDB **' );
});
// ------------- END MODULE SCOPE VARIABLES ---------------
...
```

Configure the MongoDB server connection object, passing in the URL (`localhost`) and port.

Include the MongoDB connector.

Create the MongoDB database handle, passing in the server connection object and a set of options. As of the 1.3.6 driver, the `safe` setting has been deprecated. Setting `{ w : 1 }` should provide similar results for a single MongoDB server.

Open the database connection. Add a callback function to be executed when the connection has completed.

We can also remove basic auth from our server application, as shown in listing 8.5.

Listing 8.5 Remove basic auth from our server application—webapp/app.js

```
/*
 * app.js - Express server with routing
*/
...
// ------------- BEGIN SERVER CONFIGURATION ---------------
```

```
app.configure( function () {
  app.use( express.bodyParser() );
  app.use( express.methodOverride() );
  app.use( express.static( __dirname + '/public' ) );
  app.use( app.router );
});
...
```

The line **app.use(express.basicAuth('user', 'spa'));** has been deleted.

Now we can start our server application (`node app.js` at the command prompt) and see the following output:

```
Express server listening on port 3000 in development mode
** Connected to MongoDB **
```

Now that we've connected our server application to MongoDB, let's explore basic Create-Read-Update-Delete (CRUD) operations.

8.3.3 Use MongoDB CRUD methods

Before we update our server application further, we'd like to get comfortable with MongoDB CRUD methods. Let's open a terminal and start the MongoDB shell by typing `mongo`. We can then *create* some documents in a collection (using the `insert` method) as shown in listing 8.6. Our input is shown in **bold**:

Listing 8.6 Create some documents in MongoDB

```
> use spa;
switched to db spa
> db.user.insert({
  "name" : "Mike Mikowski",
  "is_online" : false,
  "css_map":{"top":100,"left":120,
    "background-color":"rgb(136, 255, 136)"
  }
});

> db.user.insert({
  "name" : "Mr. Joshua C. Powell, humble humanitarian",
  "is_online": false,
  "css_map":{"top":150,"left":120,
    "background-color":"rgb(136, 255, 136)"
  }
});

> db.user.insert({
  "name": "Your name here",
  "is_online": false,
  "css_map":{"top":50,"left":120,
    "background-color":"rgb(136, 255, 136)"
  }
});

> db.user.insert({
  "name": "Hapless interloper",
```

```
  "is_online": false,
  "css_map":{"top":0,"left":120,
    "background-color":"rgb(136, 255, 136)"
  }
});
```

We can *read* these document to ensure they have been added correctly (using the `find` method) as shown in listing 8.7. Our input is shown in **bold**:

Listing 8.7 Read documents from MongoDB

```
> db.user.find()
{ "_id" : ObjectId("5186aae56f0001debc935c33"),
  "name" : "Mike Mikowski",
  "is_online" : false,
  "css_map" : {
    "top" : 100, "left" : 120,
    "background-color" : "rgb(136, 255, 136)"
  }
},
{ "_id" : ObjectId("5186aaed6f0001debc935c34"),
  "name" : "Mr. Josh C. Powell, humble humanitarian",
  "is_online" : false,
  "css_map" : {
    "top" : 150, "left" : 120,
    "background-color" : "rgb(136, 255, 136)"
  }
}
{ "_id" : ObjectId("5186aaf76f0001debc935c35"),
  "name" : "Your name here",
  "is_online" : false,
  "css_map" : {
    "top" : 50, "left" : 120,
    "background-color" : "rgb(136, 255, 136)"
  }
}
{ "_id" : ObjectId("5186aaff6f0001debc935c36"),
  "name" : "Hapless interloper",
  "is_online" : false,
  "css_map" : {
    "top" : 0, "left" : 120,
    "background-color" : "rgb(136, 255, 136)"
  }
}
```

Note that MongoDB automatically adds a unique ID field, named `_id`, to any document that's `inserted`. Hmm, though the `name` field for one of our authors is obviously correct (although perhaps an understatement), it seems too formal. Let's remove the stuffiness and *update* the document (using the `update` method) as shown in listing 8.8. Our input is shown in **bold**:

Listing 8.8 Update a document in MongoDB

```
> db.user.update(
  { "_id" : ObjectId("5186aaed6f0001debc935c34") },
  { $set : { "name" : "Josh Powell" } }
);

db.user.find({
  "_id" : ObjectId("5186aaed6f0001debc935c34")
});

{ "_id" : ObjectId("5186aaed6f0001debc935c34"),
  "name" : "Josh Powell",
  "is_online" : false,
  "css_map" : {
    "top" : 150, "left" : 120,
    "background-color" : "rgb(136, 255, 136)"
  }
}
```

We couldn't help but notice that a *hapless interloper* has entered our database. Like a red-shirted crew member in a *Star Trek* landing party, a hapless interloper shouldn't make it past the end of a scene. We'd hate to break with tradition, so let's dispatch this interloper forthwith and *delete* the document (using the `remove` method) as shown in listing 8.9. Our input is shown in **bold**:

Listing 8.9 Delete a document from MongoDB

```
> db.user.remove(
  { "_id" : ObjectId("5186aaff6f0001debc935c36") }
);

> db.user.find()
{ "_id" : ObjectId("5186aae56f0001debc935c33"),
  "name" : "Mike Mikowski",
  "is_online" : false,
  "css_map" : {
    "top" : 100, "left" : 120,
    "background-color" : "rgb(136, 255, 136)"
  }
}
{ "_id" : ObjectId("5186aaed6f0001debc935c34"),
  "name" : "Josh Powell",
  "is_online" : false,
  "css_map" : {
    "top" : 150, "left" : 120,
    "background-color" : "rgb(136, 255, 136)"
  }
}
{ "_id" : ObjectId("5186aaf76f0001debc935c35"),
  "name" : "Your name here",
  "is_online" : false,
  "css_map" : {
    "top" : 50, "left" : 120,
```

```
    "background-color" : "rgb(136, 255, 136)"
  }
}
```

We've now completed the Create-Read-Update-Delete operations using the MongoDB console. Now let's update our server application to support these operations.

8.3.4 Add CRUD to the server application

Because we're using Node.js, the interaction with MongoDB is going to be different than most other languages because JavaScript is event-based. Now that we have some documents in the database to play around with, let's update our router to use MongoDB to fetch a list of user objects, as shown in listing 8.10. Changes are shown in **bold**:

Listing 8.10 Update our router to retrieve a user list—webapp/routes.js

```
/*
 * routes.js - module to provide routing
*/
...
// ---------------- BEGIN PUBLIC METHODS ------------------
configRoutes = function ( app, server ) {
  ...
  app.get( '/:obj_type/list', function ( request, response ) {
    dbHandle.collection(
      request.params.obj_type,
      function ( outer_error, collection ) {
        collection.find().toArray(
          function ( inner_error, map_list ) {
            response.send( map_list );
          }
        );
      }
    );
  });
  ...
};

module.exports = { configRoutes : configRoutes };
// ----------------- END PUBLIC METHODS -------------------
...
```

Use the dbHandle object to retrieve the collection specified in :obj_type in the URL, and pass in a callback to be executed.

Find all documents in the (dbHandle.collection) collection and transform the results into an array.

Send the list of JSON objects back to the client.

Before looking at the results in your browser, you may want to get a browser extension or add-on that makes the JSON more human-readable. We use *JSONView 0.0.32* on Chrome and *JSONovich 1.9.5* on Firefox. Both of these are available through the respective vendor add-on sites.

We can start our application by typing `node app.js` in the terminal. When we point our browser to http://localhost:3000/user/list, we should see a JSON document presentation similar to figure 8.3:

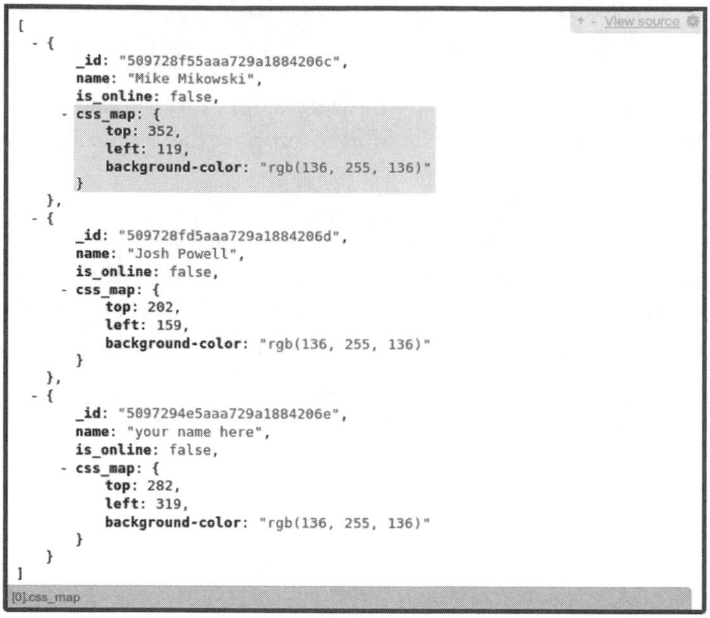

```
[
  - {
        _id: "509728f55aaa729a1884206c",
        name: "Mike Mikowski",
        is_online: false,
      - css_map: {
            top: 352,
            left: 119,
            background-color: "rgb(136, 255, 136)"
        }
    },
  - {
        _id: "509728fd5aaa729a1884206d",
        name: "Josh Powell",
        is_online: false,
      - css_map: {
            top: 202,
            left: 159,
            background-color: "rgb(136, 255, 136)"
        }
    },
  - {
        _id: "5097294e5aaa729a1884206e",
        name: "your name here",
        is_online: false,
      - css_map: {
            top: 282,
            left: 319,
            background-color: "rgb(136, 255, 136)"
        }
    }
]
[0].css_map
```

Figure 8.3 Response from MongoDB through Node.js to client

We can now add the remaining CRUD operations as shown in listing 8.11. Changes are shown in **bold**:

Listing 8.11 Add the MongoDB driver and CRUD to our router—`routes.js`

```
/*
 * routes.js - module to provide routing
*/
...
// ------------ BEGIN MODULE SCOPE VARIABLES --------------
'use strict';
var
  configRoutes,
  mongodb     = require( 'mongodb' ),

  mongoServer = new mongodb.Server(
    'localhost',
    mongodb.Connection.DEFAULT_PORT
  ),
  dbHandle    = new mongodb.Db(
    'spa', mongoServer, { safe : true }
  ),

  makeMongoId = mongodb.ObjectID;
// ------------- END MODULE SCOPE VARIABLES ---------------

// ---------------- BEGIN PUBLIC METHODS ------------------
configRoutes = function ( app, server ) {
  app.get( '/', function ( request, response ) {
    response.redirect( '/spa.html' );
  });
```

Copy the ObjectID function into a `makeMongoId` module-scope variable. This is a convenience. Note that we now open the database connection at the end of the module.

```
app.all( '/:obj_type/*?', function ( request, response, next ) {
  response.contentType( 'json' );
  next();
});

app.get( '/:obj_type/list', function ( request, response ) {
  dbHandle.collection(
    request.params.obj_type,
    function ( outer_error, collection ) {
      collection.find().toArray(
        function ( inner_error, map_list ) {
          response.send( map_list );
        }
      );
    }
  );
});

app.post( '/:obj_type/create', function ( request, response ) {
  dbHandle.collection(
    request.params.obj_type,
    function ( outer_error, collection ) {
      var
        options_map = { safe: true },
        obj_map     = request.body;

      collection.insert(
        obj_map,
        options_map,
        function ( inner_error, result_map ) {
          response.send( result_map );
        }
      );
    }
  );
});

app.get( '/:obj_type/read/:id', function ( request, response ) {
  var find_map = { _id: makeMongoId( request.params.id ) };
  dbHandle.collection(
    request.params.obj_type,
    function ( outer_error, collection ) {
      collection.findOne(
        find_map,
        function ( inner_error, result_map ) {
          response.send( result_map );
        }
      );
    }
  );
});

app.post( '/:obj_type/update/:id', function ( request, response ) {
  var
    find_map = { _id: makeMongoId( request.params.id ) },
    obj_map  = request.body;
```

Add the capability to list every user. This was shown earlier in the section. Don't add it twice.

Insert the document into MongoDB. The `safe` option specifies that the callback won't be executed until after the document is successfully inserted into MongoDB; otherwise the callback will be executed immediately without waiting for a success response. It's up to you if you want to be quicker or safer. This isn't strictly required here, as we had set our default `safe` option when we configured the database handle. Also see our earlier note about the new w option which deprecates the `safe` option.

Use the `findOne` method provided by the Node.js MongoDB driver to find and return the first document matching the search parameters. Since there should be only one object of a particular ID, one is all we need returned.

```
    dbHandle.collection(
      request.params.obj_type,
      function ( outer_error, collection ) {
        var
          sort_order = [],
          options_map = {
            'new' : true, upsert: false, safe: true
          };

        collection.findAndModify(
          find_map,
          sort_order,
          obj_map,
          options_map,
          function ( inner_error, updated_map ) {
            response.send( updated_map );
          }
        );
      }
    );
  });

  app.get( '/:obj_type/delete/:id', function ( request, response ) {
    var find_map = { _id: makeMongoId( request.params.id ) };

    dbHandle.collection(
      request.params.obj_type,
      function ( outer_error, collection ) {
        var options_map = { safe: true, single: true };

        collection.remove(
          find_map,
          options_map,
          function ( inner_error, delete_count ) {
            response.send({ delete_count: delete_count });
          }
        );
      }
    );
  });
};

module.exports = { configRoutes : configRoutes };
// ----------------- END PUBLIC METHODS -------------------

// ------------- BEGIN MODULE INITIALIZATION --------------
dbHandle.open( function () {
  console.log( '** Connected to MongoDB **' );
});
// -------------- END MODULE INITIALIZATION ---------------
```

Use the `findAndModify` method provided by the Node.js MongoDB driver. This method will find all documents matching the search criteria and replace them with the object found in `obj_map`. Yes, we know the name is misleading, but we didn't write the MongoDB driver, now did we?

Use the `remove` method to remove all documents matching the attributes of the object map. We pass in `single: true` as an option so that it only deletes one document at most.

Add a module initialization section.

We now have user CRUD operations working from the client through the Node.js server and into MongoDB and back again. Now we would like the application to validate data received from the client.

8.4 Validate client data

MongoDB doesn't have a mechanism to define what can and can't be added to a collection. We'll need to validate client data ourselves before saving it. We want our data transfer to work as shown in figure 8.5:

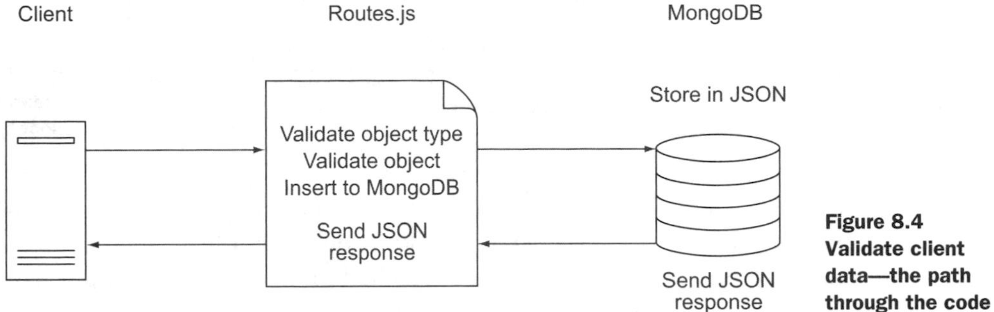

Figure 8.4 Validate client data—the path through the code

Our first step is to define what types of objects are valid.

8.4.1 Validate the object type

As it is now, we're accepting any route and passing objects to MongoDB without even verifying if it's an allowable type. For example, a POST to create a horse will work. The following is an example using `wget`. Our input is shown in **bold**:

```
# Create a new MongoDB collection of horses
wget http://localhost:3000/horse/create \
  --header='content-type: application/json' \
  --post-data='{"css_map":{"color":"#ddd"},"name":"Ed"}'\
  -O -

# Add another horse
wget http://localhost:3000/horse/create \
  --header='content-type: application/json' \
  --post-data='{"css_map":{"color":"#2e0"},"name":"Winney"}'\
  -O -

# Check the corral
wget http://localhost:3000/horse/list -O -
  [ {
    "css_map": {
      "color": "#ddd"
    },
    "name": "Ed",
    "_id": "51886ac7e7f0be8d20000001"
  },
  {
    "css_map": {
      "color": "#2e0"
    },
    "name": "Winney",
    "_id": "51886adae7f0be8d20000002"
  }]
```

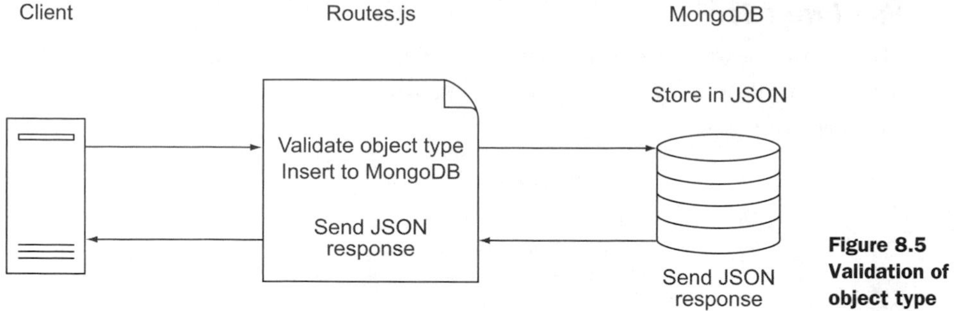

Figure 8.5 Validation of object type

This is even worse than it may appear. MongoDB will not only store the document, but it'll *create a completely new collection* (as it did in our example), which consumes a fair amount of resources. We couldn't go to production like this, as a simple script kiddie could easily overwhelm the server(s) in minutes by running a script that creates thousands of new MongoDB collections.[3] We should allow access only to approved object types, as shown in figure 8.5.

This is easy enough to implement. We can create a map of allowable object types and then check against it in the router. Let's modify the routes.js file to do this, as shown in listing 8.12. Changes are shown in **bold**:

Listing 8.12 Validate the incoming routes—routes.js

```
/*
 * routes.js - module to provide routing
*/
...
// ------------ BEGIN MODULE SCOPE VARIABLES --------------
'use strict';
var
...
  makeMongoId = mongodb.ObjectID,
  objTypeMap  = { 'user': {} };<=
// ------------- END MODULE SCOPE VARIABLES ---------------

// ---------------- BEGIN PUBLIC METHODS ------------------
configRoutes = function ( app, server ) {
  app.get( '/', function ( request, response ) {
    response.redirect( '/spa.html' );
  });

  app.all( '/:obj_type/*?', function ( request, response, next ) {
    response.contentType( 'json' );
    if ( objTypeMap[ request.params.obj_type ] ) {
      next();
    }
    else {
      response.send({ error_msg : request.params.obj_type
```

Declare and assign a map of allowed object types.

If the object type (:obj_type) is defined in the object type map, move on to the next route handler.

If the object type (:obj_type) is not defined in the object type map, send a JSON response telling the client this is an invalid route.

[3] On my 64-bit developer box, each *nearly empty* collection grabs around 64MB of disk space.

```
          + ' is not a valid object type'
        });
      }
    });
  ...
```

We don't want to stop with just ensuring the object type is allowed. We also want to ensure the client data is structured as we expect. Let's do that next.

8.4.2 Validate the object

The browser client sends a JSON document to the server to represent an object. As many readers are surely aware, JSON has displaced XML for many web APIs because it's more compact and often easier to process.

One stellar feature that XML provides is the ability to define a *Document Type Definition (DTD)* that describes allowable content. JSON has a similar, although less mature, standard that can ensure document content similar to a DTD. It's called a *JSON schema.*

JSV is a validator that uses a JSON schema. It can be used in the browser and the server, so we don't have to write or maintain two separate (and always subtly conflicting) validation libraries. Here are the steps we need to validate our objects:

- Install the JSV node module
- Create a JSON schema
- Load JSON schemas
- Create a validation function
- Validate incoming data

Our first step is to install JSV.

INSTALL THE JSV NODE MODULE

Update the package.json file to include JSV 4.0.2. It should now look like listing 8.13:

Listing 8.13 Update the manifest to include JSV—webapp/package.json

```
{ "name"    : "SPA",
  "version" : "0.0.3",
  "private" : true,
  "dependencies" : {
    "express"   : "3.2.x",
    "mongodb"   : "1.3.x",
    "socket.io" : "0.9.x",
    "JSV" : "4.0.x"
  }
}
```

When we run `npm install`, `npm` should pick up the changes and install JSV.

CREATE A JSON SCHEMA

Before we can validate a user object, we must decide what properties are allowed and what values they might take. The JSON schema provides us a nice, standard mechanism to describe these constraints, as shown in listing 8.14. Be sure to pay careful attention to the annotations, as they explain the constraints.

Listing 8.14 Create the user schema—webapp/user.json

```
{ "type" : "object",
  "additionalProperties" : false,
  "properties" : {
    "_id" : {
      "type"      : "string",
      "minLength" : 25,
      "maxLength" : 25
    },
    "name" : {
      "type"      : "string",
      "minLength" : 2,
      "maxLength" : 127
    },
    "is_online" : {
      "type"      : "boolean"
    },
    "css_map": {
      "type" : "object",
      "additionalProperties" : false,
      "properties" : {
        "background-color" : {
          "required"  : true,
          "type"      : "string",
          "minLength" : 0,
          "maxLength" : 25
        },
        "top" : {
          "required" : true,
          "type"     : "integer"
        },
        "left" : {
          "required" : true,
          "type"     : "integer"
        }
      }
    }
  }
}
```

Annotations:

- This object represents the schema for an `object` (`"type" : "object"`). Note that it could represent the constraints for a Boolean, an integer, a string, or an array.
- The `object` type can accept or deny properties not explicitly declared. If `false`, the validator won't allow undeclared properties. The correct choice is almost always `false`.
- The `properties` value provides a map of properties for the object schema, keyed by property name.
- The `_id` property is a string, and must be 25 characters in length (`"minLength" : 25, "maxLength" : 25`).
- The `name` property is similar to `_id`, although it allows a variable length.
- The `is_online` property must be `true` or `false`.
- The `css_map` property must be an object, and doesn't allow undeclared properties.
- The `css_map` object's `background-color` property is required, is a string, and may be up to 25 characters long.
- The `css_map` object's `top` property must exist and must be an integer.
- The `css_map` object's `left` property must exist and must be an integer.

You may have noticed that we have defined a schema that constrains an object and constrains an object *within* that object. This illustrates how a JSON schema can be infinitely recursive. JSON schemas may extend other schemas too, much like XML. If you want to learn more about JSON schemas, check out the official website at json-schema.org. Now we can load our schema and ensure any user object we receive contains only the data we allow.

LOAD JSON SCHEMAS

Let's load our schema documents into memory when the server is started. This will avoid expensive file seeks while our server application is running. We can load one schema document per object type defined in the object type map (`objTypeMap`) as shown in listing 8.15. Changes are shown in **bold**:[4]

Listing 8.15 Load schemas in our router—webapp/routes.js

```
/*
 * routes.js - module to provide routing
*/
...
// ------------ BEGIN MODULE SCOPE VARIABLES --------------
'use strict';
var
  loadSchema, configRoutes,
  mongodb     = require( 'mongodb' ),
  fsHandle    = require( 'fs'      ),

  mongoServer = new mongodb.Server(
    'localhost',
    mongodb.Connection.DEFAULT_PORT
  ),
  dbHandle    = new mongodb.Db(
    'spa', mongoServer, { safe : true }
  ),

  makeMongoId = mongodb.ObjectID,
  objTypeMap  = { 'user': {} };
// ------------- END MODULE SCOPE VARIABLES ---------------

// --------------- BEGIN UTILITY METHODS ------------------
loadSchema = function ( schema_name, schema_path ) {
  fsHandle.readFile( schema_path, 'utf8', function ( err, data ) {
    objTypeMap[ schema_name ] = JSON.parse( data );
  });
};
// ---------------- END UTILITY METHODS -------------------

// ---------------- BEGIN PUBLIC METHODS ------------------
...
// ----------------- END PUBLIC METHODS -------------------

// ------------- BEGIN MODULE INITIALIZATION --------------
dbHandle.open( function () {
  console.log( '** Connected to MongoDB **' );
});

// load schemas into memory (objTypeMap)
(function () {
  var schema_name, schema_path;
  for ( schema_name in objTypeMap ) {
    if ( objTypeMap.hasOwnProperty( schema_name ) ) {
      schema_path = __dirname + '/' + schema_name + '.json';
```

Include the file system module.

Create a `loadSchema` utility to read in a file and store it into the object type map (`objTypeMap`).

Read a file for each object type defined in `objTypeMap`. In this case we have one object type: `user`.

[4] Windows users will need to replace forward slashes (/) with double back slashes (\\) for file system paths.

```
        loadSchema( schema_name, schema_path );
      }
    }
  }());
  // -------------- END MODULE INITIALIZATION --------------
```

Parse the data in the file into a JSON object and store it in the object map. We use an external function (`loadSchema`) as it's generally bad practice to declare a function within a loop, and JSLint will complain.

Now that we have our schemas loaded, we can create a validation function.

CREATE A VALIDATION FUNCTION

Now that we have the `user` JSON schema loaded, we want to compare incoming client data against the schema. Listing 8.16 shows a simple function to do just that. Changes are shown in **bold**:

Listing 8.16 Add a function to validate documents—webapp/routes.js

```
/*
 * routes.js - module to provide routing
*/
...
// ------------ BEGIN MODULE SCOPE VARIABLES --------------
'use strict';
var
  loadSchema, checkSchema, configRoutes,
  mongodb     = require( 'mongodb' ),
  fsHandle    = require( 'fs'      ),
  JSV         = require( 'JSV'     ).JSV,

  mongoServer = new mongodb.Server(
    'localhost',
    mongodb.Connection.DEFAULT_PORT
  ),
  dbHandle    = new mongodb.Db(
    'spa', mongoServer, { safe : true }
  ),
  validator   = JSV.createEnvironment(),

  makeMongoId = mongodb.ObjectID,
  objTypeMap  = { 'user': {} };
// ------------- END MODULE SCOPE VARIABLES ---------------

// --------------- BEGIN UTILITY METHODS ------------------
loadSchema = function ( schema_name, schema_path ) {
  fsHandle.readFile( schema_path, 'utf8', function ( err, data ) {
    objTypeMap[ schema_name ] = JSON.parse( data );
  });
};

checkSchema = function ( obj_type, obj_map, callback ) {
  var
    schema_map = objTypeMap[ obj_type ],
```

Include the JSV module.

Create the JSV validator environment.

The validator takes three arguments: the `object`, the object schema name to validate against (`obj_type`), and a `callback` function.

```
    report_map = validator.validate( obj_map, schema_map );

  callback( report_map.errors );
};
// ---------------- END UTILITY METHODS -------------------

// ---------------- BEGIN PUBLIC METHODS ------------------
...
```

Once the validation has been run, invoke the `callback` with the list of errors. If the error list is empty, the object is valid.

Now that we have a JSON schema loading and a validation function, we can validate incoming client data.

VALIDATE INCOMING CLIENT DATA

Now we can complete validation. We just need to adjust the routes that accept client data—create and update—to use the validator. In each case, we want to perform the requested action if the list of errors is empty. Otherwise we want to return an error report, as shown in listing 8.17. Changes are shown in **bold**:

Listing 8.17 Create and update routes with validation—`webapp/routes.js`

```
/*
 * routes.js - module to provide routing
*/
...
// ---------------- BEGIN PUBLIC METHODS ------------------
configRoutes = function ( app, server ) {
  ...
  app.post( '/:obj_type/create', function ( request, response ) {
    var
      obj_type = request.params.obj_type,
      obj_map  = request.body;

    checkSchema(
      obj_type, obj_map,
      function ( error_list ) {
        if ( error_list.length === 0 ) {
          dbHandle.collection(
            obj_type,
            function ( outer_error, collection ) {
              var options_map = { safe: true };

              collection.insert(
                obj_map,
                options_map,
                function ( inner_error, result_map ) {
                  response.send( result_map );
                }
              );
            }
          );
        }
        else {
          response.send({
            error_msg  : 'Input document not valid',
            error_list : error_list
          });
```

Call the validation function (`checkSchema`) defined in the last section, using the object type, the object map, and a callback function as arguments.

```
        }
      }
    );
  });

  ...

  app.post( '/:obj_type/update/:id', function ( request, response ) {
    var
      find_map = { _id: makeMongoId( request.params.id ) },
      obj_map  = request.body,
      obj_type = request.params.obj_type;

    checkSchema(
      obj_type, obj_map,
      function ( error_list ) {
        if ( error_list.length === 0 ) {
          dbHandle.collection(
            obj_type,
            function ( outer_error, collection ) {
              var
                sort_order = [],
                options_map = {
                  'new' : true, upsert: false, safe: true
                };

              collection.findAndModify(
                find_map,
                sort_order,
                obj_map,
                options_map,
                function ( inner_error, updated_map ) {
                  response.send( updated_map );
                }
              );
            }
          );
        }
        else {
          response.send({
            error_msg  : 'Input document not valid',
            error_list : error_list
          });
        }
      }
    );
  });
  ...
};

module.exports = { configRoutes : configRoutes };
// ---------------- END PUBLIC METHODS ------------------
...
```

Check to see if the error list is empty. If it is, then create or update the object as before.

If the error list isn't empty, send an error report.

Now that we have completed validation, let's see how we've done. First we should make sure all our modules pass JSLint (`jslint user.json app.js routes.js`), and then start the application (`node app.js`). Then we can use our deft `wget` skills to `POST` bad and good data, as shown in listing 8.18. Our input is shown in **bold**:

Listing 8.18 POST bad and good data using deft wget skills

```
# Try invalid data
wget http://localhost:3000/user/create \
  --header='content-type: application/json' \
  --post-data='{"name":"Betty",
    "css_map":{"background-color":"#ddd",
    "top" : 22 }
  }' -O -

--2013-06-07 22:20:17--  http://localhost:3000/user/create
Resolving localhost (localhost)... 127.0.0.1
Connecting to localhost (localhost)|127.0.0.1|:3000... connected.
HTTP request sent, awaiting response... 200 OK
Length: 354 [application/json]
Saving to: â€˜STDOUTâ€™
...
{ "error_msg": "Input document not valid",
  "error_list": [
    {
      "uri": "urn:uuid:8c05b92a...",
      "schemaUri": "urn:uuid:.../properties/css_map/properties/left",
      "attribute": "required",
      "message": "Property is required",
      "details": true
    }
  ]
}
...
# Oops, we missed the "left" property.  Let's fix that:
wget http://localhost:3000/user/create \
  --header='content-type: application/json' \
  --post-data='{"name":"Betty",
    "css_map":{"background-color":"#ddd",
    "top" : 22, "left" : 500 }
  }' -O -
--2013-05-07 22:24:02--  http://localhost:3000/user/create
Resolving localhost (localhost)... 127.0.0.1
Connecting to localhost (localhost)|127.0.0.1|:3000... connected.
HTTP request sent, awaiting response... 200 OK
Length: 163 [application/json]
Saving to: â€˜STDOUTâ€™
...
  {
    "name": "Betty",
    "css_map": {
      "background-color": "#ddd",
      "top": 22,
      "left": 500
    },
    "_id": "5189e172ac5a4c5c68000001"
  }
...
# Success!
```

Updating a user with wget is left as an exercise for the reader.

In the next section we'll move the CRUD capability into a separate module. This will result in cleaner, easier to understand, and more maintainable code.

8.5 Create a separate CRUD module

At this point, the logic for CRUD operations and routing is contained in the routes.js file as shown in figure 8.6.

We have the server accepting calls from the client, validating the data, and saving it to the database. The only way to validate and save the data is through calling the routes with an HTTP call. If this were all we needed for the application, then it'd probably makes sense to stop here with no further abstraction. But our SPA will need to create and modify objects through web socket connections as well. Therefore, we'll create a CRUD module that has all of the logic for validating and managing our documents in the database. The router will then use the CRUD module for any required CRUD operations.

Before we create the CRUD module, we want to emphasize why we waited until now to create it. We like to keep our code as direct and simple as possible, but not simpler. If we have to do an operation only once in the code, we prefer to usually have it inline or at least as a local function. But when we find that we need to perform an operation two or more times, we want to abstract it. Though this may not save initial coding time, it almost always saves maintenance time, as we centralize the logic into a single routine and avoid subtle errors that can result in variances in implementation. Of course, it takes good judgment to determine how far to take this philosophy. For example, we feel abstracting all for loops is generally not a good idea even though it's thoroughly possible with JavaScript.

After we move the MongoDB connection and validations over to a separate CRUD module, our router will no longer be concerned with the implementation of data storage and will act more like a controller: it dispatches requests to other modules instead of performing actions itself, as shown in figure 8.7.

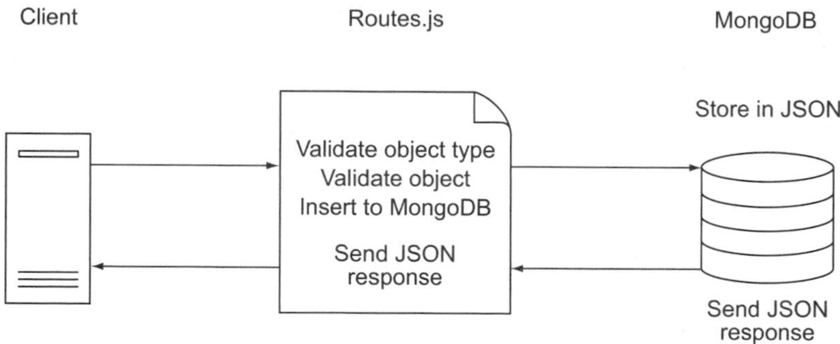

Figure 8.6 Path through code

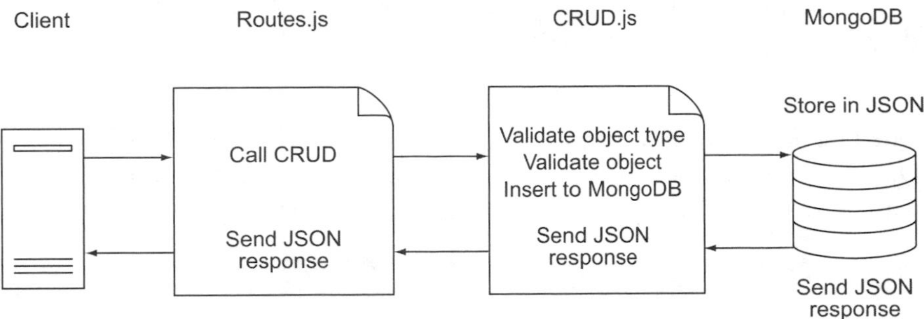

Figure 8.7 Code path on the server

Our first step in creating the CRUD module will be to prepare the file structure.

8.5.1 Prepare the file structure

Our file structure has remained consistent since the beginning of this chapter. Now that we need to add an additional module, we need to rethink it a bit. Our current structure is shown in listing 8.19:

Listing 8.19 Our current file structure

```
chapter_8
`-- webapp
    |-- app.js
    |-- node_modules/
    |-- package.json
    |-- public
    |   |-- css/
    |   |-- js/
    |   `-- spa.html
    |-- user.json
    `-- routes.js
```

We'd rather keep our modules in a separate directory called lib. This will tidy up the webapp directory and keep our modules out of the node_modules directory. The node_modules directory should only contain external modules added through `npm install` so that it can be deleted and recreated without interfering with our modules. Listing 8.20 shows how we want to structure our files. Changes are shown in **bold**:

Listing 8.20 A new and enlightened file structure

```
chapter_8
`-- webapp
    |-- app.js
    |-- lib
    |   |-- crud.js
    |   |-- routes.js
    |   `-- user.json
    |-- node_modules/
    |-- package.json
```

```
    |-- public
        |-- css/
        |-- js/
        `-- spa.html
```

Our first step toward file enlightenment is to move our routes file into webapp/lib. Once we've done that, we need to update our server application to point to the new path, as shown in listing 8.21. Changes are shown in **bold**:

Listing 8.21 Revise app.js to require moved routes.js—webapp/app.js

```
/*
 * app.js - Express server with routing
*/
...
// ------------ BEGIN MODULE SCOPE VARIABLES --------------
'use strict';
var
  http    = require( 'http'          ),
  express = require( 'express'       ),
  routes  = require( './lib/routes' ),
  app     = express(),
  server  = http.createServer( app );
// ------------- END MODULE SCOPE VARIABLES ---------------
...
```

Our next step is to include the CRUD module in our routes module, as shown in listing 8.22. Changes are shown in **bold**:

Listing 8.22 Adjust the routes module to require CRUD—webapp/lib/routes.js

```
/*
 * routes.js - module to provide routing
*/
...
// ------------ BEGIN MODULE SCOPE VARIABLES --------------
'use strict';
var
  loadSchema, checkSchema, configRoutes,
  mongodb     = require( 'mongodb' ),
  fsHandle    = require( 'fs'      ),
  JSV         = require( 'JSV'     ).JSV,
  crud        = require( './crud'  ),
  ...
```

We can create our CRUD module and sketch its API. We'll use `module.exports` to share the CRUD methods, as shown in listing 8.23.

Listing 8.23 Create the CRUD module—webapp/lib/crud.js

```
/*
 * crud.js - module to provide CRUD db capabilities
*/
```

```
/*jslint         node    : true, continue : true,
  devel  : true, indent  : 2,    maxerr   : 50,
  newcap : true, nomen   : true, plusplus : true,
  regexp : true, sloppy  : true, vars     : false,
  white  : true
*/
/*global */

// ------------ BEGIN MODULE SCOPE VARIABLES --------------
'use strict';
var
  checkType,     constructObj, readObj,
  updateObj,     destroyObj;
// ------------- END MODULE SCOPE VARIABLES ---------------

// ---------------- BEGIN PUBLIC METHODS ------------------
checkType    = function () {};
constructObj = function () {};
readObj      = function () {};
updateObj    = function () {};
destroyObj   = function () {};

module.exports = {
  makeMongoId : null,
  checkType   : checkType,
  construct   : constructObj,
  read        : readObj,
  update      : updateObj,
  destroy     : destroyObj
};
// ----------------- END PUBLIC METHODS -----------------

// ------------- BEGIN MODULE INITIALIZATION --------------
console.log( '** CRUD module loaded **' );
// -------------- END MODULE INITIALIZATION ---------------
```

Use `construct` as our method name because `create` is a root method on the JavaScript `Object` prototype.

Use `destroy` as our method name because `delete` is a reserved word in JavaScript.

When we start the server with `node app.js` it should run without any errors:

```
** CRUD module loaded **
Express server listening on port 3000 in development mode
** Connected to MongoDB **
```

Note that we've added two public methods beyond basic CRUD operations. The first is `makeMongoId`, which provides the capability to make a MongoDB ID object. The second is `checkType`, which we intend to use to check allowable object types. Now that we have our files in place, we can move our CRUD logic into the proper module.

8.5.2 Move CRUD into its own module

We can complete the CRUD module by copying our methods from the routes module and then replacing the HTTP-specific parameters with general ones. We won't go into the minutia as we feel the conversion is obvious. The completed module is shown in listing 8.24. Please pay attention to the annotations as they provide some additional insight:

Listing 8.24 Move logic to our CRUD module—webapp/lib/crud.js

```
/*
 * crud.js - module to provide CRUD db capabilities
*/

/*jslint         node    : true, continue : true,
  devel  : true, indent  : 2,    maxerr   : 50,
  newcap : true, nomen   : true, plusplus : true,
  regexp : true, sloppy  : true, vars     : false,
  white  : true
*/
/*global */

// ------------ BEGIN MODULE SCOPE VARIABLES --------------
'use strict';
var
  loadSchema,   checkSchema,  clearIsOnline,
  checkType,    constructObj, readObj,
  updateObj,    destroyObj,

  mongodb     = require( 'mongodb' ),
  fsHandle    = require( 'fs'      ),
  JSV         = require( 'JSV'     ).JSV,

  mongoServer = new mongodb.Server(
    'localhost',
    mongodb.Connection.DEFAULT_PORT
  ),
  dbHandle    = new mongodb.Db(
    'spa', mongoServer, { safe : true }
  ),
  validator   = JSV.createEnvironment(),

  objTypeMap  = { 'user' : {} };
// ------------- END MODULE SCOPE VARIABLES ---------------

// ---------------- BEGIN UTILITY METHODS -----------------
loadSchema = function ( schema_name, schema_path ) {
  fsHandle.readFile( schema_path, 'utf8', function ( err, data ) {
    objTypeMap[ schema_name ] = JSON.parse( data );
  });
};

checkSchema = function ( obj_type, obj_map, callback ) {
  var
    schema_map = objTypeMap[ obj_type ],
    report_map = validator.validate( obj_map, schema_map );

  callback( report_map.errors );
};

clearIsOnline = function () {
  updateObj(
    'user',
    { is_online : true  },
    { is_online : false },
    function ( response_map ) {
```

- Include libraries required for CRUD per webapp/lib/routes.js.
- Create the database connection variables (mongodb and dbHandle) and the JSON schema validator per webapp/lib/routes.js.
- Declare the allowable object types map (objTypeMap) per webapp/lib/routes.js.
- Add schema loading and checking utilities per webapp/lib/routes.js.
- Create a clearIsOnline method to be executed once MongoDB is connected. It ensures all users are marked as offline when the server is started.

```
      console.log( 'All users set to offline', response_map );
    }
  );
};
// ---------------- END UTILITY METHODS ----------------

// ---------------- BEGIN PUBLIC METHODS ----------------
checkType = function ( obj_type ) {
  if ( ! objTypeMap[ obj_type ] ) {
    return ({ error_msg : 'Object type "' + obj_type
      + '" is not supported.'
    });
  }
  return null;
};

constructObj = function ( obj_type, obj_map, callback ) {
  var type_check_map = checkType( obj_type );
  if ( type_check_map ) {
    callback( type_check_map );
    return;
  }

  checkSchema(
    obj_type, obj_map,
    function ( error_list ) {
      if ( error_list.length === 0 ) {
        dbHandle.collection(
          obj_type,
          function ( outer_error, collection ) {
            var options_map = { safe: true };

            collection.insert(
              obj_map,
              options_map,
              function ( inner_error, result_map ) {
                callback( result_map );
              }
            );
          }
        );
      }
      else {
        callback({
          error_msg  : 'Input document not valid',
          error_list : error_list
        });
      }
    }
  );
};

readObj = function ( obj_type, find_map, fields_map, callback ) {
  var type_check_map = checkType( obj_type );
  if ( type_check_map ) {
    callback( type_check_map );
    return;
```

Create a method to check if an object type, for example, `user` or `horse`, is supported by this module. At present `user` is the only supported object type. (annotates `checkType = function`)

Move logic to create (`construct`) an object from `webapp/lib/routes.js` to this module. Use the same logic but adjust to be more general. This facilitates calls from the routes module and other modules. (annotates `constructObj = function`)

Add logic to ensure the requested object type is supported. If not, return a JSON error document. (annotates `if ( type_check_map )` in `constructObj`)

Create the `read` method per `webapp/lib/routes.js`. Adjust the logic to be more general. (annotates `readObj = function`)

Ensure the requested object type is supported. If not, return a JSON error document. (annotates `if ( type_check_map )` in `readObj`)

```
    }

    dbHandle.collection(
      obj_type,
      function ( outer_error, collection ) {
        collection.find( find_map, fields_map ).toArray(
          function ( inner_error, map_list ) {
            callback( map_list );
          }
        );
      }
    );
  };

  updateObj = function ( obj_type, find_map, set_map, callback ) {
    var type_check_map = checkType( obj_type );
    if ( type_check_map ) {
      callback( type_check_map );
      return;
    }

    checkSchema(
      obj_type, set_map,
      function ( error_list ) {
        if ( error_list.length === 0 ) {
          dbHandle.collection(
            obj_type,
            function ( outer_error, collection ) {
              collection.update(
                find_map,
                { $set : set_map },
                { safe : true, multi : true, upsert : false },
                function ( inner_error, update_count ) {
                  callback({ update_count : update_count });
                }
              );
            }
          );
        }
        else {
          callback({
            error_msg  : 'Input document not valid',
            error_list : error_list
          });
        }
      }
    );
  };

  destroyObj = function ( obj_type, find_map, callback ) {
    var type_check_map = checkType( obj_type );
    if ( type_check_map ) {
      callback( type_check_map );
      return;
    }

    dbHandle.collection(
```

Create the update method per webapp/lib/routes.js. Adjust the logic to be more general.

Ensure the requested object type is supported. If not, return a JSON error document.

Create the delete (destroy) method per webapp/lib/routes.js. Adjust the logic to be more general.

Ensure the requested object type is supported. If not, return a JSON error document.

```
      obj_type,
      function ( outer_error, collection ) {
        var options_map = { safe: true, single: true };

        collection.remove( find_map, options_map,
          function ( inner_error, delete_count ) {
            callback({ delete_count: delete_count });
          }
        );
      }
    );
  };

  module.exports = {
    makeMongoId : mongodb.ObjectID,
    checkType   : checkType,
    construct   : constructObj,
    read        : readObj,
    update      : updateObj,
    destroy     : destroyObj
  };
  // ----------------- END PUBLIC METHODS -----------------

  // ------------- BEGIN MODULE INITIALIZATION --------------
  dbHandle.open( function () {
    console.log( '** Connected to MongoDB **' );
    clearIsOnline();
  });

  // load schemas into memory (objTypeMap)
  (function () {
    var schema_name, schema_path;
    for ( schema_name in objTypeMap ) {
      if ( objTypeMap.hasOwnProperty( schema_name ) ) {
        schema_path = __dirname + '/' + schema_name + '.json';
        loadSchema( schema_name, schema_path );
      }
    }
  }());
  // -------------- END MODULE INITIALIZATION ---------------
```

Neatly export all our public methods.

Call the `clearIsOnline` method once MongoDB is connected.

Initialize the in-memory schema storage per `webapp/lib/routes.js`.

The routes module now becomes much simpler, as most logic and many dependencies have been moved to the CRUD module. A revised routes file should look like listing 8.25. Changes are shown in **bold**:

Listing 8.25 Our modified routes module—`webapp/lib/routes.js`

```
/*
 * routes.js - module to provide routing
*/

/*jslint         node    : true, continue : true,
  devel  : true, indent  : 2,    maxerr   : 50,
  newcap : true, nomen   : true, plusplus : true,
  regexp : true, sloppy  : true, vars     : false,
  white  : true
```

```
*/
/*global */

// ------------ BEGIN MODULE SCOPE VARIABLES --------------
'use strict';
var
  configRoutes,
  crud        = require( './crud' ),
  makeMongoId = crud.makeMongoId;
// ------------- END MODULE SCOPE VARIABLES ---------------

// ---------------- BEGIN PUBLIC METHODS ------------------
configRoutes = function ( app, server ) {
  app.get( '/', function ( request, response ) {
    response.redirect( '/spa.html' );
  });

  app.all( '/:obj_type/*?', function ( request, response, next ) {
    response.contentType( 'json' );
    next();
  });

  app.get( '/:obj_type/list', function ( request, response ) {
    crud.read(
      request.params.obj_type,
      {}, {},
      function ( map_list ) { response.send( map_list ); }
    );
  });

  app.post( '/:obj_type/create', function ( request, response ) {
    crud.construct(
      request.params.obj_type,
      request.body,
      function ( result_map ) { response.send( result_map ); }
    );
  });

  app.get( '/:obj_type/read/:id', function ( request, response ) {
    crud.read(
      request.params.obj_type,
      { _id: makeMongoId( request.params.id ) },
      {},
      function ( map_list ) { response.send( map_list ); }
    );
  });

  app.post( '/:obj_type/update/:id', function ( request, response ) {
    crud.update(
      request.params.obj_type,
      { _id: makeMongoId( request.params.id ) },
      request.body,
      function ( result_map ) { response.send( result_map ); }
    );
  });

  app.get( '/:obj_type/delete/:id', function ( request, response ) {
    crud.destroy(
```

Most variable declarations are moved to the CRUD module and removed here.

Remove the utilities section.

Remove the object-type check here, as this is now handled by the CRUD module. It's much safer to rely on the CRUD module to do this check.

Use the CRUD module `read` method to get an object list. The response from the CRUD module can be data or an error. In either case, return the results unaltered.

Use the CRUD module `construct` method to create a user. Return the results unaltered.

Use the CRUD module `read` method to get a single object. Return the results unaltered. Note that this is different than our prior read method, as a successful response returns a single object inside an array.

Use the CRUD module `update` method to update a single object. Return the results unaltered.

Use the CRUD module `destroy` method to remove a single object. Return the results unaltered.

```
      request.params.obj_type,
      { _id: makeMongoId( request.params.id ) },
      function ( result_map ) { response.send( result_map ); }
    );
  });
};

module.exports = { configRoutes : configRoutes };
// ----------------- END PUBLIC METHODS -------------------
```

Remove the initialization section.

Export our configuration method as before.

Now our routes module is much smaller and uses the CRUD module to service routes. And, perhaps more importantly, our CRUD module is ready to be used by the chat module we'll build in the next section.

8.6 Build the Chat module

We want our server application to provide chat capabilities to our SPA. Until now, we've been building out the client, UI, and supporting framework on the server. See figure 8.8 to see how our application should look once chat is implemented.

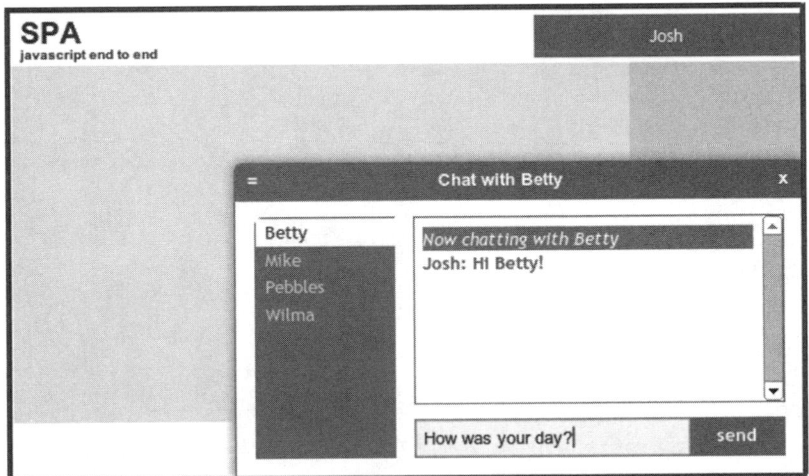

Figure 8.8 Finished Chat application

We'll have a working chat server by the end of this section. We'll start by creating a chat module.

8.6.1 Start the chat module

Socket.IO should be installed in our webapp directory already. Please ensure your webapp/package.json manifest has the correct modules listed:

```
{ "name"     : "SPA",
  "version" : "0.0.3",
  "private" : true,
  "dependencies" : {
    "express"    : "3.2.x",
    "mongodb"    : "1.3.x",
    "socket.io"  : "0.9.x",
    "JSV"        : "4.0.x"
  }
}
```

Once our manifest matches the example, we can run `npm install`, and `npm` will ensure `socket.io` and all other required modules are installed.

Now we can build our chat messaging module. We want to include the CRUD module because we're certain we'll need it for our messages. We'll construct a `chatObj` object and export it using `module.exports`. At first this object will have a single method called `connect` that will take the `http.Server` instance (`server`) as an argument and will begin listening for socket connections. Our first pass is shown in listing 8.26:

Listing 8.26 Our first pass at the chat messaging module—webapp/lib/chat.js

```
/*
 * chat.js - module to provide chat messaging
*/

/*jslint         node    : true, continue : true,
  devel  : true, indent  : 2,    maxerr   : 50,
  newcap : true, nomen   : true, plusplus : true,
  regexp : true, sloppy  : true, vars     : false,
  white  : true
*/
/*global */

// ------------ BEGIN MODULE SCOPE VARIABLES --------------
'use strict';
var
  chatObj,
  socket = require( 'socket.io' ),
  crud   = require( './crud'    );
// ------------- END MODULE SCOPE VARIABLES ---------------

// ---------------- BEGIN PUBLIC METHODS ------------------
chatObj = {
  connect : function ( server ) {
    var io = socket.listen( server );
    return io;
  }
};

module.exports = chatObj;
// ----------------- END PUBLIC METHODS -------------------
```

You may recall from chapter 6 that the client will be sending messages to the server—`adduser`, `updatechat`, `leavechat`, `disconnect`, and `updateavatar`—using the `/chat` namespace. Let's set up our chat client to handle these messages as shown in listing 8.27. Changes are shown in **bold**:

Listing 8.27 Set up our app and outline message handlers—webapp/lib/chat.js

```
/*
 * chat.js - module to provide chat messaging
*/
...
// ---------------- BEGIN PUBLIC METHODS ------------------
chatObj = {
  connect : function ( server ) {
    var io = socket.listen( server );

    // Begin io setup
    io
      .set( 'blacklist' , [] )
      .of( '/chat' )
      .on( 'connection', function ( socket ) {
        socket.on( 'adduser',      function () {} );
        socket.on( 'updatechat',   function () {} );
        socket.on( 'leavechat',    function () {} );
        socket.on( 'disconnect',   function () {} );
        socket.on( 'updateavatar', function () {} );
      }
    );
    // End io setup

    return io;
  }
};

module.exports = chatObj;
// ----------------- END PUBLIC METHODS -------------------
```

Configure Socket.IO not to blacklist or `disconnect` any other message. Enabling `disconnect` allows us to be notified when a client is dropped using the Socket.IO heartbeat.

Configure Socket.IO to respond to messages in the `/chat` namespace.

Define a function that's invoked when a client connects on the `/chat` namespace.

Create handlers for messages in the `/chat` namespace.

Let's return to the routes module, where we'll include the chat module and then use the `chat.connect` method to initialize the Socket.IO connection. We provide the `http.Server` instance (`server`) as the argument, as shown in listing 8.28. Changes are shown in **bold**:

Listing 8.28 Update the routes module to initialize chat—webapp/lib/routes.js

```
/*
 * routes.js - module to provide routing
*/
...
// ------------ BEGIN MODULE SCOPE VARIABLES --------------
'use strict';
var
  configRoutes,
  crud        = require( './crud' ),
  chat        = require( './chat' ),
  makeMongoId = crud.makeMongoId;
// ------------- END MODULE SCOPE VARIABLES ---------------

// ---------------- BEGIN PUBLIC METHODS ------------------
```

```
configRoutes = function ( app, server ) {
  ...
  chat.connect( server );
};

module.exports = { configRoutes : configRoutes };
// ----------------- END PUBLIC METHODS -------------------
```

When we start the server with `node app.js` we should see `info - socket.io started` in the Node.js server log. We can also access http://localhost:3000 as before to manage user objects or view our application in the browser.

We've declared all our message handlers, but now we need to make them respond. Let's start with the `adduser` message handler.

> **Why web sockets?**
>
> Web sockets have some distinct advantages over other near-real-time communication techniques used in the browser:
>
> - A web socket data frame requires only two bytes to maintain a data connection, whereas an AJAX HTTP call (used in long-polling) often transfers kilobytes of information per frame (the actual amount varies according to the number and size of cookies).
> - Web sockets compare favorably to long-polling. They typically use about 1-2% of the network bandwidth and have one-third the latency. Web sockets also tend to be more firewall-friendly.
> - Web sockets are full-duplex, whereas most other solutions are not and require the equivalent of two connections.
> - Unlike Flash sockets, web sockets work on any modern browser on nearly any platform—including mobile devices like smart phones and tablets.
>
> Though Socket.IO favors web sockets, it's comforting to know that it'll negotiate the best connection possible if web sockets aren't available.

8.6.2 Create the adduser message handler

When a user attempts to sign in, the client sends an `adduser` message with user data to our server application. Our `adduser` message handler should:

- Try to find the user object with the provided username in MongoDB using the CRUD module.
- If an object with the requested username is found, use the found object.
- If an object with the requested username *is not* found, create a new user object with the provided username and insert it into the database. Use this newly created object.

- Update the user object in MongoDB to indicate the user is online (`is_online: true`).
- Update the `chatterMap` to store the user ID and a socket connection as key-value pairs.

Let's implement this logic as shown in listing 8.29. Changes are shown in **bold**:

Listing 8.29 Create the `adduser` message handler—`webapp/lib/chat.js`

```
/*
 * chat.js - module to provide chat messaging
*/
...
// ------------ BEGIN MODULE SCOPE VARIABLES --------------
'use strict';
var
  emitUserList, signIn, chatObj,
  socket = require( 'socket.io' ),
  crud   = require( './crud'    ),

  makeMongoId = crud.makeMongoId,
  chatterMap  = {};
// ------------- END MODULE SCOPE VARIABLES ---------------

// ---------------- BEGIN UTILITY METHODS -----------------
// emitUserList - broadcast user list to all connected clients
//
emitUserList = function ( io ) {
  crud.read(
    'user',
    { is_online : true },
    {},
    function ( result_list ) {
      io
        .of( '/chat' )
        .emit( 'listchange', result_list );
    }
  );
};

// signIn - update is_online property and chatterMap
//
signIn = function ( io, user_map, socket ) {
  crud.update(
    'user',
    { '_id'     : user_map._id },
    { is_online : true         },
    function ( result_map ) {
      emitUserList( io );
      user_map.is_online = true;
      socket.emit( 'userupdate', user_map );
    }
  );

  chatterMap[ user_map._id ] = socket;
```

Annotations:

- **Add a `chatterMap` to correlate user IDs to socket connections.** (points to `chatterMap = {};`)
- **Declare the utility methods, `emitUserList` and `SignOn`.** (points to `emitUserList, signIn, chatObj,`)
- **Add the `emitUserList` utility to broadcast the list of online people to all connected clients.** (points to `emitUserList = function ( io ) {`)
- **Broadcast the list of online people as a `listchange` message. Provide the new list of online people as data.** (points to `.emit( 'listchange', result_list );`)
- **Add the `signIn` utility to sign in an existing user by updating their status (`is_online : true`).** (points to `signIn = function ( io, user_map, socket ) {`)
- **Once the user is signed in, call `emitUserList` to broadcast the list of online people to all connected clients.** (points to `function ( result_map ) {`)
- **Add the user to the `chatterMap` and save the user ID as an attribute on the socket so it's easily accessible.** (points to `chatterMap[ user_map._id ] = socket;`)

```
    socket.user_id = user_map._id;
  };
  // ---------------- END UTILITY METHODS ----------------

  // ---------------- BEGIN PUBLIC METHODS ----------------
  chatObj = {
    connect : function ( server ) {
      var io = socket.listen( server );

      // Begin io setup
      io
        .set( 'blacklist' , [] )
        .of( '/chat' )
        .on( 'connection', function ( socket ) {

          // Begin /adduser/ message handler
          // Summary   : Provides sign in capability.
          // Arguments : A single user_map object.
          //   user_map should have the following properties:
          //     name    = the name of the user
          //     cid     = the client id
          // Action    :
          //   If a user with the provided username already exists
          //     in Mongo, use the existing user object and ignore
          //     other input.
          //   If a user with the provided username does not exist
          //     in Mongo, create one and use it.
          //   Send a 'userupdate' message to the sender so that
          //     a login cycle can complete.  Ensure the client id
          //     is passed back so the client can correlate the user,
          //     but do not store it in MongoDB.
          //   Mark the user as online and send the updated online
          //     user list to all clients, including the client that
          //     originated the 'adduser' message.
          //
          socket.on( 'adduser', function ( user_map ) {
            crud.read(
              'user',
              { name : user_map.name },
              {},
              function ( result_list ) {
                var
                  result_map,
                  cid = user_map.cid;

                delete user_map.cid;

                // use existing user with provided name
                if ( result_list.length > 0 ) {
                  result_map     = result_list[ 0 ];
                  result_map.cid = cid;
                  signIn( io, result_map, socket );
                }

                // create user with new name
```

Document the adduser message handler.

Update the adduser message handler to accept a user_map object from the client.

Use the crud.read method to find all users with the provided username.

If a user object with the provided username is found, call the signIn utility using the found object. The signIn utility will send an updateuser message to the client and provide the user_map as data. It will also call emitUserList to broadcast the list of online people to all connected clients.

If a user with the provided username is not found, create a new object and store it in the MongoDB collection. Add the user object to the `chatterMap` and save the user ID as an attribute on the socket so it is easily accessible. Then call `emitUserList` to broadcast the list of online people to all connected clients.

```
              else {
                user_map.is_online = true;
                crud.construct(
                  'user',
                  user_map,
                  function ( result_list ) {
                    result_map     = result_list[ 0 ];
                    result_map.cid = cid;
                    chatterMap[ result_map._id ] = socket;
                    socket.user_id = result_map._id;
                    socket.emit( 'userupdate', result_map );
                    emitUserList( io );
                  }
                );
              }
            }
          );
        });
        // End /adduser/ message handler

        socket.on( 'updatechat',   function () {} );
        socket.on( 'leavechat',    function () {} );
        socket.on( 'disconnect',   function () {} );
        socket.on( 'updateavatar', function () {} );
      }
    );
    // End io setup

    return io;
  }
};

module.exports = chatObj;
// ----------------- END PUBLIC METHODS -------------------
```

It can take a while to adjust to the callback method of thinking, but typically when we call a method, and when that method finishes, the callback we provided gets executed. In essence it turns procedural code like so:

```
var user = user.create();

if ( user ) {
  //do things with user object
}
```

Into event-driven code like this:

```
user.create( function ( user ) {
    // do things with user object
});
```

We use callbacks because many function calls in Node.js are asynchronous. In the preceding example, when we invoke `user.create`, the JavaScript engine will keep on executing the subsequent code without waiting for the invocation to complete. One guaranteed way to use the results immediately after they're ready is to use a callback.[5] If you're familiar with the jQuery AJAX call, it uses the callback mechanism:

```
$.ajax({
  'url': '/path',
  'success': function ( data ) {
    // do things with data
  }
});
```

We can now point our browser to localhost:3000 and sign in. We encourage those playing along at home to give it a try. Now let's get people chatting.

8.6.3 Create the updatechat message handler

A fair amount of code was required to implement sign-in. Our application now keeps track of users in MongoDB, managing their state, and broadcasts a list of online people to all connected clients. Handling chat messaging is comparatively simple, especially now that we have the sign-in logic complete.

When the client sends an `updatechat` message to our server application, it's requesting delivery of a message to someone. Our `updatechat` message handler should:

- Inspect the chat data and retrieve the recipient.
- Determine if the intended recipient is online.
- If the recipient is online, send the chat data to the recipient on their socket.
- If the recipient is *not online*, send new chat data to the sender on their socket. The new chat data should notify the sender that the intended recipient is not online.

Let's implement this logic as shown in listing 8.30. Changes are shown in **bold**:

Listing 8.30 Add the `updatechat` message handler—`webapp/lib/chat.js`

```
/*
 * chat.js - module to provide chat messaging
*/
...
// ---------------- BEGIN PUBLIC METHODS ------------------
chatObj = {
  connect : function ( server ) {
    var io = socket.listen( server );

    // Begin io setup
    io
      .set( 'blacklist' , [] )
      .of( '/chat' )
```

5 Another mechanism is called *promises*, and is generally more flexible than vanilla callbacks. Promise libraries include Q (`npm install q`) and Promised-IO (`npm install promised-io`). jQuery for Node.js also provides a rich and familiar set of promise methods. Appendix B shows the use of jQuery with Node.js.

```
    .on( 'connection', function ( socket ) {

      ...
      // Begin /adduser/ message handler
      ...
      socket.on( 'adduser', function ( user_map ) {
        ...
      });
      // End /adduser/ message handler

      // Begin /updatechat/ message handler
      // Summary   : Handles messages for chat.
      // Arguments : A single chat_map object.
      //  chat_map should have the following properties:
      //    dest_id   = id of recipient
      //    dest_name = name of recipient
      //    sender_id = id of sender
      //    msg_text  = message text
      // Action    :
      //   If the recipient is online, the chat_map is sent to her.
      //   If not, a 'user has gone offline' message is
      //     sent to the sender.
      //
      socket.on( 'updatechat', function ( chat_map ) {
        if ( chatterMap.hasOwnProperty( chat_map.dest_id ) ) {
          chatterMap[ chat_map.dest_id ]
            .emit( 'updatechat', chat_map );
        }
        else {
          socket.emit( 'updatechat', {
            sender_id : chat_map.sender_id,
            msg_text  : chat_map.dest_name + ' has gone offline.'
          });
        }
      });
      // End /updatechat/ message handler

      socket.on( 'leavechat',    function () {} );
      socket.on( 'disconnect',   function () {} );
      socket.on( 'updateavatar', function () {} );
    }
  );
  // End io setup

  return io;
 }
};

module.exports = chatObj;
// ----------------- END PUBLIC METHODS -------------------
```

Document the updatechat message handler.

If the intended recipient is online (the user ID is in the chatterMap), forward the chat_map to the recipient client through the appropriate socket.

Add the chat_map argument which contains the chat data from the client.

If the intended recipient is not online, return a new chat_map to the sender to indicate the requested recipient is no longer online.

We can now point our browser to localhost:3000 and sign in. If we sign in to another browser window as a different user, we can pass messages back and forth. As always, we encourage those playing along at home to give it a try. The only capabilities that don't yet work are disconnect and avatars. Let's take care of disconnect next.

8.6.4 Create disconnect message handlers

A client can close the session one of two ways. First, the user may click on their username in the top-right corner of the browser window to sign out. This sends a `leavechat` message to the server. Second, the user may close the browser window. This results in a `disconnect` message to the server. In either case, Socket.IO does a good job of cleaning up the socket connection.

When our server application receives a `leavechat` or a `disconnect` message, it should take the same two actions. First, it should mark the person associated with the client as offline (`is_online : false`). Second, it needs to broadcast the updated list of online people to all connected clients. This logic is shown in listing 8.31. Changes are shown in **bold**:

Listing 8.31 Add disconnect methods—webapp/lib/chat.js

```
/*
 * chat.js - module to provide chat messaging
*/
...
// ------------ BEGIN MODULE SCOPE VARIABLES --------------
'use strict';
var
  emitUserList, signIn, signOut, chatObj,
  socket = require( 'socket.io' ),
  crud   = require( './crud'    ),

  makeMongoId = crud.makeMongoId,
  chatterMap  = {};
// ------------- END MODULE SCOPE VARIABLES ---------------

// ---------------- BEGIN UTILITY METHODS -----------------
...
// signOut - update is_online property and chatterMap
//
signOut = function ( io, user_id ) {
  crud.update(
    'user',
    { '_id'     : user_id },
    { is_online : false   },
    function ( result_list ) { emitUserList( io ); }
  );
  delete chatterMap[ user_id ];
};
// ----------------- END UTILITY METHODS ------------------

// ---------------- BEGIN PUBLIC METHODS ------------------
chatObj = {
  connect : function ( server ) {
    var io = socket.listen( server );

    // Begin io setup
    io
      .set( 'blacklist' , [] )
      .of( '/chat' )
```

Sign out a user by setting the `is_online` attribute to false.

After a user signs out, emit the new online people list to all connected clients.

The signed-out user is removed from the `chatterMap`.

```
      .on( 'connection', function ( socket ) {

        ...
        // Begin disconnect methods
        socket.on( 'leavechat', function () {
          console.log(
            '** user %s logged out **', socket.user_id
          );
          signOut( io, socket.user_id );
        });

        socket.on( 'disconnect', function () {
          console.log(
            '** user %s closed browser window or tab **',
            socket.user_id
          ); signOut( io, socket.user_id );
        });
        // End disconnect methods

        socket.on( 'updateavatar', function () {} );
      }
    );
    // End io setup

    return io;
  }
};

module.exports = chatObj;
// ----------------- END PUBLIC METHODS -------------------
```

Now we can open up multiple browser windows, point them to http://localhost:3000, and sign in as different users by clicking at the top-right corner of each window. We can then send message between users. We did intentionally leave one flaw as an exercise for our readers: the server application will allow the same user to log in on multiple clients. This shouldn't be possible. You should be able to fix this by inspecting the `chatterMap` in the `adduser` message handler.

We have one feature yet to implement: synchronizing avatars.

8.6.5 Create the updateavatar message handler

Web socket messaging can be used for all kinds of server-client communication. When we need near-real-time communication with the browser, it's often the best choice. To demonstrate another use of Socket.IO, we've built avatars into our chat that users can move around the screen and change color. When anyone changes an avatar, Socket.IO immediately pushes those updates to other users. Let's walk through what that looks like in figures 8.9, 8.10, and 8.11.

The client-side code for this has been demonstrated in chapter 6, and we've arrived at the moment where we put it all together. The server-side code to enable this is dramatically small now that we've set up the Node.js server, MongoDB, and Socket.IO. We just add a message handler adjacent to the others in lib/chat.js as shown in listing 8.32:

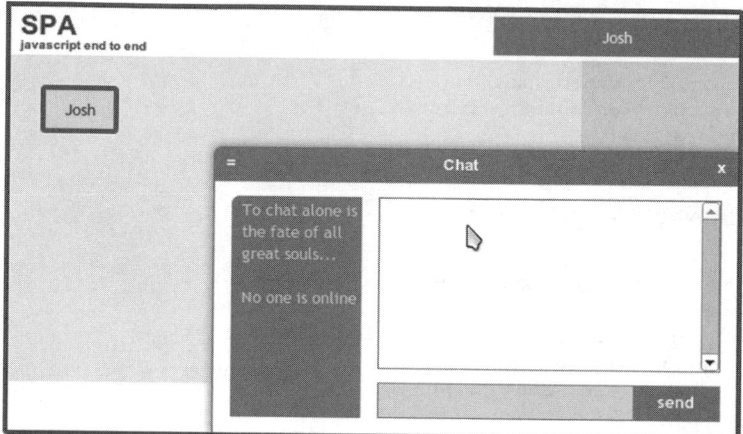

Figure 8.9 Avatar when signing in

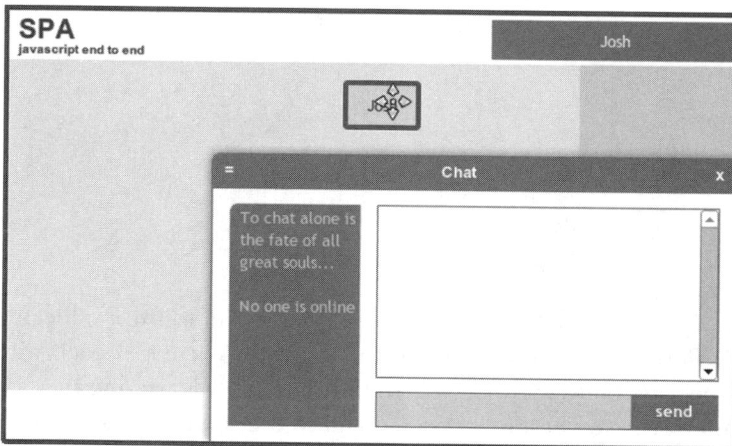

Figure 8.10 Moving an avatar

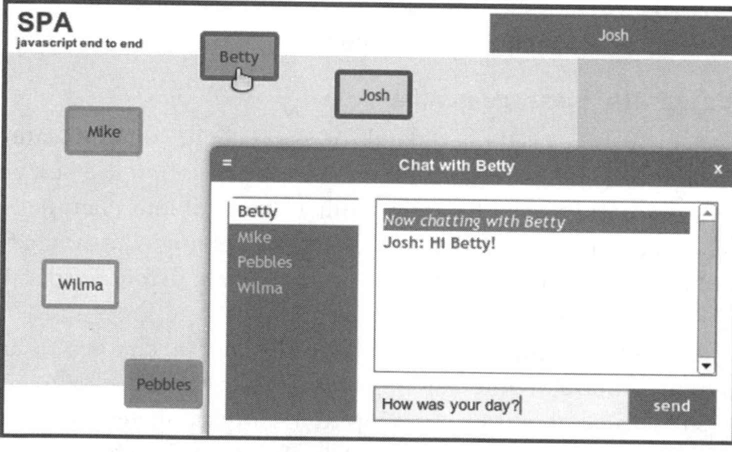

Figure 8.11 Avatars when others are signed in

Listing 8.32 Behold the avatars—webapp/lib/chat.js

```
/*
 * chat.js - module to provide chat messaging
*/
...
// ---------------- BEGIN PUBLIC METHODS ------------------
chatObj = {
  connect : function ( server ) {
    var io = socket.listen( server );

    // Begin io setup
    io
      .set( 'blacklist' , [] )
      .of( '/chat' )
      .on( 'connection', function ( socket ) {

        ...

        // End disconnect methods

        // Begin /updateavatar/ message handler
        // Summary : Handles client updates of avatars
        // Arguments : A single avtr_map object.
        //   avtr_map should have the following properties:
        //   person_id = the id of the persons avatar to update
        //   css_map = the css map for top, left, and
        //     background-color
        // Action :
        //   This handler updates the entry in MongoDB, and then
        //   broadcasts the revised people list to all clients.
        //
        socket.on( 'updateavatar', function ( avtr_map ) {
          crud.update(
            'user',
            { '_id' : makeMongoId( avtr_map.person_id ) },
            { css_map : avtr_map.css_map },
            function ( result_list ) { emitUserList( io ); }
          );
        }); // End /updateavatar/ message handler
      }
    );
    // End io setup

    return io;
  }
};

module.exports = chatObj;
// ----------------- END PUBLIC METHODS -------------------
```

Let's start the server with `node app.js`, point our browser to http://localhost:3000/, and sign in. Let's also open a second browser window and sign in with a different user name. At this point we may only see one avatar because the two may overlap. We can move an avatar by using a long-press-drag motion. We can change its color by clicking or tapping on it. This works on desktops and touch devices. In any case, our server application synchronizes the avatars in near-real time.

Messaging is the key to near-real-time collaboration. With web sockets, we can create applications where distant people can work together to solve a puzzle, design an engine, or draw a picture—the possibilities are endless. This is the promise of the real-time web, and we're seeing more of it every day.

8.7 Summary

In this chapter we set up MongoDB, connected it to Node.js, and performed some basic CRUD operations. We introduced MongoDB and discussed its many benefits and pitfalls. We've also demonstrated how to validate data before inserting it into the database using the same code that the client uses. This reuse saves us the familiar pain of writing a validator for the server in one language and rewriting it in JavaScript for the browser.

We introduced Socket.IO and showed how to use it to provide chat messaging. We moved our CRUD capabilities into a separate module so it could easily service both the HTTP API and Socket.IO. And we used messaging to provide near-real-time synchronization of avatars across many clients.

In the next chapter we'll take a look at how we make our SPA ready for production. We'll review some of the problems we have encountered when hosting SPAs, and discuss how we can solve them.

9 Readying our SPA for production

This chapter covers

- Optimizing SPAs for search engines
- Using Google Analytics
- Placing static content on a content delivery network (CDN)
- Logging client errors
- Caching and cache busting

This chapter builds on code we've written in chapter 8. We recommend copying the entire directory structure of that chapter into a new "chapter_9" directory and updating the files there.

We've finished writing a responsive SPA using a well-tested architecture, but some challenges remain that are less about programming and more about operations.

We need to adjust our SPA so that users can use Google and other search engines to find what they need. Our web server needs to interact with the *crawler* robots that index our content differently because the crawlers don't execute the JavaScript our SPA uses to generate the content. We also want to use analytics tools.

On a traditional website, analytics data is typically collected through a JavaScript snippet added to every HTML page. Because all of the HTML in an SPA is generated by JavaScript, we need a different approach.

We also want to want to adjust our SPA to provide detailed logging on traffic, user behavior, and errors. Server logging provides much of this insight on traditional websites. SPAs move most of the user interaction logic to the client, so a different approach is required. We want our SPA to be very responsive. One method to improve response time is to use a content delivery network (CDN) to serve static files and data. Another method is to use HTTP and server caching.

Let's get started by making our SPA content searchable.

9.1 Optimize our SPA for search engines

When Google and other search engines index websites, they don't execute JavaScript. This seems to put SPAs at a tremendous disadvantage compared to a traditional website. Not being on Google could easily mean the death of a business, and this daunting pitfall could tempt the uninformed to abandon SPAs.

SPAs actually have an advantage over traditional websites in search engine optimization (SEO) because Google and others have recognized the challenge. They have created a mechanism for SPAs to not only have their dynamic pages indexed, but also optimize their pages specifically for crawlers. This section focuses on the biggest search engine, Google, but other large search engines such as Yahoo and Bing support the same mechanism.

9.1.1 How Google crawls an SPA

When Google indexes a traditional website, its web crawler (called a *Googlebot*) first scans and indexes the content of the top-level URI (for example, www.myhome.com). Once this is complete, it then it follows all of the links on that page and indexes those pages as well. It then follows the links on the subsequent pages, and so on. Eventually it indexes all the content on the site and associated domains.

When the Googlebot tries to index an SPA, all it sees in the HTML is a single empty container (usually an empty `div` or `body` tag), so there's nothing to index and no links to crawl, and it indexes the site accordingly (in the round circular "folder" on the floor next to its desk).

If that were the end of the story, it would be the end of SPAs for many web applications and sites. Fortunately, Google and other search engines have recognised the importance of SPAs and provided tools to allow developers to provide search information to the crawler that can be better than traditional websites.

The first key to making our SPA crawlable is to realize that our server can tell if a request is being made by a crawler or by a person using a web browser and respond accordingly. When our visitor is a person using a web browser, respond as normal, but for a crawler, return a page optimized to show the crawler exactly what we want to in a format the crawler can easily read.

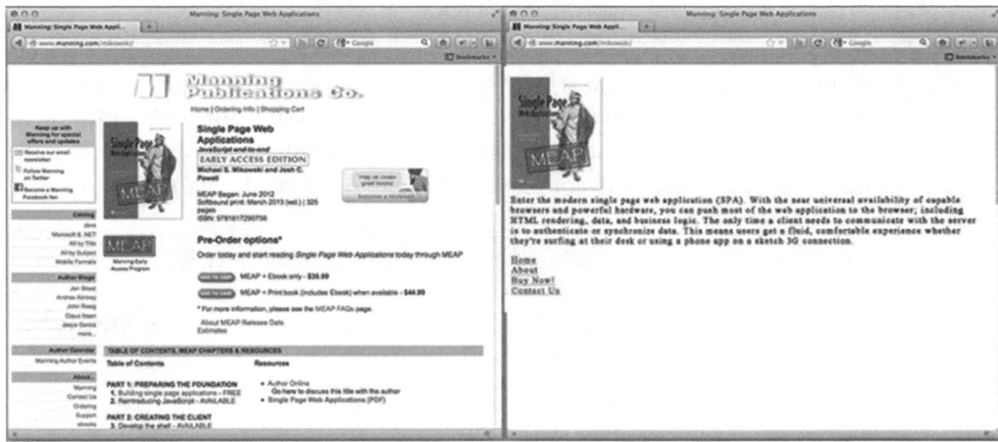

Figure 9.1 Client and crawler views of a home page

For the home page of our site, what does a crawler-optimized page look like? It's probably our logo or other primary image we'd like appearing in search results, some SEO-optimized text explaining what the application does, and a list of HTML links to only those pages we want Google to index. What the page doesn't have is any CSS styling or complex HTML structure applied to it. Nor does it have any JavaScript, or links to areas of the site we don't want Google to index (like legal disclaimer pages or other pages we don't want people to enter through a Google search). Figure 9.1 shows how a page might be presented to a browser and to the crawler.

The links on the page aren't followed by the crawler the same way a person follows links because we apply the special characters `#!` (pronounced *hash bang*) in our URI anchor component. For instance, if in our SPA a link to the user page looks like `/index.htm#!page=user:id,123`, the crawler would see the `#!` and know to look for a web page with the URI `/index.htm?_escaped_fragment_=page=user:id,123`. Knowing that the crawler will follow the pattern and look for this URI, we can program the server to respond to that request with an HTML snapshot of the page that would normally be rendered by JavaScript in the browser. That snapshot will be indexed by Google, but anyone clicking on our listing in Google search results will be taken to `/index.htm#!page=user:id,123`. The SPA JavaScript will take over from there and render the page as expected.

This provides SPA developers with the opportunity to tailor their site specifically for Google and specifically for users. Instead of having to write text that's both legible and attractive to a person and understandable by a crawler, pages can be optimized for each without worrying about the other. The crawler's path through our site can be controlled, allowing us to direct people from Google search results to a specific set of entrance pages. This will require more work on the part of the engineer to develop, but it can have big pay-offs in terms of search result position and customer retention.

At the time of this writing, the Googlebot announces itself as a crawler to the server by making requests with a user-agent string of `Googlebot/2.1 (+http://www.googlebot.com/bot.html)`. Our Node.js application can check for this user agent string in the middleware and send back the crawler-optimized home page if the user agent string matches. Otherwise, we can handle the request normally. Alternatively, we could hook it into our routing middleware as shown in listing 9.1:

Listing 9.1 Detect a Googlebot and serve alternative content in the `routes.js` file

```
...
var agent_text = 'Enter the modern single page web application(SPA).'
  + 'With the near universal availability of capable browsers and '
  + 'powerful hardware, we can push most of the web application to'
  + ' the browser; including HTML rendering, data, and business '
  + 'logic. The only time a client needs to communicate with the '
  + 'server is to authenticate or synchronize data. This means users'
  + ' get a fluid, comfortable experience whether they\'re surfing '
  + 'at their desk or using a phone app on a sketch 3G connection.'
  + '<br><br>'
  + '<a href="/index.htm#page=home">;Home</a><br>'
  + '<a href="/index.htm#page=about">About</a><br>'
  + '<a href="/index.htm#page=buynow">Buy Now!</a><br>'
  + '<a href="/index.htm#page=contact us">Contact Us</a><br>';

app.all( '*', function ( req, res, next ) {
  if ( req.headers['user-agent'] ===
      'Googlebot/2.1 (+http://www.googlebot.com/bot.html)' ) {
    res.contentType( 'html' );
    res.end( agent_text );
  }
  else {
    next();
  }
});
...
```

The HTML to be provided to the web crawler (annotation on `var agent_text`)

Detect the Googlebot by looking at the user agent string; other crawlers use a different user agent that with some research can be targeted as well. If the crawler is detected, the `contentType` is set to HTML and the text is sent to it, bypassing the normal routing code.

If the user agent isn't a crawler, call `next()` to proceed to the next route for normal processing.

This arrangment seems like it would be complicated to test, since we don't own a Googlebot. Google offers a service to do this for publicly available production websites as part of its Webmaster Tools (http://support.google.com/webmasters/bin/answer.py?hl=en&answer=158587), but an easier way to test is to spoof our user-agent string. This used to require some command-line hackery, but Chrome Developer Tools makes this as easy as clicking a button and checking a box:

1 Open the Chrome Developer Tools by clicking the button with three horizontal lines to the right of the Google Toolbar, and then selecting Tools from the menu and clicking on Developer Tools.

2. In the lower-right corner of the screen is a gears icon: click on that and see some advanced developer options such as disabling cache and turning on logging of `XmlHttpRequests`.
3. In the second tab, labelled Overrides, click the check box next to the User Agent label and select any number of user agents from the drop-down from Chrome, to Firefox, to IE, iPads, and more. The Googlebot agent isn't a default option. In order to use it, select Other and copy and paste the user-agent string into the provided input.
4. Now that tab is spoofing itself as a Googlebot, and when we open any URI on our site, we should see the crawler page.

Obviously, different applications will have different needs with regard to what to do with web crawlers, but always having one page returned to the Googlebot is probably not enough. We'll also need to decide what pages we want to expose and provide ways for our application to map the `_escaped_fragment_=key=value` URI to the content we want to show them. Whatever the case, this book should provide you with the tools to decide how to best abstract the crawler content for your application. You may want to get fancy and tie the server response in to the front end framework, but we usually take the simpler approach here and create custom pages for the crawler and put them in a separate router file for crawlers.

There are also a lot more legitimate crawlers out there, so once we've adjusted our server for the Google crawler we can expand to include them as well.

9.2 The cloud and third-party services

Many companies have services that help build and manage applications, which can save a great deal of development and maintenance. If we're a smaller operation, we may want to take advantage of some of these services. Three important services—site analytics, client logging, and CDNs—are particularly important for SPA development.

9.2.1 Site analytics

An important tool in the web developer's toolbelt is the ability to acquire analytics about the site they're working on. With traditional websites, developers have come to depend on tools like Google Analytics and New Relic to provide detailed analysis of how people are using the sites and to find any bottlenecks in application or business performance (how effectively the site is generating sales). A slightly different approach using the same tools will make them every bit as effective on an SPA.

Google Analytics provides a simple way to get statistics about how popular our SPA and its various states are, as well as how traffic is coming to our site. We can use Google Analytics in a traditional website by pasting a snippet of JavaScript code onto every HTML page on the site and making a few small modifications to categorize pages. We could use this approach with our SPA, but then we'd only get analytics on the initial page load. There are two paths we can use to enable our SPA to take full advantage of Google Analytics:

1 Use Google Events to track hashtag changes
2 Use Node.js to record server-side

We'll begin by looking at Google Events.

GOOGLE EVENTS

Google has long recognized the need to record and classify events on pages—SPA development may be fairly new, but Ajax has been around a long time (in web years, a really long time... since 1999!). Tracking events is easy, though it's more manual work then tracking page views. In a traditional website, the snippet of JavaScript code makes a call to `_trackPageView` on the `_gaq` object. It allows us to pass in custom variables to set information about the page the snippet is on. That call sends the information to Google by requesting an image and passing along parameters on the end of the request. Those parameters are used by Google's servers to process information about that page view. Using Google Events makes a different call on the `_gaq` object: it calls `_trackEvent` and takes some parameters. `_trackEvent` then loads an image with some parameters on the end of it that Google uses to process the information about that event.

The steps to set up and use event tracking are fairly straightforward:

1 Set up tracking for our site on the Google Analytics site.
2 Call the `_trackEvent` method.
3 View the reports.

The `_trackEvent` method takes two required parameters and three optional ones:

```
_trackEvent(category, action, opt_label, opt_value, opt_noninteraction)
```

The parameter details are:

- `category` is required and is used to name the group of events this belongs to. It will show up in our reporting to categorize events.
- `action` is required and defines the specific action we're tracking with each event.
- `opt_label` is an optional parameter used to add additional data about the event.
- `opt_value` is an optional parameter used to provide numerical data about the event.
- `opt_noninteraction` is an optional parameter used to tell Google not to use this event in bounce rate calculations.

For example, if in our SPA we want to track when a user opens a chat window, we might make the following `_trackEvent` call:

```
_trackEvent( 'chat', 'open', 'home page' );
```

This call would then show up in reports letting us know that a chat event occurred, the user opened the chat window, and the user did this on the home page. Another call might be:

```
_trackEvent( 'chat', 'message', 'game' );
```

This would record that a chat event occurred, the user sent a message, and did it on the game page. Like the traditional website approach, it's up to the developer to decide how to organize and track different events. As a shortcut, instead of coding each event into the client-side models, we can insert the `_trackEvent` calls into the client-side router (the code that watches the hashtag for changes) and then parse those changes into categories, actions, and labels and call the `_trackEvent` method using those changes as parameters.

SERVER-SIDE GOOGLE ANALYTICS

Tracking on the server side is useful if we want to get information about what data is being requested from the server, but it can't be used to track client interactions that don't make requests to the server side, which there's quite a bit of in SPAs. It may seem less useful because it can't track client-side actions, but it's useful to be able to track requests that are making it past the client cache. It can help us track down server requests that are running too slow and other behaviors. Though this is still able to provide helpful insights, if we have to choose one, we go with the client.

Since JavaScript is used on the server, it seems likely that we could modify the Google Analytics code to be used from the server. It's not only possible, but like many things that seem like a good idea, it has probably already been implemented by the community. A quick search turns up *node-googleanalytics* and *nodealytics* as community-developed projects.

9.2.2 Logging client-side errors

In a traditional website, when there's an error on the server, it's written to a log file. In an SPA, when a client hits a similar error, there's nothing in place to record it. We'll have to either manually write code to track errors ourselves or look to a third-party service for help. Handling it ourselves gives us the flexibility to do whatever we want to with the error, but using a third-party service gives us the opportunity to spend our time and resources on something else. Besides, they've likely implemented far more than we'd have time to. It's also not all or nothing—we can use a third-party service and then if there are errors we want tracked or escalated in a way that the service doesn't provide, we can implement the desired capability ourselves.

THIRD-PARTY CLIENT LOGGING

There are several third-party services that collect and aggregate errors and metrics data generated by our application:

- *Airbrake* specializes in Ruby on Rails applications, but has experimental JavaScript support.
- *Bugsense* specializes in mobile application solutions. Their product works with JavaScript SPAs and native mobile applications. If we have a mobile-focused application, they may be a good choice.
- *Errorception* is dedicated to logging JavaScript errors and is therefore a good choice for an SPA client. They're not as established as Airbrake or Bugsense but

we like their moxy. *Errorception* keeps a developer blog (http://blog.errorception.com), where we can gain insight on JavaScript error logging.

- *New Relic* is fast becoming an industry standard for web application performance monitoring. Its performance monitoring includes error logging and performance metrics for each step of the request/response cycle, from how long the query took in the database to how long the browser took to render the CSS styles. The service provides an impressive amount of insight into performance on both the client and the server.

At the time of writing, we tend to prefer New Relic or Errorception. Whereas New Relic provides more data, we've found Errorception superior when dealing with JavaScript errors, as well as easy to set up.

LOGGING CLIENT-SIDE ERRORS MANUALLY

When it comes down to it, all these services use one of these two methods to send JavaScript errors:

1. Catching errors with the `window.onerror` event handler.
2. Surrounding code with a `try/catch` block and sending back what it catches.

The `window.onerror` event is the basis of most of the third-party applications. `onerror` fires for runtime errors, but not for compilation errors. `onerror` is somewhat controversial because of uneven browser support and potential security holes, but it's a major weapon in our arsenal for logging client-side JavaScript errors.

```
<script>
  var obj;
  obj.push( 'string' );          // Results in an error because there's no push method on undefined.

  windor.onerror = function ( error ) {
    // do something with the error   // The error is accessible inside this block; the attributes on the error object vary by browser.
  }

</script>
```

The `try/catch` method requires wrapping a `try/catch` block around the main call in our SPA. This will catch any synchronous errors generated by our application; unfortunately it'll also prevent them from bubbling up to `window.onerror` or being displayed in the error console. It won't catch any errors in asynchronous calls like those made in event handlers or in `setTimeout` or `setInterval` functions. That means having to wrap all of the code in our asynchronous function with a `try/catch` block.

```
<script>
  setTimeout( function () {
    try {
      var obj;
      obj.push( 'string' );
    } catch ( error ) {
      // do something with error
```

```
    }
  }), 1);
</script>
```

Having to do that for all of our asynchronous calls would get tedious, and prevent reporting of the errors to the console. Wrapping code in a `try/catch` block also prevents the code in that block from being compiled in advance, causing it to run slower. A good compromise approach for an SPA is to wrap our `init` call in a `try/catch` block, log the error to the console inside the catch, and send it off via Ajax, then use `window.onerror` to catch all of our asynchronous errors and send them off via Ajax. No need to log the asynchronous errors to the console manually because they'll still appear there on their own.

```
<script>
    $(function () {
      try {
        spa.initModule( $('#spa') );
      } catch ( error ) {
        // log the error to the console
        // then send it to a third party logging service
      }
    });

    window.onerror = function ( error ) {
      // do something with asynchronous errors
    };

  </script>
```

Now that we understand which errors are happening on the client, we can focus on how to deliver content to site visitors more quickly.

9.2.3 Content delivery networks

A *content delivery network (CDN)* is a network set up to deliver static files as quickly as possible. It could be as simple as a single Apache server sitting next to our application server, or a worldwide infrastructure with dozens of data centers. In any case, it makes sense to have a separate server set up to deliver our static files, so as to not burden our application server with that task. Node.js is particularly ill-suited to delivering large static content files (images, CSS, JavaScript), because this usage can't take advantage of the asynchronous nature of Node.js. Apache, with its pre-fork, is much better suited.

Because we're well-versed in Apache, we *could* throw together our own "one-server CDN" until we get ready to scale the site; otherwise there are many third-party CDNs we can use. Three big ones are Amazon, Akamai, and Edgecast. Amazon has the Cloudfront product, and Akamai and Edgecast resell through other companies like Rackspace, Distribution Cloud, and others. In fact, there are so many CDN companies out there that there's a website dedicated to selecting the right provider: www.cdnplanet.com.

Another benefit of using a globally distributed CDN is that our content is served from the closest server, making the time it takes to serve up those files much shorter. When we consider the performance benefits, using a CDN is often an easy choice.

9.3 Caching and cache busting

Caching is incredibly important to making our application run fast. There's no faster form of data retrieval than client-side caching, and server caching is often far superior to having to request and calculate the same information over again. There are many places in our SPA that have the potential to cache data and thus speed up that part of our application. We'll go through them all:

- Web storage
- HTTP caching
- Server caching
- Database caching

It's crucial to think about data freshness when caching. We don't want to be serving stale data to our applications users, but at the same time we want to be responding to requests as quickly as possible.

9.3.1 Caching opportunities

Each of these caches has different responsibilities and interacts with the client to speed up the application in different ways.

- *Web storage* stores strings in the client and is accessible to the application. Use these to store finished HTML from data already retrieved from the server and processed.
- *HTTP caching* is client-side caching that stores responses from the server. There's a lot of detail to learn in order to properly control this style of caching, but after learning and implementing it, we'll get a lot of caching almost for free.
- *Server caching* with Memcached and Redis are often used to cache processed server responses. This is the first form of caching that can store data for different users so that if one user requests some information, it's already cached the next time someone else requests it, saving a trip to the database.
- *Database caching*, or query caching, is used by databases to cache the results of a query so that if it's turned on, subsequent identical queries return the cache instead of gathering the data again.

Figure 9.2 shows a typical request/response cycle with all of the caching opportunities. We can see how each level of caching can speed up the response by shortcutting the cycle at various stages. HTTP caching and database caching are the simplest to implement, usually only requiring the setting of some configurations, whereas web storage and server caching are more involved, requiring more effort on the part of the developer.

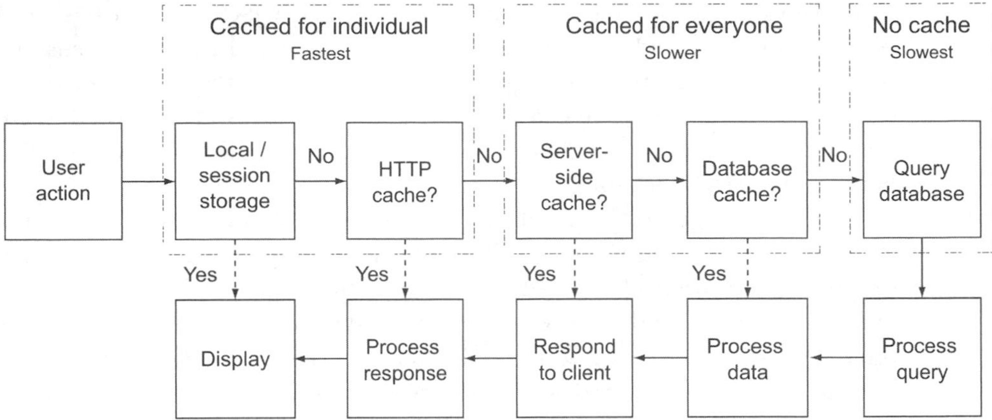

Figure 9.2 Shortcutting the request/response cycle with caching

9.3.2 Web storage

Web storage, also known as *DOM storage*, comes in two types: local and session storage. They're supported by all modern browsers, including IE8+. They're simple key/value stores where both the key and the value must be a string. Session storage only stores the data for the current tab session—closing the tab will close the session and clear the data. Local storage will keep the storage cached with no expiration date. In either case, the data is only available to the web page that stored it. For the SPA, this means that the entire site has access to the storage. One excellent way to use web storage is to store processed HTML strings, enabling a request to bypass the entire request/response cycle and proceed directly to displaying the result. Figure 9.3 shows the details.

We use local storage to store non-sensitive information that we want to persist beyond the current browser session. We use session storage to store data that won't persist beyond the current session.

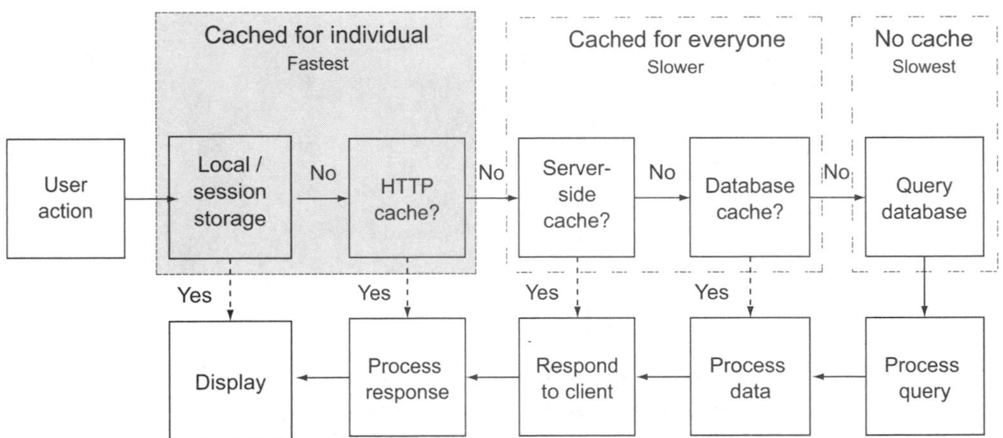

Figure 9.3 Web storage

Since web storage can only save string values, typically JSON or HTML is saved. Saving JSON is redundant with using an HTTP cache in an SPA, which we'll discuss in the next section, and still requires some processing to be used. Often it's better practice to store an HTML string so we can save the client the processing required to create it in the first place. This kind of storage can be abstracted into a JavaScript object, which handles the particulars for us.

Session storage only stores data for the current session, so we can sometimes get away with not thinking too much about the stale data problem—but not always. When we do need to worry about stale data, one method used to force a data refresh is to encode the time into the cache key. If we want data to expire every day, we can include the day's date in the key. If we want the data to expire every hour, we can encode the hour in there as well. This won't handle every scenario, but is probably the simplest in terms of execution, as shown in listing 9.2:

Listing 9.2 Encoding the time in the cache key

```
SPA.storage = (function () {

  var generateKey = function ( key ) {
    var date     = new Date(),
        datekey  = new String()
                 + date.getYear()
                 + date.getMonth()
                 + date.getDay();
    return key + datekey;
  };

  return {

    'set': function ( key, value ) {
      sessionStorage.setItem( generateKey( key ), value );
    },

    'get': function ( key ) {
      return sessionStorage.getItem( generateKey( key ) );
    },

    'remove': function ( key ) {
      sessionStorage.removeItem( generateKey( key ) );
    },

    'clear': function () {
      sessionStorage.clear();
    }
  }
})();
```

Appends the current date on the key, forcing the session to only cache the data for one day. It's a quick trick to make sure that the cached data isn't returned after a certain interval.

These methods abstract the `sessionStorage`, so that we can replace it with `localStorage` (or anything else) at a later date without having to change all of our code. They also call `generateKey` to append the date, so we don't have to code that in to every storage usage.

9.3.3 *HTTP caching*

HTTP caching occurs when the browser caches data sent to it from the server, according to some attributes the server set in the header or according to an industry standard set of default caching guidelines. Though it can be slower than web storage

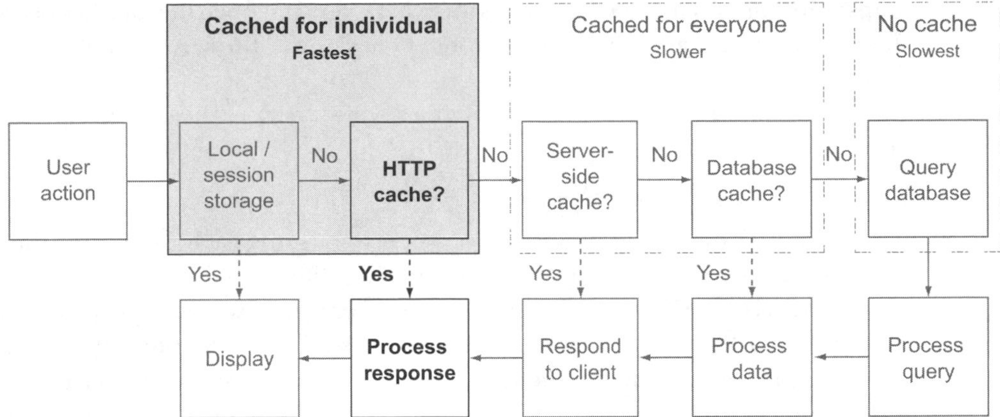

Figure 9.4 HTTP caching

because the results still need to be processed, it's often much simpler and still faster than server-side caching. Figure 9.4 shows where HTTP caching sits in the request/response cycle.

HTTP caching is used to store server responses in the client, to keep from doing another round trip. There are two patterns that it can follow:

1. Serve directly from cache without checking the server for freshness.
2. Check the server for freshness and serve from cache if fresh, and from server response if stale.

Serving directly from cache without checking for freshness of data is the quickest, because we forgo a round trip to the server. This is safer to do for images, CSS, and JavaScript files, but we can also set our application up so that it'll cache data for a length of time as well. For example, if we have an application that only updates some kinds of data once a day at midnight, then we could direct clients to cache data until just after midnight.

Sometimes that doesn't provide up-to-date enough information. In those cases the browser can be instructed to check back with the server to see if the data is still fresh.

Let's get down to the nitty-gritty and see how this caching works. HTTP caching works by having the client look at the headers of the response sent from the server. There are three primary attributes that the client looks for: `max-age`, `no-cache`, and `last-modified`. Each of these contributes toward telling the client how long to cache the data.

MAX-AGE

In order for the client to use data from its cache without attempting to contact the server, the header of the initial response must have the `max-age` set in the `Cache-Control` header. This value tells the client how long to cache the data before making another request. The `max-age` value is in seconds. This is both a powerful capability and a potentially dangerous one. It's powerful because it's the quickest possible way to access data;

apps running with data cached in this way will be very fast once the data has been loaded. It's dangerous because the client no longer checks with the server for changes, so we'll have to be deliberate with them.

When using Express, we can set the `Cache-Control` header with the `max-age` attribute.

```
res.header("Cache-Control", "max-age=28800");
```

Once the cache is set in this way, the only way to bust the cache and force the client to make a new request is to change the name of the file.

Obviously, changing the names of files every time we push to production isn't desirable. Fortunately, changing parameters passed in to the file will bust the cache. This is typically done by appending a version number or some integer that our build system increments with every deployment. There are many ways to accomplish this, but the one we prefer is to have a separate file that has our incrementing value in it and append that number onto the end of our filename. Because the index page is static, we can set up our deployment tool to generate the finished HTML file and include the version number on the end of our includes. Let's take a look at listing 9.3 for an example of what the cache buster would look like in the finished HTML.

Listing 9.3 Bust the `max-age` cache

```
<html>
<head>
  <link rel="stylesheet" type="text/css"
        href="/path/to/css/file?version=1.1 /><      <-- The cache buster, version=1.1
  <script src="/path/to/js/file?version=1.1"></script>
</head>
<body>

</body>
</html>
```

Another use of `max-age` is to set it to 0, which tells the client that the content should always be revalidated. When this is set, the client will always check with the server to make sure that the content is still valid, but the server is still free to reply with a 302 response, informing the client that the data isn't stale and should be served from cache. A side effect of setting `max-age=0` is that intermediate servers—those servers sitting between the client and the end server—can still respond with a stale cache as long as they also set a warning flag on the response.

Now, if we wish to prevent the intermediate servers from ever using its cache, then we'll want to look into the `no-cache` attribute.

NO-CACHE

The `no-cache` attribute, according to the spec, works in a manner similar enough to setting `max-age=0` to be confusing. It tells the client to revalidate with the server before using the data in cache, but it also tells intermediate servers that they can't serve up stale content, even with a warning message. An interesting situation has come up in the last few years, because IE and Firefox have started to interpret this setting to mean they shouldn't cache this data under any circumstances. That means the client won't even ask the server if the data it last received is fresh before reserving it; the client won't ever store the data in its cache. That can make resources loaded with the `no-cache` header to be unnecessarily slow. If the desired behavior is to prevent clients from caching the resource, then the `no-store` attribute should be used instead.

NO-STORE

The `no-store` attribute informs clients and intermediate servers to never store any information about this request/response in their cache. Though this helps improve the privacy of such transmissions, it's by no means a perfect form of security. In properly implemented systems, any trace of the data will be gone; there's a chance that the data could pass through improperly or maliciously coded systems and is vulnerable to eavesdropping.

LAST-MODIFIED

If no `Cache-Control` is set, then the client depends on an algorithm based on the `last-modified` date to determine how long to cache the data. Typically this is one-third of the time since the `last-modified` date. So, if an image file was last modified three days ago, when it's requested, the client will default to serving it from cache for one day before checking with the server again. This results in a largely random amount of time a resource will be served from cache, dependent on how long it has been since the file was last pushed to production.

There are many other attributes dealing with caches, but mastering these basic attributes will significantly speed up application load time. HTTP caching enables clients of our application to serve up resources it has seen before without needing to request the information again, or with a minimum of overhead in asking the server if the resource is still fresh. This speeds up our application on subsequent requests, but what about identical requests made by other clients? HTTP caching doesn't help there; instead the data will need to be cached on the server.

9.3.4 Server caching

The fastest way for a server to respond to a client-side request with dynamic data is to serve it from a cache. This removes the processing time it takes to query the database and marshal the query response into a JSON string. Figure 9.5 shows where server caching fits into the request/response cycle.

Two popular methods of caching data on the server are Memcached and Redis. According to memcached.org, "Memcached is an in-memory key-value store for small chunks of arbitrary data." It's purpose-built as a temporary cache of data retrieved from a database, API call, or processed HTML. When the server runs out of memory, it'll automatically start dropping data based on a least recently used (LRU) algorithm. Redis is an *advanced key-value store* and can be used to store more complex data structures, such as strings, hashes, lists, sets, and sorted sets.

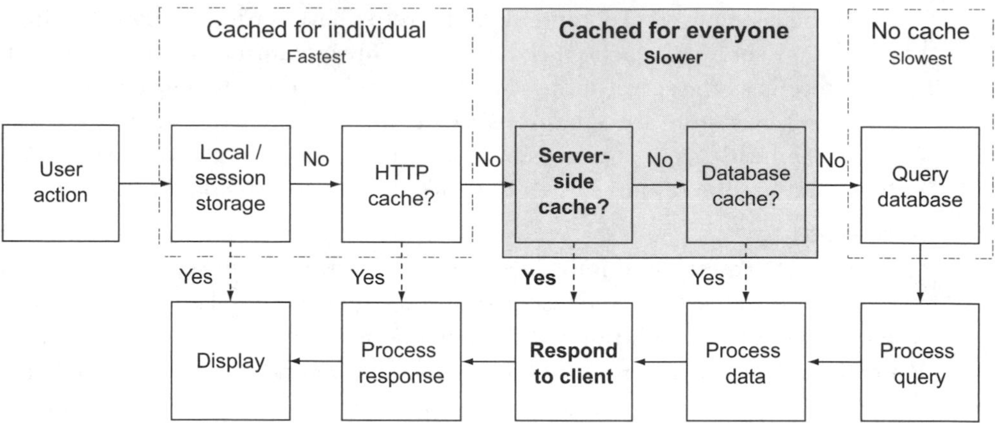

Figure 9.5 Server caching

The overall idea for the cache is to reduce server load and speed response time. When a request for data is received, the application first checks whether the response for this query has been stored in cache. If the application finds the data, it serves it to the client. If the data isn't cached, it instead makes a comparatively expensive database query and transforms the data into JSON. It then stores the data in the cache and replies to the client with the results.

When we use a cache, we must consider when the cache needs to be "busted." If only our application writes to the cache, then it can either clear or regenerate the cache when the data changes. If other applications also write to the cache, then we need them to update the cache as well. There are a few methods to work around this:

1. We can invalidate caches after a set length of time and force a refresh of the data. If we do this once an hour then there will be up to 24 times throughout the day with a cache-free response. Obviously, this won't work for all applications.
2. We can check the last updated time of the data, and if it's the same or earlier than the cache timestamp. This will take longer to process than the first option, but it may not take as long as a complex request takes, and we'll be assured that the data is fresh.

Which option we choose is dependent on the needs of our application.

Server caching is overkill for our SPA. MongoDB offers excellent performance for our sample data set. And we don't process the MongoDB response—we just pass it along to the client.

So when should we consider adding server caching to our web application? When we find our database or web server is becoming a bottleneck. Usually it'll reduce the load on both the server and the database, and improve response time. It's certainly worth trying before purchasing an expensive new server. But remember that server caching requires another service (like Memcached or Redis) that will need to be monitored and maintained, and it also adds complexity to our application.

Node.js has drivers for both Memcached and Redis. Let's add Redis to our application and use it to cache data about our users. We can visit http://redis.io and follow the instructions to install Redis on our system. Once installed and running, we can confirm it's available by starting the Redis shell with the command `redis-cli`.

Let's update the `npm` manifest to install the Redis driver as shown in listing 9.4. Changes are shown in **bold**:

Listing 9.4 Update the `npm` manifest to include redis—`webapp/package.json`

```
{ "name"    : "SPA",
  "version" : "0.0.3",
  "private" : true,
  "dependencies" : {
    "express"   : "3.2.x",
    "mongodb"   : "1.3.x",
    "socket.io" : "0.9.x",
    "JSV"       : "4.0.x",
    "redis"     : "0.8.x"
  }
}
```

Before we get started, let's think about what we'll need to be able to do with a cache. Two things that come to mind are *setting* a cache key-value pair and *getting* the cache value by key. We also will probably want to be able to *delete* a cache key. With that, let's set up the node module by creating a cache.js file in the lib directory and filling it in with the node module pattern and methods to get, set, and delete from the cache. See listing 9.5 for how to connect Node.js to Redis and set up the skeleton of the cache file.

Listing 9.5 Start the redis cache—`webapp/cache.js`

```
/*
 * cache.js - Redis cache implementation
*/

/*jslint         node    : true, continue : true,
  devel  : true, indent  : 2,    maxerr   : 50,
  newcap : true, nomen   : true, plusplus : true,
  regexp : true, sloppy  : true, vars     : false,
  white  : true
*/
/*global */

// ------------ BEGIN MODULE SCOPE VARIABLES --------------
'use strict';
var
  redisDriver = require( 'redis' ),
  redisClient = redisDriver.createClient(),
  makeString, deleteKey, getValue, setValue;
// ------------- END MODULE SCOPE VARIABLES ---------------

// ---------------- BEGIN PUBLIC METHODS ------------------
deleteKey = function ( key ) {};
```

```
getValue = function ( key, hit_callback, miss_callback ) {};

setValue = function ( key, value ) {};

module.exports = {
  deleteKey : deleteKey,
  getValue  : getValue,
  setValue  : setValue
};
// ---------------- END PUBLIC METHODS ------------------
```

Now, let's start filling in these methods; the finished methods are in listing 9.6. We'll start with `setValue` because that one is the simplest. Redis has a lot of different data types that, depending on the type of data we're caching, could be useful. For this example, we'll stick with the basic string key-value pair. Using the Redis driver to set a value is as simple as calling `redis.set( key, value );`. There's no callback, because we're going to assume this method works and let the call work asynchronously and discard failures. We could do something fancier and increment a value in Redis to keep track of failures if we wanted to. We encourage interested readers to explore this approach.

The `getValue` method takes three arguments: the `key` to search for, a callback for a cache hit (`hit_callback`), and a callback for a cache miss (`miss_callback`). When this method is invoked, it requests that Redis return the value associated with the key. If there's a hit (the value is not `null`), it invokes the `hit_callback` with the value as its argument. If there's a miss (the value is `null`), it invokes the `miss_callback`. Any logic for querying a database is left to the caller, as we want this code focused on caching.

The `deleteKey` method calls `redis.del` and passes in the Redis key. We don't use a callback because we'll be doing this asynchronously and assume it works.

The `makeString` utility is used to convert keys and values before we present them to Redis. We need this, because otherwise the Redis Node driver would use the `toString()` method on keys and values. This results in strings that look something like `[Object object]`, which isn't what we want.

Our updated cache module is shown in listing 9.6. Changes are shown in **bold**:

Listing 9.6 Final Redis cache file—`webapp/lib/cache.js`

```
/*
 * cache.js - Redis cache implementation
*/
...
// ----------- BEGIN MODULE SCOPE VARIABLES -------------
'use strict';
var
  redisDriver = require( 'redis' ),
  redisClient = redisDriver.createClient(),
  makeString, deleteKey, getValue, setValue;
// ------------- END MODULE SCOPE VARIABLES --------------

// --------------- BEGIN UTILITY METHODS -----------------
makeString = function ( key_data ) {
  return (typeof key_data === 'string' )
```

The `makeString` method is used to convert objects to a JSON string; otherwise the Redis client calls the `toString()` method on the input, which creates keys like `[Object object]` which aren't useful.

```
      ? key_data
      : JSON.stringify( key_data );
};
// ---------------- END UTILITY METHODS ------------------

// ---------------- BEGIN PUBLIC METHODS ------------------
deleteKey = function ( key ) {
  redisClient.del( makeString( key ) );
};

getValue = function ( key, hit_callback, miss_callback ) {
  redisClient.get(
    makeString( key ),
    function( err, reply ) {
      if ( reply ) {
        console.log( 'HIT' );
        hit_callback( reply );
      }
      else {
        console.log( 'MISS' );
        miss_callback();
      }
    }
  );
};

setValue = function ( key, value ) {
  redisClient.set(
    makeString( key ), makeString( value )
  );
};

module.exports = {
  deleteKey : deleteKey,
  getValue  : getValue,
  setValue  : setValue
};
// ----------------- END PUBLIC METHODS ------------------
```

The deleteKey method uses the Redis del command to delete a key and its value.

The getValue method takes the key and two callback methods as arguments. The first callback is invoked if a match is found, otherwise the second callback is invoked.

The setValue method uses the Redis set command for storing a string. Redis has different commands, depending on the type of object being stored; it does more than just store strings, which makes for a more flexible caching system.

Now that we have the cache file set, we can take advantage of it in the crud.js file by adding five lines of code, as seen in listing 9.7. Changes are shown in **bold**:

Listing 9.7 Reading from the cache—webapp/lib/crud.js

```
/*
 * crud.js - module to provide CRUD db capabilities
*/
...
// ------------ BEGIN MODULE SCOPE VARIABLES --------------
'use strict';
var
  ...
  JSV         = require( 'JSV'      ).JSV,
  cache       = require( './cache' ),

  mongoServer = new mongodb.Server(
  ...
```

Include the cache module in our CRUD module.

```
// ------------ END MODULE SCOPE VARIABLES --------------
...
// --------------- BEGIN PUBLIC METHODS -----------------
...
readObj = function ( obj_type, find_map, fields_map, callback ) {
  var type_check_map = checkType( obj_type );
  if ( type_check_map ) {
    callback( type_check_map );
    return;
  }
  cache.getValue( find_map, callback, function () {
    dbHandle.collection(
      obj_type,
      function ( outer_error, collection ) {
        collection.find( find_map, fields_map ).toArray(
          function ( inner_error, map_list ) {
            cache.setValue( find_map, map_list );
            callback( map_list );
          }
        );
      }
    );
  });
};
...

destroyObj = function ( obj_type, find_map, callback ) {
  var type_check_map = checkType( obj_type );
  if ( type_check_map ) {
    callback( type_check_map );
    return;
  }
  cache.deleteKey( find_map );
  dbHandle.collection(
    obj_type,
    function ( outer_error, collection ) {
      var options_map = { safe: true, single: true };
      collection.remove( find_map, options_map,
        function ( inner_error, delete_count ) {
          callback({ delete_count: delete_count });
        }
      );
    }
  );
};

...
// ---------------- END PUBLIC METHODS ------------------
...
```

Add a `cache.getValue` call, and pass the previous call to `mongo` in the callback to be executed in case of a cache miss.

Use `find_map` as our cache key.

Add the item to the cache with a call to `cache.setValue` when there's a cache miss.

Close the `cache.getValue` call.

Remove the search key from Redis using the `cache.deleteKey` method when we delete an object from the database.

We ensure that the key is removed from the Redis database when an object is deleted. But this is far from ideal. It doesn't ensure that all instances of cached data are deleted; it only ensures that the cached data associated with the *key used to delete the item* is removed. We could, for example, delete an employee *by ID* who was just fired, but the user might still log in and cause havoc in the system because the information might be cached using a *username-and-password* key. The same issue can happen when updating an object.

This isn't an easy problem to resolve and is one reason why server caching is often put off until it's necessary to invest the time in it to scale the system. Some possible solutions include expiring cached records after a length of time (minimizes the cache mismatch window), clearing the entire user cache when deleting or updating a user (safer, but results in more cache misses), or manually keeping track of cached objects (more error-prone for developers).

There are many more opportunities and challenges in server caching—enough to fill a book on its own—but hopefully this is enough to get you started. Now let's take a look at the final caching method: caching data in the database.

9.3.5 Database query caching

Query caching happens when the database caches the results to particular queries. In relational databases, this is particularly important because of the need to translate the results into a form that the application can read. The query cache stores this translated result. Take a look at figure 9.6 to see where query caching resides in the request/response cycle.

With MongoDB, this is handled automatically for us using the file system of the OS. Instead of caching the results to a particular query, MongoDB tries to hold the entire index in memory, resulting in extremely quick queries when the entire dataset can be held in memory. MongoDB, or rather the operating system's subsystem memory, will dynamically allocate memory based on the needs of the server. That means MongoDB will have the entire supply of free RAM available to it without having to guess how much to allocate, and will automatically free up memory for other processes when it's

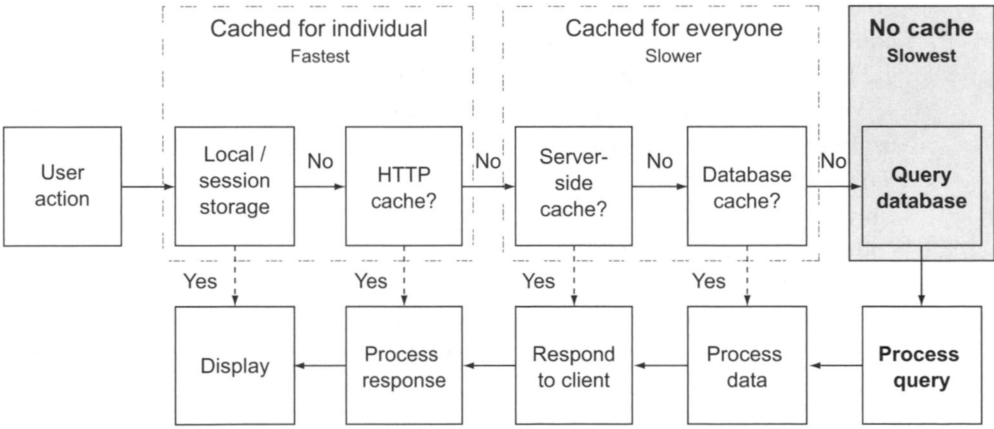

Figure 9.6 Query caching

needed. Caching behavior such as Least Recently Used algorithms work according to the behavior of the operating system.

9.4 Summary

In this chapter, we answered some common questions that occur when hosting an SPA website. We showed how we can adjust our SPA so it can be indexed by a search engine, how to use analytics tools (like Google Analytics), and how to log application errors to a server. Finally, we discussed how to cache at every layer of the application, what practical benefit each layer of caching provides, and how to take advantage of it.

Our advice on how to build a robust, testable, and scalable SPA is nearly complete. We strongly encourage you to read appendices A and B, as both cover important topics that are covered in significant depth. Appendix A shows the code standards we used throughout most of the book; appendix B shows how to use test modes and automation to easily identify, isolate, and fix software defects.

In part 1 of this book, we built our first SPA and discussed why SPAs are an excellent choice for many websites. In particular, SPAs can provide an incredibly responsive and interactive user experience that a traditional website can't touch. Next we reviewed some JavaScript programming concepts that need to be understood to successfully implement a large-scale SPA.

In part 2, we proceeded to design and implement an SPA using a well-tested architecture. We didn't use a "framework" library because we wanted to illustrate the inner workings of an SPA. You should be able to use this architecture to develop your own SPA, or tackle the challenge of learning one of the many framework libraries with the experience necessary to judge if it provides the tools you need.

In part 3, we set up a Node.js and MongoDB server to provide a CRUD backend for our SPA. We used Socket.IO to provide responsive and lightweight full-duplex communication between client and server. We also eliminated the marshalling of data between data formats that we often see in traditional websites.

In the end, we find ourselves with an entire stack that uses JavaScript as its language and JSON as its data format. This elegant simplicity provides benefits that are compounded at each step of the development process. For example, the use of a single language provides the opportunity to move and share code between the client and server, which can signicantly reduce the size and complexity of our code. It also saves us time and avoids confusion, as there is little context switching between languages or data formats. And the benefits extend into testing, as not only can we have significantly less code to test, but we can also use the same test framework for almost all the code without the overhead and expense of a browser test suite.

We hope that you've enjoyed the book and learned as much as we did writing it. The best way to continue learning about single page web applications is to continue developing them. We've tried hard to provide you with all the tools you need to do it using JavaScript end-to-end.

appendix A JavaScript coding standard

This appendix covers:

- Exploring why a coding standard is important
- Laying out and documenting code consistently
- Naming variables consistently
- Isolating code using namespaces
- Organizing files and ensuring consistent syntax
- Validating code using JSLint
- Using of a template that embodies the standard

Coding standards are contentious. Almost everyone agrees you should have one, but few seem to agree on what the standard should be. Let's consider why a coding standard is especially important for JavaScript.

A.1 Why we need a coding standard

Having a well-defined standard for a loosely typed, dynamic language like JavaScript is almost certainly more important than with stricter languages. JavaScript's very flexibility can make it a Pandora's box of coding syntax and practice. Whereas stricter languages provide structure and consistency inherently, JavaScript requires discipline and an applied standard to achieve the same effect.

What follows is the standard we've used and revised over many years. It's fairly comprehensive and cohesive, and we use it consistently throughout the book. Its presentation here isn't very concise because we've added many explanations and examples. Most of it has been condensed into a three-page cheat-sheet found at https://github.com/mmikowski/spa.

We're not presumptive enough to think this coding standard is right for everyone: you should use or ignore this standard for your work as you see fit. In any event, we hope the concepts discussed will encourage you to review your own practices. We strongly recommend any team agree on a standard before embarking on a large project to avoid experiencing their own Tower of Babble.

Experience and research show we'll spend more time maintaining code than writing it. Our standard therefore favors readability over speed of creation. We've found that code which is written to be understood tends to be more carefully considered and better constructed the first time around.

We've found that a successful coding standard:

- Minimizes the chance of coding errors.
- Results in code suitable for large-scale projects and teams—consistent, readable, extensible, and maintainable.
- Encourages code efficiency, effectiveness, and reuse.
- Encourages the use of JavaScript's strengths and avoids its weaknesses.
- Is used by all members of the development team.

Martin Fowler once famously said, "Any fool can write code that a computer can understand. Good programmers write code that humans can understand." Though well-defined and comprehensive standards don't ensure human-readable JavaScript, they sure can help—just as dictionaries and grammar guides help ensure human-readable English.

A.2 Code layout and comments

Laying out your code in a consistent and considered manner is one of the best way to increase comprehension. It's also one of the more contentious issue in code standards.[1] So when you read this section, relax. Have a decaf latte, get a spearmint tea-leaf pedicure, and open your mind. It'll be fun. Really.

A.2.1 Lay out your code for readability

What if we omitted all headers, punctuation, spacing and capitalization from this book? Well, the book would have come out months earlier, but our audience would

[1] Legions of developers have spent countless hours rabidly flaming each other over the use of tabs alone—search the internet for "tabs versus spaces" if you need more proof.

probably find it unintelligible. Perhaps that is why our editor insisted that we format and apply conventions to our writing so that you, dear reader, would have a fighting chance at understanding the content.

JavaScript code has two audiences that need to understand it—the machines that will execute it and the humans who will maintain or extend it. Typically, our code will be read by humans many more times than it's written. We format and apply conventions to our code so that our fellow developers (and that includes ourselves a few weeks from now) will have a fighting chance at understanding the content.

USE CONSISTENT INDENTATION AND LINE LENGTHS

We probably all have noticed the text columns in a newspaper are between 50 and 80 characters in length. Lines longer that 80 characters are progressively harder for the human eye to follow. Bringhurst's authoritative book, *The Elements of Typographic Style*, recommends line lengths between 45-75 characters for optimal reading comprehension and comfort, with 66 considered the optimal.

Longer lines are also hard to read on computer displays. Today more and more web pages have multi-column layouts—even though this is notoriously expensive to implement well. The only reason a web developer is going to go though such trouble is if there's a problem with long lines (or if they get paid by the hour).

Proponents for wider tab stops (4-8 spaces) say it makes their code more legible. But they often also advocate long line lengths to compensate for the wide tabs. We take the other approach: short tab width (2 spaces) and shortish line length (78 characters) work together to provide a narrower, more legible document with significant content per line. The short tab stop also recognizes that an event-driven language like JavaScript is typically more indented than a purely procedural language due to the proliferation of callbacks and closures.

- **Indent two spaces** per code level.
- **Use spaces, not tabs** to indent as there's not a standard for the placement of tab stops.
- **Limit lines to 78 characters.**

Narrower documents also work better across all displays, allowing an individual to open six views of files concurrently on two high-definition displays, or easily read a single document on the smaller screens found on notebooks, tablets, or smart phones. They also fit nicely as listings on e-readers or in a printed book format, which makes our editor much happier.[2]

ORGANIZE YOUR CODE IN PARAGRAPHS

English and other written languages are presented in paragraphs to help the reader understand when one topic is complete and another is to be presented. Computer languages also benefit from this convention. These paragraphs can be annotated as a

[2] The line length limit for listings in this book is actually 72 characters, and losing those last six characters was painful.

whole. Through the appropriate use of white space[3] our JavaScript can read like a well-formated book.

- **Organize your code in logical paragraphs** and place blank lines between each.
- **Each line should contain at most one statement or assignment** although we do allow multiple variable declarations per line.
- **Place white space between operators** and variables so that variables are easier to spot.
- **Place white space after every comma.**
- **Align like operators** within paragraphs.
- **Indent comments** the same amount as the code they explain.
- **Place a semicolon at the end of every statement.**
- **Place braces around all statements in a control structure.** Control structures include `for`, `if`, and `while` constructs, among others. Perhaps the most common violation of this guideline is to omit braces for a single line `if` statement. Don't do this. Always use braces so it's easy to add statements without accidentally introducing bugs.

Listing A.1 Not like this

```
// initialize variables
var first_name='sally';var rot_delta=1;
var x_delta=1;var y_delta=1; var coef=1;
var first_name = 'sally', x, y, r, print_msg, get_random;
// put important text into div id sl_foo
print_msg = function ( msg_text ) {
// .text() prevents xss injection
  $('#sl').text( msg_text )
};
// get a random number
get_random = function ( num_arg ){
  return Math.random() * num_arg;
};
// initialize coordinates
x=get_random( 10 );
y=get_random( 20 );
r=get_random( 360 );
// adjust coordinates
x+=x_delta*coef;
y+=y_delta*coef;
r+=rot_delta*coef;
if ( first_name === 'sally' ) print_msg('Hello Sally!)
```

This comment states the obvious. (// initialize variables)

We should not make multiple assignments on a single line. (var first_name='sally';var rot_delta=1;)

This comment is easily outdated. (// put important text into div id sl_foo)

Every comment should be indented the same level as the code it describes. (// .text() prevents xss injection)

This statement is not terminated with a semicolon. ($('#sl').text(msg_text))

We cannot easily see the comment because it is hidden in a mass of text. (// initialize coordinates)

These equations are hard to read. (x+=x_delta*coef;)

All `if` statements should use braces. (if (first_name === 'sally') ...)

[3] White space is any combination of space, line breaks, or tabs. But don't use tabs.

Listing A.2 But like this

```
var
  x, y, r, print_msg, get_random,
  coef       = 0.5
  rot_delta  = 1,
  x_delta    = 1,
  y_delta    = 1,
  first_name = 'sally'
  ;

// function to write text to message container
print_msg = function ( msg_text ) {
  // .text() prevents xss injection
  $('#sl').text( msg_text );
};

// function to return a random number
get_random = function ( num_arg ) {
  return Math.random() * num_arg;
};

// initialize coordinates
x = get_random(  10 );
y = get_random(  20 );
r = get_random( 360 );

// adjust to offsets
x += x_delta   * coef;
y += y_delta   * coef;
r += rot_delta * coef;

if ( first_name === 'sally' ){ print_msg('Hello Sally!); }
```

Remove the obvious comment. (annotates `var`)

Put one or more declarations on a single line, but only one assignment per line.

Indent the comment the same level as the paragraph described.

Add an empty line before the next paragraph. Change the comment to describe the paragraph.

Add the missing semicolon. All statements should be terminated with semicolons.

Add an empty line before the next paragraph. Change the comment to describe the paragraph.

Add another paragraph. Paragraphs make comments much easier to see.

Add spaces and align like elements to make similar statements more readable.

Use braces for all `if` statements and control structures.

When we lay out our code, we want to aim for clarity and not reduced byte-count. Once our code reaches production, our JavaScript will be concatenated, minified, and compressed before it reaches our users. As a result, the tools we use to aid comprehension—white space, comments, and more descriptive variable names—will have little to no effect on the performance.

BREAK LINES CONSISTENTLY

We should place a statement on a single line if it doesn't exceed the maximum line length. But that is often not possible, so we have to break it into two or more lines. These guidelines will help reduce errors and improve cognition:

- **Break lines before operators** as one can easily review all operators in the left column.
- **Indent subsequent lines** of the statement one level, for example two spaces in our case.
- **Break lines after comma separators.**
- **Place a closing bracket or parenthesis on its own line.** This clearly indicates the conclusion of the statement without forcing the reader to scan horizontally for the semicolon.

Listing A.3 Not like this

It's so easy to miss a trailing "+" on ragged line endings.

Placing commas in front has merit, but it's not our standard.

Where does the statement end? Keep scanning for that semicolon...

```
long_quote = 'Four score and seven years ago our ' +
  'fathers brought forth on this continent, a new '
  'nation conceived in Liberty, ' +
  'and dedicated to the proposition that ' +
  'all men are created equal.';

cat_breed_list = ['Abyssinian' , 'American Bobtail'
 , 'American Curl' , 'American Shorthair' , 'American Whiterhair'
 , 'Balinese', 'Balinese-Javanese'  , 'Birman' , 'Bombay'  ];
```

Listing A.4 But like this

Line up the operators on the left side.

Trailing commas are easier to maintain.

Place the closing bracket on its own line. The next statement is easy to spot.

```
long_quote = 'Four score and seven years ago our '
  + 'fathers brought forth on this continent, a new '
  + 'nation, conceived in Liberty, '
  + 'and dedicated to the proposition that '
  + 'all men are created equal.';

cat_breed_list = [
  'Abyssinian',         'American Bobtail',    'American Curl',
  'American Shorthair', 'American Whiterhair', 'Balinese',
  'Balinese-Javanese',  'Birman',              'Bombay'
];
```

We'll install JSLint a little later in this appendix, which will help us check our syntax.

USE K&R STYLE BRACKETING

K&R style bracketing balances the use of vertical space with readability. It should be used when formatting objects and maps, arrays, compound statements, or invocations. A compound statement contains one or more statements enclosed in curly braces. Examples include `if`, `while`, and `for` statements. An invocation like `alert( 'I have been invoked!' );` calls a function or a method.

- **Prefer single lines** when possible. For example, do not unnecessarily break a short array declaration into three lines when it can fit on one.
- **Place the opening** parenthesis, brace or bracket at the end of the opening line.
- **Indent the code inside the delimiters** (parenthesis, brace, or bracket) one level—for example, two spaces.
- **Place the closing** parenthesis, brace or bracket on its own line with the same indentation as the opening line.

Listing A.5 Not like this

This is awfully sparse and long.

```
var invocation_count, full_name, top_fruit_list,
  full_fruit_list, print_string;

invocation_count = 2;
full_name = 'Fred Burns';
top_fruit_list =
```

```
[
  'Apple',
  'Banana',
  'Orange'
];

full_fruit_list =
[ 'Apple','Apricot','Banana','Blackberry','Blueberry',
  'Currant','Cherry','Date','Grape','Grapefruit',
  'Guava','Kiwi','Kumquat','Lemon','Lime',
  'Lychee','Mango','Melon','Nectarine','Orange',
  'Peach','Pear','Pineapple','Raspberry','Strawberry',
  'Tangerine'  ,'Ugli'
];

print_string = function ( text_arg )
{
  var char_list = text_arg.split(''), i;

  for ( i = 0; i < char_list.length; i++ )
  {
    document.write( char_list[i] );
  }

  return true;
};

print_string( 'We have counted '
  + String( invocation_count )
  + ' invokes to date!
);
```

What a mess! Try to pick out a fruit using human eyes.

The GNU style bracketing results in longer pages.

Listing A.6 But like this

```
var
  run_count,        full_name,   top_fruit_list,
  full_fruit_list, print_string;

run_count = 2;
full_name = 'Fred Burns';

top_fruit_list  = [ 'Apple', 'Banana', 'Orange' ];
full_fruit_list = [
  'Apple',      'Apricot',    'Banana',     'Blackberry', 'Blueberry',
  'Currant',    'Cherry',     'Date',       'Grape',      'Grapefruit',
  'Guava',      'Kiwi',       'Kumquat',    'Lemon',      'Lime',
  'Lychee',     'Mango',      'Melon',      'Nectarine',  'Orange',
  'Peach',      'Pear',       'Pineapple',  'Raspberry',  'Strawberry',
  'Tangerine', 'Ugli'
];

print_string = function ( text_arg ) {
  var text_arg, char_list, i;

  char_list = input_text.split('');

  for ( i = 0; i < char_list.length; i++ ) {
    document.write( char_list[i] );
  }
```

Vertical alignment does wonders for readability.

These all fit on one line.

Match the closing bracket to the overhang in K&R bracketing.

```
    return true;
  };

  print_string( 'We have counted '
    + String( run_count )
    + ' invocations to date!
  );
```

Adjusting elements to line up vertically really helps comprehension, but also can be time-consuming if you don't have a powerful text editor. Vertical text selection—as provided by Vim, Sublime, WebStorm, and others—is helpful in aligning values. WebStorm even provides tools to auto-align map values, which is a great time-saver. If your editor doesn't allow for vertical selection, we highly recommend you consider changing editors.

USE WHITE SPACE TO DISTINGUISH FUNCTIONS AND KEYWORDS

Many languages have the concept of an article—words like *an*, *a* or *the*. One purpose of an article is to alert the reader or listener that the next word will be a noun or noun phrase. White space can be used with functions and keywords for a similar effect.

- **Follow a function with no space** between the function keyword and the opening left parenthesis, `(`.
- **Follow a keyword with a single space** and then its opening left parenthesis, `(`.
- **When formatting a `for` statement**, add a space after each semicolon.

Listing A.7 Not like this

```
mystery_text = get_mystery ('Hello JavaScript Denizens');
for(x=1;x<10;x++){console.log(x);}
```

Is get_mystery a keyword or a custom function?

The lack of spaces makes for a blob of text.

Listing A.8 But like this

```
mystery_text = get_mystery( 'Hello JavaScript Denizens' );
for ( x = 1; x < 10; x++ ) { console.log( x ); }
```

Nestled parenthesis means this is a function.

Spaces make this more readable.

This convention is common with other dynamic languages like Python, Perl, or PHP.

QUOTE CONSISTENTLY

We *prefer single quotes* over double quotes for string delimiters, as the HTML standard attribute delimiter is double quotes. And HTML is typically quoted often in SPAs. HTML delimited with single quotes requires less character escaping or encoding. The result is shorter, easier to read, and less likely to have errors.

Listing A.9 Not like this

```
html_snip = "<input name=\"alley_cat\" type=\"text\" value=\"bone\">";
```

Listing A.10 But like this

```
html_snip = '<input name="alley_cat" type="text" value="bone">';
```

Many languages like Perl, PHP, and Bash have the concept of interpolating and non-interpolating quotes. *Interpolating quotes* expand variable values found inside, whereas *non-interpolating quotes* don't. Typically, double quotes (`"`) are interpolating, and single quotes (`'`) are not. JavaScript quotes never interpolate, yet both single and double quotes may be used with no variance in behavior. Our use is therefore consistent with other popular languages.

A.2.2 Comment to explain and document

Comments can be even more important than the code they reference because they can convey critical details that aren't otherwise obvious. This is especially evident in event-driven programming, as the number of callbacks can make tracing code execution a big time sink. This doesn't mean that adding more comments is always better. Strategically placed, informative, and well-maintained comments are highly valued, whereas a clutter of inaccurate comments can be worse than no comments at all.

EXPLAIN CODE STRATEGICALLY

Our standard is intended to minimize comments and maximize their value. We minimize comments by using conventions to make the code as self-evident as possible. We maximize their value by aligning them to the paragraphs they describe and ensuring their content is of value to the reader.

Listing A.11 Not like this

```
var
  welcome_to_the  = '<h1>Welcome to Color Haus</h1>',
  houses_we_use   = [ 'yellow','green','little pink' ],
  the_results, make_it_happen, init;

// get house spec
var make_it_happen = function ( house ) {
  var
    sync = houses_we_use.length,
    spec = {},
    i;

  for ( i = 0; i < sync; i++ ) {
    ...
    // 30 more lines
  }
  return spec;
};

var init = function () {
  // houses_we_use is an array of house colors.
```

```
  // make_it_happen is a function that returns a map of building specs
  //
  var the_results = make_it_happen( houses_we_use );

  // And place welcome message into our DOM
  $('#welcome').text( welcome_to_the );
  // And now our specifications
  $('#specs').text( JSON.stringify( the_results ) );
};

init();
```

Listing A.12 But like this

```
var
  welcome_html      = '<h1>Welcome to Color Haus</h1>',
  house_color_list = [ 'yellow','green','little pink' ]
  spec_map, get_spec_map, run_init;

// Begin /get_spec_map/
// Get a specification map based on colors
get_spec_map = function ( color_list_arg ) {
  var
    color_count = color_list_arg.length,
    spec_map    = {},
    i;
  for ( i = 0; i < color_count; i++ ) {
    // ... 30 more lines
  }
  return spec_map;
};
// End /get_spec_map/

run_init = function () {
  var spec_map = getSpecMap( house_color_list );

  $('#welcome').html( welcome_html );
  $('#specs').text( JSON.stringify( spec_map ) );

};

run_init();
```

Use consistent and meaningful variable names instead of comments to explain as much as possible.

Use `Begin` and `End` delimiters to clearly define longer sections.

Consistent, meaningful variable names can provide *more* information with *fewer* comments. Our section on variable naming appears a little later in the appendix, but let's look at a few highlights. Variables that refer to functions all have a verb as their first word—`get_spec_map`, `run_init`. Other variables are named to help us understand their content—`welcome_html` is an HTML string, `house_color_list` is an array of color names, and `spec_map` is a map of specifications. This helps reduce the number of comments we need to add or maintain to make the code understandable.

Document your APIs and TODOs

Comments can also provide more formal documentation for your code. We need to be careful though—documentation about general architecture shouldn't be buried in one of dozens of JavaScript files, but instead should go into a dedicated architecture document. But documentation about a function or an object API can and often should be placed right next to the code.

- **Explain any non-trivial function** by specifying its *purpose*, the *arguments* or *settings* it uses, the values it *returns*, and any exception it *throws*.
- **If you disable code,** explain why with a comment of the following format: `// TODO date username - comment`. The user name and date are valuable in deciding the freshness of the comment, and can be also used by automated tools to report on TODO items in the code base.

Listing A.13 Example of API documentation for a function

```
// BEGIN DOM Method /toggleSlider/
// Purpose    : Extends and retracts chat slider
// Required Arguments :
//   * do_extend (boolean) true extends slider, false retracts
// Optional Arguments :
//   * callback (function) executed after animation is complete
// Settings  :
//   * chat_extend_time,   chat_retract_time
//   * chat_extend_height, chat_retract_height
// Returns   : boolean
//   * true  - slider animation activated
//   * false - slider animation not activated
// Throws    : none
//
toggleSlider = function( do_extend, callback ) {
  //   ...
};
// END DOM Method /toggleSlider/
```

Listing A.14 Example of disabled code

```
// BEGIN TODO 2012-12-29 mmikowski - debug code disabled
// alert( warning_text );
//  ... (lots more lines) ...
//
// END TODO 2012-12-29 mmikowski - debug code disabled
```

Some people say you should always delete code immediately and recover it from source control if you need it again. But we have found that commenting-out code which we'll *likely* need again is more efficient than trying to find the version where the disabled code was pristine and then merging it back. After the code has been disabled for a while, you can safely remove it.

A.3 Variable names

Ever notice how books often include an ad-hoc naming convention in their code listings? For example, you'll see lines like `person_str = 'fred';`. The author typically does this because he doesn't want to insert a clumsy, time-and-focus-sapping reminder later about what the variable represents. The name is self-evident.

Everyone that codes uses a naming convention, whether they realize it or not.[4] A good naming convention provides the greatest value when all members of a team understand it and use it. When they do, they're liberated from dull code tracing and arduous comment maintenance, and can instead focus on the purpose and logic of the code.

A.3.1 Reduce and improve comments with a naming convention

Consistent and descriptive names are extremely important for enterprise-class JavaScript applications, as they can greatly speed cognition and also help avoid common errors. Consider this completely valid and realistic JavaScript code:

Listing A.15 Example A

```
var creator = maker( 'house' );
```

Now let's rewrite it using our naming conventions, which we'll discuss shortly:

Listing A.16 Example B

```
var make_house = curry_build_item({ item_type : 'house' });
```

Example B certainly seems more descriptive. With our convention, we can tell the following:

- `make_house` is an object constructor.
- The called function is a currying function—it employs a closure to maintain a state and returns a function.
- The called function takes a string argument that indicates a `type`.
- The variables are local in scope.

Now we could figure all of that out for example A by looking at the context of the code. Maybe it'll take us 5, 30, or 60 minutes to trace all the functions and variables. And then *we'll need to remember it all* while working with or around this code. Not only will we lose time, but we might lose focus on what we're trying to accomplish in the first place.

This avoidable expense will be incurred *every time* a new developer works with this code. And remember, after a few weeks away from this code, any developer—including the original author—is effectively a new developer. Obviously, this is horribly inefficient and error-prone.

Lets see how example A would look if we used comments to provide the same amount of meaning as in example B:

Listing A.17 Example A with comments

```
// 'creator' is an object constructor we get by
// calling 'maker'. The first positional argument
```

[4] A bit like "if you choose not to decide you still have made a choice" ("Freewill" by Rush, *Permanent Waves* album, 1980)

```
// of 'maker' must be a string, and it directs
// the type of object constructor to be returned.
// 'maker' uses a closure to remember the type
// of object the returned function is to
// meant to create.

var creator = maker( 'house' );
```

Not only is example A with comments much more verbose than example B, it also took much longer to write, probably because we tried to convey the same amount of information as the naming convention. It gets worse: the comments are prone to become inaccurate over time as the code changes and developers exert their laziness. Let's say we decide to change a few names a few weeks later:

Listing A.18 Example A with comments after variable name changes

```
// 'creator' is an object constructor we get by
// calling 'maker'. The first positional argument
// of 'maker' must be a string, and it directs
// the type of object constructor to be returned.
// 'maker' uses a closure to remember the type
// of object the returned function is to
// meant to create.

var maker = builder( 'house' );
```

Whoops! wrong name.

Incorrect—it's builder now.

Darn it ... builder not maker, better fix this.

Arrghh! Let someone else fix this—I've got new code to write!

Oh dear, we forgot to update the comments that referenced the variable names we just changed. Now the comments are completely wrong and misleading. Not only that, but all these comments obscure the code because the listing is *nine times* longer. It would be better to have no comments at all. Compare that to if we wanted to change variable names in example B:

Listing A.19 Example B with the names changed

```
var make_abode = curry_make_item({ item_type : 'abode' });
```

These revisions are immediately correct, as *there are no comments to adjust.* As this shows, a well-considered naming convention is a great way to self-document code *by the original author,* with greater precision and without a clutter of comments that are near-impossible to maintain. It helps speed development, improve quality, and ease maintenance.

A.3.2 *Use naming guidelines*

A variable name can convey a lot of information, as we have illustrated above. Let's step through some guidelines we've found most useful.

USE COMMON CHARACTERS

Though much of our team might think it clever to name a variable `queensrÿche_album_name`, those who try to find the ÿ key on their keyboard might have different and significantly more negative opinions. It's better to limit variable names to characters available on most of the world's keyboards.

- **Use a-z, A-Z, 0-9, undescore, and $** characters in variable names.
- **Don't begin a variable name with a number.**

Communicate variable scope

Our JavaScript files and modules have a one-to-one correspondence, similar to Node.js (we detail this later in the appendix). We've found it useful to distinguish between variables that are available anywhere in the module, and those that have a more limited scope.

- **Use camel case when the variable is full-module scope** (it can be accessed anywhere in a module namespace).
- **Use underscores when the variable is not full-module scope** (variables local to a function within a module namespace).
- **Make sure all module scope variables have at least two syllables** so that the scope is clear. For example, instead of using a variable called `config` we can use the more descriptive and obviously module-scoped `configMap`.

Recognize that variable type is important

Just because JavaScript allows you to play fast and loose with variable types doesn't mean you should. Consider the following example:

Listing A.20 Implicit conversion of type

```
var x = 10, y = '02', z = x + y;
console.log ( z ); // '1002'
```

In this case, JavaScript converts `x` into a string and concatenates it to `y (02)` to get the string `1002`. Which is probably not what was intended. The results of type conversion can have more profound effects as well:

Listing A.21 The dark side of type conversion

```
var
  x = 10,
  z = [ 03, 02, '01' ],
  i , p;

for ( i in z ) {
  p = x + z[ i ];
  console.log( p.toFixed( 2 ) );
}

// Output:
// 13.00
// 12.00
// TypeError: Object 1001 has no method 'toFixed'
```

We've found that *unintentional* type conversion like this is much more common than *intentional*, and this often leads to difficult to find and solve bugs. We hardly ever *purposely* change a variable's type because (among other reasons) doing so is almost always too confusing or difficult to manage to be worth the benefit. [5] Therefore, when we name our variables, we often want to convey the variable type we intend it to contain

NAMING BOOLEANS

When a boolean represents a state, we use the word `is`; for example, `is_retracted` or `is_stale`. When we use a boolean to direct an action, say as in a function argument, we use the word `do`, as in `do_retract` or `do_extend`. And when we use a boolean to indicate ownership, we use `has`; for example, `has_whiskers` or `has_wheels`. Table A.1 shows some examples.

Table A.1 Example regular expression names

Indicator	Local scope	Module scope
`bool` [generic]	`bool_return`	`boolReturn`
`do` (requests action)	`do_retract`	`doRetract`
`has` (indicates inclusion)	`has_whiskers`	`hasWhiskers`
`is` (indicates state)	`is_retracted`	`isRetracted`

NAMING STRINGS

Our earlier example shows that it's useful if we know we're using a string variable. Table A.2 is a chart of indicators that we commonly use with strings.

Table A.2 Example string name

Indicator	Local scope	Module scope
`str [generic]`	`direction_str`	`directionStr`
`id (identifier)`	`email_id`	`emailId`
`date`	`email_date`	`emailDate`
`html`	`body_html`	`bodyHtml`
`msg (message)`	`employee_msg`	`employeeMsg`
`name`	`employee_name`	`employeeName`
`text`	`email_text`	`emailText`
`type`	`item_type`	`itemType`

NAMING INTEGERS

JavaScript doesn't expose integers as a supported variable type, but there are many instances where the language won't work properly unless we provide an integer. When

[5] More recent versions of Firefox's JavaScript JIT compiler recognize this fact and use a technique called *type inference* to realize a 20-30% performance gain in real-world code.

iterating over an array, for example, the use of a floating-point number as an index doesn't work right:

```
var color_list = [ 'red', 'green', 'blue' ];

color_list[1.5] = 'chartreuse';

console.log( color_list.pop() ); // 'blue'
console.log( color_list.pop() ); // 'green'
console.log( color_list.pop() ); // 'red'
console.log( color_list.pop() ); // undefined - where did 'chartreuse' go?
console.log( color_list[1.5] );  // oh, there it is

console.log( color_list ); // shows [1.5: "chartreuse"]
```

Other built-ins also expect integer values, like the string `substr()` method. So when it's important that the number you're using is an integer, you can use indicators, as shown in table A.3.

Table A.3 Example integer names

Indicator	Local scope	Module scope
`int` [generic]	`size_int`	`sizeInt`
none (convention)	`i, j, k`	(not allowed in module scope)
`count`	`employee_count`	`employeeCount`
`index`	`employee_index`	`employeeIndex`
time (milliseconds)	`retract_time`	`retractTime`

NAMING NUMBERS

We can use other indicators (see table A.4) if it's important to understand that we're dealing with non-integer numbers.

Table A.4 Example number names

Indicator	Local scope	Module scope
num [generic]	`size_num`	`sizeNum`
none (convention)	`x, y, z`	(not allowed in module scope)
`coord` (coordinate)	`x_coord`	`xCoord`
`ratio`	`sales_ratio`	`salesRatio`

NAMING REGULAR EXPRESSIONS

We typically prefix a regular expression with `regex`, as in table A.5.

Table A.5 Example regular expression names

Indicator	Local scope	Module scope
`regex`	`regex_filter`	`regexFilter`

NAMING ARRAYS

Here are a few guidelines we have found useful in naming arrays:

- **An array variable name should be a singular noun followed by the word "list".**
- Prefer the noun-"List" form for module-scoped arrays.

Table A.6 shows some examples.

Table A.6 Example array names

Indicator	Local scope	Module scope
`list`	`timestamp-list`	`timestampList`
`list`	`color_list`	`colorList`

NAMING MAPS

JavaScript doesn't officially have a `map` data type—it just has objects. But we've found it useful to distinguish between simple objects used only to store data (`maps`) and full-featured objects. This map structure is analogous to a `map` in Java, a `dict` in Python, an *associative array* in PHP, or a `hash` in Perl.

When we name a map, we usually want to emphasize the developer's intent and include the word `map` in the name. Typically, the structure is a noun followed by the word `map`, and it's always singular. See table A.7 for example map names.

Table A.7 Example map names

Indicator	Local scope	Module scope
`map`	`employee_map`	`employeeMap`
`map`	`receipt_timestamp_map`	`receiptTimestampMap`

Sometimes the key of a map is an unusual or a distinguishing feature. In such cases, we indicate the key in the name, for example, `receipt_timestamp_map`.

NAMING OBJECTS

Objects typically have a concrete "real world" analog and we name them accordingly:

- **An object variable name should be a noun** followed by an optional modifier—`employee` or `receipt`.
- **Make sure a module-scoped object variable name has two syllables** or more so the scope is clear—`storeEmployee` or `salesReceipt`.
- **Prefix jQuery objects with a $.** This is a common convention these days, and jQuery objects (or collections as they're sometimes called) are prevalent in SPAs.

Table A.8 shows some examples.

Table A.8 Example object names

Indicator	Local scope	Module scope
none (singular noun)	`employee`	`storeEmployee`
none (singular noun)	`receipt`	`salesReceipt`
`$`	`$area_tabs`	`$areaTabs`

If we expect a jQuery collection to contain multiple entries, we make it plural.

NAMING FUNCTIONS

A function almost always performs an action on an object. Therefore we always like to place the action verb as the first part of a function name:

- **Name functions should always include a verb followed by a noun**, for example, `get_record` or `empty_cache_map`.
- **Module-scoped functions should always contain two or more syllables** so the scope is clear, for example, `getRecord` or `emptyCacheMap`.
- **Use consistent verb meanings**. Table A.9 shows consistent meanings for common verbs.

Table A.9 Example function names

Indicator	Meaning of indicator	Local scope	Module scope
`fn` [generic]	Generic function indicator.	`fn_sync`	`fnSync`
`curry`	Return a function as specified by argument(s).	`curry_make_user`	`curryMakeUser`
`destroy`, `remove`	Remove a data structure, such as an array. Implies that data references will be tidied up as needed.	`destroy_entry`, `remove_element`	`destroyEntry`, `removeElement`
`empty`	Remove some or all members of a data structure without removing the container—for example, remove all elements of an array but leave the array intact.	`empty_cache_map`	`emptyCacheMap`
`fetch`	Return data fetched from an external source, such as from an AJAX or web socket call.	`fetch_user_list`	`fetchUserList`
`get`	Return data from an object or other internal data structure.	`get_user_list`	`getUserList`
`make`	Return newly constructed object (doesn't use the `new` operator)	`make_user`	`makeUser`

Table A.9 Example function names *(continued)*

Indicator	Meaning of indicator	Local scope	Module scope
`on`	Event handler. The event should be a single word as in the HTML markup.	`on_mouseover`	`onMouseover`
`save`	Save data to an object or other internal data structure.	`save_user_list`	`saveUserList`
`set`	Initialize or update values as provided by arguments.	`set_user_name`	`setUserName`
`store`	Send data to an external source for storage, for example via an AJAX call.	`store_user_list`	`storeUserList`
`update`	Similar to `set`, but has a "was previously initialized" connotation	`update_user_list`	`updateUserList`

We've found the `make` constructor verb, and the distinctions between `fetch/get` and `store/save`, especially valuable in communicating intent across a development team. Also, using `onEventname` for event handlers has become common and useful. The general form is *on<eventname><modifier>* where the modifier is optional. Note that we keep the event name as a single word. For example, `onMouseover` *not* `onMouseOver`, or `on_dragstart` *not* `on_drag_start`.

NAMING VARIABLES WITH UNKNOWN TYPES

Sometimes we really don't know what data types our variables contain. There are two situations where this is common:

- **We're writing a polymorphic function**—one that accepts multiple data types.
- **We're receiving data from an external data source**, such as an AJAX or web socket feed.

In these cases, the primary feature of the variable is the uncertainty of its data type. We've settled on a practice of ensuring the word `data` is in the name (see table A.10).

Table A.10 Example data names

Local scope	Module scope	Notes
`http_data`, `socket_data`	`httpData`, `socketData`	Unknown data type received from an HTTP feed or web socket
`arg_data, data`	`---`	Unknown data type received as an argument

Now that we've reviewed our naming guidelines, let's put them to use.

A.3.3 Put the guidelines to use

Let's compare an object prototype before and after we apply naming guidelines.

Listing A.22 Not like this

```
doggy = {
  temperature   : 36.5,
  name          : 'Guido',
  greeting      : 'Grrrr',
  speech        : 'I am a dog',
  height        : 1.0,
  legs          : 4,
  ok            : check,
  remove        : destroy,
  greet_people  : greet_people,
  say_something : say_something,
  speak_to_us   : speak,
  colorify      : flash,
  show          : render
};
```

- We have no idea what `temperature` is—a method, a string, or an object? If it's a number, what are the units—F or C?
- This property is also misleading. We might guess a string or a method. (speech)
- `legs` implies a collection, like an array or a map. Yet here it's used to store an integer count.
- The methods mapping is horrible—there's no parallel structure between the keys and the function that is referenced, so tracing through the code is a nightmare. Also, the function names don't always indicate an action. The worst offender is probably `ok`, which implies a boolean status. But it isn't.

Listing A.23 But like this

```
dogPrototype = {
  body_temp_c    : 36.5,
  dog_name       : 'Guido',
  greet_text     : 'Grrrr',
  speak_text     : 'I am a dog',
  height_in_m    : 1.0,
  leg_count      : 4,

  check_destroy  : checkDestroy,
  destroy_dog    : destroyDog,
  print_greet    : printGreet,
  print_name     : printName,
  print_speak    : printSpeak,
  show_flash     : showFlash,
  redraw_dog     : redrawDog
};
```

- The name indicator tells us we have a string value, as do the text values below it. (dog_name)
- Providing units in the name lets us know we have a number and its scale. (body_temp_c)
- Count indicates an integer value. (leg_count)
- Action verbs indicate we have methods. Note how the names are aligned, which helps when tracing through the code.

These examples are snippets from two web page examples—`listings/apx0A/bad_dog.html` and `listings/apx0A/good_dog.html` found in the book resources. You're encouraged to download and compare them to see which is more comprehensible and maintainable.

A.4 Variable declaration and assignment

Variables can be assigned to functions pointers, object pointers, array pointers, strings, numbers, null, or undefined. Some JavaScript implementations may make internal distinctions between integers, 32-bit signed, and 64-bit double-precision floating point numbers, but there's no formal interface to enforce this typing.

- **Use {} or []** instead of `new Object()` or `new Array()` to create a new object, map, or array. Remember, a map is a simple data-only object with no methods. If you require object inheritance, use the `createObject` utility shown in chapter 2 and in Section A.5 of this appendix.
- **Use utilities to copy objects and arrays.** Simple variables such as booleans, strings, or numbers are copied when they'are assigned. For example, `new_str = this_str` will copy the underlying data (in this case, a string) to `new_str`. Complex variables in JavaScript, such as arrays and objects, are *not* copied when they're assigned; instead the pointer to the data structure is copied. For example, `second_map = first_map`, will result in `second_map` pointing to the same data as `first_map`, and any manipulations of `second_map` will be reflected in `first_map`. Copying arrays and objects correctly is not always obvious or easy. We highly recommend the use of well-tested utilities for this purpose, such as those provided by jQuery.
- **Explicitly declare all variables first** in the functional scope using a single `var` keyword. JavaScript scopes variables by function and doesn't provide block scope. Therefore if you declare a variable anywhere within a function, it'll be initialized with a value of `undefined` immediately on invocation of the function. Placing all the variable declarations first recognizes this behavior. It also makes the code easier to read and to detect undeclared variables (which are never acceptable).

```
var getMapCopy = function ( arg_map ) {
  var key_name, result_map, val_data;      // Declarations only—many per line

  result_map = {};                         // Assignment only—one per line

  for ( key_name in arg_map ) {
    if ( arg_map.hasOwnProperty( key_name ) ) {
      val_data = arg_map[ key_name ];      // Conditional assignment
      if ( val_data ) { result_map[ key_name ] = val_data; }
    }
  }

  return result_map;
};
```

Declaring a variable is *not* the same as assigning a value to it: *declaring* informs the JavaScript engine that the variable exists within a scope. *Assigning* provides the variable a value (instead of `undefined`). As a convenience, you may combine declaration and assignment with the `var` statement, but it's not required.

- **Don't use blocks** as JavaScript doesn't provide block scope.[6] Defining variables in blocks can confuse programmers who are experienced with other C family languages. Define variables in functional scope instead.
- **Assign all functions to variables.** This reinforces the fact that JavaScript treats functions as first-class objects.

---

[6] This is mostly true, but Firefox's JavaScript, as of version 1.7, introduced the `let` statement, which can be used to provide block scope. But it's not supported by all major browsers and, therefore, should be ignored.

```
// BAD
 function getMapCopy( arg_map ) { ... };
// GOOD
 var getMapCopy = function ( arg_map ) { ... };
```

- **Use named arguments** whenever requiring three or more arguments in a function, as positional arguments are easy to forget and aren't self-documenting.

```
// BAD
 var coor_map = refactorCoords( 22, 28, 32, 48);
// BETTER
 var coord_map = refactorCoords({ x1:22, y1:28, x2:32, y2:48 });
```

- **Use one line per variable assignment.** Order them alphabetically or in logical groups when possible. *More than one declaration* may be placed on a single line:

```
// vars for lasso and drag function
var
  $cursor         = null, // current highlighted list item
  scroll_up_intid = null, // interval Id for scroll up
  index, length, ratio
  ;
```

Declaration and assignment

Multiple declarations on a single line

A.5 Functions

Functions play a central role in JavaScript: they organize code, provide a container for variable scope, and they provide an execution context which can be used to construct prototype-based objects. So though we have few guidelines for functions, we hold them quite dear.

- **Use the factory pattern for object constructors**, as it better illustrates how JavaScript objects actually work, is fast, and can be used to provide class-like capabilities like object count.

```
var createObject, extendObject,
  sayHello, sayText, makeMammal,
  catPrototype, makeCat, garfieldCat;

// ** Utility function to set inheritance
// Cross-browser method to inherit Object.create()
//   Newer js engines (v1.8.5+) support it natively

var objectCreate = function ( arg ) {
  if ( ! arg ) { return {}; }
  function obj() {};
  obj.prototype = arg;
  return new obj;
};

Object.create = Object.create || objectCreate;

// ** Utility function to extend an object
extendObject = function ( orig_obj, ext_obj ) {
  var key_name;
  for ( key_name in ext_obj ) {
```

```
    if ( ext_obj.hasOwnProperty( key_name ) ) {
      orig_obj[ key_name ] = ext_obj[ key_name ];
    }
  }
};

// ** object methods...
sayHello = function () {
  console.warn( this.hello_text + ' says ' + this.name );
};

sayText = function ( text ) {
  console.warn( this.name + ' says ' + text );
};

// ** makeMammal constructor
makeMammal = function ( arg_map ) {
  var mammal = {
    is_warm_blooded : true,
    has_fur         : true,
    leg_count       : 4,
    has_live_birth  : true,
    hello_text      : 'grunt',
    name            : 'anonymous',
    say_hello       : sayHello,
    say_text        : sayText
  };
  extendObject( mammal, arg_map );
  return mammal;
};

// ** use mammal constructor to create cat prototype
catPrototype = makeMammal({
  has_whiskers : true,
  hello_text   : 'meow'
});

// ** cat constructor
makeCat = function( arg_map ) {
  var cat = Object.create( catPrototype );
  extendObject( cat, arg_map );
  return cat;
};

// ** cat instance
garfieldCat = makeCat({
  name       : 'Garfield',
  weight_lbs : 8.6
});

// ** cat instance method invocations
garfieldCat.say_hello();
garfieldCat.say_text('Purr...');
```

- **Avoid pseudoclassical object constructors**—those that take a `new` keyword. If you call such a constructor without the `new` keyword, the global namespace gets corrupted. If you *must* keep such a constructor, its first letter should be capitalized so it may be recognized as a pseudo classical constructor.

- **Declare all functions before they are used**—remember that declaring functions is *not* the same as *assigning a value* to them.
- **When a function is to be invoked immediately**, wrap the function in parenthesis so that it's clear that the value being produced is the result of the function and not the function itself: `spa.shell = (function () { ... }());`

A.6 Namespaces

Much early JavaScript code was relatively small and used alone on a single web page. These scripts could (and often *did*) use global variables with few repercussions. But as JavaScript applications have become more ambitious and third-party libraries have become common, the chance that someone else is going to want the global `i` variable rises steeply. And when two code bases claim the same global variable, all hell can break loose.[7]

We can greatly minimize this problem by using only a single global function inside of which all our other variables are scoped as illustrated here:

```
var spa = (function () {
  // other code here

  var initModule = function () {
    console.log( 'hi there' );
  };

  return { initModule : initModule };
}());
```

We call this single global function (`spa`, in this example) our *namespace*. The function we assign to it executes on load, and of course, any local variables assigned within that function won't be available to the global namespace. Note that we did make the `initModule` method available. So other code can call the initialization function, but it can't access anything else. And it has to use our `spa` prefix:

```
// from another library, call the spa initialization function
spa.initModule();
```

We can subdivide the namespace so that we aren't forced to cram a 50KB application into a single file. For example, we can create the namespaces of `spa`, `spa.shell`, and `spa.slider`:

```
// In the file spa.js:
var spa = (function () {
  // some code here
}());

// In the file spa.shell.js:
var spa.shell = (function () {
```

[7] The author once worked on an application where a third-party library suddenly and mistakenly claimed the global variable `util` (they should have used JSLint...). Though our application had only three namespaces, `util` was one of them. The conflict crashed our application, and it took four hours to diagnose and work around the problem. We were significantly less than happy.

```
  // some code here
}());

// In the file spa.slider.js:
var spa.slider = (function () {
 // some code here
}());
```

This namespacing is key to creating manageable code in JavaScript.

A.7 File names and layout

Namespacing is the foundation of our file naming and layout. Here are the general guidelines:

- **Use jQuery** for DOM manipulations.
- **Investigate third-party code** like jQuery plugins before building your own—balance the cost of integration and bloat versus the benefits of standardization and code consistency.
- **Avoid embedding JavaScript** code in HTML; use external libraries instead.
- **Minify, obfuscate, and gzip** JavaScript and CSS before go-live. For example, use Uglify to minify and obsfucate Javascript during preparation, and use Apache2/mod_gzip to gzip the files on delivery.

JavaScript file guidelines are as follows:

- **Include third-party JavaScript files first** in our HTML so their functions may be evaluated and made ready for our application.
- **Include our JavaScript files next**, in order of namespace. You can't load namespace `spa.shell`, for example, if the root namespace, `spa`, has not yet been loaded.
- **Give all JavaScript files a .js suffix**.
- **Store all static JavaScript files** under a directory called `js`.
- **Name JavaScript files** according to the namespace they provide, one namespace per file. Examples:

  ```
  spa.js        // spa.*        namespace
  spa.shell.js  // spa.shell.*  namespace
  spa.slider.js // spa.slider.* namespace
  ```

- **Use the template** to start any JavaScript module file. One is found at the end of this appendix.

We maintain a parallel structure between JavaScript and CSS files and class names:

- **Create a CSS file for each JavaScript file** that generates HTML. Examples:

  ```
  spa.css        // spa.*        namespace
  spa.shell.css  // spa.shell.*  namespace
  spa.slider.css // spa.slider.* namespace
  ```

- **Give all CSS files a .css suffix.**

- **Store all CSS files** under a directory called *css*.
- **Prefix CSS selectors** according to the name of the module they support. This practice helps greatly to avoid unintended interaction with classes from third-party modules. Examples:

```
spa.css defines #spa, .spa-x-clearall
spa.shell.css defines
  #spa-shell-header, #spa-shell-footer, .spa-shell-main
```

- **Use <namespace>-x-<descriptor>** for state-indicator and other shared class names. Examples include `spa-x-select` and `spa-x-disabled`. Place these in the root namespace stylesheet, for example `spa.css`.

These are simple guidelines and easy to follow. The resulting organization and consistency make the correlation between CSS and JavaScript much easier to understand.

A.8 Syntax

This section is a survey of JavaScript syntax and the guidelines we follow.

A.8.1 Labels

Statement labels are optional. Only these statements should be labeled: `while`, `do`, `for`, `switch`. Labels should always be uppercase and should be a singular noun:

```
var
  horseList  = [ Anglo-Arabian', 'Arabian', 'Azteca', 'Clydsedale' ],
  horseCount = horseList.length,
  breedName, i
  ;

HORSE:
for ( i = 0; i < horseCount; i++ ) {
  breedName = horseList[ i ];
  if ( breedName === 'Clydsedale' ) { continue HORSE; }
  // processing for non-bud horses follows below
  // ...
}
```

A.8.2 Statements

Common JavaScript statements are listed next, along with our suggested use.

CONTINUE

We avoid use of the `continue` statement unless we use a label. It otherwise tends to obscure the control flow. The inclusion of a label also makes `continue` more resilient.

```
// discouraged
 continue;

// encouraged
 continue HORSE;
```

DO

A `do` statement should have the following form:

```
do {
  // statements
} while ( condition );
```

Always end a do statement with a semicolon.

FOR

A for statement should have one of the forms illustrated next:

```
for ( initialization; condition; update ) {
  // statements
}

for ( variable in object ) {
  if ( filter ) {
    // statements
  }
}
```

The first form should be used with arrays and with loops of a known number of iterations.

The second form should be used with objects and maps. Be aware that members with attributes and methods added to the prototype of the object will be included in the enumeration. Use the hasOwnProperty method to filter the true properties:

```
for ( variable in object ) {
  if ( object.hasOwnProperty( variable ) ) {
    // statements
  }
}
```

IF

The if statement should have one of the forms illustrated as follows. An else keyword should begin its own line:

```
if ( condition ) {
  // statements
}

if ( condition ) {
  // statements
}
else {
  // statements
}

if ( condition ) {
  // statements
}
else if ( condition ) {
  // statements
}
else {
  // statements
}
```

RETURN

A `return` statement shouldn't use parentheses around the return value. The `return` value expression must start on the same line as the `return` keyword in order to avoid semicolon insertion.

SWITCH

A `switch` statement should have the following form:

```
switch ( expression ) {
  case expression:
    // statements
  break;
  case expression:
    // statements
  break;
  default:
   // statements
}
```

Each group of statements (except the default) should end with `break`, `return`, or `throw`; fall-through should only be used with great caution and accompanying comments, and even then you should rethink the need for it. Is the terseness really worth the trade-off in legibility? Probably not.

TRY

A `try` statement should have one of the following forms:

```
try {
  // statements
}
catch ( variable ) {
  // statements
}

try {
  // statements
}
catch ( variable ) {
  // statements
}
finally {
  // statements
}
```

WHILE

A `while` statement should have the following form:

```
while ( condition ) {
  // statements
}
```

`While` statements should be avoided as they tend to induce endless loop conditions. Favor using the `for` statement when possible.

WITH

The `with` statement should be avoided. Use the `object.call()` family of methods instead to adjust the value of `this` during function invocation.

A.8.3 *Other syntax*

Of course there's more to JavaScript than just labels and statements. Here are some additional guidelines we follow:

AVOID THE COMMA OPERATOR

Avoid the use of the comma operator (as found in some `for` loop constructs). This doesn't apply to the comma separator, which is used in object literals, array literals, var statements, and parameter lists.

AVOID ASSIGNMENT EXPRESSIONS

Avoid using assignments in the condition part of `if` and `while` statements—don't write `if ( a = b ) { ...` as it's not clear if you intended to test for equality or a successful assignment.

ALWAYS USE === AND !== COMPARISONS

It is almost always better to use the `===` and `!==` operators. The `==` and `!=` operators do type coercion. In particular, don't use `==` to compare against falsey values. Our JSLint configuration doesn't allow type coercion. If you want to test if a value is truthy or falsey, use a construct like this:

```
if ( is_drag_mode ) { // is_drag_mode is truthy!
  runReport();
}
```

AVOID CONFUSING PLUSES AND MINUSES

Be careful to not follow a `+` with a `+` or a `++`. This pattern can be confusing. Insert parentheses between them to make your intention clear.

```
// confusing:
total = total_count + +arg_map.cost_dollars;

// better:
 total = total_count + (+arg_map.cost_dollars);
```

This prevents the `+ +` from being misread as `++`. The same guideline applies for the minus sign, `-`.

DON'T USE EVAL

Be careful—`eval` has evil aliases. Don't use the `Function` constructor. Don't pass strings to `setTimeout` or `setInterval`. Use a parser instead of `eval` to convert JSON strings into internal data structures.

A.9 *Validating code*

JSLint is a JavaScript validation tool written and maintained by Douglas Crockford. It's very popular and useful in spotting code errors and ensuring fundamental guidelines are followed. If you're creating professional-grade JavaScript, you should be using

JSLint or a similar validator. It helps us avoid numerous types of bugs and significantly shortens development time.

A.9.1 Install JSLint

1. Download the latest jslint4java distribution, such as `jslint4java-2.0.2.zip`, from http://code.google.com/p/jslint4java/
2. Unpack and install per the instructions for your platform.

> **If you're running OS X or Linux**
>
> You may move the jar file, for example `sudo mv jslint4java-2.0.2.jar /usr/local/lib/`, and then create the following wrapper in `/usr/local/bin/jslint`:
>
> ```
> #!/bin/bash
> # See http://code.google.com/p/jslint4java/
>
> for jsfile in $@;
> do /usr/bin/java \
>   -jar /usr/local/lib/jslint4java-2.0.1.jar \
>   "$jsfile";
> done
> ```
>
> Make sure jslint is executable—`sudo chmod 755 /usr/local/bin/jslint`

If you have Node.js installed, you may install a different version like so: `npm install -g jslint`. This version runs much faster, although it's untested with the listings in this book.

A.9.2 Configure JSLint

Our module template includes the configuration for JSLint. These settings are used to match our coding standard:

```
/*jslint          browser : true, continue : true,
  devel  : true, indent  : 2,    maxerr   : 50,
  newcap : true, nomen   : true, plusplus : true,
  regexp : true, sloppy  : true, vars     : false,
  white  : true
*/
/*global $, spa, <other external vars> */
```

- `browser : true`—Allow browser keywords like `document`, `history`, `clearInterval`, and so on.
- `continue : true`—Allow the `continue` statement.
- `devel : true`—Allow development keywords like `alert`, `console`, and so forth.
- `indent : 2`—Expect two-space indentation.
- `maxerr : 50`—Abort JSLint after 50 errors.
- `newcap : true`—Tolerate leading underscores.
- `nomen : true`—Tolerate uncapitalized constructors.

- plusplus : true—Tolerate ++ and --.
- regexp : true—Allow useful but potentially dangerous regular expression constructions.
- sloppy : true—Don't require the use strict pragma.
- vars : false—Don't allow multiple var statements per functional scope.
- white : true—Disable JSLint's formatting checks.

A.9.3 Use JSLint

We can use JSLint from the command line whenever we want to check code validity. The syntax is:

```
jslint filepath1 [filepath2, ... filepathN]
# example: jslint spa.js
# example: jslint *.js
```

We've written a git commit hook to test all changed JavaScript files before allowing a commit into the repository. The following shell script can be added as repo/.git/hooks/pre-commit.

```
#!/bin/bash

# See www.davidpashley.com/articles/writing-robust-shell-scripts.html
# unset var check
set -u;
# exit on error check
# set -e;

BAIL=0;
TMP_FILE="/tmp/git-pre-commit.tmp";
echo;
echo "JSLint test of updated or new *.js files ...";
echo "  We ignore third_party libraries in .../js/third_party/...";
git status \
  | grep '.js$' \
  | grep -v '/js/third_party/' \
  | grep '#\s\+\(modified\|new file\)' \
  | sed -e 's/^#\s\+\(modified\|new file\):\s\+//g' \
  | sed -e 's/\s\+$//g' \
  | while read LINE; do
      echo -en "  Check ${LINE}: ... "
      CHECK=$(jslint $LINE);
      if [ "${CHECK}" != "" ]; then
        echo "FAIL";
      else
        echo "pass";
      fi;
    done \
  | tee "${TMP_FILE}";

echo "JSlint test complete";
if grep -s 'FAIL' "${TMP_FILE}"; then
  echo "JSLint testing FAILED";
  echo "  Please use jslint to test the failed files and ";
```

```
    echo "  commit again once they pass the check.";
    exit 1;
  fi
  echo;
  exit 0;
```

You may need to modify it somewhat for your purposes. Also, please ensure it's executable (in Mac or Linux, `chmod 755 pre-commit`).

A.10 A template for modules

Experience has shown that breaking a module into consistent sections is a valuable practice. It assists our comprehension and navigation, and it reminds us of good coding practice. The template we've settled on after hundreds of modules over many projects is shown next, with some sample code sprinkled in:

Listing A.24 Recommended module template

```
/*
 * module_template.js
 * Template for browser feature modules
*/
/*jslint         browser : true, continue : true,
  devel  : true, indent  : 2,    maxerr   : 50,
  newcap : true, nomen   : true, plusplus : true,
  regexp : true, sloppy  : true, vars     : false,
  white  : true
*/
/*global $, spa */
spa.module = (function () {
  //--------------- BEGIN MODULE SCOPE VARIABLES -------------
  var
    configMap = {
      settable_map : { color_name: true },
      color_name   : 'blue'
    },
    stateMap  = { $container : null },
    jqueryMap = {},

    setJqueryMap, configModule, initModule;
  //---------------- END MODULE SCOPE VARIABLES --------------

  //------------------- BEGIN UTILITY METHODS -----------------
  // example : getTrimmedString
  //-------------------- END UTILITY METHODS ------------------

  //--------------------- BEGIN DOM METHODS -------------------
```

Include purpose, author, and copyright information in the header. This ensures this information is not lost regardless of any file transfer method.

Include JSLint settings in the header. We recommend a commit-hook to ensure only JavaScript that passes JSLint can be submitted to a code repository.

Create a namespace for the module using a self-executing function. This prevents accidental creation of global JavaScript variables. Only one namespace should be defined per file, and the file name should correlate precisely. For example, if the module provides the `spa.shell` namespace, the file name should be `spa.shell.js`.

Declare and initialize modules-scope variables. We commonly include `configMap` to store module configurations, `stateMap` to store run-time state values, and `jqueryMap` to cache jQuery collections.

Group all private utility methods in their own section. These methods don't manipulate the Document Object Model (DOM) and therefore don't require a browser to run. If a method has utility beyond a single module, we should move it to a shared utility library such as `spa.util.js`.

Group all private DOM methods in their own section. These methods access and modify the DOM and therefore require a browser to run. An example DOM method might move a CSS sprite. The `setJqueryMap` method should be used to cache jQuery collections.

Group all private event handlers in their own section. These methods handle events such as a button click, a key press, a browser window resize, or receipt of a web socket message. Event handlers should generally call DOM methods to adjust the DOM instead of making changes themselves.

Group all callback methods in their own section. If we have callbacks, we usually place them between event handlers and public methods. They're quasi-public methods, since they're used by external modules to which they have been provided.

Group all public methods in their own section. These methods are part of a module's public interface. This section should include the `configModule` and `initModule` methods if they're provided.

Neatly return the public methods in an object.

```
  // Begin DOM method /setJqueryMap/
  setJqueryMap = function () {
    var $container = stateMap.$container;

    jqueryMap = { $container : $container };
  };
  // End DOM method /setJqueryMap/
  //---------------------- END DOM METHODS ---------------------

  //------------------- BEGIN EVENT HANDLERS -------------------
  // example: onClickButton = ...
  //-------------------- END EVENT HANDLERS --------------------


  //------------------- BEGIN PUBLIC METHODS -------------------
  // Begin public method /configModule/
  // Purpose    : Adjust configuration of allowed keys
  // Arguments  : A map of settable keys and values
  //   * color_name - color to use
  // Settings   :
  //   * configMap.settable_map declares allowed keys
  // Returns    : true
  // Throws     : none
  //
  configModule = function ( input_map ) {
    spa.butil.setConfigMap({
      input_map    : input_map,
      settable_map : configMap.settable_map,
      config_map   : configMap
    });
    return true;
  };
  // End public method /configModule/

  // Begin public method /initModule/
  // Purpose    : Initializes module
  // Arguments  :
  //  * $container the jquery element used by this feature
  // Returns    : true
  // Throws     : nonaccidental
  //
  initModule = function ( $container ) {
    stateMap.$container = $container;
    setJqueryMap();
    return true;
  };
  // End public method /initModule/

  // return public methods
  return {
    configModule : configModule,
    initModule   : initModule
  };
  //------------------- END PUBLIC METHODS ---------------------
}());
```

A.11 Summary

A good coding standard is required for one or many developers to work most effectively. The standard we present is comprehensive and cohesive, but we recognize it may not be right for every team. In any event, we hope it encourages our readers to think about common issues and how a convention may solve or mitigate them. We strongly advise any team to agree on a standard before embarking on a large project.

Code will be read many times more than it will be written, so we optimize for readability. We limit our lines to 78 characters and use a two-space indentation. We don't allow tab stops. We group our lines into logical paragraphs to help readers understand our intent, and we break lines consistently. K&R style is used for bracketing, and whitespace is used to differentiate keywords from functions. We prefer to use the single quote when defining string literals. We favor conventions over comments to convey what the code is doing. Descriptive and consistent variable names are key to conveying our intent without over-using comments. When we comment, we document strategically by paragraph. Non-trivial internal interfaces are documented consistently.

We protect our code from unwanted interaction with other scripts through the use of namespaces. Self-executing functions are used to provide namespaces. We subdivide our root namespace to organize our code and provide reasonable file size and scope. Our JavaScript files each contain a single namespace, and their filename reflects the namespace they provide. We create a parallel namespace for CSS selectors and files.

We installed and configured JSLint. Our code is always validated using JSLint before we allow it to be checked into our code base. We use consistent settings for validation. We presented a module template that embodies many of the conventions presented and that includes our JSLint settings in the header.

A coding standard is meant to liberate developers from menial tasks through the introduction of a common dialect and consistent structure. This allows them to instead focus their creative energy on the logic that matters. A good standard provides a clarity of intent crucial for the success of large-scale projects.

appendix B
Testing an SPA

This appendix covers

- Setting up test modes
- Selecting a test framework
- Setting up nodeunit
- Creating a test suite
- Adjusting SPA modules for test settings

This appendix builds on code we've completed in chapter 8. Before starting, you should have the project files from chapter 8, as we'll be adding to them. We recommend you copy the entire directory structure you created in chapter 8 into a new "appendix_B" directory and update them there.

We're fans of test-driven development and have worked *gonzo* projects where the *generation* of tests was automated. A permutation tool was used to automatically generate thousands of regression tests by simply describing the APIs and their expected behavior. If a developer modified code, it had to pass the regression tests before it could be checked in to the repository. And when a new API was introduced, the developer added the description to the configuration, and hundreds or thousands of new tests were generated automatically. This practice resulted in exceptional quality, as code coverage was great, and we rarely had a regression of any sort.

Although we love these sorts of regression tests, we won't be so ambitious in this appendix. We only have enough space and time to get your feet wet, not give you a bath. Instead we'll set up test modes, discuss their use, and then create a test suite using jQuery and a test framework. We're testing later than we'd like for a real project—we prefer to write our tests along with our code because it helps clarify what the code is supposed to do. And, as if to prove the point, we found and fixed two issues while writing this appendix.[1] Now let's discuss the test modes we want for an SPA.

B.1 Set up test modes

We use at least four different test modes when developing an SPA. These modes should generally be used in the order presented:

1. Test the Model without a browser using fake data (mode 1).
2. Test the user interface using fake data (mode 2).
3. Test the Model without a browser using live data (mode 3).
4. Test the Model and user interface using live data (mode 4).

We need to be able switch easily between test modes so we may quickly identify, isolate, and solve issues. A corollary to this goal is that we should use the same code for all modes. We want to run tests without a browser (modes 1 and 3), and with a browser (modes 2 and 4).

Figure B.1 shows the modules used when we test the Model without a browser using fake data (mode 1). This test mode should typically be used first to ensure the Model API works exactly as designed.

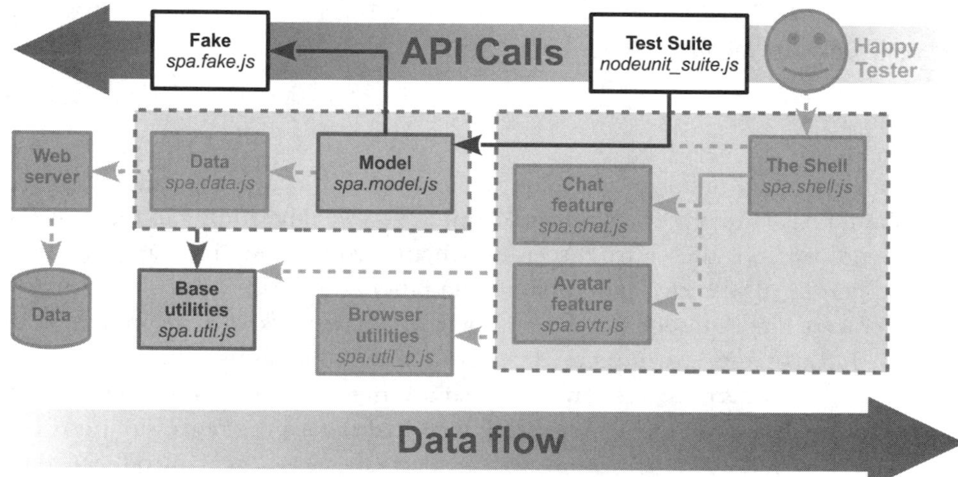

Figure B.1 Testing the Model without a browser using fake data (mode 1)

[1] If you must know, they were: 1) The online person list wasn't being properly cleared on sign-out, and 2) calls to `spa.model.chat.get_chatee()` were returning an out-of-date object after the chatee's avatar had been updated. Both bugs are fixed in chapter 6.

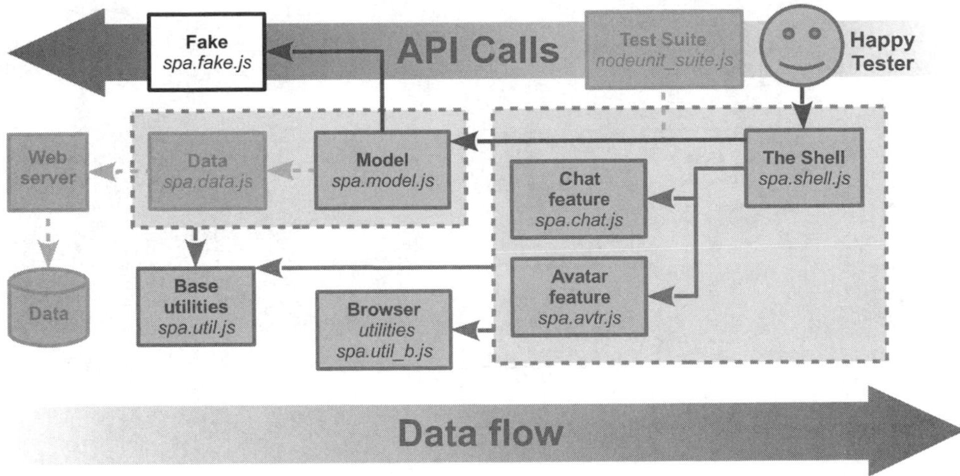

Figure B.2 Testing the View and Controller using fake data (mode 2)

Figure B.2 shows the modules used when we test the user interface using fake data (mode 2). This is a great mode to isolate View- and Controller-related bugs after the Model has been tested.

Figure B.3 shows the modules used when we test the Model without a browser using live data (mode 3). This helps isolate problems with the server API.

Figure B.4 shows the modules used when we test the user interface using live data (mode 4). This allows the user to test the full stack, and is really the full application. Test freaks (or aspiring freaks like ourselves) call this *integration testing*.

We minimize the number of issues we find in mode 4 if we do a good job testing with the other modes. And once we do find an issue in mode 4, we should try to

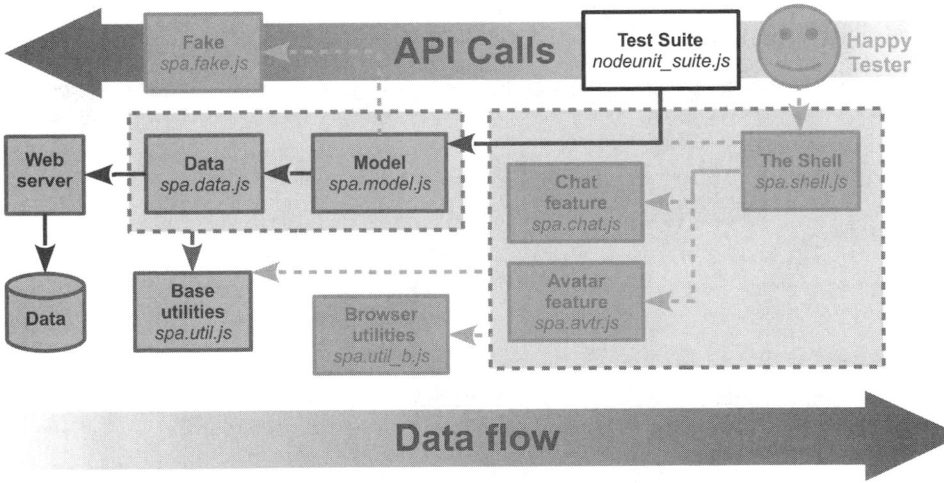

Figure B.3 Testing the Model using the test suite and live data (mode 3)

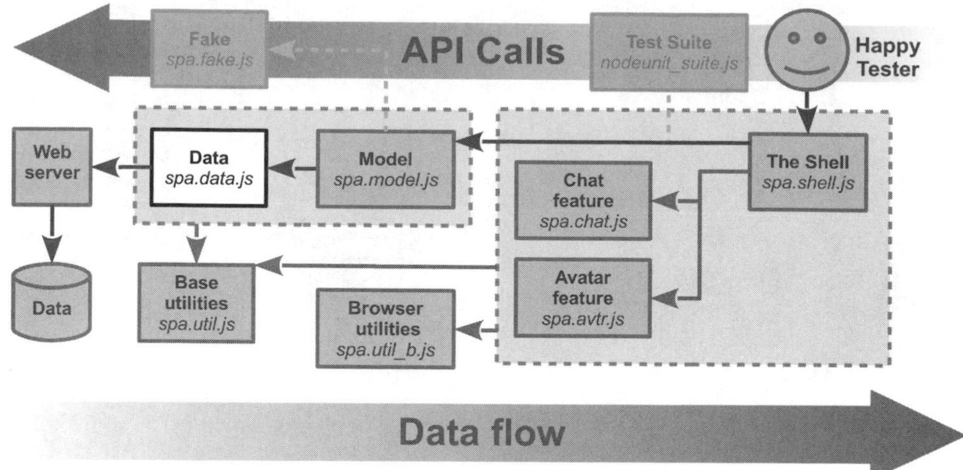

Figure B.4 Integration testing with live data (mode 4)

isolate it in a simpler mode, starting at mode 1. When it comes to resolving issues effectively, mode 4 is like the moon—it's an interesting place to visit, but you don't want to live there.

In this section, we'll make the changes necessary so we can use the browser interface with both live and fake data (modes 2 and 4). Here's what we need to do:

- Create the `spa.model.setDataMode` Model method to switch between fake and live data.
- Update the Shell to inspect the value of a URI query argument, `fake`, during initialization. Have it then set the data mode using `spa.model.setDataMode`.

The `spa.model.setDataMode` method is easy to add to the Model, as we only need to change the module-scope `isFakeData` variable. The following listing shows the update. Changes are shown in **bold**:

Listing B.1 Add `setDataMode` to the Model—webapp/public/js/spa.model.js

```
...
spa.model = (function () {
  'use strict';
  var
    configMap = { anon_id : 'a0' },
    stateMap  = { ...
    },
    isFakeData = true,          // Default to fake data.

    personProto, makeCid, clearPeopleDb, completeLogin,
    makePerson, removePerson, people, chat, initModule,
    setDataMode;
...
  setDataMode = function ( arg_str ) {     // Set the isFakeData module-scope variable.
```

```
    isFakeData = arg_str === 'fake'
      ? true : false;
  };

  return {
    initModule  : initModule,
    chat        : chat,
    people      : people,
    setDataMode: setDataMode          <-- Add to export list.
  };
}());
```

Our next step is to adjust the Shell to read the URI query arguments on initialization and then call `spa.model.setDataMode` (you know, the method we just added). This change is surgical, as shown in the following listing. Changes are shown in **bold**:

Listing B.2 Set data mode in the Shell—webapp/public/js/spa.shell.js

```
...
  //------------------- BEGIN PUBLIC METHODS -------------------
  // Begin Public method /initModule/
  ...
  //
  initModule = function ( $container ) {
    var data_mode_str;

    // set data to fake if URI query argument set
    data_mode_str
      = window.location.search === '?fake'
      ? 'fake' : 'live';
    spa.model.setDataMode( data_mode_str );

    // load HTML and map jQuery collections
    stateMap.$container = $container;
    $container.html( configMap.main_html );
    setJqueryMap();
    ...
```

First let's enter our webapp directory and install the modules (`npm install`) and then start the node application (`node app.js`). When we open our browser document with the `fake` flag (`http://localhost:3000/spa.html?fake`), fake data will be used with the interface (mode 2).[2] If we open the browser document without the `fake` flag (`http://localhost:3000/spa.html`), live data will be used instead (mode 4). In the upcoming sections we'll discuss how to test our SPA without the browser (modes 1 and 3). First, let's decide on a test framework.

B.2 Select a test framework

We've designed our SPA architecture so we may easily test the Model without the use of a browser. We've found that when the Model works exactly as designed, the expense to fix user interface bugs tends to be trivial. We've also found that humans are often (but not always) more effective at interface testing than scripts are.

[2] Yes, we *know* the query argument parsing is a hack. In production we'd use a much more robust library routine.

Instead of a browser, we'll use Node.js to test the Model. This will allow us to easily and automatically run test suites during development and prior to deployment. And because we're not dependent on a browser, tests are simpler to write, maintain, and extend.

Node.js has many test frameworks that have years of use and refinement. Let's be wise and use one instead of hacking our own. Here's a list of some that we found interesting for one reason or another:[3]

- *jasmine-jquery*—Can "watch" jQuery events.
- *mocha*—Popular and similar to nodeunit but with better reporting.
- *nodeunit*—Popular, with simple yet powerful tools.
- *patr*—Uses promises (similar to jQuery `$.Deferred` objects) for asynchronous testing.
- *vows*—Popular asynchronous BDD framework.
- *zombie*—Popular full-stack headless featuring a WebKit engine.

Zombie is inclusive and is intended to test the user interface as well as the Model. It even includes its own instance of the WebKit rendering engine so tests can check rendered elements. We won't pursue this kind of testing here because it's expensive and tedious to install, set up, and maintain—and this is an appendix, *not another book*. Although we find jasmine-jquery and patr interesting for the reasons listed here, we feel they don't have the level of support we need. Mocha and vows are popular, but we want to start simpler.

This leaves us with nodeunit, which is popular, powerful, simple, and also integrates nicely with our IDE. Let's set it up.

B.3 Set up nodeunit

Before we can install nodeunit, we need to ensure Node.js is installed as outlined in chapter 7. Once Node.js is available, we need to install two `npm` packages to get nodeunit ready to run our test suite:

- `jquery`—We need to install the Node.js version of jQuery because our Model uses global custom events, and this requires jQuery and the jquery.event.gevent plugin. As an added bonus, installation of this package provides a mocked browser environment. So if we wanted to test DOM manipulation we could.
- `nodeunit`—This provides the nodeunit command-line tool. When we run our test suite, we'll use the `nodeunit` command instead of `node`.

We like to install these packages system-wide so they can be used by all Node.js projects. We may do so using the `-g` switch and installing them as root (or administrator, if you're on Windows). The following should work for Linux and Mac:

[3] See https://github.com/joyent/node/wiki/modules#testing for an exhaustive list.

Listing B.3 Installing jQuery and nodeunit system-wide

```
$ sudo npm install -g jquery
$ sudo npm install -g nodeunit
```

Note that you may need to tell your execution environment where to find the system Node.js libraries by setting the `NODE_PATH` environment variable. In Linux or Mac, this can be done by adding to your ~/.bashrc file:

```
$ echo 'export NODE_PATH=/usr/lib/node_modules' >> ~/.bashrc
```

This will ensure the `NODE_PATH` is set every time you start a new terminal session.[4] Now that we have Node.js, jQuery, and nodeunit installed, let's prepare our modules for testing.

B.4 Create the test suite

As of chapter 6, we have all the ingredients for successful testing of our Model using known data (thanks to the Fake module) and a well-defined API. Figure B.5 shows how we plan to test the Model:[5]

Before we can start testing, we need to get Node.js to load our modules. Let's do that next.

B.4.1 Get Node.js to load our modules

Node.js handles global variables differently than browsers. Unlike browser JavaScript, variables in a file are local by default. Effectively, Node.js wraps all library files in an

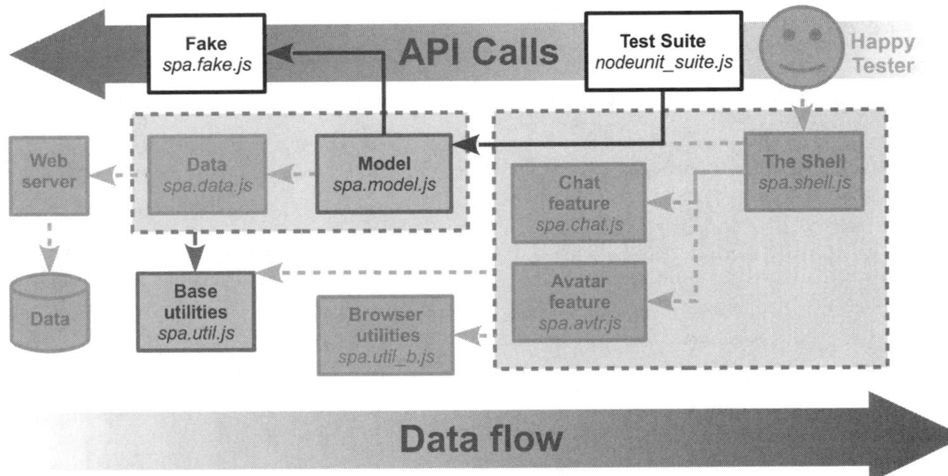

Figure B.5 Testing the Model using the test suite and fake data (mode 1)

[4] For a currently running session, type `export PATH=/usr/lib/node_modules`. Depending on how Node.js is installed, the path may vary. On Mac, you might try /usr/local/share/npm/lib/node_modules.

[5] The astute interloper will notice that this figure is a lazy, pixel-perfect copy of one presented earlier. We should get paid by the column-inch...

anonymous function. The way we make a variable available across all modules is to make it a property of the top-level object. And the-top level object in Node.js is not `window`, like it is in browsers, but is instead called—wait for it—`global`.

Our modules are designed for use by the browser. But with ingenuity, we can have Node.js use them with little modification. Here's how we do it: our entire application runs in the single namespace (object) of `spa`. So if we declare a `global.spa` attribute in our Node.js test script before we load our modules, everything should work as expected.

Now before all that evaporates from our short-term memories, let's start our test suite, webapp/public/nodeunit_suite.js, as shown in the following listing.

Listing B.4 Declare our namespace in the test suite—webapp/public/nodeunit_suite.js

```
/*
 * nodeunit_suite.js
 * Unit test suite for SPA
 *
 * Please run using /nodeunit <this_file>/
*/

/*jslint         node   : true, continue : true,
  devel  : true, indent : 2,    maxerr   : 50,
  newcap : true, nomen  : true, plusplus : true,
  regexp : true, sloppy : true, vars     : false,
  white  : true
*/
/*global spa */

// our modules and globals
global.spa    = null;
```

Add the `node: true` switch to have JSLint assume the Node.js environment.

Create a `global.spa` attribute so the SPA modules can use the `spa` namespace when they load.

We only need to adjust the root JavaScript file (webapp/public/js/spa.js) to finish loading our modules. Our adjustment allows the test suite to use the correct global spa variable as shown in the next listing. Changes are shown in **bold**:

Listing B.5 Adjust our root SPA JavaScript—webapp/public/js/spa.js

```
/*
 * spa.js
 * Root namespace module
*/
...
/*global $, spa:true */

spa = (function () {
  'use strict';
  var initModule = function ( $container ) {
    spa.data.initModule();
    spa.model.initModule();

    if ( spa.shell && $container ) {
      spa.shell.initModule( $container );
    }
  };

  return { initModule: initModule };
}());
```

Add `spa: true` to the configuration so that JSLint will allow us to assign to the `spa` global variable.

Remove the `var` declaration.

Adjust the application so that it can run without the user interface (the Shell).

Now that we've created a `global.spa` variable, we can load our modules much like we did with our browser document (webapp/public/spa.html). First we'll load our third-party modules like jQuery and TaffyDB, and make sure *their* global variables are also available (`jQuery`, `$`, and `TAFFY`, if you must know). Then we can load our jQuery plugins and then our SPA modules. We won't load our Shell or feature modules, because we don't need them to test the Model. Let's update our unit test file while these thoughts still linger in our consciousness. Changes are shown in **bold**:

Listing B.6 Adding the libraries and our modules—webapp/public/nodeunit_suite.js

```
...
/*global $, spa */

// third-party modules and globals
global.jQuery = require( 'jquery' );
global.TAFFY  = require( './js/jq/taffydb-2.6.2.js' ).taffy;
global.$      = global.jQuery;
require( './js/jq/jquery.event.gevent-0.1.9.js' );

// our modules and globals
global.spa = null;
require( './js/spa.js'       );
require( './js/spa.util.js'  );
require( './js/spa.fake.js'  );
require( './js/spa.data.js'  );
require( './js/spa.model.js' );

// example code
spa.initModule();
spa.model.setDataMode( 'fake' );

var $t = $( '<div/>' );
$.gevent.subscribe(
  $t, 'spa-login',
  function ( event, user ){
    console.log( 'Login user is:', user );
  }
);

spa.model.people.login( 'Fred' );
```

Whoops, we got ambitious and snuck in a short test script at the end of our listing. Although we eventually want to use nodeunit to run this file, we'll use Node.js to run it first to ensure it's loading the libraries properly. Indeed, when we run our test suite using Node.js we see something like this:

```
$ node nodeunit_suite.js
Login user is: { cid: 'id_5',
  name: 'Fred',
  css_map: { top: 25, left: 25, 'background-color': '#8f8' },
  ___id: 'T000002R000003',
  ___s: true,
  id: 'id_5' }
```

If you're playing along at home, please be patient. It takes three seconds before we see any output because the Fake module pauses that long before completing a sign-in request. And it takes another eight seconds after the output for Node.js to finish running. That's because Fake module uses timers when emulating the server (timers are created by the `setTimeout` and `setInterval` methods). Until those timers are complete, Node.js considers the program "running" and doesn't exit. We'll come back to this issue later. Now let's get familiar with nodeunit.

B.4.2 Set up a single nodeunit test

Now that we have Node.js loading our libraries, we can focus on setting up our nodeunit tests. First let's get comfortable with nodeunit all by itself. The steps to running a successful test are as follows:

- Declare the test functions.
- In each test function, tell the `test` object how many assertions to expect using `test.expect( <count> )`.
- In each test, run the assertions; for example `test.ok( true );`.
- At the end of each test, tell the test object that this test is complete using `test.done()`.
- Export the list of tests to be run *in order*. Each test will be run only after the prior test is complete.
- Run the test suite using `nodeunit <filename>`.

Listing B.7 shows a nodeunit script using these steps for a single test. Please read the annotations as they provide helpful insight:

Listing B.7 Our first nodeunit test—webapp/public/nodeunit_test.js

```
/*jslint node : true, sloppy : true, white : true */

// A trivial nodeunit example

// Begin /testAcct/
var testAcct = function ( test ) {
  test.expect( 1 );
  test.ok( true, 'this passes' );
  test.done();
 };
// End /testAcct/

module.exports = { testAcct : testAcct };
```

- Declare a test function called `testAcct`. We can name a test whatever we want; it just has to be a function that takes a `test` object as its only argument.
- Tell the test object that we plan to run a single assertion.
- Invoke our first (and only) assertion in this example.
- Invoke `test.done()` so that nodeunit may proceed to the next test (or exit).
- Export our tests in the order we want `nodeunit` to run them.

When we run `nodeunit nodeunit_test.js` we should see the following output:

```
$ nodeunit_test.js
✔ testAcct

OK: 1 assertions (3ms)
```

Now let's combine our nodeunit experience with the code we want tested.

B.4.3 Create our first real test

We'll now convert our first example into a real test. We can use nodeunit and jQuery deferred objects to avoid the pitfalls of testing event-driven code. First, we rely on the fact that nodeunit won't proceed to a new test until the prior test declares it's finished by executing `test.done()`. This makes testing easier to write and understand. Second, we can use a deferred object in jQuery to invoke `test.done()` only after the required `spa-login` event has been published. This then allows the script to proceed to the next test. Let's update our test suite as shown in listing B.8. Changes are shown in **bold**:

Listing B.8 Our first real test—webapp/public/nodeunit_suite.js

```
...
// our modules and globals
global.spa = null;
require( './js/spa.js'        );
require( './js/spa.util.js'   );
require( './js/spa.fake.js'   );
require( './js/spa.data.js'   );
require( './js/spa.model.js' );

// Begin /testAcct/ initialize and login
var testAcct = function ( test ) {
  var $t, test_str, user, on_login,
    $defer = $.Deferred();

  // set expected test count
  test.expect( 1 );

  // define handler for 'spa-login' event
  on_login = function (){ $defer.resolve(); };

  // initialize
  spa.initModule( null );
  spa.model.setDataMode( 'fake' );

  // create a jQuery object and subscribe
  $t = $('<div/>');
  $.gevent.subscribe( $t, 'spa-login', on_login );

  spa.model.people.login( 'Fred' );

  // confirm user is no longer anonymous
  user     = spa.model.people.get_user();
  test_str = 'user is no longer anonymous';
  test.ok( ! user.get_is_anon(), test_str );

  // declare finished once sign-in is complete
  $defer.done( test.done );
};
// End /testAcct/ initial setup and login

module.exports = { testAcct : testAcct };
```

When we run the test suite using nodeunit ./nodeunit_suite.js we should see the following output:

```
$ nodeunit nodeunit_test.js
✔ testAcct

OK: 1 assertions (3320ms)
```

Now that we've successfully implemented a single test, let's map out the tests we want to have in our suite and discuss how we'll ensure they execute in the correct sequence.

B.4.4 Map the events and tests

When we tested the Model manually in chapters 5 and 6, waiting for some process to complete before typing in the next test came naturally. It's obvious to humans that we must wait for sign-in to complete before we can test messaging. But this isn't obvious to a test suite.

We must map out a sequence of events and tests for our test suite to work. One benefit of writing test suites is that it makes us analyze and understand our code more completely. Sometimes we find more bugs when writing tests than when running them.

Let's first design a test plan for our suite. We want to test the Model as our imaginary user, Fred, puts our SPA through its paces. Here is what we'd like Fred to do, with labels:

- testInitialState—Test the initial state of the Model.
- loginAsFred—Sign in as Fred and test the user object before the process completes.
- testUserAndPeople—Test the online-user list and the user details.
- testWilmaMsg—Receive a message from Wilma and test the message details.
- sendPebblesMsg—Change the chatee to Pebbles and send her a message.
- testMsgToPebbles—Test the content of the message sent to Pebbles.
- testPebblesResponse—Test the content of a response message sent by Pebbles.
- updatePebblesAvtr—Update data for Pebbles' avatar.
- testPebblesAvtr—Test the update of Pebbles' avatar.
- logoutAsFred—Sign out as Fred.
- testLogoutState—Test the state of the Model after sign-out.

Our test framework, nodeunit, runs tests in the order presented, and won't proceed to the next test until the prior test has declared that it has finished. This works to our advantage, as we want to ensure that specific events have occurred before certain tests are run. For example, we want a user sign-in event to occur before we test the online person list. Let's map out our test plan with the events that need to occur before we can proceed from each test, as shown in listing B.9. Note that our test names match the labels from our plan exactly, and they're human-readable:

Listing B.9 Test plan with blocking events detailed

```
// Begin /testInitialState/
  // initialize our SPA
  // test the user in the initial state
  // test the list of online persons
  // proceed to next test without blocking
// End /testInitialState/

// Begin /loginAsFred/
  // login as 'Fred'
  // test user attributes before login completes
  // proceed to next test when both conditions are met:
  //   + login is complete (spa-login event)
  //   + the list of online persons has been updated
  //     (spa-listchange event)
// End /loginAsFred/

// Begin /testUserAndPeople/
  // test user attributes
  // test the list of online persons
  // proceed to next test when both conditions are met:
  //   + first message has been received (spa-updatechat event)
  //     (this is the example message from 'Wilma')
  //   + chatee change has occurred (spa-setchatee event)
// End /testUserAndPeople/

// Begin /testWilmaMsg/
  // test message received from 'Wilma'
  // test chatee attributes
  // proceed to next test without blocking
// End /testWilmaMsg/

// Begin /sendPebblesMsg/
  // set_chatee to 'Pebbles'
  // send_msg to 'Pebbles'
  // test get_chatee() results
  // proceed to next test when both conditions are met:
  //   + chatee has been set (spa-setchatee event)
  //   + message has been sent (spa-updatechat event)
// End /sendPebblesMsg/

// Begin /testMsgToPebbles/
  // test the chatee attributes
  // test the message sent
  // proceed to the next test when
  //   + A response has been received from 'Pebbles'
  //     (spa-updatechat event)
// End /testMsgToPebbles/

// Begin /testPebblesResponse/
  // test the message received from 'Pebbles'
  // proceed to next test without blocking
// End /testPebblesResponse/

// Begin /updatePebblesAvtr/
  // invoke the update_avatar method
  // proceed to the next test when
```

```
  //   + the list of online persons has been updated
  //      (spa-listchange event)
// End /updatePebblesAvtr/

// Begin /testPebblesAvtr/
  // get 'Pebbles' person object using get_chatee method
  // test avatar details for 'Pebbles'
  // proceed to next test without blocking
// End /testPebblesAvtr/

// Begin /logoutAsFred/
  // logout as fred
  // proceed to next test when
  //   + logout is complete (spa-logout event)
// End /logoutAsFred/

// Begin /testLogoutState/
  // test the list of online persons
  // test user attributes
  // proceed without blocking
// End /testLogoutState/
```

This plan is linear and easy to understand. In the next section, we'll put our plan into practice.

B.4.5 Create the test suite

We can now add some utilities and incrementally add tests to our suite. At each step we'll run the suite to check our progress.

ADD TESTS FOR INITIAL STATE AND SIGN-IN

We'll begin our test suite by writing some utilities and adding our first three tests to check the initial Model state, have Fred sign in, and then check the user and person list attributes. We've found that tests typically fall into two categories:

1. Validation tests where many assertions (like `user.name === 'Fred'`) are used to check the correctness of program data. These tests often don't block.
2. Control tests that perform actions like signing in, sending a message, or updating an avatar. These tests rarely have many assertions and often block progress until an event-based condition is met.

We've found it is best to embrace this natural division, and we name our tests accordingly. Validation tests are named `test<something>`, and the control tests are named after what they do, like `loginAsFred`.

The `loginAsFred` test requires that the sign-in be complete *and* the list of online users be updated before allowing nodeunit to proceed to the `testUserAndPeople` test. This is accomplished by having the `$t` jQuery collection subscribe handlers for the `spa-login` and `spa-listchange` events. The test suite then uses jQuery deferred objects to ensure these events occur *before* `loginAsFred` executes `test.done()`.

Let's update the test suite as shown in listing B.10. As always, please read the annotations as they provide additional insight. The comments we built for our test plan in listing B.9 are shown in **bold**:

Listing B.10 Add our first two tests—webapp/public/nodeunit_suite.js

```
...
/*global $, spa */

// third-party modules and globals
...

// our modules and globals
...

var
  // utility and handlers
  makePeopleStr, onLogin, onListchange,

  // test functions
  testInitialState, loginAsFred, testUserAndPeople,

  // event handlers
  loginEvent, changeEvent, loginData, changeData,

  // indexes
  changeIdx = 0,

  // deferred objects
  $deferLogin      = $.Deferred(),
  $deferChangeList = [ $.Deferred() ];

// utility to make a string of online person names
makePeopleStr = function ( people_db ) {
  var people_list = [];
  people_db().each(function( person, idx ) {
    people_list.push( person.name );
  });
  return people_list.sort().join( ',' );
};

// event handler for 'spa-login'
onLogin = function ( event, arg ) {
  loginEvent = event;
  loginData  = arg;
  $deferLogin.resolve();
};

// event handler for 'spa-listchange'
onListchange = function ( event, arg ) {
  changeEvent = event;
  changeData  = arg;
  $deferChangeList[ changeIdx ].resolve();
  changeIdx++;
  $deferChangeList[ changeIdx ] = $.Deferred();
};

// Begin /testInitialState/
testInitialState = function ( test ) {
  var $t, user, people_db, people_str, test_str;
  test.expect( 2 );

  // initialize our SPA
  spa.initModule( null );
```

Declare the first three test methods using descriptive names so that our report reads easily.

Create the `makePeopleStr` utility. As you might gather from the name, this makes a string containing the names of the people found in a TaffyDB collection. This enables the suite to test the list of online people with a simple string comparison.

Create a method to handle an `spa-login` custom global event. When this is executed, it invokes `$deferLogin .resolve()`.

Create a method to handle an `spa-listchange` custom global event. When this is executed, it invokes `$deferChangeList[idxChange] .resolve()`, and then pushes a new jQuery deferred object into `$deferChangeList` for subsequent `spa-listchange` events.

```
    spa.model.setDataMode( 'fake' );

    // create a jQuery object
    $t = $('<div/>');

    // subscribe functions to global custom events
    $.gevent.subscribe( $t, 'spa-login',      onLogin      );
    $.gevent.subscribe( $t, 'spa-listchange', onListchange );

    // test the user in the initial state
    user     = spa.model.people.get_user();
    test_str = 'user is anonymous';
    test.ok( user.get_is_anon(), test_str );

    // test the list of online persons
    test_str = 'expected user only contains anonymous';
    people_db  = spa.model.people.get_db();
    people_str = makePeopleStr( people_db );
    test.ok( people_str === 'anonymous', test_str );

    // proceed to next test without blocking
    test.done();
  };
  // End /testInitialState/

  // Begin /loginAsFred/
  loginAsFred = function ( test ) {
    var user, people_db, people_str, test_str;
    test.expect( 6 );

    // login as 'Fred'
    spa.model.people.login( 'Fred' );
    test_str = 'log in as Fred';
    test.ok( true, test_str );

    // test user attributes before login completes
    user     = spa.model.people.get_user();
    test_str = 'user is no longer anonymous';
    test.ok( ! user.get_is_anon(), test_str );

    test_str = 'usr name is "Fred"';
    test.ok( user.name === 'Fred', test_str );

    test_str = 'user id is undefined as login is incomplete';
    test.ok( ! user.id, test_str );

    test_str = 'user cid is c0';
    test.ok( user.cid === 'c0', test_str );

    test_str   = 'user list is as expected';
    people_db  = spa.model.people.get_db();
    people_str = makePeopleStr( people_db );
    test.ok( people_str === 'Fred,anonymous', test_str );

    // proceed to next test when both conditions are met:
    //   + login is complete (spa-login event)
    //   + the list of online persons has been updated
    //     (spa-listchange event)
    $.when( $deferLogin, $deferChangeList[ 0 ] )
      .then( test.done );
```

Make a jQuery collection, `$t`, which we can use to subscribe handlers to custom global events.

Subscribe to the jQuery custom global events needed to confirm completion of `loginAsFred`. The event `spa-login` is handled by `onLogin`, and the `spa-listchange` event is handled by `onListchange`.

The `testInitialState` test proceeds without blocking the next test by unconditionally invoking `test.done()`.

Have `loginAsFred` use jQuery deferred objects to ensure required events have completed before declaring `test.done`. The sign-in process must be completed (`$deferLogin.is_resolved() === true`) and the online person list must have been updated (`$deferChangeList[ 0 ].is_resolved === true`). The `$.when( <deferred objects> ).then( <function> )` statement implements this logic.

```
};
// End /loginAsFred/

// Begin /testUserAndPeople/
testUserAndPeople = function ( test ) {
  var
    user, cloned_user,
    people_db, people_str,
    user_str, test_str;
  test.expect( 4 );

  // test user attributes
  test_str = 'login as Fred complete';
  test.ok( true, test_str );

  user        = spa.model.people.get_user();
  test_str    = 'Fred has expected attributes';
  cloned_user = $.extend( true, {}, user );

  delete cloned_user.___id;
  delete cloned_user.___s;
  delete cloned_user.get_is_anon;
  delete cloned_user.get_is_user;

  test.deepEqual(
    cloned_user,
    { cid     : 'id_5',
      css_map : { top: 25, left: 25, 'background-color': '#8f8' },
      id      : 'id_5',
      name    : 'Fred'
    },
    test_str
  );

  // test the list of online persons
  test_str = 'receipt of listchange complete';
  test.ok( true, test_str );

  people_db  = spa.model.people.get_db();
  people_str = makePeopleStr( people_db );
  user_str = 'Betty,Fred,Mike,Pebbles,Wilma';
  test_str = 'user list provided is expected - ' + user_str;

  test.ok( people_str === user_str, test_str );

  test.done();
};
// End /testUserAndPeople/

module.exports = {
  testInitialState  : testInitialState,
  loginAsFred       : loginAsFred,
  testUserAndPeople : testUserAndPeople
};
// End of test suite
```

Test the attributes of the signed-in user and the online person list.

Don't block the `testUserAndPeople` test from proceeding at this time because there isn't a test that follows it. We'll change that when we add more tests.

Export the tests in the order we'd like them executed. When we run our test suite using `nodeunit`, the test names will be displayed.

When we run our test suite (`nodeunitnodeunit_suite.js`) we should see output like so:

```
$ nodeunit nodeunit_suite.js
✔ testInitialState
✔ loginAsFred
✔ testUserAndPeople

OK: 12 assertions (4223ms)
```

The suite takes about 12 seconds to return control to the console because JavaScript has active timers that need to complete. Don't worry about that—it'll be a non-issue by the time we complete the test suite. Now let's add tests for message transactions.

ADD TESTS FOR MESSAGE TRANSACTIONS

We'll now add the next four tests from our test plan. These are a nice logical group, as they all test issues with sending and receiving messages. The tests include `testWilmaMsg`, `sendPebblesMsg`, `testMsgToPebbles`, and `testPebblesResponse`. We feel the names provide a good summary of what each test does.

When we add our tests, we'll need a few more jQuery deferred objects to ensure serial progression. Listing B.11 shows this implementation. Please read the annotations as they detail how blocking is accomplished on these new tests. All changes are shown in **bold**:

Listing B.11 Add tests for message transactions—webapp/public/nodeunit_suite.js

```
...
var
  // utility and handlers
  makePeopleStr, onLogin, onListchange,
  onSetchatee,   onUpdatechat,                 <-- Declare two new event handlers.

  // test functions
  testInitialState,    loginAsFred,    testUserAndPeople,
  testWilmaMsg,        sendPebblesMsg, testMsgToPebbles,   <-- Declare four new test names.
  testPebblesResponse,

  // event handlers                    Declare variables to hold event handler data.
  loginEvent, changeEvent, chateeEvent, msgEvent,
  loginData, changeData, msgData, chateeData,

  // indexes
  changeIdx = 0, chateeIdx = 0, msgIdx = 0,    <-- Declare index variables for deferred object lists.

  // deferred objects                  Declare lists of jQuery deferred objects used by event handlers.
  $deferLogin      = $.Deferred(),
  $deferChangeList = [ $.Deferred() ],
  $deferChateeList = [ $.Deferred() ],
  $deferMsgList    = [ $.Deferred() ];

// utility to make a string of online person names

...

// event handler for 'spa-updatechat'   <-- Add the global custom event handler for spa-updatechat. This will get called when a new message is received or sent.
onUpdatechat = function ( event, arg ) {
  msgEvent = event;
  msgData  = arg;
  $deferMsgList[ msgIdx ].resolve();
```

Add the global custom event handler for `spa-setchatee`. This will get called when the chatee is changed for any reason. The chatee could change if the user selects a new chatee, or if the current chatee goes offline, or if we receive a message from a person different than the current chatee.

Have the jQuery collection `$t` subscribe the `onSetchatee` handler for the `spa-setchatee` custom global event.

Have the jQuery collection `$t` subscribe the `onUpdatechat` handler for the `spa-updatechat` custom global event.

Don't proceed from the `testUserAndPeople` test until after the first message has been processed and the first chatee change has occurred. Use jQuery deferred objects and the `$.when().then()` construct to implement this blocking.

Add the test to check the message from Wilma along with the new chatee attributes.

```
    msgIdx++;
    $deferMsgList[ msgIdx ] = $.Deferred();
  };

  // event handler for 'spa-setchatee'
  onSetchatee = function ( event, arg ) {
    chateeEvent = event;
    chateeData  = arg;
    $deferChateeList[ chateeIdx ].resolve();
    chateeIdx++;
    $deferChateeList[ chateeIdx ] = $.Deferred();
  };

  // Begin /testInitialState/
  testInitialState = function ( test ) {
    ...
    // subscribe functions to global custom events
    $.gevent.subscribe( $t, 'spa-login',      onLogin      );
    $.gevent.subscribe( $t, 'spa-listchange', onListchange );
    $.gevent.subscribe( $t, 'spa-setchatee',  onSetchatee  );
    $.gevent.subscribe( $t, 'spa-updatechat', onUpdatechat );
    ...
  };
  // End /testInitialState/

  ...
  // Begin /testUserAndPeople/
  testUserAndPeople = function ( test ) {
    ...
    test.ok( people_str === user_str, test_str );

    // proceed to next test when both conditions are met:
    //   + first message has been received (spa-updatechat event)
    //     (this is the example message from 'Wilma')
    //   + chatee change has occurred (spa-setchatee event)
    $.when($deferMsgList[ 0 ], $deferChateeList[ 0 ] )
      .then( test.done );
  };
  // End /testUserAndPeople/

  // Begin /testWilmaMsg/
  testWilmaMsg = function ( test ) {
    var test_str;
    test.expect( 4 );

    // test message received from 'Wilma'
    test_str = 'Message is as expected';
    test.deepEqual(
      msgData,
      { dest_id: 'id_5',
        dest_name: 'Fred',
        sender_id: 'id_04',
        msg_text: 'Hi there Fred!  Wilma here.'
      },
      test_str
    );

    // test chatee attributes
```

```
    test.ok( chateeData.new_chatee.cid  === 'id_04' );
    test.ok( chateeData.new_chatee.id   === 'id_04' );
    test.ok( chateeData.new_chatee.name === 'Wilma' );

    // proceed to next test without blocking
    test.done();
  };
  // End /testWilmaMsg/

  // Begin /sendPebblesMsg/
  sendPebblesMsg = function ( test ) {
    var test_str, chatee;
    test.expect( 1 );

    // set_chatee to 'Pebbles'
    spa.model.chat.set_chatee( 'id_03' );

    // send_msg to 'Pebbles'
    spa.model.chat.send_msg( 'whats up, tricks?' );

    // test get_chatee() results
    chatee = spa.model.chat.get_chatee();
    test_str = 'Chatee is as expected';
    test.ok( chatee.name === 'Pebbles', test_str );

    // proceed to next test when both conditions are met:
    //   + chatee has been set (spa-setchatee event)
    //   + message has been sent (spa-updatechat event)
    $.when( $deferMsgList[ 1 ], $deferChateeList[ 1] )
      .then( test.done );
  };
  // End /sendPebblesMsg/

  // Begin /testMsgToPebbles/
  testMsgToPebbles = function ( test ) {
    var test_str;
    test.expect( 2 );

    // test the chatee attributes
    test_str = 'Pebbles is the chatee name';
    test.ok(
      chateeData.new_chatee.name === 'Pebbles',
      test_str
    );

    // test the message sent
    test_str = 'message change is as expected';
    test.ok( msgData.msg_text === 'whats up, tricks?', test_str );

    // proceed to the next test when
    //   + A response has been received from 'Pebbles'
    //     (spa-updatechat event)
    $deferMsgList[ 2 ].done( test.done );
  };
  // End /testMsgToPebbles/

  // Begin /testPebblesResponse/
  testPebblesResponse = function ( test ) {
    var test_str;
```

Proceed from the `testWilmaMsg` test to the next without blocking.

Add the `sendPebblesMsg` test where Fred sets Pebbles as the chatee and sends her a message. Like most tests that perform actions, there are few assertions and the code blocks progress until events have occurred.

Don't proceed from the `sendPebblesMsg` test until after the second message has been processed and the second chatee change has occurred. Use jQuery deferred objects and the `$.when().then()` construct to implement this blocking.

Add the test to check the message sent to Pebbles.

Don't proceed from the `testMsgToPebbles` test until after the third message (Pebbles' response) has been processed.

Add the `testPebblesResponse` test to check the message sent from Pebbles.

```
  test.expect( 1 );

  // test the message received from 'Pebbles'
  test_str = 'Message is as expected';
  test.deepEqual(
    msgData,
    { dest_id: 'id_5',
      dest_name: 'Fred',
      sender_id: 'id_03',
      msg_text: 'Thanks for the note, Fred'
    },
    test_str
  );

  // proceed to next test without blocking
  test.done();
};
// End /testPebblesResponse/

module.exports = {
  testInitialState     : testInitialState,
  loginAsFred          : loginAsFred,
  testUserAndPeople    : testUserAndPeople,
  testWilmaMsg         : testWilmaMsg,
  sendPebblesMsg       : sendPebblesMsg,
  testMsgToPebbles     : testMsgToPebbles,
  testPebblesResponse  : testPebblesResponse
};
// End of test suite
```

Proceed from testPebblesResponse without blocking.

Add the new tests to our suite.

When we run our test suite (nodeunitnodeunit_suite.js) we should see output like so:

```
$ nodeunit nodeunit_suite.js
✔ testInitialState
✔ loginAsFred
✔ testUserAndPeople
✔ testWilmaMsg
✔ sendPebblesMsg
✔ testMsgToPebbles
✔ testPebblesResponse

OK: 20 assertions (14233ms)
```

The suite takes just as long to return from execution as before, but now we see the new tests. Specifically, the suite is now waiting for, and then testing, the message Wilma sends to the user. Now let's add more tests to complete our test suite.

ADD TESTS FOR AVATARS, SIGN-OUT, AND SIGNED-OUT STATE

We'll now complete our test suite by adding the four remaining tests from our plan. Again, we use deferred objects to ensure certain events are received before we allow one test to proceed to another. Listing B.12 shows the additional tests. Changes are shown in **bold**:

Listing B.12 Additional tests—webapp/public/nodeunit_suite.js

```
...
var
  // utility and handlers
  makePeopleStr, onLogin,      onListchange,
  onSetchatee,   onUpdatechat, onLogout,

  // test functions
  testInitialState,    loginAsFred,         testUserAndPeople,
  testWilmaMsg,        sendPebblesMsg,      testMsgToPebbles,
  testPebblesResponse, updatePebblesAvtr,   testPebblesAvtr,
  logoutAsFred,        testLogoutState,

  // event handlers
  loginEvent, changeEvent, chateeEvent, msgEvent, logoutEvent,
  loginData, changeData, msgData, chateeData, logoutData,
  ...

  $deferMsgList    = [ $.Deferred() ],
  $deferLogout     = $.Deferred();

...
// event handler for 'spa-setchatee'
...
// event handler for 'spa-logout'
onLogout = function ( event, arg ) {
  logoutEvent = event;
  logoutData  = arg;
  $deferLogout.resolve();
};

// Begin /testInitialState/
testInitialState = function ( test ) {
  ...
  $.gevent.subscribe( $t, 'spa-updatechat', onUpdatechat );
  $.gevent.subscribe( $t, 'spa-logout',     onLogout     );

  // test the user in the initial state
...
// End /testPebblesResponse/

// Begin /updatePebblesAvtr/
updatePebblesAvtr = function ( test ) {
  test.expect( 0 );

  // invoke the update_avatar method
  spa.model.chat.update_avatar({
    person_id : 'id_03',
    css_map   : {
      'top' : 10, 'left' : 100,
      'background-color' : '#ff0'
    }
  });

  // proceed to the next test when
  //   + the list of online persons has been updated
  //     (spa-listchange event)
  $deferChangeList[ 1 ].done( test.done );
```

```
};
// End /updatePebblesAvtr/

// Begin /testPebblesAvtr/
testPebblesAvtr = function ( test ) {
  var chatee, test_str;
  test.expect( 1 );

  // get 'Pebbles' person object using get_chatee method
  chatee = spa.model.chat.get_chatee();

  // test avatar details for 'Pebbles'
  test_str = 'avatar details updated';
  test.deepEqual(
    chatee.css_map,
    { top : 10, left : 100,
      'background-color' : '#ff0'
    },
    test_str
  );

  // proceed to next test without blocking
  test.done();
};
// End /testPebblesAvtr/

// Begin /logoutAsFred/
logoutAsFred = function( test ) {
  test.expect( 0 );

  // logout as fred
  spa.model.people.logout();

  // proceed to next test when
  //   + logout is complete (spa-logout event)
  $deferLogout.done( test.done );
};
// End /logoutAsFred/

// Begin /testLogoutState/
testLogoutState = function ( test ) {
  var user, people_db, people_str, user_str, test_str;
  test.expect( 4 );

  test_str = 'logout as Fred complete';
  test.ok( true, test_str );

  // test the list of online persons
  people_db  = spa.model.people.get_db();
  people_str = makePeopleStr( people_db );
  user_str   = 'anonymous';
  test_str   = 'user list provided is expected - ' + user_str;

  test.ok( people_str === 'anonymous', test_str );

  // test user attributes
  user     = spa.model.people.get_user();
  test_str = 'current user is anonymous after logout';
  test.ok( user.get_is_anon(), test_str );
```

```
    test.ok( true, 'test complete' );

    // Proceed without blocking
    test.done();
  };
  // End /testLogoutState/

  module.exports = {
    testInitialState      : testInitialState,
    loginAsFred           : loginAsFred,
    testUserAndPeople     : testUserAndPeople,
    testWilmaMsg          : testWilmaMsg,
    sendPebblesMsg        : sendPebblesMsg,
    testMsgToPebbles      : testMsgToPebbles,
    testPebblesResponse   : testPebblesResponse,
    updatePebblesAvtr     : updatePebblesAvtr,
    testPebblesAvtr       : testPebblesAvtr,
    logoutAsFred          : logoutAsFred,
    testLogoutState       : testLogoutState
  };
  // End of test suite
```

When we run our test suite (`nodeunitnodeunit_suite.js`) we should see output like so:

```
$ nodeunit nodeunit_suite.js
✔ testInitialState
✔ loginAsFred
✔ testUserAndPeople
✔ testWilmaMsg
✔ sendPebblesMsg
✔ testMsgToPebbles
✔ testPebblesResponse
✔ updatePebblesAvtr
✔ testPebblesAvtr
✔ logoutAsFred
✔ testLogoutState

OK: 25 assertions (14234ms)
```

We've completed the test suite according to our plan. We can run this suite automatically before checking updates into a repository (think "commit hook"). Such a practice shouldn't slow us down but instead *accelerate* our development by preventing regressions and ensuring quality. This is an example of designing quality *into* a product instead of testing the product only after it has been "finished."

Alas, one glaring problem remains: the test suite currently never exits. Sure, the terminal shows 25 assertions being completed, but control is never returned to the terminal or any other calling process. This prevents us from automating the run of the test suite. In the next section we'll discuss why this happens and what we can do about it.

B.5 Adjust SPA modules for tests

One troublesome question Node.js (and by extension, nodeunit) encounters is *how does it know when execution of a test suite is complete?* This is an example of the classic computer science *halting problem*, and isn't trivial in any event-driven language. In general, Node.js considers an application complete when it can find no code to execute and it has no pending transactions.

Up to this point, our code has been designed for continuous use without consideration for an exit condition outside of closing the browser tab. When a tester uses mode 2 (testing in a browser using fake data) and signs out, our Fake module starts a `setTimeout` in anticipation of another sign-in.

Our test suite, like some film genres, requires an explicit ending. Therefore, if we intend to *ever* see our test suite complete this side of a `SIGTERM` or `SIGKILL`, we need to use a *test setting*.[6] A test setting is a configuration or directive required for testing, but not required for "production" use.

As you might gather, we'd rather minimize test settings so we can prevent them from introducing their own bugs. Sometimes, they're unavoidable. In this case we need a test setting to stop our Fake module from constantly respawning timers. This will allow our suite to exit so we can use scripts to automate the run of the test suite and interpret the results.

We can perform the following steps to prevent Fake from restarting timers after sign-out:

- In the test suite, add a `true` argument to the sign-out call like so: `spa.model.people( true )`. This directive (which we call the *do_not_reset* flag) informs the Model that after a sign-out, we don't want it to reset values in preparation for another sign-in.
- In the Model's `spa.model.people.logout` method, accept an optional `do_not_reset` argument. Pass this value as the single argument to the `chat._leave` method.
- In the Model's `spa.model.chat._leave` method, accept an optional `do_not_reset` argument. Pass this value as the data when sending the `leavechat` message to the back end.
- Change Fake (webapp/public/js/spa.fake.js) to ensure the `leavechat` callback treats the received data as a `do_not_reset` flag. When the `leavechat` callback sees that the data it received has the value of `true`, it should *not* restart timers after sign-out.

Though that's more work than we'd hoped (we were looking for *no additional work*), this only requires minor surgery on three files. Let's start with the test suite and add the `do_not_reset` directive to our `logout` method call as shown in listing B.13. The one-word addition is shown in **bold**:

6 Let's be clear—we need this program to exit because our automated commit hook will rely on analysis of the exit code. No exit means no exit code, which means no automation, which of course is unacceptable.

Listing B.13 Add do_not_reset to suite—webapp/public/nodeunit_suite.js

```
...
// Begin /logoutAsFred/
logoutAsFred = function( test ) {
  test.expect( 0 );

  // logout as fred
  spa.model.people.logout( true );

  // proceed to next test when
  //   + logout is complete (spa-logout event)
  $deferLogout.done( test.done );
};
// End /logoutAsFred/
...
```

Now let's add the do_not_reset argument in the Model as shown in the following listing. Changes are shown in **bold**:

Listing B.14 Add do_not_reset to the Model—webapp/public/js/spa.model.js

```
 ...
 people = (function () {
   ...
   logout = function ( do_not_reset ) {
     var user = stateMap.user;

     chat._leave( do_not_reset );
     stateMap.user = stateMap.anon_user;
     clearPeopleDb();

     $.gevent.publish( 'spa-logout', [ user ] );
   };
   ...
 }());
 ...
 chat = (function () {
   ...
   _leave_chat = function ( do_not_reset ) {
     var sio = isFakeData ? spa.fake.mockSio : spa.data.getSio();
     chatee  = null;
     stateMap.is_connected = false;
     if ( sio ) { sio.emit( 'leavechat', do_not_reset ); }
   };
   ...
 }());
 ...
```

Finally, let's update the Fake module to consider the do_not_reset directive when sending a leavechat message. Changes are shown in **bold**:

Listing B.15 Add do_not_reset to Fake—webapp/public/js/spa.fake.js

```
...
mockSio = (function () {
```

```
...
emit_sio = function ( msg_type, data ) {
  ...
  if ( msg_type === 'leavechat' ) {
    // reset login status
    delete callback_map.listchange;
    delete callback_map.updatechat;

    if ( listchange_idto ) {
      clearTimeout( listchange_idto );
      listchange_idto = undefined;
    }
    if ( ! data ) { send_listchange(); }
  }
  ...
```

After the updates, we can run `nodeunit nodeunit_suite.js` and watch the test suit run *and exit*:

```
$ nodeunite nodeunit_suite.js
✔ testInitialState
✔ loginAsFred
✔ testUserAndPeople
✔ testWilmaMsg
✔ sendPebblesMsg
✔ testMsgToPebbles
✔ testPebblesResponse
✔ updatePebblesAvtr
✔ testPebblesAvtr
✔ logoutAsFred
✔ testLogoutState

OK: 25 assertions (14234ms)
$
```

The exit code of the suite will be the number of failed assertions. Therefore if all the tests pass, the exit code will be 0 (we can inspect the exit code on Linux and Mac using `echo $?`). A script can use this exit status (and other output) to do things like block the deployment of a build, or send an email to a concerned developer or project manager.

B.6 Summary

Testing is a practice that helps us develop faster and better. A well-run project is designed from the start for multiple test modes, and tests are written with the code to help identify and resolve issues quickly and efficiently. Almost everyone has worked at some time on a project where each advancement seemed to come with a matching failure in stuff that *used* to work. Consistent, early, and well-designed tests can prevent regressions and facilitate rapid progress.

This appendix showed four test modes and discussed how to set them up and when to use them. We selected nodeunit as our test framework. We were then able to test our Model without the use of a web browser. When we created our test suite, we used jQuery deferred objects and test directives to ensure our tests occurred in the correct sequence. Finally, we showed how to adjust modules so tests can be successfully run in a test environment.

We hope you found our presentation enlightening and inspirational. Happy testing!

index

Symbols

A

B

C

D

E

F

G

N

O

P

Q

R

S

RELATED MANNING TITLES

Secrets of the JavaScript Ninja
by John Resig and Bear Bibeault

ISBN: 978-1-933988-69-6
392 pages, $39.99
December 2012

Third-Party JavaScript
by Ben Vinegar and Anton Kovalyov

ISBN: 978-1-617290-54-1
288 pages, $44.99
March 2013

Sass and Compass in Action
by Wynn Netherland, Nathan Weizenbaum, Chris Eppstein, and Brandon Mathis

ISBN: 978-1-617290-14-5
240 pages, $44.99
July 2013

Node.js in Action
by Mike Cantelon, Marc Harter, TJ Holowaychuk, and Nathan Rajlich

ISBN: 978-1-617290-57-2
300 pages, $44.99
September 2013

For ordering information go to www.manning.com